Challenge Cancer
and **WIN**!

Kim Dalzell, PhD, RD, LD

Challenge Cancer and **WIN**!

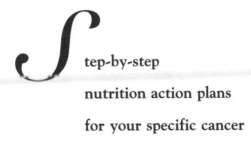

Step-by-step

nutrition action plans

for your specific cancer

Kim Dalzell, PhD, RD, LD

NutriQuest Press
Round Lake, Illinois

You can order this book from BookMasters, Inc.: 800 247-6553

Important Notice to Readers!

This book provides information about natural healing options that may be used as adjuvant therapy to conventional medical care. Information presented in this book is intended to help you make informed decisions about your nutritional needs, not as a substitute for or to countermand the advice given to you by your physician.

The author and publisher are not responsible for any adverse effects or consequences associated with the use of any of the recommendations in this book. Because each individual is unique, it is important that the reader consult with a qualified healthcare professional before making major changes in diet, exercise patterns, or consumption of supplements.

ISBN: 0-9712558-7-3

Illustrations: Steve Ferchaud

Editor: Peter Bumpus w/indypub, LLC

PRINTED IN THE UNITED STATES OF AMERICA

Do you have a health tip, nutritious recipe, or testimonial about how nutrition has helped you? I'd love to hear from you! Please write: NutriQuest Press, P.O. Box 874, Round Lake, IL 60073 or email: nutriquest@att.net. Thank you!

To Leslie and every person with cancer I have worked with.
Your strength and resolve show the rest of us the importance
of a falling snowflake, a child's whisper, a quiet morning,
and a new day.

Table of Contents

Acknowledgments   xi
Preface   xiii

Section One: Are You Ready?

Chapter 1: Strategies for Success   1
Sizing Up the Competition   3
Your Best Defense   4
Six Steps to Success   4

Chapter 2: Are You Running on Empty?   19
Malnutrition Myths   20
Self-Assessment: Are You at Risk for Malnutrition?   23
Avoid Malnutrition   24
Common Laboratory Tests   28
How's Your Diet?   34
Food Records   34
Advanced Nutritional Support   41

Chapter 3: Is Your Digestion Off Track?   45
An Incredible Journey — The Nickel Tour   45
A Finicky Tract   46
Self-Assessment: How's Your Gut?   47
First Aid Station   49
Eat for Less Stress   81

Section Two: Get Set!

Chapter 4: At the Starting Block – Nutrition 101   87
The Nutrients   87
Counting Calories   93
Lessons in Label Reading   100
Out of the Kitchen   104
Self-Assessment: Mastering Restaurant Menus   108

Chapter 5: Stats on Fats   111
The Cancer Connection to Fat   111
Counting Fat Grams   113

Table of Contents

Self-Assessment: Helping Yourself to Hidden Fats?   114

Trimming the Fat   115

Fats: The Good, the Bad, and the Ugly   117

Chapter 6: A Sweet Victory   **129**

Does Sugar Feed Cancer?   129

Self-Assessment: How Sweet Are You?   133

So Long, Sweets!   138

Sugar Substitutes   141

Alternative Sweeteners   143

Chapter 7: Plants To Help You Advance   **145**

The Power of Plants   146

On Your Way to Five-a-Day   147

Fabulous Phytochemicals   150

Self-Assessment: Are You Eating Your Way to Five-a-Day?   157

Putting Plants into Your Diet   158

Chapter 8: Fast Forward with Fiber   **165**

What is Fiber?   165

How Fiber Fights Cancer   168

Self-Assessment: Finding Fiber   171

How To Increase Your Fiber Intake   172

Bean Basics   174

In the Granary   176

Fiber Supplements   180

Chapter 9: Step Up to Soy   **183**

Soy Beneficial!   184

Can Soy Stop Cancer?   185

Soy and Estrogen-Dependent Cancers   186

Self-Assessment: How Soy Savvy Are You?   188

Soy Many Products!   190

Cooking with Soy   194

Chapter 10: Dietary Supplements – Gaining a Competitive Edge   **199**

Do You Need Dietary Supplements?   199

Supplements During Treatment   200

Supplements That Fight Cancer   203

How To Become Supplement Savvy   227

What Should You Tell Your Doctor?   232

Chapter 11: Cooling Off   235

Living in a Toxic World   235
How You Can Safely Detoxify   237
The Detox Diet   238
Juicing   241
Food Safety   248
Self-Assessment: How Safe Are You?   249
Toxic Food Additives   250
Environmental Pollutants Linked to Cancer   252
A Nontoxic Lifestyle   255

Section Three: Go!

Nutrition Action Plans   259

Which Plan Is Right for You?   259
Bladder Cancer   262
Breast Cancer   273
Colorectal Cancer   285
Upper Digestive Tract Cancer (Esophagus, Oral Cavity, Stomach) 297
Gynecological Cancer (Cervical, Endometrial, Ovarian, Uterine) 309
Leukemia   321
Lung Cancer   331
Melanoma   342
Non-Hodgkin's Lymphoma   353
Pancreatic Cancer   364
Prostate Cancer   375
Other Cancers   386

Appendix   397
Endnotes   417
Glossary   447
Resources   449
Index   453

List of Charts

Percent Weight Loss and Risk   26

High Calorie, High Protein Supplemental Drinks   40

Natural Pharmacy Quick Reference Guide   83

Cuisine Quick Change   106

How Sugars Stack Up   132

Power Chemo!   202

Dietary Hurdles for Eating Well   242

Potent Protectors   247

Bladder Cancer Quick Reference Guide to Eating Right   268

Breast Cancer Quick Reference Guide to Eating Right   280

Colorectal Cancer Quick Reference Guide to Eating Right   292

Upper Digestive Cancer Quick Reference Guide to Eating Right   304

Gynecological Cancer Quick Reference Guide to Eating Right   316

Leukemia Quick Reference Guide to Eating Right   326

Lung Cancer Quick Reference Guide to Eating Right   337

Melanoma Quick Reference Guide to Eating Right   348

Non-Hodgkin's Lymphoma Quick Reference Guide to Eating Right   359

Pancreatic Cancer Quick Reference Guide to Eating Right   370

Prostate Cancer Quick Reference Guide to Eating Right   381

Other Cancer Quick Reference Guide to Eating Right   391

Acknowledgments

To Mark, for your continued support and belief in me throughout our years together. You've been a steadfast, comforting light in my life.

To David and Kathryn. Because of you, I live intentionally, love unconditionally, worry endlessly, and thank God repeatedly. You are the greatest gifts of all!

A special thanks to my friends and coworkers at Cancer Resource Center, Midwestern Regional Medical Center, and Cancer Treatment Centers of America for their gracious assistance and encouragement.

Preface

I LOVE A GOOD CHALLENGE — perhaps that's why I enjoy working with cancer patients. Despite the advances in conventional medicine, a cancer diagnosis still causes everyone to wonder, "Why?" The scientific community has only recently and somewhat reluctantly acknowledged that nutrients in food can affect cancer.

Still, many physicians are unwilling to entertain the notion that diet can positively impact disease. Herein lies the source of my personal challenge: It is difficult to sell a new way of eating to those with cancer when their doctors suggest that nutrition doesn't play a role in the cancer process.

I've put a lot of time and effort into convincing patients and their doctors otherwise. Researchers in nutrition and oncology have sufficiently determined (from population studies, test tube experiments, and clinical trials) that certain nutrients are linked to specific cancers. Unfortunately, this information seems to get lost in the hands of healthcare professionals and government agencies. I have rarely found a lay person who is aware of these promising findings! And so I began my crusade to spread the word.

I have over a decade of experience as a hospital-based registered dietitian and have completed advanced degrees in clinical and holistic nutrition. I have developed educational materials, conducted community seminars, written for company newsletters and Web sites, and have been a featured guest on radio and television programs. I have talked with folks from all over the world who want to learn how food can fuel recovery from cancer. My counseling style is much like a coach's. In addition to providing vital information, I encourage, motivate, and reinforce good habits. And I don't stop with my patients, either. I talk with family members, friends, and physicians in an effort to mesh integrative approaches to healing with real world living and conservative medical treatment. Over the years I have discovered what patients and family members really want to know — useful, effective nutritional strategies that will help them challenge their cancer and win!

This book is the much-needed, essential guide to therapeutic nutrition for cancer patients who want a step-by-step action plan to help them eat to beat cancer. Practical nutritional recommendations make it easy to apply cancer-fighting principles to your life. *Challenge Cancer and Win!* was written because I want to send a loud and clear message to those who have been diagnosed with cancer: Health, hope, and healing are available for those who wish to be proactive in the race against cancer. The restorative power of nature's bounty awaits!

Section I

Are You Ready?

— 1 —

Strategies for Success

Taking Action Through Diet

THIS BOOK IS ABOUT TAKING ACTION against cancer. If you can protect your immune system and improve your overall health, you stand a much better chance of enjoying a longer, higher quality life than if you succumb to the idea that cancer means debilitation and death. Cancer can be a fierce competitor, but, just like anything else,

— 1 —

if you know what you're up against and become proactive, you stand a better chance of defeating it.

In the United States, the incidence of most kinds of cancer continues to rise. While the reasons for this trend are not totally clear, research findings suggest a causal relationship between various nutritional factors and cancer. With over eleven years of clinical experience with cancer patients, and after a thorough review of the scientific literature, I am convinced that eating right and following healthful lifestyle practices can limit treatment side effects, strengthen immunity, and stop cancer from growing.

This book blends current research findings with practical advice about diet and supplements. Not only will you know *why* you should eat right, you'll know *how* to eat right. By following the nutritional suggestions in this book, you will give yourself a winning advantage over cancer.

Cancer patients interested in nutrition are often confused by conflicting information, invariably leading to the question, "What foods should I be eating to beat my cancer?" Based on the most prominent research findings for each particular cancer diagnosis, I have designed nutrition action plans that will help you choose foods and specific nutrients. Some of the nutritional recommendations also stem from population studies that carry probable implications for a specific cancer.

I've included the latest research findings available for the most prevalent cancers. Unfortunately, there are less common cancers that haven't been studied for potential nutritional correlations. If you have a cancer not linked to a nutrition action plan, it is because more research is needed before certain dietary habits or specific nutrients can be linked with your cancer. For this reason, you should follow the nutritional guidelines for "Other Cancers."

Special features such as "Coach's Corner," "Getting the Edge," and other tips of the trade were born out of working with thousands of cancer patients who told me what they needed to know in order to get the most out of their diet and supplements.

Whether you have been recently diagnosed, have experienced a recurrence, or are on the road to recovery, now is the time to send a powerful message to your body and mind that you are prepared to stop cancer in its tracks.

Sizing Up the Competition

Cancer begins when a normal cell becomes genetically damaged because of poor diet, unhealthy lifestyle habits, or other cancer-promoting factors that encourage free radical activity. Free radicals are highly reactive (unstable) molecules that damage normal cells during their quest for stability. Altered (damaged) cells pass on mutations when they divide.

Oncogenes, quiet genes that are spurred into action during mutation, produce abnormal proteins that can initiate cancer. Tumor suppressor genes also play a role in cancer. If suppressor gene activity is lost through cellular mutation, cancer cell growth and division can't be regulated. It is the failure of these and other built-in preventive mechanisms that allows precancerous cells to become detectable tumors with the potential for metastasis.

Genetic mutations provide cancer cells with adaptive characteristics that are very different than normal cells:

- Normal cells have regulators that influence their growth. Cancer cells can grow without growth regulators or in spite of growth inhibitors.
- Normal cells have a built-in termination code. Cancer cells are not programmed to die, so they continue to proliferate into a large tumor.

- Cancer cells have the ability to develop a blood supply and establish growth at a distant site. This is the most lethal step as cancer progresses.
- Cancer cells can change. Variations of the cancer cells may be resistant to chemotherapy or radiation. Others can evade immune system recognition by disguising themselves.

Your Best Defense

While cellular mutations occur all the time, in the vast majority of cases, the body's immune system destroys these abnormal cells. Researchers believe that everyone probably develops a cancerous cell nine to ten times in their lifetime. If this is true, why do some people "grow" cancer, while others do not?

Understanding the immune system is the key to answering this question. When the immune system is intact, a mutated cell is recognized as foreign, then it is attacked and destroyed. When the immune system is weak, the body is subject to fatigue and illness and can't prevent a precancerous cell from becoming an abnormal cellular growth.

The immune system protects the body from bacteria, viruses, and other harmful organisms. Toxins in foods and the environment, poor diet, stress, and free radicals contribute to a decline in immune system function. You can strengthen your immune system by being proactive, reducing stress, exercising, practicing spirituality, eating right, and thinking positively.

Six Steps to Success

Are you doing everything you can to beat your cancer? Can you fight cancer with more than surgery, chemotherapy, or radiation? You might be getting the best medical treatment, but are you using every available tool to boost your immune system and reclaim your health? Running a good race involves more than donning a pair of Nikes. Wellness increases when you take care of all your needs.

Step 1: Be Proactive

When you have cancer, you have very important decisions to make. While working with many cancer patients over the years, I have observed some behaviors that can help make your treatment experience much more positive and beneficial:

- Don't take the advice of only one person at your insurance company regarding your benefits. If you ask the same question to five people, you often get five different answers. Pursue an answer until the information you receive is consistent. Otherwise, you may end up confused about medical benefits or financial matters.
- Get a second opinion about your treatment options. Don't ask two doctors who work together what they think; ask two doctors from two different facilities what they think. You will be surprised how variable treatment approaches can be!
- Keep a copy of every blood test, scan, and progress note in your medical record. You can request a copy of your entire medical record from a hospital's medical records department. Possessing all of your medical information, which is legally yours any time you ask for it, will help you feel more in control and can help you move quickly to another doctor or treatment facility should that be required. I've talked with patients who have waited over six weeks to get their medical records. Meanwhile, they were not receiving any treatment. Why put your life on hold?

- Make sure you know your exact diagnosis. You will have a hard time getting accurate information or appropriate help for your cancer if you are unable to relay this specific detail. For example, dietary recommendations for breast cancer will differ depending on whether or not cell growth is affected by estrogen.
- Get on the Internet or to the bookstore. Talk with others. Learn everything you can about your cancer and research your treatment options. Don't try to become a cancer expert, just familiarize yourself with what you are up against. That way, you'll have a better idea about what questions to ask the next time you visit your doctor.
- Communicate frequently with your doctor. Insist on it. There is nothing more frustrating and isolating than not being able to talk with the man or woman responsible for formulating your treatment plan. Learn the best way to contact your healthcare providers. For example, my patients have a hard time getting me by phone because I'm usually on another call (really!). They know they should fax or e-mail me when they want a quick response. If you don't get the quick response you are looking for, try communicating your request in a different way. Instead of phoning, fax your questions. Instead of faxing, e-mail your questions. Better yet, instead of guessing, ask your doctor how he or she prefers to be contacted.
- Ask your doctor about getting full body scans completed when you are first diagnosed. Some facilities conduct head-to-toe scans on all patients, but other facilities do not. Although some tests have limited diagnostic value, they can provide a baseline for measuring

future cancer activity, if there is any, and they can silence your fears that something might have been missed.

- Be an educator. Help others to help themselves. If something has worked for you, made you feel better, or helped you cope, share that information with others who are likely to have similar experiences. Each time you share your gift of knowledge, you are reinforcing what you have learned, and you are rebuilding your own strength. Giving to others is extremely empowering to the mind, the spirit, and the immune system.

- Attend support group meetings even if you feel like you already have a tremendous support system. As much as your family or friends love and support you, they don't have a clue about what you are truly going through. The only people who can really connect with you are those who are going through the same thing you are. Camaraderie can help make a bad day a little better and a good day a little sweeter.

Step 2: Reduce Stress

Your thoughts, attitudes, emotions, and state of health are intricately related. Numerous studies have demonstrated that stress can slow the body's healing, increasing susceptibility to disease. Stress related to cancer treatment can also change immune system response, for instance:

- Preoperative radiation and surgery of esophageal cancer patients caused natural killer cell activity to decline.[1]
- Patients with lung cancer who received chest radiation had impaired immunological competence.[2]

- Surgery alone, or with chemotherapy, reduced immunity in breast cancer patients.[3]

By changing how you react to stressors in your life, you may be able to influence the state of your health and the course of your disease. One study reported that 80 percent of patients with a "fighting spirit" were healthy and disease-free at the end of five years, compared to only 20 percent of patients who seemed to have a fatalistic attitude toward cancer.[4]

The first step to wellness involves communicating with your body so that you can become as physically well as possible. There are a number of ways to accomplish this:

- Get enough rest. Fatigue or lack of energy may persist well beyond the completion of treatment. Get plenty of rest and don't push yourself. Have realistic expectations about getting back to your pretreatment energy level.
- Try some form of relaxation. Relaxation techniques such as meditation and yoga have reduced pain by half in patients with chronic pain.[5] Massage therapy can also relieve chronic pain and create feelings of vitality and tranquility.[6]
- Take a mini-vacation. Women with breast cancer who attended a mountain retreat experienced an increase in overall quality of life that was maintained for up to six months following the retreat.[7] If you can't get away for a weekend, consider taking one afternoon or evening per week for a little respite.
- Remain in contact. Social isolation breeds depression, which can impair immune functioning. Reports show that cancer or chronically ill patients have enhanced psychological well-being when they become involved in religious activities, join support groups, and express their emotions.[8]

- Seek humor to enhance your health. Laughter reduces stress, improves mood, enhances creativity, reduces pain, and improves immunity.[9]

Step 3: Move Your Body

A number of recent studies showed that physical inactivity, when combined with excess body weight, is a risk factor for several cancers, including colorectal, lung, uterine, cervical, prostate, and postmenopausal breast cancers.[10] Several proposed mechanisms explain how exercise can help prevent cancer or promote recovery from the cancer process:

- Moderate exercise boosts the activity of lymphocytes and macrophages, which destroy cancer cells.[11]
- A lean body mass, coupled with physical activity, lowers insulin and glucose levels. These growth factors can suppress immunity and stimulate tumor growth.
- Exercise can make the body more sensitive to insulin, helping the body to use energy from foods more effectively.[12] This may help lessen the severity of cancer cachexia, a detrimental malnourished state.
- Physical activity may stimulate bowel movements, reducing the amount of time cancer-causing agents or toxins reside in your colon.
- Exercise may help prevent hormonally based cancers by decreasing estrogen production.

Based on guidelines put forth by the American College of Sports and Medicine, you should exercise three to five days per week at 50 to 80 percent of your maximum heart rate, for at least fifteen to sixty minutes. Complement your aerobic conditioning with a basic strength training program to develop muscle tone and strength. Don't forget to warm up, because cold muscles can cause strain or tiny tears in muscle tissue.

Always obtain medical clearance from your doctor before you begin an exercise regimen. A physical therapist or exercise physiologist can discuss correct exercise techniques and provide you with a specific program that will safely and effectively meet your

Gold Medal Action

Motivation to Move

- Don't quit exercising once you start. It is far too easy to let large lapses of time go by before you restart an exercise program.
- Set realistic goals. Don't try to run a 10K race if you've just begun jogging.
- Set a routine. Schedule a time to exercise just as you would schedule an important meeting.
- Don't feel guilty if you miss a session or two. Negative feelings hinder motivation and immunity.
- Use distractions such as reading, listening to music, or watching television to make the time go by faster.
- Do what you like. You are much more likely to stick to an exercise program if you find an activity that you look forward to.
- Get a partner. Exercising with a mate can keep you motivated and provide an opportunity for socializing.

health goals. Certain activities may need to be limited in individuals at risk for lymphedema and those with metastasis to the bones.

Step 4: Nurture Your Spiritual Side

A review of the literature shows a consistent link between religion and better mental and physical health.[13] It appears that individuals with strong spiritual beliefs are more likely to be healthier and live longer than those who are less religious. Hospitalized patients who nurture their spiritual side heal faster and tend to have more hope, strength, comfort, and peace.

Organized religion or personal spirituality can affect health in a number of ways:

- People who attend religious services and pray regularly tend to be happier than people who never or rarely attend church.[14]
- People with serious medical illnesses who practice some form of religion have less stress and are more hopeful. They are less likely to feel defeated and overwhelmed by any negative health experiences.[15]
- Religious faith can positively influence emotions and help people with chronic illness cope with life-changing events.[16]
- Experts suggest that practicing some form of religion provides chronically ill patients with a much needed social outlet and support system.

Whether you choose to express your faith through church attendance, prayer, meditation, or by observing nature, spirituality can be a sound way to cope with your cancer treatment and recovery.

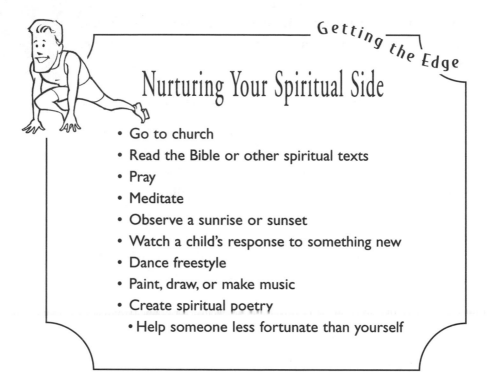

Getting the Edge

Nurturing Your Spiritual Side

- Go to church
- Read the Bible or other spiritual texts
- Pray
- Meditate
- Observe a sunrise or sunset
- Watch a child's response to something new
- Dance freestyle
- Paint, draw, or make music
- Create spiritual poetry
  - Help someone less fortunate than yourself

Step 5: Eat Right

What you put into your mouth can affect your health in some pretty amazing ways. Both dietary excesses and deficiencies play a role in cancer development.

Diets low in protein, vitamins A, E, B_6, and folate are associated with reduced immunocompetence.[17] Since protein is found in every cell, it makes sense that a protein deficiency or rapid protein turnover caused by cancer treatment would hinder the immune system. Diets high in saturated fat and refined sugar also suppress immunity.

Eating right can help you prevent cancer and restore your body during and after cancer treatment. For example, chemicals found in common foods such as soybeans or tangerines can stop the development of cancer cells, prevent tumors from spreading, reduce

treatment side effects, enhance chemotherapy and radiation benefits, and support immunity. Changing your diet now can give you
the best chance for a complete recovery!

There is a harsh reality about eating better. New dietary habits
don't always last, despite the best intentions. Life tends to get busy,
or your family insists on fried chicken every Sunday. Permanently
changing your dietary and lifestyle habits can be challenging.
Living well is a conscious choice that requires a renewed commit-
ment each day. Here are some tips to help you successfully change
your diet:

Plan your meals. Count on spending more time, energy, and
money on your meals. It will take you longer to make out your
shopping list, because you'll have to sit down and make out a
menu ahead of time. You will spend more time reading labels. Be
prepared for some sticker shock, too. If you opt to purchase
organic or hormone-free products, your grocery bill can easily
increase by 30 percent.

Meal Planning Basics

- Set aside time to plan your family's meals each week.
  Spread out your cookbooks and begin to formulate
  your meals featuring a variety of entrees, side dishes,
  vegetables, and fruits.
- Consider the seasonal availability of produce. To break
  the monotony of eating apples and citrus fruits in the
  winter, consider using frozen berries or canned fruit
  once in a while.
- Add variety to your meals. Mix flavors, colors, textures,
  and shapes. Vary your preparation methods (stir-fry one
  day, bake the next). Offer a particular meal no more
  than twice a month—unless it is a family favorite!

- Honor your family's food preferences, customs, and special needs. If they don't eat what you prepare, food will go to waste, and you'll be less motivated to try new recipes.
- Don't assume you will need to purchase your foods from a health food store. Healthier versions of breads, cereals, and snacks, and soy products and hormone-free animal products are available in most large grocery stores.
- Try new foods at least once. Or, if you have tried a particular food and didn't like it, don't write it off. Try a different brand, or try it prepared in a different way. Look through cookbooks for recipes that include fruits or vegetables that you might not eat alone, but would be willing to try mixed into something.
- Disguise healthy foods if you have to. Mix soy milk in with skim milk, add textured vegetable protein crumbles into ground beef or turkey recipes, and hide vegetables in sauces. Don't say a word, just smile and serve.
- Choose food over pills. If you think that taking dietary supplements will somehow make up for poor dietary choices, you are wrong. No amount of vitamins, minerals, or herbal concoctions will provide your body with the necessary components to function properly. First and foremost, your body needs wholesome, nutritious food. Nutritional supplements work together with a healthful diet to repair cells, regenerate the immune system, and fight cancer.
- Avoid feeling guilty. If the voice inside your head tells you it's okay to have that piece of chocolate, then have it and don't think twice about it. Negative or guilty

thoughts may be as detrimental to your immune system as eating poorly. It is fine to periodically indulge in your favorite foods. This will help to keep you sane and prevent you from feeling deprived. Deprivation tends to lead to total dietary destruction. Indulge too often, though, and you will not experience the health benefits you desire. Remember that what you eat will most often shape your overall health.

- Avoid rigid dietary rituals, especially if you have lost a significant amount of weight. If you, or others, suspect that your eating habits may be damaging your health, seek the help of a healthcare practitioner who can make sure you are meeting your nutritional needs.

Step 6: Build a Winning Character

I have noticed that people who nurtured their psychological, spiritual, and physical needs were more likely to breeze through treatment and maintain a stronger immune system than those who only used standard cancer treatment modalities. Here are some of these people's winning characteristics that you should try to emulate:

- They didn't believe that a diagnosis of cancer meant death.
- They believed in nutritional therapy and made major dietary changes.
- They followed a dietary supplement regimen, as discussed with a qualified healthcare professional.
- They enlisted the help of their family and friends to help them keep their new dietary habits.
- They became an active participant in their medical care.

- They were labeled "high maintenance" patients because they continually communicated their concerns or questions to their physicians.
- They practiced stress reduction techniques.
- They routinely exercised.
- They developed a spiritual connection.
- They wanted to share their experiences and motivate others.
- They exhibited patience and had realistic expectations.
- They knew that there was more than one way to treat their illness, so they sought second and sometimes third opinions about their medical care.
- They stopped destructive lifestyle habits.
- They did not see cancer as limiting, but freeing.
- They were hopeful and looked forward to the future.
- They had some form of social support, either from family, friends, caregivers, or support group members.
- They explored opportunities for personal growth.
- They laughed.
- They acted on their desire to be healthier and stronger.
- They did not question why they got cancer, but focused on how to change its course.
- They did not dwell on any past medical blunders, personal lifestyle choices, insurance frustrations, or other negative issues in their lives.
- They did not blame themselves for their cancer.

As You Begin Your Race...

While nutritional therapy is the focus of this book, it is apparent that a holistic approach to cancer will increase your chances for a complete recovery. Whatever strategies you employ to beat cancer, remember that even small changes can have a big impact on your health. Keep your mind tuned to the positive experiences as you make dietary and lifestyle changes. Ultimately, it is up to you to evaluate your progress and determine your success. Keep your eyes focused on the finish line and don't look back.

It's time to begin your race against cancer. Are you ready? Get set! Go!

– 2 –

Are You
Running on Empty?

"Make hunger thy sauce, as a medicine for health."
– *Thomas Tusser, 1524*

Malnutrition

THE STATISTICS ARE QUITE SOBERING: Over 40 percent of cancer patients die from causes related to malnutrition, not from cancer itself.[1] If you aren't adequately nourished or are depleted of protein or other nutrients, you may be suffering from malnutrition.

Why is malnutrition such a threat? Cancer causes changes that can alter the level of nutrients your body requires for optimal functioning. Side effects associated with chemotherapy, radiation, and surgery can complicate your ability to eat, absorb, or utilize foods. The final insult comes when a malnourished body can't support treatment goals. When you are poorly nourished, your current treatment may not be as effective, or you might not be able to tolerate further treatments.

Over time, inadequate or improper dietary habits can wreak havoc on the healthiest individuals, even "healthy" cancer patients. If you don't address dietary deficiencies, cachexia ensues. Think of cachexia as a downward spiral. Every cell in your body requires many nutrients to work effectively. Without the proper fuel, cells can't do their jobs, and debilitation begins. Without an opportunity for rebuilding, the chances of recovery are greatly reduced.

Before you dismiss malnutrition as a condition for the weak and debilitated, understand that even minor degrees of undernutrition are associated with a marked increased risk of hospital admissions and death.[2] Between 40 and 80 percent of all cancer patients develop some degree of clinical malnutrition.[3]

Malnutrition Myths

Myth #1: You Know When You Are Malnourished

Malnutrition is not always as physically obvious as you might think. When you picture someone who is malnourished, do you see a thin, frail, weakened individual sitting in a wheelchair? Certainly, underweight individuals can be malnourished, but weight alone is not a good indicator of the internal health changes brought about by poor eating or cancer.[4] If you are able to pinch more than an inch, you could still be suffering from the consequences of poor nutrition. My clinical experience has taught me that many overweight folks also need nutritional intervention during their cancer treatment.

Myth #2: It Is Easy To Regain Weight

Many people feel they can "pull through" the rest of their treatment, then gain back any weight they might have lost in the process. Unfortunately, for most cancer patients, putting weight back on can be an overwhelming, difficult task.

Myth #3: Nutrition Doesn't Impact Your Cancer Outcome

Some physicians feel that nutrition is not important when it comes to cancer, but there is a link between eating right and sustaining yourself during and after cancer treatment. The diagnosis of cancer and the treatment may contribute in several ways to the risk of malnutrition:

- Your metabolism may change. Increased levels of calories and nutrients may be needed to help your body rebuild itself.
- Your body may not be functioning at its best. The digestive tract can become sluggish, hindering clearance of toxic substances from the body.
- Your treatment may predispose you to nutritional problems. Physical, debilitating side effects associated with your treatment regimen can leave you weak and unable to eat much.
- You may experience dietary anxiety. If you have read conflicting nutritional approaches to cancer, you may be confused or fearful about what to eat.

- You may have social challenges. Depression and isolation can diminish appetite and compromise the body's natural defenses.

Coach's Corner

Randall was a robust man in his late fifties who had been diagnosed with lung cancer. I remember how he meandered down the hospital corridor, cowboy hat perched on his head, with a swagger that would rival John Wayne's. Randall had a hearty laugh and a demeanor to match.

Randall initially tolerated his chemotherapy well. As several weeks went by, however, his appetite decreased and he began to lose weight. When I asked Randall if he would like to try a special shake to help him regain some strength and weight, he refused. Real cowboys, he explained, don't need help.

A few months later, Randall was thirty-five pounds lighter. He used a rustic, carved wooden cane to walk. About that time Randall agreed to receive nutritional therapy. Efforts were made to help Randall regain some health and energy, but he had lost a significant amount of weight very quickly and had developed a lung infection. Unfortunately, Randall was unable to recover his health, and he died a few months later. His primary diagnosis: malnutrition. Randall joined the numerous ranks of "cancer" victims who lost their lives to the seemingly benign condition of poor nutrition.

Self-Assessment: Are You at Risk for Malnutrition?

*Complete this personal checklist to determine whether
you may be at risk for malnutrition.*

Malnutrition Risk Survey

(Circle your answer)

1. I am underweight.   Yes   No
2. I have lost weight recently.   Yes   No
3. I have had a recent change in my appetite.   Yes   No
4. I do not have an appetite.   Yes   No
5. It doesn't take much food to make me feel full.   Yes   No
6. Some foods taste or smell unusual.   Yes   No
7. I have difficulty swallowing or chewing.   Yes   No
8. I have frequent nausea or vomiting.   Yes   No
9. I have frequent bouts of diarrhea or constipation.   Yes   No
10. I often have gas, bloating, cramping, or heartburn.   Yes   No
11. I have a malabsorption disease of my gastrointestinal tract,
    such as celiac disease, parasites, Crohn's disease, and so forth.
    Yes   No
12. I have had a recent illness or infection.   Yes   No
13. I have had surgery to remove some part of my gastrointestinal
    tract.   Yes   No
14. I am retaining water in my ankles or stomach area.   Yes   No
15. I receive tube or intravenous feedings.   Yes   No
16. My energy level is less than it used to be.   Yes   No
17. I am on medications that decrease my appetite.   Yes   No
18. I am on a restricted diet (low salt, diabetic).   Yes   No

Total: Yes _____   No _____

Survey Interpretation

The number of yes answers positively correlates to an increased risk for malnutrition that can profoundly interfere with your cancer treatment and recovery. Every yes answer can significantly detract from your overall well-being. If you feel you are at risk for malnutrition based on this questionnaire, immediately seek medical advice.

Avoid Malnutrition

You can take several steps to make sure your nutritional status is up to par:

1. Address the weakening effects of poor nutrition before they become an issue. This point is best illustrated with a story about a woman with pancreatic cancer who received a feeding tube during surgery. Her surgeon encouraged her to eat and use the tube in an emergency. She went home and was unable to eat very much, but she did not use the tube. After three weeks, she had lost fifteen pounds. Why choose to ignore your nutritional needs? Be prepared to address them right from the start. Communicate with your doctor. Discuss your risk for malnutrition with your healthcare providers and let them know you are concerned about your nutritional status. A clinical dietitian should be following your progress throughout your treatment and should be available to discuss your dietary needs or concerns. If you haven't met with a dietitian — ask! A dietitian or nutritionist can help you identify risk factors and devise solutions to any special needs related to your diet.

2. Ignore advice to "eat whatever you want." Have you been told to eat whatever you want in order to keep your weight up?

Instead, consider how nourishing your food is or whether your diet is detrimental to the immune system. Although it is better to eat something rather than nothing, what you eat can make a difference in your cancer outcome. If you eat rich, thick ice cream milkshakes and cream soups in an attempt to maintain your weight, you are not providing your body what it needs to rid itself of cancer. With a little planning and some knowledge, you can make better meals that are quick to prepare, taste good, are easy to digest, and support normal cell division and immune function.

3. Maintain your weight. Weight loss is frequently used to evaluate early malnutrition and impacts the survival time of newly diagnosed cancer patients even more than their chemotherapy regimen.[5] If you lose as little as 5 percent of your current body weight, your health and cancer recovery can be compromised.

Unintentional weight loss can occur at any stage of a cancer diagnosis or treatment plan. While a few pounds here or there probably aren't critical and most likely reflect a shifting fluid balance, it is important to be aware of weight change trends. Don't think that you can "starve" the cancer. Rapid or progressive weight loss usually signals lost muscle mass, impaired immunity, and free radical generation, and presents the greatest risk for complications that reduce the survival and quality of life for many cancer patients. The percentage of weight loss and the rate of loss are both critical for determining whether negative health consequences may arise. The following diagram shows that as weight loss continues, the risk of health complications and death increases:[6]

Percent Weight Loss and
the Risk for Increased Morbidity and Mortality

0% None	30% Serious
10% Limited	40% Life threatening
20% Significant	>40% Lethal

If you think your weight loss may be affecting your health, ask your dietitian to determine your percent weight loss, or see Appendix 2 for an equation to calculate this for yourself. Based on your risk, you may wish to consult with a nutritionist.

4. Lose weight safely if you are overweight. Obesity, as well as undernutrition, can play a role in the disease process. Excess weight has been linked to a higher risk of many kinds of cancer (endometrial, kidney, *postmenopausal* breast, and possibly colon) and other degenerative diseases. If weight reduction is a health goal, limit your weight loss to no more than one to two pounds per week. When you have cancer, it is essential that you consult with a nutritionist who will help you determine realistic and safe goals for gradual weight loss.

5. Learn what your needs are. I'm always shocked to hear that most patients do not know what their calorie and protein requirements are. Knowing what your body requires makes it easier to define your dietary goals. If you would like to know specifically what your energy and protein needs are, I suggest you contact the hospital dietitian or nutritionist. Nutritional professionals routinely calculate these requirements for every patient, so don't hesitate to ask.

If you need assistance finding a dietitian in your area, call the American Dietetic Association. Their number is listed in the resource section of this book. A dietitian can enter specific information about your height, weight, age, gender, activity, and stress factors into a calculation and provide you with a reliable estimate of what your energy and protein requirements are.

Appendix 3 provides an equation and worksheet to help you calculate your energy and protein needs if you prefer to do it on your own and don't mind some math. Keep in mind that the general calculation provides you with an estimate of your baseline calorie and protein requirements; in some individuals, cancer or treatment may cause requirements to be greater than usual.

6. Monitor your progress. Anyone who undergoes chemotherapy, radiation, or surgery has had their blood drawn at one point or another. Laboratory tests convey a general cell response trend that helps the doctor determine when changes in your treatment plan are necessary.

If you become familiar with a few of the laboratory results, you will be able to get more involved in your treatment. Looking at the numbers on a laboratory test can help you create a picture in your mind of what is going on inside of you. This visualization can be very powerful for proactive healing.

I recommend that you maintain your own copy of blood tests and talk to your doctor about the results. Ask your doctor:

- What does this specific blood test tell about me?
- Why would this particular laboratory result be abnormal?
- Are any of my reported symptoms associated with this abnormal laboratory value? If so, can anything be done to improve that value?
- Will this abnormal laboratory result affect my treatment? If so, how?
- How often will I be getting my blood drawn for these tests?
- Where can I get a copy of my results each time my blood is drawn?

Remember, your doctor uses these blood tests to help determine how to best treat you. The results of a single laboratory test should be interpreted cautiously. Sometimes, laboratory tests can be falsely elevated or depressed depending on factors such as fluid balance, prescription medication use, organ dysfunction, trauma, and other nonnutritive factors. Through consistent monitoring, your doctor is able to obtain a more accurate picture of how your body is responding to your treatment. If you feel you aren't getting satisfactory answers to your questions about your blood work, find a nurse or dietitian to address your concerns. Both of these healthcare professionals have a general knowledge of what physiological alterations cause a particular laboratory test to register as abnormal and may be able to answer your questions sufficiently.

Common Laboratory Tests

Laboratory tests help gauge your overall health and screen for any problems. The complete blood count (CBC) and chemistry panel have some components that correlate directly with nutritional status. Appendix 4 contains a sample CBC and chemistry panel for your reference during this section.

Complete Blood Count (CBC)

The CBC is a basic screening test that provides diagnostic information about your various blood cells. The CBC includes a white blood cell count (WBC) and differential (the proportions of the different kinds of white blood cells with specific functions in the body's defense), red blood cell count (RBC), hemoglobin, and hematocrit. The CBC counts you should pay close attention to include the WBC, RBC, hemoglobin, and hematocrit.

WBCs

Your white blood cells rescue you from invading bacteria, viruses, and other foreign substances. When your WBC count is high, you may have an infection. When it is consistently low, your doctor may decide to withhold treatment until your numbers rise. Here are some of the most common interventions to increase WBC production:

- Neupogen, an injectable prescription drug that stimulates production of white blood cells.
- Dietary analysis to determine the adequacy of calorie and protein intake, which provide essential building materials for all cells.
- Supplements to support the immune system such as echinacea, astragalus, zinc, thymus glandular extract, vitamin C, and other antioxidants. Ask your healthcare professional for recommendations regarding these supplements.

RBCs

Red blood cells circulate in the body, transporting and distributing substances to meet the needs of specific body tissues. Hemoglobin measures the oxygen carrying capacity of the red blood cells, and hematocrit is a measurement of the volume of red blood cells in a volume of blood.

Cancer treatment can shorten the life span of your blood cells, creating symptoms of anemia, represented by a characteristic drop in RBC, hemoglobin, and hematocrit counts. Anemia can also arise from a diet low in iron, certain amino acids, and B vitamins. These changes can lead to fatigue, intolerance to cold, poor energy production, and pale skin color. If your blood cell levels are very low, the doctor may recommend a blood transfusion. Current therapies used to increase your RBC, hemoglobin, and hematocrit include:

- Epogen, an injectable prescription drug that is used to boost RBC production.
- Dietary analysis to determine the adequacy of calorie and protein intake. (Surely, this is not a surprise by now!)
- Supplements such as vitamin C, hydrolyzed liver extract, B vitamins (particularly B_{12} and folate), and iron, which are essential for healthy production of blood cells. Ask your healthcare professional for recommendations regarding these supplements.

Anemia

Because there are many reasons for anemia, it is best to have a definitive clinical determination of the underlying cause. If you are anemic, ask for serum ferritin (to determine iron stores), folate, and B_{12} level lab tests. These will help your healthcare provider determine what kind of vitamin therapy is appropriate for your anemia.

If you have been diagnosed with anemia, you may or may not need iron. Don't take iron until you find out from your healthcare professional whether you need to. Unused iron can be detrimental to cancer patients because it becomes a pro-oxidant in the body, causing cellular damage.[7]

On the other hand, if you are iron deficient, iron supplements can increase oxygen and nutrient flow to tissues, aiding the rebuilding process. Long-term iron supplementation is usually not necessary, so ask that a CBC be drawn periodically to determine whether continuing your iron supplement is appropriate.

Getting the Edge

Effectively Combating Iron Deficiency Anemia

When iron deficiency sets in, a cancer-fighting diet doesn't come close to providing enough iron to do the trick. Consuming a diet low in animal protein (where highly absorbable iron is found) or high in fiber makes it difficult for your body to absorb adequate amounts of iron. A supplement is almost always needed. Combine an iron-rich diet with an iron supplement for fastest recovery.

Iron is found in eggs, fish, meat, poultry, green leafy vegetables, whole grains, almonds, avocados, beets, brewer's yeast, dates, kelp, kidney beans, lentils, millet, peaches, pears, dried prunes, raisins, soybeans, and watercress.

Chemistry Panel

The chemistry panel, often called a metabolic panel or metabolic profile, provides a view of the overall function of specific organs. There are many components within this test, but for our purposes, I will discuss the one used to ascertain malnutrition risk. The chemistry panel can tell you much more, and if you are so inclined, you may want to ask your doctor, nurse, or dietitian to help you decipher the meaning of other values. Fischbach's *Laboratory Diagnostic Tests* is an excellent reference for those who prefer to learn about laboratory values on their own.

Strengths and Weaknesses of Iron

Gold Medal Action

When purchasing an over-the-counter iron supplement, choose iron in the form of ferrous succinate or fumarate. These highly absorbable forms of iron are tolerated well and are not expensive. Recommended dosage for iron deficiency is 30 mg of elemental iron twice a day. You can enhance iron absorption by combining iron-rich foods or supplements with foods containing vitamin C.

Avoid taking iron supplements with coffee, tea, calcium supplements, or a high fiber meal. These items contain compounds that bind with iron, rendering it unabsorbable. Some individuals with a sensitive stomach may have difficulty tolerating iron supplements. Reducing and then gradually increasing the dosage may help. Taking iron with meals can decrease the possibility of iron intolerance symptoms such as diarrhea, stomach pain, heartburn, gas, and vomiting.

Protein Status

Serum albumin is considered a fairly reliable indicator of protein status, especially when looking at malnutrition in later stages. Serum prealbumin can be used to determine earlier stage protein deficiencies, but most doctors do not routinely order this lab test. Ask whether this test would help the doctor assess your overall health status.

Albumin is a carrier protein that is also responsible for maintaining normal distribution of water within the body. If you notice edema (water retention) around your abdomen or extremities, you may not be getting adequate calories or protein in your diet.

Serum albumin levels lower than 3.5 mg/dl are correlated with an increased risk of malnutrition. What can you do if your albumin is low? First, follow up with your healthcare professional to create a plan of action to stabilize this component. Your nutritionist may have you evaluate your diet for calorie and protein adequacy. Often, a high-calorie protein supplement is suggested when the albumin drops below this level.

Quick Bites

Super Smoothie!

Serves. 1

- 2 scoops high-calorie, high-protein powder such as Gainers Fuel 1000 or Atkins Shake Mix
- 8 oz fluid (lite soy milk, skim milk, 100% fruit juice, water)
- 3 or 4 ice cubes
- 1/2 cup frozen or fresh fruit (strawberries, pineapple, blueberries)

Mix in a blender and enjoy. Provides approximately 400 calories and 20 grams of protein per serving.

Need more calories? Try these delicious, nutritious add-ins: 2 Tbs ground flaxseeds, 2 Tbs wheat germ, 8 oz plain non-fat yogurt, 1/4 cup powdered milk, 2 oz silken tofu, 1 scoop isolated soy or whey protein powder.

How's Your Diet?

Most people falsely perceive that they eat pretty well. The truth is, the standard American diet is nutritionally weak. A large survey on dietary habits showed that respondents consumed less than the recommended daily allowance (RDA) of six of the eleven nutrients studied![8] Other national consumption studies confirm that average Americans are typically deficient in vitamins A and C, and minerals such as calcium and magnesium.[9,10]

Food Records

Food records are a tool for determining the adequacy of your diet. Often, you can eyeball whether or not you are consuming enough calories, protein, or other nutrients. Whether you believe that you eat right or not, I encourage you to complete a food record. Compare your completed food records to your specific nutrition action plan to ascertain whether you are eating as well as you can for your specific cancer.

To determine whether you are consuming enough of a specific nutrient, such as calcium or vitamin C, you can refer to a food composition book. I recommend purchasing a food composition book, which contains a wealth of nutritional data, including calorie, protein, fat, vitamin, and mineral content for most foods. Nutrient composition tables are also available through the United States Department of Agriculture. See the resource section for their Web site address.

Blank food record intake sheets are provided in Appendix 5.

How To Complete a Food Record

- Record what you eat for two or three days.
- Record usual foods consumed to ensure accurate representation.
- Record food amounts in common measurements, such as ounces, cups, teaspoons, and so forth. Avoid vague measurements such as "a handful" or "a big bowl."
- List all condiments, such as sugar, jelly, margarine, mayonnaise, and so on. They contain calories too!
- Record all fluids consumed, including water.

Sample Completed Food Record

Name: Mary Kay Eatright

Date: Tuesday

Food Eaten (include serving sizes/amounts):

Breakfast

1 omelet (prepared with vegetable cooking spray)

    2 eggs

    1 oz cheddar cheese

    1/2 cup diced vegetables (green peppers, mushrooms, onions, red peppers, potatoes)

2 pieces whole grain toast

1 teaspoon butter

1/2 grapefruit

1 cup green tea

8 oz purified water

Chapter 2

Lunch

Turkey sandwich
    2 slices whole grain bread
    1/2 tsp mustard
    3 oz turkey breast
    lettuce, tomato, onion slice
fresh fruit cup (1 cup assorted orange, tangerine, strawberry, and banana slices)
1/2 cup cooked broccoli
1 cup green tea
8 oz purified water

Snack

10 raw almonds
1 medium red apple
8 oz purified water

Dinner

1 cup whole wheat spaghetti noodles
1/2 cup marinara sauce
1 cup salad (mixed greens, cucumber, tomato, onion, carrots)
1 Tbs olive oil, 1 tsp balsamic vinegar
1/2 cup cooked green beans
1 whole grain dinner roll
1 tsp butter
1 cup green tea
8 oz purified water

Gold Medal Action

Problem Solving for a Poor Diet

Need help with your diet? Try the following suggestions to help you meet your nutritional goals:

- Eat small, frequent meals.
- Choose soft textures or puree your foods in a blender.
- Avoid foods containing lactose (milk products).
- Take digestive enzymes with all your meals.
- Talk to your healthcare provider about an appetite stimulant.
- Choose calorie dense, healthy foods.
- Try commercial high-calorie, high-protein drinks. Choose a product that best meets your nutritional goal.
- Talk to your healthcare provider about nutrition support.
- Find a dining partner. You tend to eat more when you aren't socially isolated.
- Place smaller portions of food on your plate to avoid feeling overwhelmed.
- Don't drink empty calorie liquids like water or herbal teas before a meal. They will help you fill up, but not help you fill out.

Consolidated Calories!

Add healthy calories to your diet by eating more of these foods:

Fruits: Currants and raisins, dates and figs, and dried apples and apricots make great cereal toppers. Eat more bananas, cherries, canned fruit in juice, fruit juice bars, mangoes, pineapple, and plantains. Drink 100% fruit juice with all of your meals.

Vegetables: Starchy vegetables such as corn, lima beans, parsnips, peas, potatoes, squash, succotash, and sweet potatoes help you cram in the calories.

Breads and Cereals: Eat more calorie-packed cereals such as All-Bran, Bran-Buds, Fruitful Bran, Fruit Squares, and low-fat granolas. Choose quinoa, whole grain breads and pastas, and wild or brown rice. Add wheat germ to cereals, yogurt, and salads.

Dairy: Don't load up on whole-fat dairy products. Instead, choose nonfat cheeses and yogurts. Add extra calcium and calories by mixing dry milk powder into foods.

Meats and Proteins: Beans brimming with calories include garbonzo, kidney, navy, and pinto. Eat more bluefish, chubb, herring, mackerel, salmon, sardines, swordfish, and tuna, which contain healthy fats. Try lite soy milk, tempeh, textured vegetable protein, and lite tofu.

Fats: Add extra virgin olive or canola oil to beans, greens, pasta, potatoes, chicken, or fish. Choose tuna packed in oil. Top salads or sandwiches with slices of avocado.

Not All Supplemental Drinks Are the Same!

In keeping with healthy diet principles, I recommand avoiding Boost Plus or Carnation Instant Breakfast, which contain too much sugar and fat. Better high-protein choices include Gainers Fuel 1000 and Atkins Shake Mix. Of course, taste is the most important factor. After all, you have to drink the supplement to get the nutritional benefit!

Gold Medal Action

Revving Up Your Appetite

Don't bother fixing a five-course gourmet meal! If you don't feel like eating, you will not be tempted by mounds of sumptuous food. If your appetite continues to drag, ask your physician or nutritionist for details about prescription medications that can help you recover lost weight and regain your desire to eat.

- Prednisone, a corticosteriod hormone given in small doses, has helped to stimulate appetite.
- Megace, used up to four times per day, has promoted significant weight gain in immunocompromised individuals.[11,12]
  - Marinol, a controlled drug, has reduced nausea and helped to stabilize weight.[13]

High Calorie, High Protein Supplemental Drinks

Protein Formula (8 oz serving)	Form	Calories	Protein	Fat	Sugars	Fiber	Source	Lactose-Free?
Atkins Shake Mix	Powder	170 cal	24 gm	8 gm	0 gm	0 gm	Casein, egg	No
Boost	Premixed	240 cal	10 gm	4 gm	23 gm	0 gm	Milk	No
Boost High Protein	Premixed	240 cal	15 gm	6 gm	14 gm	0 gm	Milk	No
Boost Plus	Premixed	360 cal	14 gm	14 gm	20 gm	<1 gm	Milk	No
Carnation Instant Breakfast	Premixed	176 cal	10 gm	2 gm	27 gm	2 gm	Milk	No
Ensure	Premixed	250 cal	9 gm	6 gm	14 gm	0 gm	Soy	Yes
Ensure Fiber FOS	Premixed	250 cal	9 gm	6 gm	12 gm	3 gm	Soy	Yes
Ensure High Protein	Premixed	230 cal	12 gm	6 gm	19 gm	0 gm	Soy	Yes
Ensure Plus	Premixed	360 cal	13 gm	11 gm	16 gm	0 gm	Soy	Yes
Gainers Fuel 1000	Powder	175 cal	8 gm	<1 gm	19 gm	0 gm	Milk, egg	No
Nutrament	Premixed	240 cal	11 gm	7 gm	31 gm	0 gm	Soy	No
Total Balance	Powder	190 cal	14 gm	6 gm	15 gm	2 gm	Soy, whey	No

SOURCE: *Product labels*

Advanced Nutritional Support

If high-calorie shakes, appetite stimulants, and other dietary modifications don't help you maintain your weight, you may need advanced nutritional support. Advanced nutritional support used as a complementary therapy to basic cancer treatment can decrease the risk of further deterioration, improve some nutritional and immunological parameters, avoid health complications associated with malnutrition, and enhance quality of life.[14] Nutritional support techniques used in cancer patients have reduced complication rates of surgery by 33 percent![15] Additionally, survival rates improved, without affecting tumor growth.[16] Take note of this fact: Some doctors avoid using advanced nutritional support fearing that they will feed the cancer. Today, we know that just isn't so!

How do you know whether you are a candidate for advanced nutrition support? The malnutrition self-assessment, along with the professional assessment of your healthcare providers, can be valuable tools to ascertain what type of nutritional support you need. Advanced nutritional support can be delivered into your gastrointestinal tract (enteral feeding) or blood vessels (parenteral feeding).

Enteral Feedings

Enteral feedings, commonly called tube feedings, are best suited for people who can still eat, digest, and assimilate foods through their gastrointestinal tract. A tube is placed surgically or by an endoscope in an outpatient procedure. This form of advanced nutritional support is the most cost-effective and best for optimal delivery of nutrients to your body. The rule of thumb is, if the gut works, use it. So, if your gastrointestinal tract is functioning, this method of nutritional support is appropriate for you.

Enteral feeding is most often selected for those who

- Consistently eat less than 1,000 calories per day,
- Have oral–mechanical or physiological obstruction that makes it difficult to eat and digest food (e.g., head and neck cancers, swallowing difficulties due to radiation of the esophagus, etc.),
- Have metabolic dysfunction where it is difficult to digest or absorb foods,
- Have dramatically increased needs due to rapid cell destruction or tumor-induced hypermetabolism, and
- Do not have intractable vomiting or diarrhea, intestinal blockage, or gastrointestinal bleeding.

Talk to your oncologist and a gastroenterologist if you feel that you would be a good candidate for this type of nutritional support. If you are scheduled for gastrointestinal tract surgery, it would make sense to ask your surgeon whether a feeding tube could be placed at that time. This forethought could save you an outpatient procedure and limit your exposure to infectious pathogens.

If you require a tube feeding, your doctor will talk to you about tube placement techniques and will review any potential complications. Your nutritionist and physician will decide which feeding formula will be infused through the tube. There are many kinds of enteral feeding formulas, including formulas that contain nutrients such as glutamine or omega-3 fatty acids. Patients receiving these immune-enhancing formulas experience fewer infections and spend significantly less time in the hospital.[17]

Prior to hospital discharge, your nurse will explain how to care for your tube and how to administer your feedings. Arrangements are usually made for home healthcare agencies to deliver supplies and formula for tube feedings to your home. Your job will be to monitor and report your tolerance to the suggested tube-feeding regimen. You must let your healthcare provider or home health nurse know if you are not able to comply with the recommended tube-feeding regimen. If you are nauseated, in pain, or unable to infuse the required amount of formula, you must inform your healthcare providers immediately so that your nutritional progress is not compromised.

Coach's Corner

Robin weighed 120 pounds when she discovered that she had stomach cancer. This was not her usual weight; she had lost nearly 50 pounds two months prior to her diagnosis. During surgery, a feeding tube was placed. Prior to discharge, a feeding regimen was established. About six months after her tube placement, I got a call from Stan, Robin's husband. He was frantic. Robin's weight had plummeted to 89 pounds. Stan told me that Robin had been taking only three of the required six cans of formula per day. Robin and Stan both thought that she would eventually be able to tolerate the recommended six feedings per day, so they put off discussing this discrepancy with the home health nurse and Robin's doctor. Robin was unable to recover from her debilitating weight loss.

Healthcare providers are responsible for monitoring your progress when you are on nutritional support; however, it is your responsibility to keep them informed of any circumstances that keep you from completing your prescribed regimen.

Intravenous Feeding

Intravenous feeding, often called total parenteral nutrition (TPN), is reserved for individuals who are unable to assimilate nutrients through the gastrointestinal tract. Nutrients in a liquid solution are infused intravenously.

Total parenteral nutrition requires a surgeon to place a catheter into either a peripheral vein (for short-term feedings) or a central vein such as the subclavian or internal jugular vein (for long-term feedings). As with any surgical procedure, there is an increased risk of infection, so care must be taken to keep the catheter site clean.

Candidates for parenteral nutrition must have

- A non-functional gastrointestinal tract,
- Functioning organs to handle nutrient metabolism,
- The need for bowel rest,
- Severe malnutrition, and
- The inability to eat for five or more days.

As with enteral nutritional therapies, there are different routes and methods of administration, formulas, and complications associated with TPN. Your surgeon and nurse will review all of this information with you prior to your discharge from the hospital. Total parenteral nutrition can be administered at home, and home health agencies provide appropriate follow-up care. TPN and home health care for TPN are covered by most health insurance policies.

— 3 —

Is Your Digestion Off Track?

"Health is not simply the absence of sickness."
– Hannah Green

An Incredible Journey – The Nickel Tour

EVER WONDER WHAT HAPPENS to that twelve-ounce porterhouse steak after you've eaten it? Let's take a walk down the digestive tract and find out.

The process of digestion begins with the sight and smell of food. In fact, the brain signals enzymes in your mouth to be released just at the thought of food. After the food is chewed, mixed with saliva, and swallowed, it travels down the esophagus, a long pipe extending from the throat to the top of the stomach. The stomach is the key to the whole digestive process, releasing hydrochloric acid to break apart proteins. The stomach muscles contract to churn the food into a mixture called chyme. Digestive enzymes secreted from the pancreas work on the partially digested food particles to prepare them for absorption in the small intestine.

About 90 percent of all nutrients are absorbed by the intestines and distributed to cells throughout your body. Fluid and a few other nutrients are absorbed in the colon. Whatever the body doesn't use is eliminated through the colon, and any waste is expelled out of the rectum. Digestion is much more complicated than this, but even with this brief overview, it is easy to see that many steps are required for food to be formulated into body fuel.

A Finicky Tract

There are many opportunities for cancer treatment, or the cancer itself, to affect the intricate functioning of the GI tract. Chemotherapy and radiation have the potential to interrupt the delicate chemical and physical mechanisms needed for the digestion and absorption of food. Because the gastrointestinal tract has rapid cellular turnover, it can be affected by cell-destroying treatments more severely than other parts of the body.

Diarrhea, constipation, excessive bloating and cramping, and other uncomfortable and potentially serious side effects can be very challenging obstacles to health. The risk of malnutrition is increased, especially in cancers of the head or neck. Chewing or swallowing problems occur with treatment involving the surgical removal or chemical destruction of the tongue, neck muscles, salivary glands, or tooth structures. Radiation to the chest can adversely affect the function of the esophagus. Strictures, which are involuntary closures of the esophagus, make swallowing or food passing into the stomach impossible.

Additional negative side effects include gastroesophageal reflux and achalasia, a lack of enzyme activity, and early satiety due to physical blockage caused by tumor invasion into the GI tract wall. Appendix 6 outlines the side effects associated with various chemotherapies.

Self-Assessment: How's Your Gut?

The benefits of eating a healthy, well-balanced diet can be reduced when your GI tract can't adequately digest, absorb, transport, or assimilate nutrients into the cells of your body. Do you experience any of the below GI complaints? These physical symptoms are often linked to GI tract dysfunction.

GI Dysfunction Survey
(Circle your answer)

1. Are you or have you been on antibiotics?   Yes   No
2. Do you consistently have bad breath?   Yes   No
3. Do you feel bloated after a meal?   Yes   No
4. Does your tongue have a thick, white coating on it?   Yes   No
5. Do you have chronic constipation?   Yes   No
6. Do you often experience abdominal cramping?   Yes   No
7. Do you have poor dental health?   Yes   No
8. Do you frequently have diarrhea or undigested food in your stools?   Yes   No

9. Do you have a dry mouth or difficulty swallowing?   Yes   No

10. Do you have greasy, fatty stools?   Yes   No

11. Do you have heartburn or belch frequently?   Yes   No

12. Do you have food sensitivities or allergies?   Yes   No

13. Do you have difficulty digesting milk or milk products? Yes   No

14. Do you have mouth sores or ulcers?   Yes   No

15. Do you have nausea or vomiting?   Yes   No

16. Do you have pain or bowel spasms after you eat?   Yes   No

17. Are you experiencing taste changes?   Yes   No

18. Do you have a burning sensation in your stomach that is relieved when you eat?   Yes   No

Total: Yes ____   No ____

Survey Interpretation

The questions above reflect the conditions and symptoms that can be associated with gastrointestinal dysfunction as a result of cancer treatment or other health-related factors. The greater your number of yes answers, the more likely your nutritional status will be affected by weakened GI tract activity. GI tract dysfunction can potentially interfere with your cancer treatment and prolong your recovery. Even one yes answer can detract from your overall well-being and may significantly affect your health.

If you experience any of these symptoms on a regular basis, seek the advice of a healthcare professional. Do not dismiss your GI problems as minor inconveniences. There are effective conventional and natural therapies that can help GI dysfunction and improve well-being.

In this chapter, the symptoms for common cancer treatments and the therapies for each are outlined. Natural therapies sufficiently resolve many GI disorders, so you may want to try nutritional approaches before taking prescription medication. Always discuss your treatment decisions with your medical doctor.

First Aid Station
GI Obstacle: Antibiotic Use

Antibiotics are used to fight off infections. Unfortunately, they can interrupt the normal balance of beneficial bacteria in the intestinal tract. Altered bacterial counts impair digestion and food absorption, increase the risk of urinary tract infections, and provide a breeding ground for candida. Candida is a yeast normally present in the body that can grow out of control and cause health problems. Gastrointestinal symptoms associated with the lack of "friendly" bacteria in your colon include gas, bloating, and constipation.

First Aid

- Eat plain, nonfat yogurt to establish healthy friendly bacterial counts. Yogurt should contain active live cultures.
- Eat more dietary fiber to nourish friendly bacteria.
- Drink at least 64 oz of purified water per day.
- Take probiotics. Probiotic capsules contain live cells that can help optimize gut bacterial counts.
- Support the immune system. Thymus glandular extracts, vitamins C and E, zinc, selenium, echinacea, astragalus, and Chinese mushrooms have proven immune-stimulating activity.

- See your doctor. If your symptoms have not significantly improved by the time you have finished your antibiotic course, follow up with your doctor. You may need a stronger medication or additional testing.

Gold Medal Action

Say Yes to Yogurt!

Yogurt contains several types of bacteria, including the strains lactobacillus and bifidobacterium, which have tumor-killing activity![1]

Quick Bites

Fruit n' Nut Sundaes

Serves: 4

- 4 cups of bite-sized pieces of fresh fruit (pitted cherries, blueberries, peaches, strawberries, kiwi fruit)
- 1/3 cup peach low-fat yogurt
- 1/4 cup raw almond slivers

Combine fruit in a medium bowl, spoon into 4 serving dishes.

Top with yogurt; sprinkle almonds on top.

Dig in and enjoy!

Getting the Edge

Good Bugs!

Do you want to keep your GI tract healthy, but need to get rid of that bacterial infection? It is safe to begin a probiotic such as acidophilus as soon as you start antibiotic treatment. Make sure you take the antibiotic and the probiotic at different times of the day to avoid negating the effect of your medicine.

GI Obstacle: Bad Breath

Bad breath is more than just a social embarrassment. Halitosis is linked to several digestive disorders, including constipation, low levels of stomach acid, and altered gut bacteria levels.

First Aid

- See your dentist. Periodontal disease or tooth infections can contribute to bad breath. Replace your toothbrush and brush your tongue regularly to limit bacterial buildup.
- Eat a high-fiber diet. Toxins left in the colon can cause bad breath.
- Take probiotic capsules that contain live cells. Friendly bacteria encourage detoxification through regular elimination.
- Drink at least 64 oz of purified water per day. Adequate fluid intake is essential for healthy elimination.

- Test for low stomach acid. Hypochlorhydria (low stomach acid) has been linked to several GI problems, including bad breath. You can test for low stomach acid yourself by taking betaine HCl capsules with food. If your symptoms are relieved, you probably have low stomach acid. If your symptoms get worse, you may be overproducing stomach acid and risk GI ulceration. Betaine HCl capsules are available in the digestive wellness section of health food stores.
- Exercise helps the bowels to move, aiding the body's natural detoxification process. Always seek the counsel of your doctor before you begin an exercise program.

GI Obstacle: Bloating

Bloating can be caused by overeating, food allergies, or consuming a high-fiber diet. This uncomfortable feeling of fullness can be the symptom of gut dysbiosis (bacterial imblance), involving candida, parasitic or bacterial infection, or low stomach acid and pancreatic insufficiency. Tumors that block part of the stomach or press up against the diaphragm (the muscle that is positioned between the chest and abdominal cavity) can cause bloating as well.

First Aid

- Eat small, frequent meals.
- Pace yourself at meals. Avoid overeating and limit fried foods and fatty foods. Too much food or fat slows down digestive processes, allowing foods to remain in the stomach for longer periods of time.

- Eat slowly. Don't gulp your food or chew with your mouth open. Excessive air can be trapped, causing a bloated feeling. Limit the amount of chewing gum and breath mints you eat.
- Drink plenty of fluids. Drink at least 64 oz of purified water each day to prevent bowel discomfort associated with a high-fiber diet.
- Limit the following sulfur containing foods only if they cause bloating: broccoli, cauliflower, onions, garlic, celery, apples, and eggs.
- Avoid concentrated sources of sugar, such as dried fruits, candy, syrups, jellies, and desserts. Sweets may contribute to bloating caused by yeast overgrowth.
- Limit milk and milk products if you are lactose intolerant. Lactose intolerance is a common side effect of cancer treatment. Lact-Aid products, available in grocery stores, can improve lactose intolerance.
- Consult an allergist. ELISA food allergy testing identifies food allergens, which contribute to bloating.
- Digestive enzymes, betaine HCl, and probiotics help restore optimal gut functions.
- Stressful situations can cause excessive bloating. Manage stress through behavioral modification techniques such as meditation or routine exercise.
- Follow the "Eat for Less Stress" guidelines on page 81.
- See your doctor about testing for parasites, altered bacteria levels, and candida infections, which may cause bloating.
- Reglan is often prescribed to stimulate gastrointestinal tract activity and assist with gastric emptying.

GI Obstacle: A Thick White Coating on the Tongue (Candidiasis)

Candida yeast infection, otherwise known as thrush, has a cottage cheese appearance in the mouth and is very common in cancer patients. *Candida albicans* levels can increase excessively due to widespread antibiotic use, a high-sugar diet, or depleted immune system mechanisms. A recent study revealed that *Candida albicans* was isolated in 70 percent of cancer patients with solid tumors and in 35 percent of cancer patients with hematologic diseases, such as leukemia.[2]

Oral candida infections can make eating very difficult. Other side effects include bloating, gas, fatigue, and general malaise.

First Aid

- Sugars are the food preferred by *Candida albicans*. Avoid candy, cookies, pies, sherbets, soft drinks, jellies, syrups, and dried fruits. Fruits should be temporarily eliminated and then gradually reintroduced, starting with lower sugar fruits such as cherries, strawberries, blueberries, and blackberries. Avoid milk and milk products that contain lactose (milk sugar).
- Avoid foods that contain yeast such as commercially prepared breads, cakes, cookies, and pizza.
- Limit fermented or moldy foods such as vinegar, sauerkraut, brewer's yeast, cheese, mushrooms, and peanuts.
- Restore normal GI environment with digestive enzymes, betaine HCl, and probiotics. Caprylic acid, garlic, and oregano volatile oil preparations have anti-yeast properties.
- Support the immune system with thymus glandular extracts, vitamins C, E, and zinc and selenium.

- Consult an allergist for ELISA food allergy testing. Food sensitivities are common in patients with yeast problems.
- Systemic yeast infections require overall body detoxification. Support the liver, which can be injured by candida overgrowth,[3] with supplements that repair hepatocytes, such as milk thistle, SAM, and glutathione.
- Stressful situations can exacerbate candida. Manage stress through behavioral modification techniques such as meditation or routine exercise.
- Follow the "Eat for Less Stress" guidelines on page 81.
- Nystatin is commonly prescribed for candida infections.

GI Obstacle: Constipation

Infrequent bowel movements increase the risk of toxic buildup that can contribute to cancer. Effective elimination clears harmful bile acids, dilutes carcinogens, and promotes the growth of beneficial gut bacteria.

Optimal bowel transit time (the amount of time it takes food to enter through the mouth, go through the digestive tract and exit out through the stool) is twelve to eighteen hours. If you have hard stools, difficulty defecating, or do not have a bowel movement at least twice a day, you are constipated. The main cause for constipation is poor fluid intake. Other causes for constipation include dietary intake, recent bowel surgery, and laxative abuse. Chemotherapies that may cause constipation include Navelbine and Temodal.

First Aid

- Eat a high-fiber diet, which promotes bowel regularity and protects against colon cancer.[4] Supplemental powders containing oat bran, rice bran, and psyllium attract water into feces, bulking up the stool for easy passage.

- Avoid milk and milk products if you are lactose intolerant. Lactose intolerance can cause constipation.
- Limit caffeine-containing beverages such as coffee, tea, and cocoa or chocolate products. Caffeine tends to pull water out of the colon.
- Limit binding foods such as bananas, apples, and rice.
- Drink at least 64 oz of purified water per day.
- Stimulate bowel movements by drinking warm liquids, such as broth or herbal tea, prior to meals.
- Natural laxatives include prunes, prune juice, and ground flaxseeds. Senna and cascara sagrada are cathartic herbs.
- Routine exercise may aid in the transit of food along the GI tract,[5] aiding the body's natural detoxification process. Always consult your doctor before you begin an exercise program.
- Digestive enzymes and probiotics that contain live cells will help restore GI environment. Vitamin C and magnesium promote healthy peristalsis.
- Limit the use of laxatives, as bowels can become lazy with regular use. Avoid mineral oil, which interferes with the absorption of calcium and fat-soluble vitamins.
- Explore medication alternatives to pain relievers, antidepressants, or antacids containing aluminum, which are constipating.
- See a gastroenterologist to rule out an intestinal blockage if you have small, ribbon-like stools. Bowel obstructions will usually cause severe cramping and vomiting. If left untreated, the distended bowel can rupture.

GI Obstacle: Abdominal Cramping

Painful spasms or cramping after meals occurs with food intolerances, recent gastrointestinal surgery, radiation to the GI tract, and inflammatory bowel diseases such as Crohn's and ulcerative colitis. Chemotherapies that cause abdominal cramping are Vindesine and Vincristine.

Gold Medal Action

Dynamic Digestives

Digestive enzymes help you digest your foods and kill cancer! Studies show that enzymes stimulate the release of tumor necrosis factor (TNF), a substance that selectively attacks cancer cells!'

Getting the Edge

Are you taking morphine or codeine-based medications for pain? If so, avoid psyllium fiber products such as Metamucil in order to decrease your risk of constipation and colon blockage. Natural herbal preparations that contain cascara sagrada, flaxseed, or senna may be a better option for you.

First Aid

- Gradually increase your fiber intake. Avoid the following foods only if you can't tolerate them: beans, barley, broccoli, Brussels sprouts, cabbage, cauliflower, garlic, nuts, onions, and soybeans.

- Seek professional advice if you have been diagnosed with irritable bowel or other inflammatory bowel diseases. Many nutritional deficiencies may develop with chronic GI diseases.

- Try natural antispasmodics such as chamomile, melissa, rosemary, valerian root, and magnesium.

- Support GI tract healing with digestive enzymes, probiotics, glutamine, essiac tea, aloe vera, flaxseed oil, zinc, gamma-oryzanol, and deglycyrrhizinated licorice.

- Stressful situations seem to trigger bowel symptoms Manage stress through behavioral modification techniques such as meditation or routine exercise.

- Follow the "Eat for Less Stress" guidelines on page 81.

- Consult an allergist for ELISA food allergy testing. Your doctor will help you to determine what, if any, food hypersensitivities may be contributing to your discomfort.

- Rest your bowels after surgery by consuming clear liquids or elemental diet drinks. Bowels can become tender postoperatively and need time to recover before they begin working again. Slowly transition from liquids to a low-residue solid diet (low fiber, minimal dairy products). See Appendix 7 for dietary guidelines after GI surgery.

GI Obstacle: Poor Dental Health

Poor dental health affects general health. Infections can negatively affect immune system responses, while the inability to chew can tax your digestive processes. Ill-fitting dentures cause pain and limit dietary choices, which can lead to malnutrition.

First Aid

- A complete dental exam will check and correct trouble spots. Inform your dentist that you are undergoing cancer treatment, and notify your oncologist when dental procedures are needed. Be refitted for dentures if you have lost weight, and your dentures no longer fit.
- Chop your food into smaller bites, tenderize meats, and limit raw foods. Consume shakes, soups, and other liquid foods until you resolve your dental problems.
- Avoid extremely hot or cold foods if you have temperature sensitivities. Avoid eating sugar and sticky foods that promote dental caries.
- Nutrients essential to good dental health include vitamins A and D, and the minerals calcium and phosphorus. Avoid chewable or powdered forms of vitamin C that can irritate the inside of the mouth and erode tooth enamel. Tea tree oil works as an antiseptic for tooth infections.
- You may wish to avoid dental sensitivity toothpastes, which can contain nitrates.
- If you have a tooth infection, your dentist may prescribe an antibiotic. Eat yogurt and take probiotic supplements to help balance intestinal flora.

GI Obstacle: Diarrhea

Certain physical characteristics of the stool can warn us about potential health problems. When you have diarrhea, food is whisked through your GI tract so quickly that it can't be adequately absorbed and assimilated into cells. This rapid transit of nutrients leads to weight loss, dehydration, immune system depression, physical weakness, and malnutrition.

Various chemotherapy drugs can cause diarrhea. Navelbine, Taxotere, Taxol, and 5-FU can have toxic effects on the intestinal lining of the bowels. Radiation to the pelvic area reduces digestive and absorptive capacity, often causing watery stools. Many digestive disorders, such as lactose intolerance, inflammatory bowel disease, and irritable bowel syndrome can also lead to diarrhea.

First Aid

- Completely chew your food to aid digestion. Enzymes in the digestive tract can readily break down the smaller food components of well-chewed food, ensuring optimal absorption into the intestinal wall.
- Eat a high-fiber diet or try the BRAT diet. The BRAT diet can be used for a few days to help control severe diarrhea. This diet is named for the selection of foods that bind: bananas, rice, apples, and toast.
- Rehydrate with juices (naturally high in potassium). Prolonged loss of fluids can lead to dehydration and mineral imbalance. Add soy protein or carob powders to drink mixtures. Soy powder has been used to reduce diarrhea induced by chemotherapy.[7]
- Stimulate digestive enzyme activity with pungent foods such as garlic, ginger, curry, and onions. Raw foods,

which contain live digestive enzymes, contribute to digestion as well.

- Avoid foods or drinks that stimulate loose bowels such as prunes, other dried fruits, prune juice, sugary sports drinks such as Gatorade, juices with added sugar, and so on.
- Avoid sugarless candies and gums that contain sugar alcohols such as mannitol, xylitol, or sorbitol. Even small amounts of these products can cause diarrhea.[8]
- Hot foods stimulate peristalsis so you may want to eat more cold or room temperature foods.
- Raw beans, broccoli, cauliflower, Brussels sprouts, and cabbage may be difficult to digest.
- Avoid all dairy products except for yogurt if you are lactose intolerant.
- Digestive enzymes can help with possible pancreatic digestive insufficiency. Probiotics that contain live cells can improve gastrointestinal function. Look for acidophilus supplements that contain *Saccharomyces bouldardii,* a yeast that has been used to treat diarrhea induced by antibiotics.
- Herbs used to treat parasite induced diarrhea include goldenseal, Oregon grape, and grapefruit seed extract. Zinc and B_{12} may be needed to replace losses due to excessive diarrhea.
- See a gastroenterologist to determine whether you have parasites or bacterial overgrowth.
- Antidiarrheals such as Kaopectate or Lomotil are prescribed to slow bowel movements or thicken stools. Kaopectate has no side effects, but Lomotil can cause bloating and nausea.

GI Obstacle: Dry Mouth and Difficulty Swallowing

That dry, sticky, thick-tongued feeling makes it almost impossible to eat without taking countless sips of liquid to help swallow food. Swallowing difficulties can occur with low levels of saliva, which may be caused by surgery to the salivary glands or neck region, radiation to the head and neck area, or chemotherapies that cause transitional dryness of the mouth.

First Aid

- Stimulate saliva by sucking on a lemon drop, root beer barrel, peppermint hard candy, frozen fruit juice, or ice chips. Add citrus wedges to your purified water.

Coach's Corner

Dawn, who had been diagnosed with colon cancer, contacted me because she was concerned about her fatigue and weight loss. It had been over six months since her colon surgery. She said she couldn't understand why she was losing weight because her appetite was very good, and she was eating just fine. When I asked about her bowel habits, she revealed she had been having more than ten loose bowel movements per day. No wonder Dawn was losing weight! Her food was going right through her and she was unable to digest, absorb, or utilize any nutrients. She was diagnosed and treated for parasites and was placed on a diet and natural therapies for diarrhea. Normal bowel movements resumed, and she began to gain weight.

- Take over-the-counter saliva replacements such as Oral Balance mouth moisturizing gel.
- Fill a spray bottle with water and spray liquid into your mouth periodically throughout the day.
- Eat smaller, more frequent meals and take small bites.
- Add fat-free broths to rice, potatoes, pastas, and breads. Consume more broth-based soups as meals.
- Avoid dry or salty foods, which tend to increase the need for fluid.
- Try recipes that incorporate sweet pickles, soy sauce, and other aromatic foods to stimulate the appetite and get your mouth watering.
- Visit your dentist more often; saliva is responsible for washing away bacteria from teeth surfaces. Biotene toothpaste, gum, and mouthwash is available over the counter for dry mouth and maintenance of healthy oral flora.

GI Barrier: Greasy, Fatty Stools

If your stools are large and floating, and you see a greasy film on the toilet water, you may not be sufficiently absorbing dietary fats. There can be many reasons for fat malabsorption, including pancreatic insufficiency or cancer, surgical removal of a section of the intestine, or malabsorption syndromes such as cystic fibrosis or Crohn's.

First Aid

- If you usually have greasy stools, see a gastroenterologist. A fecal fat test is used to determine whether there is excessive fat loss in the stool.
- Follow low-fat diet guidelines in Appendix 8.
- If you are losing weight, medium chain triglycerides (MCT) should be considered. MCT oil is a form of

dietary fat that provides calories without taxing the digestive process. Ask your local pharmacy whether they carry MCT oil or can order it for you. Don't exceed more than one to two tablespoons per dose.

- Change your fat-soluble vitamin E to a water-miscible form for maximum absorption. Take zinc if you have excessive diarrhea.

- Pancreatin is prescribed for pancreatic insufficiency. If you have not been placed on this medication, and you are having digestive and malabsorptive problems, you should ask your doctor for a prescription. Pancreatic enzymes can be purchased from your health food store for the same purpose.

GI Obstacle: Food Sensitivities or Allergies

Food hypersensitivities can be the result of genetics or environmental conditions such as physical trauma, excessive consumption of a particular food, and chemical toxins. When your immune system responds to a food protein or environmental contaminant as if it was damaging the body, food allergies, usually called food hypersensitivities, begin. Allergic symptoms include itchy eyes, rash, a runny nose, difficulty breathing, and gastrointestinal disturbances such as abdominal pain, diarrhea, and vomiting.

If you have several food hypersensitivities, meet with a nutritionist who can provide you with informational resources or food and ingredient lists.

First Aid

- Get tested for food hypersensitivities. See the resource listing to help you locate a board-certified allergist in your area. An ELISA blood test can tell you of any suspected allergens.

- Remove the offending food source from your diet. Read labels carefully for cereal, starch, flour, thickening agents, emulsifiers, gluten, stabilizers, hydrolyzed vegetable proteins, and so on.
- Digestive enzymes and betaine HCl can be used to ensure adequate digestion of proteins. Poorly digested proteins are the culprit behind food hypersensitivities. This is especially important for cancer patients: When proteins are partially digested, the immune system can be impaired.
- During stress, food allergies tend to develop or become worse. Manage stress through behavioral modification techniques such as meditation or routine exercise.
- Follow the "Eat for Less Stress" guidelines on page 81.

GI Obstacle: Gas or Belching

Excessive gas usually comes from swallowing too much air. Chronic problems with gas can also be a symptom of underlying food allergies or intolerances, bacterial infections, or a reduction in digestive enzymes or hydrochloric acid.

First Aid

- Avoid overeating or consuming fried foods, which slow down digestive processes. Limit broccoli, cabbage, onions, beans, and soy if they cause you gas.
- Avoid excessive air. Don't gulp your food or chew with your mouth open. Limit the amount of chewing gum or breath mints you eat.
- Avoid or limit milk or milk products if you are lactose intolerant.
- ELISA food allergy testing can identify any food sensitivities that might be causing excessive gas.

- Hypochlorhydria, or low stomach acid, can cause belching or excessive gas production. Helicobacter pylori overgrowth has been linked to low stomach acid and can increase gastric cancer risk.[9] If you have low stomach acid levels, relieve symptoms by taking betaine HCl capsules with meals or snacks. These are available in the digestive wellness section of health food stores.
- Restore gut function with probiotics and digestive enzymes with or without betaine HCl (depending on whether you have hypochlorhydria). Charcoal tablets, available at health food stores, can be used as quick relief from occasional gas.
- Limit use of over-the-counter acid reducers. Antacids may provide initial relief from gas, but long-term use leads to poor absorption of vitamin B_{12}, iron, calcium, magnesium, and zinc.

GI Obstacle: Heartburn

Symptoms of heartburn, or reflux, include an uncomfortable burning sensation in your upper chest area and a sour taste in your mouth.

Factors that contribute to or aggravate reflux include certain dietary habits, abnormal gastric acidity, stress, medication side effects, and internal physical changes due to cancer activity. Radiation to the chest cavity can cause inflammation to the upper GI tract lining or can cause the esophageal sphincter to relax, allowing acid to flow from the stomach back up into the esophagus. Chronic reflux can increase your risk of esophageal cancer.[10]

First Aid

- Follow the anti-reflux diet recommendations in Appendix 9.

- You may have heartburn because you have too much or too little gastric acid (called hypochlorhydria). If you have low stomach acid levels, your symptoms will be relieved by taking betaine HCl capsules with meals or snacks. These are available in the digestive wellness section of health food stores. If your symptoms get worse, you most likely overproduce stomach acid; you should follow the suggestions for GI ulcers.

- Support gastrointestinal tract function and healing with digestive enzymes, glutamine, essiac tea, aloe vera, flaxseed oil, zinc, gamma-oryzanol, and deglycyrrhizinated licorice.

- Take all dietary supplements with food unless you are otherwise directed. Some supplements such as fish oil and some herbal extracts can be particularly offensive if they are regurgitated.

- Stress can cause digestive upset, including reflux. Manage stress through behavioral modification techniques such as meditation or routine exercise.

- Follow the "Eat for Less Stress" guidelines on page 81.

- Recognize that physical changes may contribute to symptoms. Large tumors in the chest or trunk area can compress the diaphragm or stomach toward the heart, creating shortness of breath or a feeling of fullness. Chemotherapy, radiation, and surgery are used to reduce tumor size quickly and offer relief from internal physical changes that are causing discomfort.

- Find out how long you will need to be on Tagamet or over-the-counter antacids such as Tums. Longer term use of these agents can aggravate reflux and cause deficiencies in vitamin B_{12}, iron, calcium, magnesium, and zinc.

GI Obstacle: Milk Intolerance

Lactose intolerance is caused by a deficiency of an enzyme responsible for breaking down milk sugar. Cancer patients and the elderly typically have more difficulty digesting milk products because enzyme activity has been decreased.

Symptoms associated with lactose intolerance include bloating, abdominal cramping, diarrhea, gas, and nausea. Not everyone experiences the same level of discomfort, and many people with a lactose intolerance are able to consume small amounts of milk products without experiencing any side effects at all.

First Aid

- Test your tolerance to foods containing lactose. Exclude all sources of dairy, such as milk, cheese, butter, margarine, yogurt, puddings, custards, ice cream, frozen yogurt, whipped cream, and cream-based soups, salad

Coach's Corner

Forbidden Fruits and Other Fine Foods

Did you receive a list of "forbidden" foods from your radiation oncologist? Before eliminating any foods from your diet, test your tolerance to each food at least twice. Most people undergoing radiation can tolerate citrus fruits and juices, broccoli, cabbage, soy, and other so-called problem foods without experiencing any negative GI symptoms.

dressings, and sauces. Avoid prepared food items that contain casein, caseinate, lactose, or whey. Even some nondairy food products contain casein, so read the labels carefully! If your symptoms significantly improve, you may want to limit or avoid milk or milk products. You may be able to tolerate small amounts of foods containing milk in your diet if you reintroduce the products slowly.

- Replace cow's milk with soy or rice milk; use both for drinking and cooking.
- There is no need to avoid yogurt, which contains active live cultures that digest milk sugar. Fermented products such as buttermilk, natural or aged cheeses, and cottage cheese may also be tolerated.
- LactAid, available in commercial milk products or supplement form, is specifically formulated for consumers with lactose intolerance.
- A hydrogen breath test can be administered by your doctor to determine your level of lactose intolerance. Restrict your fiber intake during this test, as a false positive test result could occur.
- Aid your digestion with digestive enzymes, probiotics, and FOS.
- When you restrict dairy intake, you will need to take a calcium supplement.

GI Obstacle: Mouth Sores

Mouth sores are very common in people undergoing chemotherapy. Treatment with Bleomycin, Adriamycin, Taxotere, and Xeloda increase your chances of developing mouth sores. You can also develop sores in response to stress, food allergies, hormonal changes, or nutritional deficiencies. These sores can be painful and can affect eating.

First Aid

- Avoid arginine-rich foods such as beans, nuts, peas, corn, rice, barley, and oats. This amino acid suppresses L-lysine, an amino acid that retards virus growth.
- Avoid acidic tomatoes, oranges, grapefruits, and so on, which can cause a burning sensation during an active outbreak.
- A link between wheat hypersensitivity and mouth sores has been established, so if you think you might be allergic to wheat products, consult an allergist for testing.[11]
- Eat soft, bland foods. Dunk dry foods in beverages or swallow foods with a beverage.
- Alcohol and foods that are too hot or cold tend to aggravate mouth tissues.
- L-lysine, in combination with a low-arginine diet, can reduce the severity of your outbreak.[12] Topical vitamin E, zinc lozenges, B vitamins, quercetin, tea tree oil, melissa extract, slippery elm, and goldenseal have oral mucosa healing properties.
- Avoid feverfew, an herb taken for preventing migraine headaches, during an outbreak. It can activate or aggravate sores.
- Ice reduces the pain of mouth sores and has been shown in clinical settings to reduce the chances of mouth sore development. Rinse your mouth frequently with warm water. Avoid alcohol-based mouthwashes.
- Stress management. During stress, mouth sores tend to develop or become worse. Manage stress through

behavioral modification techniques such as meditation or routine exercise.

- Follow the "Eat for Less Stress" guidelines on page 81.
- Hurricaine is a swish-and-swallow topical anesthetic that tastes good and comes in a variety of flavors such as wild cherry, pina colada, and watermelon. Xylocaine is a flavored topical anesthetic that is sprayed directly into the mouth.

GI Barrier: Nausea and Vomiting

Loss of appetite due to nausea can lead to weakness and lethargy. Vomiting can be painful and cause throat discomfort. Vomiting is considered dangerous when it is severe, lasts several days, and causes dehydration.

Stomach upset that may include vomiting can be caused by many factors, including food hypersensitivities, lactose intolerance, food-borne illness, low gastric acid, chemotherapy, radiation to the brain or GI tract, other medications, and taking dietary supplements on an empty stomach. Chemotherapies most likely to cause stomach upset include Cisplatin, Cytoxan, and Dacarbazine. Some people experience a food aversion, a psychological phenomenon where you associate cancer treatment symptoms with certain foods. This makes it impossible to enjoy those foods for a while.

First Aid

- Eat small, frequent meals and avoid fatty foods. Too much food or drink will swell the stomach and create a nauseous feeling.
- Eat foods that are starchy and low in fat, such as crackers, rice, bread, and so on. These carbohydrates will help maintain normal blood sugar levels.

Coach's Corner

Sue, a tea drinker, began to drink chamomile tea to soothe her nerves before her cancer treatments. After she drank the tea, she decided to place the wet tea bags over her mouth sores. After a few ten-minute tea bag sessions, she reported less pain and fewer outbreaks.

Chamomile, which has anti-inflammatory, anti-spasmodic, and sedative properties, may provide relief for your mouth sores. Give it a try!

- Suck on root beer barrels, lemon drops, ice chips, clear juices, fruitsicles, and broths.
- Avoid eating highly spiced or flavored foods on treatment days. These foods are likely to cause food aversions.
- Avoid foods with strong odors such as broccoli, asparagus, cauliflower, onions, garlic, curry, and eggs.
- Avoid any foods that cause you heartburn or reflux.
- Stress can be a powerful influence on digestion and feelings of nausea. Manage stress through behavioral modification techniques such as meditation or routine exercise.
- Follow the "Eat for Less Stress" guidelines on page 81.
- Avoid odors. Cancer patients can be extremely sensitive to smells, including perfumes, shampoos, aftershaves, and cooking odors. Ask your friends and family members to refrain from scents, and stay out of the kitchen during cooking, if possible.
- Ginger capsules taken before and during chemotherapy have antiemetic (antinausea) actions.

- Zofran and Kytril are the most commonly used medications to combat nausea and vomiting and can be used in combination with other antinausea medications for increased effectiveness.

Breakfast Suggestions

- Ready-to-eat high-fiber cereals such as Raisin Bran, From Kashi to Good Friends, low-fat granola, and Shredded Wheat (Serve with seasonal fresh fruit and soy milk or nonfat cow's milk)
- Eggo Nutri-Grain multigrain waffles, toasted (Serve with Horizon or Stonyfield Farm's nonfat yogurt and seasonal fresh fruit)
- Pepperidge Farm's natural whole grain bagels, toasted (Serve with a boiled egg and citrus sections)
- Health Valley Strawberry Cobbler cereal bars (Serve with natural peanut butter and apple slices)

Getting the Edge

Any Ginger in That Ginger Ale?

Ginger ale is nothing more than sugar water that contains little, if any, ginger. Combat nausea with the real deal: ginger capsules. Ginger has a longstanding reputation as an antiemetic, and has been shown to be effective in both mild and severe forms of nausea and vomiting.[13]

Nauseated Just Thinking about Chemo?

Take a ginger capsule one hour before your treatment, every hour during your treatment, and one hour after your treatment. Ginger, alone or in combination with prescription antiemetics, really helps to settle the stomach!

- Natural Oven's low-fat carrot muffins (Serve with banana slices and Brazil nuts)

Lunch Suggestions

- Del Rey whole wheat tortillas (Top with heated Old El Paso vegetarian refried beans, Tofurella shredded cheese. Serve with Del Monte canned corn and kiwi slices)
- Progresso black bean soup (Serve with whole grain crackers, Bunny Luv petite carrots and Libby's lite canned pears)
- Bumble Bee solid white albacore tuna (Mix with non-fat plain yogurt and place on lettuce, tomato, and onion topped Natural Oven's multigrain bread. Serve with baked Lay's chips and pineapple slices)
- Hillshire Farm's oven roasted turkey (Cut into slices and top your grocer's ready-made salad. Toss with olive oil and balsamic vinegar. Serve with Natural Oven's whole grain roll and Mott's natural applesauce)

Fast and Easy Foods

Having one of those "stay out of the kitchen" days? Frozen or canned soups, vegetables, and fruit can create easy meals for low-energy days. Although not as healthy as whole, unprocessed foods, these alternatives will provide your body with some nutrition and allow you a much needed rest.

- Healthy Choice garden vegetable soup (Serve with Triscuit low-fat whole wheat wafers and cantaloupe wedge)

Dinner Suggestions

- Pritikin vegetarian chili with black beans (Serve with Tostito's baked chips and orange slices)
- Amy's Organic Vegetarian Grains veggie loaf frozen dinner (Serve with Libby's lite canned peach slices)
- Lean Cuisine's Skillet Sensation teriyaki chicken (Serve with seasonal fresh fruit)
- Wendy's grilled chicken sandwich, without dressing (Serve with Green Giant select broccoli, carrot, and water chestnut frozen vegetables and apple wedges)
- Uncle Ben's honey ginger chicken noodle bowl (Serve with Bird's Eye frozen baby pea blend and grapes)

GI Obstacle: Bowel Spasms

Irritable bowel syndrome, also called spastic colon or colitis, is caused by abnormally contracting bowels. These spasms lead to chronic explosive diarrhea, abdominal pain, cramping, bloating, and gas. If you have had intestinal surgery or radiation, you may temporarily experience spasms and other symptoms similar to those found in irritable bowel syndrome.

Risk of malnutrition is high for people experiencing these symptoms. The pain caused by spastic movements of the colon can hinder one's desire to eat, and consistent diarrhea limits absorption of many vital nutrients. Additional dietary protein is usually needed to compensate for malabsorption associated with irritable bowel syndrome.

First Aid

- See a doctor and a nutritionist. Do not unnecessarily restrict your daily activities to accommodate for bowel symptoms! If you are uncomfortable talking about your bowel habits to a healthcare professional, keep a diary of your symptoms, write down your questions, and give this information to your doctor.
- A high-fiber diet is recommended for people with irritable bowel syndrome.
- Lactose intolerance is often the underlying cause of irritable bowel. A hydrogen breath test can be administered by your doctor to determine your level of lactose intolerance, or you can conduct a food challenge test yourself. (See "Milk Intolerance")
- Get tested for food allergies or sensitivities. Foods that most commonly cause digestive disturbances include milk or dairy products, soy products, nuts, or wheat bran.
- Restore a normal GI environment with digestive enzymes, probiotics, and glutamine. Herbs that reduce bowel spasticity include peppermint oil, chamomile,

Gold Medal Action

Ten Minutes to the Table

No energy to cook? Here are some relatively healthy frozen food entrees. Each is low in fat and includes at least one serving of vegetables or fruit. Pop into the microwave and enjoy!

- Hain Meatless Ravioli in Marinara Sauce
- Healthy Choice Mesquite Chicken BBQ
- Healthy Choice Beef Pot Roast
- Healthy Choice Herb Baked Fish
- Lean Cuisine Cafe Classics Honey Roasted Chicken
- Uncle Ben's Rice Bowl Sweet and Sour Chicken
  - Uncle Ben's Rice Bowl Honey Dijon Chicken

rosemary, and valerian root. Excessive diarrhea may require zinc and B$_{12}$ supplements.

- Stressful situations can trigger irritable bowel symptoms. Manage stress through behavioral modification techniques such as meditation or routine exercise.
- Follow the "Eat for Less Stress" guidelines on page 81.

GI Obstacle: Taste Changes

When food doesn't taste good, you don't want to eat. Taste changes can occur with chemotherapy because taste buds are rapidly destroyed. Other situations that can alter taste sensations include radiation to the head and neck region, bacterial overgrowth of candida, mouth surgery, and nutritional deficiencies.

First Aid

- Avoid red meat, which may taste like metal. Instead, choose mild tasting fish, soy products, and lean chicken and turkey as protein sources.
- Try temperature extremes. Some people find hot foods more tolerable than cold foods, and vice versa.
- Spice up your foods with herbs, lemon juice, soy sauce, and flavor extracts. Strong, pungent odors help to stimulate the olfactory sense.
- Add citrus wedges to your purified water for a cleaner, crisper flavor.
- Use plastic utensils instead of regular flatware and avoid cooking in iron or copper cookware.

Coach's Corner

Babying Your Bowels

Have you ever burned your arm on a hot iron? Remember how inflamed and red the skin was? Your bowels are very sensitive after surgery or radiation treatments. Just as you wouldn't rub sandpaper over a burned arm, you don't want scratchy fiber from raw foods and whole grains irritating the GI tract lining. Fight the urge to eat high-fiber foods and baby those bowels back to health!

- Take zinc. Zinc deficiencies, which contribute to taste changes, have been found in many forms of squamous cancers such as head and neck, esophageal, and lung cancers.[14-16]

GI Obstacle: GI Ulcers

The stomach secretes hydrochloric acid in response to food, medications such as aspirin or nonsteroidal anti-inflammatory drugs, stress, and other stimuli. When acid is overproduced, the stomach lining can become irritated, and an ulcer can develop. If you experience a consistent burning or gnawing feeling in your stomach, you may have an ulcer.

First Aid

- Eat small, frequent meals and avoid personal food intolerances.
- Avoid gastric stimulants such as caffeine, alcohol, black pepper, garlic, cloves, and chili powder.
- Eat soft, bland foods such as brown rice, farina, oatmeal, and other soft, well-cooked whole grains. It is not necessary to limit fiber, although you may need to avoid dry, rough foods such as whole grain toasts, cold cereals, and granolas, which might irritate the GI tract lining.
- Acidic juices or fruits should be consumed on a per tolerance basis.
- Avoid the old ulcer remedy of drinking milk. Milk protein initially buffers acid, but then stimulates it.
- Promote gut healing with flaxseed mucilage, vitamin A, vitamin E, selenium, and zinc. Flavonoids decrease the production and secretion of histamine, a substance responsible for releasing gastric acid.[17]

Getting the Edge

Herbs to Make You Hungry!

The following herbs and spices may help
to jump-start your appetite:

- alfalfa
- ginger root
- ginseng
- caraway
- cayenne

- fennel seeds
- basil seeds
- peppermint
- papaya
- dill

Gold Medal Action

The Goods on Glutamine

Cancer patients often have depleted muscle levels of glutamine, a beneficial amino acid that can enhance GI function in a number of ways:[18]

- It stimulates healthy GI tract cell growth.
- It helps maintain gut barrier function.
- It prevents toxic side effects during cancer treatment.
- It may increase the effectiveness of some chemotherapy drugs.

Glutamine is available in powder form from Cambridge Nutraceuticals and can be administered orally or by tube feeding.

- Herbs such as deglycyrrhizinated licorice and aloe vera can help hasten gastric wall healing.
- Ulcers are closely linked to stress. Manage stress through behavioral modification techniques such as meditation or routine exercise.
- Follow the "Eat for Less Stress" guidelines below.
- Prevacid or Prilosec may be prescribed if you are diagnosed with a gastric ulcer. If you have an *H. pylori* infection, you may want to try Pepto-Bismol, which contains bismuth, a naturally occurring mineral that has antacid properties and helps combat *H. pylori*.

Eat For Less Stress

Too much food, the wrong kind of food, unstable eating patterns, and nutritional deficiencies can put excessive demands on your body and weaken your immune system. While you may not be able to control what is causing your stress, you can control what you put into your mouth. Changing your eating habits, along with exercise and relaxation, can help you cope with stress more positively.

- Support your adrenal glands. These glands are responsible for balancing your body during stressful times. The adrenals need potassium, vitamin B_6, vitamin C, pantothenic acid, and magnesium to do their job. Eat a varied diet rich in citrus fruits, potatoes, peppers, beans, nuts, salmon, and whole grains.
- Decrease your intake of sugar and refined carbohydrates. Eating sweets depletes the body of many nutrients, including several B vitamins, which are needed for

carbohydrate metabolism and nerve health. Sugar can also decrease white blood cell production.

- Avoid dietary stimulants. Now is the time to break the habit of a morning coffee ritual. Caffeinated drinks such as tea, coffee, and chocolate milk encourage the production of adrenaline, leading to overworked adrenals.

- Consider dietary supplementation. When the adrenal glands become overworked, you may benefit from taking an adrenal glandular extract, along with antioxidants such as vitamin E, selenium, and ginseng. You should seek the advice of a qualified healthcare professional to determine appropriate dosage recommendations.

Getting the Edge

Are Treatment Side Effects Getting You Down?

Don't accept the statement, "It's just the chemo, hang in there and you'll be fine." Too often, cancer treatment symptoms are dismissed as minor inconveniences. Many side effects can last longer than you anticipate and can lead to feelings of hopelessness. Be ready to fight back by stocking your natural medicine chest now!

Natural Pharmacy Quick Reference Guide

GI Obstacle	Stock Your Cabinet With
Antibiotic Use	probiotics
Bloating	probiotics, digestive enzymes, betaine HCl
Candida	probiotics, digestive enzymes, betaine HCl, caprylic acid, garlic, oregano oil
Constipation	probiotics, digestive enzymes, flaxseed, cascara sagrada, senna, oat and rice bran, psyllium seed, vitamin C
Cramping	digestive enzymes, probiotics, chamomile, melissa, rosemary, valerian root, peppermint oil, flaxseed oil, zinc, magnesium, gamma-oryzanol
Dental Infections	tea tree oil
Diarrhea	probiotics, digestive enzymes, betaine HCl, grapefruit seed, goldenseal, Oregon grape, zinc, vitamin B_{12}
Fat Malabsorption	MCT oil, water soluble vitamin E
Food Sensitivities	digestive enzymes, betaine HCl
Gas	probiotics, digestive enzymes, betaine HCl, charcoal tablets
Heartburn	digestive enzymes, betaine HCl, glutamine, slippery elm, aloe vera, flaxseed oil, deglycyrrhizinated licorice, gamma-oryzanol
Lactose Intolerance	digestive enzymes, betaine HCl, probiotics
Mouth Sores	lysine, vitamin E, zinc, melissa extract, slippery elm, tea tree oil, quercetin, B vitamins
Nausea and Vomiting	ginger capsules
Bowel Spasms	digestive enzymes, probiotics, glutamine, peppermint oil, chamomile, rosemary, valerian root, zinc, vitamin B_{12}
Taste Alterations	zinc
Gastric Ulcers	aloe vera, flaxseeds, deglycyrrhizinated licorice, flavonoids, vitamins A and E, zinc

Section II

Get Set!

4

At the Starting Block — Nutrition 101

"Food is an important part of a balanced diet."
— Fran Leibowitz

The Nutrients

NUTRIENTS ARE CHEMICAL SUBSTANCES FOUND IN FOOD that supply energy, build and maintain cells, and help regulate body processes. Nutrients are categorized as macronutrients or micronutrients.

Carbohydrates, protein, fat, and alcohol are considered macronutrients because they provide the body with energy. Although water doesn't provide energy, it is also considered a macronutrient because it is essential to metabolic functions.

Vitamins and minerals are considered micronutrients and are needed by the body in much smaller amounts than macronutrients. While micronutrients do not provide energy, they do help with energy transformation.

Classifying Carbs

Carbohydrates are our primary energy source. Between 50 to 60 percent of your calories should come from carbohydrates, and the majority of those should come from unprocessed whole grains. While the main emphasis for dietary change in America has focused on lowering fat intake, it is also necessary to limit the amount of refined white sugar and flour products you eat. Carbohydrates can be classified as simple or complex sugars:

- Simple sugars come in a single form, called a "monosaccharide," or as a pair, called a "disaccharide." Single sugars include glucose, fructose (fruit), and galatose (milk). Double sugars include sucrose (cane, or table, sugar), lactose (milk sugar), and maltose (malt sugar). Because these sugars are so small, they are absorbed rapidly and raise your blood sugar level quickly. High blood sugar levels tend to suppress the immune system and create an environment favorable for cancer cell growth.

- Complex sugars are known as "polysaccharides" and are made up of many sugars linked together. Complex carbohydrates (sugars), more commonly known as starches, include bread, cereal, rice, pasta, and starchy vegetables. These larger sugars take much longer to break down than the single sugars, so they enter into the bloodstream at a slower rate. Complex carbohydrates also contain fiber, which offers a number of health benefits.

Coach's Corner

Simplifying Sugars

Visualize a simple carbohydrate (sugar) as a toy made up of two spools and one dowel. Just as this simple toy can easily be pulled apart, a simple sugar can be broken down and rapidly sent into the bloodstream. Complex carbohydrates, on the other hand, might be viewed as a large assembly of spools and dowels, more intricately designed and requiring much greater effort to pull apart for use. This type of sugar takes a while to break apart and enters the bloodstream more gradually, not causing a rapid rise in blood sugar levels.

The Power of Protein

The word "protein" comes from the Greek root meaning "of first importance." Protein is a principal component of muscle tissue, genetic material, red blood cells, and digestive enzymes. Most Americans eat too much protein. Your diet should generally be between 15 to 20 percent protein.

Fueling Up!

Carbohydrates are your main energy source. If you're feeling tired, you might not be eating an adequate amount of carbohydrates. Eating regular meals and consuming between 6 and 11 servings of breads, cereals, rice, and pasta can help you maintain an optimal energy level.

The body can store small amounts of carbohydrate in the liver and muscle; however, this storage provides energy for only about one day. If you consistently do not consume enough carbohydrate, your body is forced to break down fat and then muscle to convert them to a usable form of energy. Lost muscle mass is difficult to restore, negatively affecting metabolic rate and healthy cellular regeneration. On the other hand, if you eat too many carbohydrates, the excess energy is turned into fat and stored in the body. Elevated blood levels of triglycerides, the storage form of fat, can negatively affect immunity.

Protein is vital because it provides the building blocks for your body, called "amino acids." These amino acids join together in a number of ways to create different proteins. Amino acids can be classified as essential or nonessential:

- Essential amino acids are required by the body and must be obtained from the food we eat. Eating a varied diet will help you to achieve a good balance of essential amino acids. If you do not meet your body's requirements for protein, your muscles will waste away, and you will be unable to rebuild healthy cells. (See Appendix 10 for protein food sources.)

- Nonessential amino acids are produced by our bodies. When we consume too much protein, any excess will be converted into fat for storage. A good rule of thumb is to have the protein portion of your meal take up one quarter of your dinner plate. Think of protein foods as a side dish to larger servings of grains and vegetables.

Completely Complementary

Protein can be divided into two groups: complete and incomplete.

- Complete protein contains all the essential amino acids in just the right amounts for growth and repair. Sources of complete protein include animal products such as dairy foods, eggs, fish, pork, poultry, and red meat. Although soy is a plant food, its proportion of essential amino acids closely resembles animal products, and is therefore considered a complete protein.

- Incomplete protein lacks one or more of the essential amino acids or contains them in the wrong proportion for adequate growth and repair. Sources of incomplete protein include beans, grains, nuts, and vegetables. In some cases two incomplete proteins can be combined to yield a complete protein. This combination is called a complementary protein.

Your Guide to Complementary Proteins

Do you want to build a high-quality protein? Simply match the amino acid strengths and weaknesses of individual foods. For example, nuts, seeds, and grains are generally low in the amino acid lysine and relatively high in tryptophan and the sulfur-containing amino acids. Legumes, on the other hand, are good sources of lysine and poor sources of tryptophan and sulfur-containing amino acids. By combining nuts, seeds, and grains with legumes, you can create a complementary protein that meets your body's needs.

Complementary Combinations

Legumes + Seeds and Nuts
Navy bean soup with sesame crackers
Peanut butter toast with sunflower seeds
Trail mix of peanuts, raisins, sunflower seeds

Legumes + Grains and Cereals
Baked beans and brown bread
Split pea soup and a sandwich
Red beans and rice
Pintos and corn bread
Peanuts and pretzels

Animal Protein + Vegetable Protein
Macaroni and cheese
Vegetable lasagna
Peanut butter toast and soy milk
Cheese sandwich
Tuna noodle casserole
Baked beans and veggie hot dogs

Facts on Fats

Dietary fat is, literally, the most fattening nutrient we eat. We typically consume over 40 percent of our calories from fat, but cancer and nutrition experts agree that it is best to eat no more than 20 to 30 percent of our total calories from fat.

When dietary fat is digested, it breaks down into fatty acids and glycerol. Fatty acids are the key building blocks of all fats in our body. Our body preferentially saves smaller fatty acids, such as omega-3 and omega-6, for vital hormone-like functions. The immune system is supported if the proper ratio of fatty acids is consumed. The larger fatty acids are used for energy, protecting organs, and hormone regulation.

Dietary fats can either be saturated, unsaturated, polyunsaturated, or monounsaturated. Saturated fats are easy to identify because they are derived primarily from animal sources and are generally solid at room temperature (red meat, pork, poultry, whole milk, cheese, yogurt, butter, and palm and coconut oils). Unsaturated fats come from plant sources and are soft or liquid at room temperature. Unsaturated fats are divided into polyunsaturated and monounsaturated fats. Polyunsaturated fats include sunflower, corn, safflower, sesame, and soybean oils. Monounsaturated fats include avocado, peanut, olive, and canola oils. Omega-3 fatty acids, sometimes referred to as superunsaturated fats, are found in fish and flax.

Counting Calories

A calorie is a measure of the energy in food. Our body needs energy to perform everyday functions. The amount of energy contained in a food varies with the amount of carbohydrate, protein, fat, and alcohol in it. Some foods contain only one of these nutrients, but most foods are a combination of carbohydrates, proteins, and fats.

Here's how the major nutrients add up when it comes to energy value:

- Carbohydrate: 4 calories per gram
- Protein: 4 calories per gram
- Fat: 9 calories per gram
- Alcohol: 7 calories per gram

Foods are often classified according to their calorie density. Calorie density refers to the number of calories contained in a specific amount of a food, such as one ounce. Just by looking at the assigned energy values above, you can see that foods containing large amounts of fat are more calorie dense, containing more energy than those containing large amounts of carbohydrates.

Let me give you an example of energy or calorie density. If you had a bowl full of fat, you could eat two and a half bowls of sugar or protein for the same amount of calories. This explains why eating some foods helps you pack on weight more quickly than others. It also brings up another important issue: If you are losing weight, does it make sense to eat a bunch of fat or extra sugar in order to regain your weight? Absolutely not! We know that excess amounts of fat and sugar have the ability to promote the cancer process and impact immune system response. So, it is much better to regain weight by eating higher calorie, nutrient dense foods.

How Foods Weigh In

If you are concerned about losing weight or need to regain some weight, you should be consuming higher calorie foods without all that added harmful fat and sugar. Instead of eating foods that contain a bunch of empty calories, you should eat foods that provide calories *and* nutrients. Examples of nutrient dense foods include skim milk in place of whole milk, nonfat yogurt in place of whole milk yogurt, and orange juice in place of orange soda pop. All of these lower calorie foods offer essentially the same amount of vitamins, minerals, and other nutrients as their fat- and sugar-laden, higher calorie counterparts, but don't contain the detrimental calories.

If you add up the calories, you will see that you have to eat more healthy, nutrient dense foods in order to keep your weight up or regain any weight lost. This can be difficult if your appetite is poor or if treatment side effects hinder eating. Choosing foods that pack good nutrition into smaller servings can help. Here are some other suggestions:

- Don't fill up your stomach with zero calorie, empty nutrition fluids such as coffee or tea. Instead, drink eight ounces of a weight gain shake that will provide you with calories and nutrients.
- Think about putting some or all of your vitamin supplements on hold. If you are struggling to eat, it does not make sense to fill up on pills. Most dietary supplements need to be taken with adequate amounts of food to ensure the body can use them properly. Supplements do not provide calories, nor are they a sole source of energy, so they should never take priority over real food.
- Add whey or soy protein powder or nonfat dry milk to cereals, yogurt smoothies, and other blended drinks. You can add between 50 and 110 calories per serving without significantly affecting the volume of a food product.

- Eat higher calorie, nutrient dense foods. Refer to Chapter 2, "Getting the Edge: Consolidated Calories" for suggestions about which food choices can help you to achieve this goal.

Putting It All Together

When serving up your favorite selections, you should try to dish out appropriate portion sizes from each food group. Without following portion guidelines, you can negatively affect your health by eating too much fat, animal protein, or refined sugar. What's in a serving?

- **Starches:** 1 slice bread, 3/4 cup cold cereal, 1/2 cup cooked cereal, 1/2 cup starchy vegetables (corn, potato, peas, winter squash), 1/2 cup rice or pasta, 1/4 cup baked beans
- **Vegetables:** 1/2 cup cooked, 1 cup raw, 1/2 cup vegetable juice
- **Fruits:** 4 oz juice, 1/2 banana, 1/2 cup chopped fruit, 1 small whole fruit, 2 Tbs raisins
- **Meats and Meat Substitutes:** 3 oz lean fish, poultry, pork, or beef, 1 egg, 1/2 cup dried beans or peas, 4 oz tofu, 1/4 cup tempeh, 1 Tbs peanut butter, 1 oz assorted nuts or seeds
- **Milk, Yogurt, Cheese:** 8 oz nonfat milk, 8 oz nonfat yogurt, 1 oz nonfat cheese
- **Fats:** 1 tsp margarine or butter, 1 tsp vegetable oil, 1 Tbs oil-based salad dressing, 2 tsp mayonnaise-based salad dressing, 2 Tbs gravy, 5 large olives

At the Training Table

Seven Steps to a Vegetarian Diet

- **Step One:** Eat enough food to meet your calorie requirement for the day. You will find you need to eat much more in order to maintain your weight.
- **Step Two:** Eat a variety of foods. Variety breeds longevity. If you eat the same foods every day, you will lose interest and revert back to your old eating habits. Look through vegetarian magazines and cookbooks for meal suggestions.
- **Step Three:** Replace meat, poultry, and fish with soy-based products or complementary proteins. See the complementary protein food list on page 92.
- **Step Four:** Make sure whole grains and legumes are the mainstay of your meals. Choose whole wheat pastas, brown rice, and try alternative grains such as amaranth, bulgur, and millet. Add a variety of beans, lentils, and nuts to your meals.
- **Step Five:** If desired, reduce or eliminate eggs, cheeses, and milk from your meals. Replace with soy or rice-based products.
- **Step Six:** Eat green leafy vegetables every day. Foods such as broccoli, cabbage, spinach, and leaf lettuce supply the body with the iron, calcium, and B and C vitamins often lacking in a vegetarian diet.
- **Step Seven:** Take a B complex supplement every day. Vegetarians risk a B_{12} deficiency when they completely avoid eating animal products. Consult with a nutritionist to determine whether you may be at risk for any other nutrient deficiencies.

Attack These Snacks!

The easiest choices for a snack may be concentrated fruits and juices; they satisfy quickly, but they have a tendency to contribute to fluctuating blood sugars. A quick sugar fix can leave you feeling lightheaded, fatigued, and wanting more food soon after you've eaten.

If you have to skip a meal for a medical procedure, or you aren't feeling up to eating at an appointed time, grab one of these mini-meals when you can. Snack choices should be a combination of complex carbohydrates and proteins to sustain your energy level. Here are twenty great (and easy!) snack suggestions. Take your pick and then try them all. Who said snacks have to be boring?

1. Pumpernickel bread and low-fat cottage cheese
2. Low-fat bran muffin and fruited low-fat yogurt
3. Fresh berries in season and soy milk
4. Bananas and pistachios
5. Goat cheese and endive and tomato slices
6. Apple wedges and raw almonds
7. Wheat tortilla and mashed pinto beans
8. Buckwheat mini pancakes and plain low-fat yogurt
9. Rye wafers and sesame butter
10. Dried, unsweetened mixed fruit and sunflower seeds
11. Wheat tortilla and hummus
12. Fresh veggies and low-fat yogurt dip
13. Rice cakes and peanut butter
14. Graham squares and carob-flavored soy milk
15. Grapefruit sections and hard-boiled egg
16. Low-sodium V-8 juice and wheat bagel w/low-fat cheese
17. Apple rings and peanut butter
18. Harvest grain & nut bread and fresh fruit cup
19. String cheese and seven grain bread
20. Low-fat granola w/walnuts and dried, unsweetened pineapple chunks

Variety Is the Spice of Life!

Think about what you ate for breakfast today. Now, what did you have for breakfast yesterday? Was it the same thing? If so, you aren't alone. Most Americans eat the same ten foods every day! You can't possibly get every nutrient your body needs when you limit your food choices, so get creative with the kinds of foods you put on your plate. Diversifying your diet prevents mealtime boredom and provides you with an abundance of cancer-fighting compounds!

Seasoned Bagel Chips

Carefully slice any variety of bagel into 1/4" slices. Lay the slices on a dry baking sheet. Spray each bagel slice with vegetable cooking spray and sprinkle your choice of herbs or seasoning salts on top. Suggested toppers include garlic or onion salt and cinnamon. Toast in a 350-degree oven for 9 to 12 minutes or until crisp and light brown.

Lessons in Label Reading

When producers add or change words on their labels in an effort to market their food products, it can cause confusion for health-conscious consumers. The U.S. Department of Agriculture (USDA) and the U.S. Food and Drug Administration (FDA) have created regulations and policies related to food labeling to help explain the significance of special dietary claims on food labels. However, if you've ever attempted to read a food label, you know how difficult it can be to interpret the actual health value of a product.

Ingredients are usually listed on the back of the label by their specific common or usual name (corn oil, chicken fat) in descending order by weight. The front of the label isn't so easy. As you make your way through the grocery store, you'll see phrases such as "low fat," "high fiber," and "sugarless." What do these phrases actually mean? Here are some tips on becoming label savvy:

Getting the Edge

Label Alert!

Take note of the serving sizes. If an eight-ounce box of crackers lists a serving as one ounce, and you eat half the box, you will need to multiply all numbers on the label by four to determine the total calorie and nutrient intake. Your low-fat snack might not be so low fat once you add up all the fat grams you consumed!

Calling All Fats

The total amount of fat and its classification (saturated, polyunsaturated, monounsaturated) will be listed on the "Nutritional Information" section of the food label. To follow a specific reduced-fat diet, you will need to know your fat gram allowance for the day. A dietitian can easily calculate your fat goal for you.

In the ingredients section of the label, the kind of fat is presented. For example, fat may be listed as animal fat, butter, cocoa butter, coconut or palm or palm kernel oils, cream, egg yolk solids, hardened fat or oil, vegetable shortening, hydrogenated or partially hydrogenated vegetable oil, and lard. Vegetable oil is a generic term that means the product contains primarily soybean oil or contains a mixture of several types of oils. You will want to avoid foods that contain saturated, hydrogenated, and partially hydrogenated fat and limit your intake of polyunsaturated fats.

Hidden fats are usually found in quick breads, biscuits, muffins, pancakes, doughnuts, cookies, pastries, cakes, crackers, and chips.

Labeling Terms Related to Fat

- Lite or Light: The product may contain less fat, or this term might refer to fewer calories, sugar, or salt.
- Low fat: This refers to milk products with some degree of milk fat removed. Although the product has less fat, it still contains fat.
- Lean: The product contains no more than 22.5 percent fat by weight. Often used to describe ground beef.
- Reduced calorie: This product must contain one third fewer calories than the original product. Watch serving sizes here; they may be smaller to make the claim true.

- % fat free: This indicates how much of the weight of the product comes from fat. This can be misleading. For example, 2% milk still derives 38 percent of its calories from fat.

Sugar Savvy

The "Nutritional Information" section of a label will list the total amount of carbohydrates in the product, with a separate breakdown for simple sugars and dietary fiber.

In the ingredient section, if one of the first ingredients listed is sugar, you should avoid that food. When you consume a high-sugar food, don't forget to consume it with protein food in an effort to moderate your blood sugar level. Sweeteners have many names, including brown sugar, cane sugar, corn syrup, dextrose, confectioner's sugar, fructose, fruit juice, glucose, granulated sugar, honey, invert sugar, lactose, maltose, maple sugar, molasses, raw sugar, sucrose, and turbinado sugar. Some sugars are easily recognized by the "ose" endings.

Keep in mind that natural sugars, those found in nature as part of a food, such as lactose (milk sugar) and fructose (fruit sugar), will contribute to the simple sugar and total carbohydrate content of any food. For example, plain yogurt contains fifteen grams of carbohydrate, with all of the carbohydrates coming from simple sugars. This doesn't mean that you should avoid yogurt because it is a high-sugar food, it. As it turns out, yogurt also contains a good amount of protein. This carbohydrate–protein pairing makes yogurt an excellent food choice.

Sugar alcohols, which are absorbed more slowly than regular sweeteners, include mannitol, sorbitol and xylitol. Ingesting even small amounts of products containing sugar alcohols can cause diarrhea or make it worse.

Artificial sweeteners such as acesulfame-K and Aspartame are discouraged, unless you are a diabetic and these products are necessary to help you to control your blood sugar. Saccharin has caused cancer in laboratory animals and should be avoided.

Sugar is used as a sweetener, preservative, bulking agent, fermentation aid, or flavor enhancer and can be found in jams and jellies, ice creams, baked goods, soft drinks and fruit drinks, breads, crackers, cereals and processed meats, and salad dressings.

Labeling Terms Related to Sugar

- Dietetic: This product has one ingredient that has changed from its original product. It may have fewer calories, or less sugar or fat.
- Low calorie: This product must contain fewer than forty calories per serving.
- Low in sugar: This term is not regulated by the FDA. A breakfast cereal may be low in sugar, but still may contain added sweeteners.
- No sugar added: These products are sweetened with a naturally occurring sweetener such as fruit juice or dried fruit, but are still high in simple sugars.
- Reduced calorie: This must contain one-third fewer calories than the original product.
- Sugar free: A low caloric food or one reduced in calories. It may contain artificial sweeteners or sugar alcohols.

A Few Words about Fiber

Dietary fiber is a complex carbohydrate that doesn't contain any calories because it isn't digested by the body. Dietary fiber on food labels refers to both soluble and insoluble fibers, unless they are listed separately.

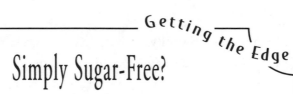

Getting the Edge

Simply Sugar-Free?

Sugar-free foods may not be the simple solution to your sweet tooth after all. If the label says sugar-free, your food may be sweetened by sugar alcohols such as mannitol or xylitol. These sweeteners don't cause as rapid a rise in blood sugar levels as sugar, but if overeaten, they can cause diarrhea and other gastrointestinal complaints. Try stevia, an herbal alternative sweetener, which doesn't affect blood sugar levels.

Foods labeled as a "source of dietary fiber" contain more than two grams of fiber per serving. A "good source of fiber" contains six or more grams of fiber per serving. An "excellent source of fiber" contains ten grams of fiber or more per serving.

Main sources of soluble and insoluble fiber include whole grain products, dried fruits, nuts, and seeds. For an in-depth discussion about roughage, see the chapter on fiber.

Out of the Kitchen

Here are some dining out strategies to help you choose foods that make the most of your menu choice:

- Never arrive hungry. Grab a healthy snack prior to leaving home or work. This will prevent you from ordering appetizers that satisfy quickly, but add tons of fat to your diet.

- Select a restaurant that you know or one that posts the menu on the outside window. Healthy menu choices should be offered or special requests honored.
- Avoid all-you-can-eat specials or buffets. You know what will happen if you don't, right? Dietary resolve can fade quickly when faced with a wide variety of sumptuous foods.
- Avoid high-fat menu descriptors:

au beurre	bearnaise	fried
au gratin	creamy	fritters
Alfredo	crispy	hollandaise
batter-dipped	carbonara	parmigiana
breaded	flaky	tempura

- Ask before you order. Find out if an item can be prepared in a more healthful manner. Get a clear explanation of ingredients and preparation methods.
- Look for heart-healthy menu items. These are usually listed as house specialties and annotated with a special symbol. Any food that is heart healthy contains less fat, cholesterol, and sodium.
- Order extra sides. To accompany your entree, order an extra helping of steamed vegetables or a large mixed green salad. Ask whether the restaurant carries any fresh or canned fruit. If it isn't on the menu, it still may be available upon request.

Chews Wisely

Don't be afraid to dine out! You can make healthy food choices almost anywhere you go! Here are some good choices at your favorite lunch spots.

Cuisine Quick Change	
Instead of	**Choose**
Quarter-Pound Burger	Small Burger and Tossed Salad
Waldorf Salad	Tossed Greens with Fresh Fruit Side Dish
Rice Pilaf or Stuffing	Baked Potato or Steamed Red Potatoes
Chicken Kiev	Chicken Marsala
Beef or Cheese Enchilada	Chicken Fajitas
Chocolate Raspberry Torte	Mixed Berries with Sorbet

Sandwich Shop

Choose fresh-sliced veggies in a pita with low-fat dressing and a cup of minestrone soup. Add fresh fruit to a chicken or turkey breast sandwich made with mustard, lettuce, and tomato. For over-stuffed sandwiches, order two extra slices of bread, remove half the filling, share with a friend or wrap in foil and refrigerate. Subway sandwich shops offer seven kinds of sandwiches that contain less than six grams of fat.

Fast Food

Order a grilled chicken breast sandwich without mayonnaise, or a single burger without cheese. Bring a piece of fresh fruit to round out the meal or try McDonald's Fruit n' Yogurt Parfait without granola. For only four grams of fat, you get a fast fruit delight guaranteed to satisfy.[1] Keep fast-food garden or grilled chicken salads healthy by topping with fat-free vinaigrettes or lemon juice.

A Fast-Food Twist

Still at the mall and in need of a snack? Auntie Anne's features whole wheat pretzels. Each five-ounce pretzel has seven grams of fiber and plenty of vitamins and minerals.[2] Keep it healthy by asking for an unsalted, unbuttered version. Add flavor by dunking it into the sweet mustard or marinara sauce dip.

Salad Bars

Broth-based soups served with fresh bread or fresh greens topped with raw veggies make a great meal. Choose low-fat salad dressings and fresh or canned fruits. Avoid marinated beans, oily pasta salads, creamy salad dressings, croutons, cheesy biscuits, or corn bread.

Asian Take-Out

Choose miso or hot and sour soup or steamed vegetable dumplings as appetizers. Try all vegetable mixtures, with or without tofu, over steamed rice or noodles. Request that vegetables be steamed or stir-fried with as little oil as possible. Use soy sauce sparingly and avoid MSG.

Pizzeria

Choose flavorful, low-fat toppings such as peppers, onions, sliced tomatoes, spinach, broccoli, or mushrooms. For extra zip, try sprinkling red peppers, garlic salt, or oregano on top. Cut the fat by requesting, "Easy on the cheese."

Self-Assessment: Mastering Restaurant Menus

How skillful are you are at choosing healthful foods from a menu? Circle the foods you'd likely order from this sample restaurant menu and compare your choices to the optimal choices listed below.

Appetizers

Chilled tomato juice
Chicken noodle soup
Shrimp cocktail
Fresh fruit cup (in season)

Dinners

Filet mignon (tenderloin of beef delicately broiled)
Turkey cutlet (lightly breaded and fried to a golden brown)
Pork chops (two large center-cut chops charbroiled)
Chicken kabobs (chunks of tender chicken breast on a skewer with mushrooms, onions, and green peppers)
Stuffed cod (delicate white fish stuffed with breaded, seasoned dressing)
Chicken livers (breaded and pan-fried)
All dinners include: your choice of potato (baked, french fried, or twice-baked) or rice; vegetable of the day; salad with choice of dressing (Italian, French, Thousand Island); hot rolls and butter.

How Did You Do?

Appetizers

The best choices for an appetizer are tomato juice or fresh fruit, because both are void of fat and chock full of beneficial plant chemicals.

Dinners

Dinner selections may have been more difficult to choose. If you chose beef, did you think about the portion size? Most filets are six to eight ounces, but other steak cuts tend to be much larger. The chicken kabobs appear to be a safe choice, as well as the pork chops. If you chose the pork, were you planning on only eating one pork chop? The stuffed cod, chicken livers, and turkey cutlet should be your last choices because they are fried or contain fatty breading. Although there are no vegetarian selections on the menu, were you planning on asking the waiter if you could order a vegetarian special request meal?

Side Orders

A baked potato is the clear winner here (remember to order butter on the side and skip the sour cream!). It is a lower fat choice than french fries or a twice-baked potato. Eat your potato with the skin on to get more fiber into your diet. If you circled the vegetable for the day, did you think about asking that it be prepared steamed, without butter? Did you choose an oil-based salad dressing instead of a cream-based dressing? Better yet, a lemon wedge and balsamic vinegar makes a flavorful, low-fat seasoning for your greens. Did you think about asking whether the rolls were available in whole wheat?

The Grand Finale

For those of you who are tempted to order dessert, I made sure this restaurant conveniently didn't offer any! Most restaurants, however, do offer dessert choices. If your sweet tooth is acting up, fresh fruit or a light sorbet are your best bites.

Stats on Fats

"The distance doesn't matter; only the first step is difficult."
– Mme. Marquise du Deffand

The Cancer Connection to Fat

A S A NATION, AMERICA IS GETTING FATTER. Not only do we eat too much, we continue to pile the same amount of fats and oils onto our plates as we did ten years ago.[1] Despite public health warnings that excessive intake of fats and oils are linked to chronic diseases, we still indulge in high-fat foods. How does all this dietary fat affect cancer?

Eating too much fat can suppress immunity and stimulate cancer cell division and growth.[2] Some fats interfere with the way our cells use oxygen, chemically altered fats are toxic to our cells, and rancid fats increase the free radicals in the body.

Research has demonstrated a definite association between dietary fat and specific cancer risks. Those who gain weight as adults have an increased risk for breast, colorectal, and endometrial cancers,[3-5] while individuals with excessive stores of body fat have been found to be at greater risk for gall bladder and renal cancers.[6,7]

If diets are high in total fat, there is an increased risk for colorectal, breast, prostate, and lung cancers.[8] Limited studies support a link between high-fat diets and bladder and endometrial cancers.[9,10]

Consuming animal fats, a primary source of saturated fats, increases your risk of breast, colorectal, endometrial, lung, and prostate cancers.[11-13] Some studies have shown an association between saturated fat, animal protein and bladder, breast, colorectal, and lung cancers.[14]

Cholesterol, another component of animal foods, is correlated to pancreatic cancer,[15] with a potential increased risk associated with endometrial cancer.[16] Diets high in omega-6 fatty acids have been shown to stimulate human prostate cancer cell growth and have led to an increased incidence of breast cancer.[17,18]

A Fat Recap

It's easy to get bogged down in technical terms, especially when it comes to trying to remember which type of fat comes from which type of food. So, here's a quick refresher to help you identify the good, the bad, and the ugliest of fats. Remember, foods usually contain a mixture of various fatty acids. The food sources below are categorized by the most prevalent type of fat.

Dietary Fat Sources

- Superunsaturated: cold water fish (salmon, tuna, mackerel, sardines, bluefish, herring) and flaxseed oils.
- Monounsaturated: avocado, peanut, olive, and canola oils.
- Polyunsaturated: sunflower, corn, safflower, cottonseed, sesame, soybean, borage, and evening primrose oils.
- Hydrogenated, partially hydrogenated and trans-fatty acid sources: margarine, shortening, refined vegetable oils; smaller amounts of trans-fatty acids naturally occur in beef and butter.
- Saturated fat sources: red meat, pork, poultry, whole milk, cheese, yogurt, butter, and palm and coconut oils.

Counting Fat Grams

Do you know what a 20-percent low-fat diet looks like? Probably not. Counting fat grams can help you visualize how much fat you are allowed for the day. To determine the number of fat grams you need, complete the worksheet in Appendix 11. Remember, a dietitian can easily calculate a fat gram goal for you if you prefer. After just a few days of counting fat grams, you will be surprised at how easy it is to accurately guess the relative amounts of fat in your favorite foods.

Appendix 12 provides a list of fat grams contained in common foods. Use this reference to help you count grams for foods without labels.

Self-Assessment: Helping Yourself to Hidden Fats?

How do you know if you are really eating a low-fat diet when so many foods contain hidden fats? Answering the questions below will help you identify food choices that may be contributing more fat to your diet than you'd like.

Dietary Fat Intake Survey

(Circle Yes or No)

1. Do you eat deep fried foods such as fish, shrimp, snack chips, french fries, etc.?   Yes   No
2. Do you eat sour cream or whipping cream?   Yes   No
3. Do you like creamy salad dressings such as Thousand Island, Ranch, etc.?   Yes   No
4. Do you eat margarine or butter on your bread or add it to cooked vegetables?   Yes   No
5. Do you add oil to cooking water?   Yes   No
6. Do you drink regular soy milk?   Yes   No
7. Do you eat olives?   Yes   No
8. Do you snack on nuts or seeds?   Yes   No
9. Do you eat red meat (beef)?   Yes   No
10. Do you eat processed meats?   Yes   No
11. Do you drink 2% or whole milk?   Yes   No
12. Do you eat cheese?   Yes   No
13. Do you eat creamy soups such as cream of broccoli or cream of chicken?   Yes   No
14. Do you add shortening when preparing baked goods?   Yes   No
15. Do you eat chips or crackers?   Yes   No

Total: Yes ____   No ____

Survey Interpretation

These questions provide you with a starting point for reducing excessive or hidden fats in your diet. Questions 1 through 5 detail high-fat dietary habits that should be changed right away. Questions 6 through 8 refer to healthy foods that are higher in fat and should be eaten in moderation. Questions 9 through 13 reveal sources of hidden fats, and questions 14 and 15 point to food sources high in trans-fatty acids. Trans-fatty acids are unhealthy fats that should be avoided.

Trimming the Fat

In your quest to cut fat, first concentrate on the obvious excessive dietary fats. For example, if you eat any deep-fried foods, lighten them up by changing preparation methods. If you aren't sure where you should begin, don't worry! Review the following suggestions to find alternative selections that contain less fat or healthier types of fat.

- Change your cooking methods. Remove fat from your menus by using cooking techniques that require no added fats. Instead of frying or sautéing your food, bake, broil, or poach it. Stir-fry with broth or vegetable juice. Nonstick vegetable sprays prevent food from sticking without contributing fat grams.
- Modify your recipes. You can reduce the fat in baked products by about one fourth to one third without affecting quality. Alternative add-ins, such as fruit puree, can reduce the total amount of fat in a product. See Appendix 13 for recipe modification tips.

- Season with herbs. Herbs and spices add interesting flavors to foods and can replace butter, sauces, and gravies. Use fresh lemon, lime, or vinegar to season salads rather than using high-fat salad dressings.
- Select slender meat cuts. Choose lean cuts of meat such as round, sirloin, and tenderloin from beef, lamb, and pork. Trim off visible fat. Decrease the use of prime grade cuts that contain more marbling. Increase your intake of fish and shellfish, which are lower in saturated fats. Avoid organ meats such as kidney, liver, and brain. Avoid processed meats such as sausage, bacon, hot dogs, and luncheon meats.
- Eat reduced-fat dairy products. Choose skim or 1% milk, low-fat yogurt, and soft cheeses such as cottage and farmer. White cheeses are typically lower in fat than yellow cheeses. Avoid cream cheese, sour cream, half-and-half, real or non-dairy whipped topping, custard-style yogurt, whole, evaporated, and condensed milks. Choose egg whites over whole eggs to avoid fat and cholesterol.
- Change the type of fat you eat. Prepare and cook foods made with monounsaturated fats such as canola and olive oils. Where possible, as in salad dressings, use olive oil more than canola oil. Olive oil contains about 25 percent more monounsaturated fatty acids than canola oil. Broth soups are more healthful than creamy soups, which contain saturated fats. Decrease butter use and avoid tropical (palm, coconut) or hydrogenated oils, including margarines or shortening. Read the labels on "health foods." Some granolas and cereal bars can be high in tropical oils or hydrogenated fats. Tropical oils,

although derived from plant sources, act like saturated fats in the body. Many of these fat spreads are full of trans-fatty acids.

- Eat "plain" starches. Choose whole grain breads, rice cakes, low-fat crackers such as matzo, zwieback, or rye krisp, whole grain pastas, dried peas, and beans. Limit packaged pancakes, waffles, biscuits, muffins, and corn bread. Avoid croissants, butter rolls, pastries, doughnuts, most snack crackers, granola-like cereals made with saturated fats, pasta, and rice dishes prepared with cream, butter, or cheese sauces.

- Pick the right kind of produce. Choose plenty of fresh, frozen, canned, or dried fruits and vegetables. Avoid those prepared with butter, cream, or other types of sauce. Avoid the temptation to add melted cheese on top of your steamed vegetables.

- Be reluctive about sweets and snacks. Choose low-fat frozen desserts such as sherbet, sorbet, Italian ice, frozen yogurt, and fruitsicles. Avoid high-fat frozen desserts such as ice cream or frozen tofu. Angel food cake, fig bars, and gingersnaps are low-fat dessert choices. Avoid packaged pies and frosted cakes. The best snacks are air-popped popcorn and pretzels. Avoid buttered microwave popcorn and potato and corn chips prepared with hydrogenated fats.

Fats: the Good, the Bad, and the Ugly

Eating less fat is a great start toward a healthy diet, but don't stop there. The type of fat you eat can affect cancer. For example, some dietary fats feed into metabolic pathways that depress natural

Hidden Fats

Fats hide where you might not suspect. Take a look at how much fat is present in the following foods. Each pat of butter is equivalent to 1 teaspoon, or 5 grams, of fat. The total number of fat grams per serving are listed in parentheses next to each product.

Pats of Butter

Dean's 2% milk, 8 oz (5)

Fibar peanut butter crunch, 1 bar (4.5)

Keebler Wheatables, 12 crackers (6)

Planter's salted almonds, 2 Tbs (15)

Progresso New England Clam Chowder, 1 cup (10)

Sargento Four Cheese Mexican blend, 1/4 cup (9)

Orville Redenbacher light popcorn * (5)

Oscar Meyer beef bologna, 1 slice (8)

Eggo frozen waffles, 2 waffles (7)

Homemade potato salad, 1/2 cup (10)

Avocado, raw, 1/2 (15)

*The serving size is one third of a bag. If you ate the whole bag, you would be eating 15 grams of fat. Reducing the serving size is one way food manufacturers qualify their product as a lower fat product. Always look at the serving size and the number of servings per container to determine whether the product is truly low in fat.

Source: Product labels

killer (NK) cells and promote inflammatory diseases such as arthritis. Other dietary fats are used by the body in positive ways, such as promoting cardiovascular health, functioning as anti-metastatic agents, and suppressing tumor growth.

All fats are not created equal. Read on to learn which fats are helpful and harmful.

Is Butter Better Than Margarine?

Butter is the better choice for several reasons. Butter, because of its fatty acid content, is perfect for high-heat cooking methods. Margarine is not suitable for frying or sautéing. Butter does contain some naturally occurring trans-fatty acids, but the hydrogenation process used to make margarine creates substantially more trans-fatty acids. Margarine is also a source of undesirable aluminum and nickel. If you are worried about environmental contaminants, you can avoid pesticide and hormones by purchasing organic butter.

The Best Fats

If there is one type of fat we tend to be "deficient" in, it would be the superunsaturated omega-3 fatty acids. Unrefined, essential fatty acids are found in cold water fish, flaxseeds, and in lesser amounts, soybeans and walnuts. These superunsaturates can slow tumor growth, decrease the metastatic properties of cancer cells, and increase cancer patient survival time.[19,20]

Not Another Fish Story

Fish oil contains the omega-3 fatty acids EPA and DHA, which have demonstrated anticancer benefits. These fatty acids stop cancer from spreading by enhancing NK cell and lymphocyte cancer kill rates.[21]

You should eat at least one meal of fish per week. Eating fish will provide you with an excellent source of protein and will help you reduce your total saturated fat intake. Most of the essential oils are found under the skin, so cold water fish are best eaten with their skins on. What kinds of fish should you be fishing for? Atlantic salmon, sardines, and farmed coho salmon and rainbow trout have between two and four omega-3 fat grams per serving. Other fish such as mackerel, flounder, halibut, and canned tuna contain less than one omega-3 fat gram per serving.

Even if you consume fish more than once a week, you should supplement your diet with omega-3 fatty acids in order to obtain therapeutic levels of these essential oils. Simply add omega-3 fatty acid oil or supplements to your nutritional regimen. This is an appealing option for those who would rather take a pill than eat fish every day. Recommended dosages range from 1,000 to 6,000 milligrams per day.

Gold Medal Action

Storing Your Oils

Although oils contain a fair amount of vitamin E to protect them from free radical damage, they will need to be stored properly to retard oxidation and extend shelf life. Light, heat, and oxygen cause fats to oxidize very quickly. Once opened, your bottle of oil should be stored in the refrigerator. Store oils in airtight containers and keep them out of the direct sun. Most oils should be used within a month or two after opening.

Flax Facts

In animal studies, flax oil has produced fewer or smaller tumors, less metastasis, and has protected against breast cancer.[22,23]

Flaxseed oil contains more omega-3 fatty acids than fish oil, but the acids in flax have to be converted in the body to EPA (the substance found in fish oil that exhibits beneficial health properties). With adequate levels of B_3, B_6, vitamin C, magnesium, and zinc, your body easily makes this conversion. One to two tablespoons of flax oil per day is a typical dosage recommendation.

Flaxseeds have many health benefits. They are rich in minerals such as potassium and magnesium, and in vitamins such as niacin, riboflavin, C and E, and carotenes. Mucilage, a water-soluble fiber

Getting the Edge

Flax Facts

Don't bite into those flaxseeds just yet! Your teeth can't possibly chew through the tough exterior of the seeds to release the valuable oil within. Instead, invest in a hand-held coffee bean grinder and grind just what you need for your meal.

Avoid the temptation of buying conveniently ground flaxseeds at the health food store. Exposure to light and oxygen can destroy flax's healthful properties!

Heat reduces the phytochemical content of flax. Use olive or canola oil for cooking and save flax oil for salad dressings and other products that don't need to be heated.

found in flax, aids constipation, moderates blood sugar levels, and soothes digestive disorders. One ounce of flaxseed meal contains a whopping eleven grams of dietary fiber. Ground-up flax can be sprinkled over cereal, blended into muffins or breads, and mixed into health shakes.

Ode to Olives

Olive oil is rich in monounsaturated fatty acids, which if taken in moderation, is a safe fat to consume. Olive oil has many healthful properties. It contains a mild vegetable mucilage that protects the digestive tract[24] and contains phenolic compounds that act as cell protectors.[25] Olive oil has been shown to prevent colon cancer cell growth in animals.[26]

Gold Medal Action

What To Look For in an Olive Oil

- The oil should be stored in a dark, opaque container.
- The label should state "extra virgin" to ensure that the oil has not been refined.
- Buy cold-pressed oil. This processing technique eliminates heat destruction of the seed or oil.
- For intense flavor and the most phytochemicals, choose the deeper golden-green oils.

A Balancing Act

Too many omega-6 fatty acids can suppress immune function and cancer growth, but too few omega-6 fatty acids can allow omega-3 fatty acid levels to rise, overstimulating the immune system. How do you know whether you are eating the right type of fat in the right amounts? Food labels will not tell you how many omega-3 or omega-6 fatty acids are present, so you can't count them as you do fat grams.

Lipid experts suggest the ratio of omega-6 to omega-3 fatty acids should be about 2:1. People in the U.S. currently consume a 14:1 ratio. A ratio of 1:1 may be beneficial for degenerative diseases such as cancer, which usually require an additional intake of omega-3 fatty acids. A favorable ratio can be achieved by balancing the diet as follows:

- Eat at least 15 percent of your daily calories from healthy fats that contain omega-3 and omega-6 fatty acids. You can accomplish this by using unrefined olive and canola oils exclusively. Avoid other added fats.

- Restrict intake of meat, dairy, and eggs. Eat fish twice a week. Consume low-fat soy products. Use limited amounts of nuts and seeds as alternative protein sources.

- Fruits, vegetables, whole grains, and legumes should make up the majority of your diet. Eat fewer processed flour or sugar products, such as cookies, pastries, and crackers.

- Take flaxseed or fish oil supplements daily.

- Supplement an animal-based diet with black current seed oil. This oil contains derivatives of both omega-6 and omega-3 fatty acids that can inhibit the cancer-promoting effects of saturated fatty acids.

The Case for Canola

Canola oil is a versatile monounsaturated fat ideal for baked products. Canola, or rapeseed, has been touted by the media as a healthy oil; however, you must purchase an unrefined oil to derive health benefits. Commercially marketed oils are refined and do not have the same health benefit as unprocessed versions. Read labels carefully, because some canola oils are partially hydrogenated as well.

Getting the Edge

Promising Products

Chickens on a typical corn-based diet lay eggs that are higher in omega-6 fatty acids. To help consumers eat better fats, Eggland's Best offers omega-3 fatty acid enriched eggs. Next, look for enriched cow's milk.

Acceptable Avocado

Another monounsaturated fat, avocado oil is usually sold in a refined form, which has destroyed its beneficial properties. A fresh avocado is a better choice for monounsaturated fat and contains other cancer-fighting nutrients such as folate, vitamin E, and fiber.

The Problem with Peanuts

Peanut oil is one of the few monounsaturated fats that is stable at higher temperatures so you can stir-fry with it and not worry about the fat breaking down. Peanut oil and other peanut products contain beta-sitosterols, a plant substance that has exhibited a protective role

At the Training Table

Avocado Accolades

Need to ripen an avocado? Here are two ways to do it. Place the avocado in a sealed plastic bag with a ripe banana and store at room temperature. Don't have a banana? Bury the avocado completely in a jar of flour. Use mashed avocado as an alternative spread for bread.

against colon, prostate, and breast cancers.[27] Peanuts also contain resveratrol, a cancer-fighting plant compound also found in red wine.[28]

With all those benefits, why would peanuts classify as a questionable fat? Peanuts have been known to contain aflatoxins, which are cancer-causing substances made by a fungus that grows inside the nut.[29] Unless you can be sure fungus-free peanuts were used, you may wish to limit all peanut products.

Use Caution with Cottonseed Oil

Cottonseed oil, rich in omega-6 fatty acids, has been found to contain toxic natural ingredients as well as pesticide residues. Research has linked reduced red blood cell integrity and impaired liver and kidney function with cottonseed oil use.[30] Read package labels carefully to make sure cottonseed oil is not in your food.

Unhealthy Fats

Normally, unsaturated fats are good for us because they have the ability to protect our cells from toxic substances. They become destructive only when they are heated by high temperature cooking methods or during the hydrogenation process. These trans-fatty acids can cause cellular mutations. Americans eat an average of five grams of trans fat per day, accounting for about 3 percent of their total energy intake.[31] That may not sound like much, but even small amounts contribute significantly to cellular damage.[32]

Any oil you buy in a regular supermarket, with the exception of extra virgin olive oil, has been chemically treated and refined by a heat process that changes the fat from helpful to hurtful. You will need to stop by your local health food store to purchase most of your unrefined oils. Once you purchase unrefined oils, make sure you store opened bottles in the refrigerator to slow fatty acid degradation. Light, heat, and oxygen quickly destroy liquid fats and can make them harmful to consume.

Research suggests that 75 percent of the trans-fatty acids consumed are derived from processed foods.[33] Go to your kitchen right

Gold Medal Action

Three Cheers for the FDA!

The Food and Drug Administration has proposed that trans-fatty acid fat grams should be listed on food labels. Trans-fatty acids are common in partially and fully hydrogenated foods and are known to cause cellular damage and contribute to heart disease. Although any new labeling requirement takes time to become effective, many food manufacturers are offering trans-free foods and may soon begin listing trans-free fatty acids on their product labels.[34]

At the Training Table

Love to Stir-Fry?

Put away the olive oil and take out some butter! The saturated fat in butter doesn't break down during high-temperature cooking, unlike the fatty acids in olive or other monounsaturated oils. Sautéing or stir-frying with vegetable oils produces unnatural trans-fatty acids that can be toxic to healthy cells.

now. Take a quick look at your pantry shelves. Do you see any products that contain hydrogenated fats? Look closely at any packaged convenience foods such as rice or pasta mixes, crackers, and ready-to-eat cereals. Next, take out the dinners, pizza, and packets of seasoned vegetables from the freezer. See any dangerous fats there? Open up your refrigerator door. Look at your dairy products, processed cheeses, coffee creamer, and margarine. Every food product you buy that contains hydrogenated or partially hydrogenated oils has health-damaging potential.

Won't Give Up Your Margarine?

Reduce the amount of trans-fatty acids in your margarine by changing from stick to tub form. Better yet, try Smart Balance, Spectrum and Brummel & Brown's margarines. They all qualify as trans-free bread spreads.

Fake Fats

Fat substitutes such as Olestra and Simplesse seem to be a dieter's dream. They replace fat in food without adding calories.

They simply pass through our GI tract undigested. Unfortunately, fat-soluble vitamins hitch a ride on fat substitutes through the GI tract, so they are not absorbed by the body either. Fat substitutes have also been found to reduce the body's ability to absorb carotenoids from fruits and vegetables. Additionally, there have been concerns about GI cramping and loose stools.[35]

The Food and Drug Administration has received thousands of reports from people who have experienced adverse reactions to eating olestra products. The big question remains: What are the long-term health implications for ingesting fat substitutes? Until we know more, it is prudent to avoid foods containing fat substitutes.

At the Training Table

Smart Seasoning Suggestions

Want to jazz up those steamed dinners without adding fat? Make your meals taste better by adding:

- Mexican salsa
- Dill
- Red onions
- Lemon or lime juice
- Dried cranberries
- Chives
- Rosemary
- Sun-dried tomatoes
- Currants
- Low-sodium soy sauce
- Crushed red pepper flakes

A Sweet Victory

"Life is like an ice-cream cone, you have to lick it one day at a time."
– *Charles M. Schulz,* as "Charlie Brown," in *Peanuts*

Does Sugar Feed Cancer?

WE ALL KNOW that simple sugars, the sweetener most often found in desserts, candies, and soft drinks, are detrimental to health. Diets high in sugar have been linked to a number of health problems, including diabetes, hypoglycemia, chronic constipation, intestinal gas, asthma, candida infections, headaches, obesity, inflammatory bowel disease, and tooth decay. Eating sugar affects cancer as well.

Researchers have been able to link processed, refined starches and sugars to increased risk of breast, colorectal, pancreatic, and stomach cancers.[1-3] A diet high in sugar contributes to cancer development in three ways:

- It elevates insulin levels.
- It creates a toxic burden.
- It negatively impacts immunity.

Insulin Response

Tumors, just like normal cells, prefer carbohydrates as their main source of energy.[4] When you eat sweets your blood sugar rises rapidly. In response to all this sugar in your blood, the insulin hormone is released by the pancreas. Insulin helps cells to use the sugar as energy and brings blood sugar levels back to normal. When you eat too much sugar, a large amount of insulin is produced and circulates in the blood. High insulin levels cause precancerous cells to gobble up sugar, accelerating their growth into fully formed cancer cells.[5]

Toxic Burden

Eating sugary foods, which have a tendency to be low in fiber, slows the movement of the GI tract and contributes to constipation. High-sugar diets also increase production of secondary bile acids. These carcinogenic compounds contribute to a toxic GI environment and have been linked to colorectal cancer.[6]

Immune Response

Nourishing the cells that protect you from foreign invaders is a number one priority. A constant threat of viral or bacterial infection, in conjunction with destructive cancer treatments, increases immune system vulnerability. Add a high-sugar diet to the equation and you short-circuit your immunity. Elevated insulin levels slow the release of growth hormones, which in turn reduce white blood cell production.[7]

Getting the Edge

Need Another Reason to Stop Eating Sweets?

Refined carbohydrates provide food for *Candida albicans*, a yeast overgrowth commonly found in cancer patients. The more advanced your cancer, the more likely you will contract a fungal infection.[8] Candidiasis causes bloating, gas, and fatigue, and can make eating a painful, difficult task.

All Sugars Are Not the Same

Regardless of what kind of carbohydrate you eat, your blood sugar will rise. The form of carbohydrate determines how high your blood sugar level will go. Simple sugars such as fruit, candy, and milk are rapidly absorbed. They raise blood sugar levels quickly. Complex carbohydrates such as starchy corn, potatoes, and breads are larger sugars that take much longer to break down to absorbable single sugars. They enter the bloodstream at a slower rate.

How Sugars Stack Up

Choose This	Instead of This
Whole Wheat Bread 68	French Baguette 95
Oatmeal 49	Corn Flakes 83
Brown Rice 55	White Rice 88
Oatmeal Cookies 55	Graham Crackers 74
Grapefruit 25	Raisins 64
Cantaloupe 65	Watermelon 72
Soybeans 14	Kidney Beans 52
Carrots 49	Beets 64
Fructose 20	Table Sugar 63

The more refined the sugar, the higher your blood sugar will rise. Take a look at the glycemic index of some common foods above.[9] The higher the glycemic index number, the more quickly your blood sugar will rise and fall. The glycemic index is a good tool to help you choose foods that don't cause sharp fluctuations in blood glucose or insulin levels.

Self-Assessment: How Sweet Are You?

Americans love sugar! Most adults get their sugar fix in the form of soft drinks, sweets, sweetened grains, milk or milk products, and fruitades.[10] While some foods are almost exclusively sugar, others contain hidden sweeteners that make it hard to know how much sugar you are eating. Answer the questions below to determine whether you are eating too many refined carbohydrates:

Dietary Sugar Intake Survey

(Circle Yes or No)

1. Do you eat white rice more often than brown rice?   Yes   No
2. Do you snack on fruit alone?   Yes   No
3. Do you eat jelly or jam?   Yes   No
4. Do you eat dried fruit?   Yes   No
5. Are you on a juicing regimen?   Yes   No
6. Do you eat low fat baked goods?   Yes   No
7. Do you use prepackaged mixes more often than you make foods from scratch?   Yes   No
8. Do you like cereals that could be classified as kids' cereal?   Yes   No
9. Do you eat canned fruit?   Yes   No
10. Do you drink regular soft drinks?   Yes   No
11. Do you drink flavored beverages such as sports drinks, teas, or sodas?   Yes   No
12. Do you eat candy as a snack or pick-me-up?   Yes   No
13. Do you eat dessert often?   Yes   No
14. Do you add some kind of sweetener to food or drink?   Yes   No
15. Do you use artificial sweeteners?   Yes   No

Total: Yes _____   No _____

Survey Interpretation

These questions were designed to provide a starting point for reducing excessive or hidden sugars in your diet. Yes answers to questions 1 and 2 point out eating habits that cause a fast release of sugar into the bloodstream. Questions 3 through 5 reveal concentrated sugar food choices. Questions 6 through 11 indicate hidden sugars lurking in your foods that you might not be aware of. Questions 12 and 13 point to overt surplus dietary sugar intake. When you choose these foods, it should not surprise you that you're eating way too much sugar! Questions 14 and 15 introduce the subject of alternative sweeteners.

Coach's Corner

Get Off the Roller Coaster!

Fast rising, free falling blood sugar levels can leave you feeling fatigued and emotionally unbalanced. You probably have a blood sugar management problem if you experience any of the following symptoms:

- Cravings for sugar or sweets
- Dizziness or irritability when you skip a meal
- Frequent urination
- Low energy early in the morning
- Restless sleep
- Thirst not relieved by drinking water

Often, combining carbohydrate and protein foods will decrease the severity or number of these symptoms.

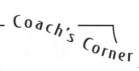

Secret Sugars

Do you think you eat a diet low in sugar? Conduct a little label research in your kitchen pantry. Hidden sugars may be lurking in your favorite foods! Take a look at how sweet many foods are. Each spoon symbol is equivalent to about 4 grams of sugar. The total number of sugar grams per serving is listed in parentheses next to each product.

Teaspoons of Sugar

Ocean Spray Cran-Grape Juice (41)

Gatorade Frost Thirst Quencher (14)

Five Alive frozen beverage mix (28)

Starbuck's Low Fat Frappuccino (31)

Quaker Apple-Cinnamon Oatmeal (12)

General Mills Multi-Grain Chex (12)

Nabisco Multi-Grain Crackers (4)

Campbell's Tomato Garden Soup (12)

Prego Traditional Spaghetti Sauce (7)

Columbo Strawberry Yogurt (35)

Mott's Mixed Berry Applesauce (21)

Source: Product labels

The Sugar-Insulin Connection

Your blood sugar response to certain foods is very unique. Your own physiology has a lot to do with how quickly a food is digested and then released into your bloodstream. Here are some suggestions for balancing blood sugar levels.

- Avoid foods that trigger blood sugar peaks. Limit sugary confections, desserts, and other sweet treats.
- Eat high-fiber foods. Diets rich in fiber create a slow, even energy uptake. Choose whole grain breads, buckwheat pasta, and brown rice in place of white bread, pasta, and rice products.
- Combine high-sugar foods with protein. The release of sugar into the bloodstream is slowed down when meat, eggs, or other protein sources accompany potatoes, fruit, or other carbohydrates. Don't eat fruit or drink fruit juice alone; combine with nuts or seeds.
- If you have dessert, eat it at the end of a protein-based meal.

Thorough descriptions of carbohydrates and proteins are given in Chapter 4 to help you distinguish between the two. The snacking suggestions will show you how to combine starches with proteins. This rule of food combining is one of your best defenses against initiating cancer cell growth and suppressing the immune system.

Concentrated Sugars

Watch the amount of juice, dried fruit, and sugary condiments you eat! All of these foods contribute concentrated carbohydrates to your diet and raise levels of sugar in your blood.

Juicing is very popular among people who want an easy way to consume large quantities of fruits and vegetables. While juicing does have its benefits, it has a disadvantage as well. Fruit and vegetable juices can raise blood sugar levels dramatically. The rule of food combining applies here as well. If you are going to juice, you should consume your juice with a protein based meal or snack, or add protein powder to the juice mixture. If you want to integrate this practice into your nutrition action plan, you can read about juicing in Chapter 11, "Cooling Off."

Dried fruit, usually thought of as a healthy snack food, qualifies as a high-sugar food because it contains concentrated sources of natural sugars. Why the emphasis on dried fruit and not fresh fruit?

The sugar contribution from the same amount of fresh fruit and dried fruit differs substantially. For example, one cup of grapes contains almost 4 teaspoons of sugar. One cup of raisins, on the other hand, contains 28 teaspoons of sugar! Dried fruit packs a lot of sugar into a little package. You don't have to give up raisins, prunes, figs, and other dried fruits, just limit them. Save dried fruits, which are easy to tote around, for emergency situations when you are not able to eat fresh fruits.

Jams, jellies, marmalades, syrups, and glazes are all examples of sugary condiments. All of these products contain a large amount of sugar that, when heated into a liquid, becomes concentrated. One tablespoon of grape jelly contains a whopping six teaspoons of sugar!

Sweetened condiments should be avoided because even small amounts of sugar contribute significantly to the total dietary carbohydrate load.

Hidden Sugars

Typically, any food that has been processed and packaged by the food industry contains added refined sugars. These sweeteners can hide just about anywhere! The only way you are going to find hidden sugars is to look for them. Sugar goes by a number of names, so inspect the ingredient section of food labels for the following terms: sugar, sucrose, dextrose, fructose, powdered sugar, maple sugar, brown sugar, corn syrup, levulose, high fructose corn syrup, honey, milk sugar, lactose, and maltose.

Soft drinks, flavored beverages, and fruit drinks are loaded with sugar. Did you know that one can of soda contains between 7 and 10 teaspoons of sugar? Most colorful sports drinks used to replace sodium and potassium after strenuous workouts contain tons of sugar. The only time to drink a sports drink is when you are dehydrated from severe diarrhea or vomiting. Check the label on flavored bottled waters. Usually, they contain a sweetener as a flavor enhancer.

Canned fruits come packed in heavy, light, and fruit-juice-based syrups. Make sure you take a good long look at the label and purchase the fruit that is packed in juice or light syrup. Choosing "lite" fruits will reduce your intake of sugar by at least 50 percent.

Low-fat bakery products such as crackers, cookies, and cakes are often high in sugar. While there is less fat in these products, the fat has been replaced with sugar. Consider preparing baked goods from scratch to control the amount of sugar in them.

Children's cereals are very high in sugar, but adults' cereals can be too. A peek at the labels of some granolas and oat bran cereals will convince you of this.

So Long, Sweets!

Having a sweet tooth can be hard on your body. A diet high in sugar requires tapping into your body stores of calcium, phosphorus, chromium, magnesium, cobalt, copper, zinc, and manganese in order to produce the enzymes necessary to metabolize the carbohydrates.

If the threat of health complications and poor nutrition doesn't provide the motivation necessary to cut back your sugar intake, keep the bigger picture in mind. Is that candy bar or can of soda pop really worth a depressed immune system and potential cancer growth?

Getting the Edge

Parting Is Such Sweet Sorrow

Sugar consumption in America continues to rise and soft drinks are only one of the culprits. To cut out concentrated or hidden sweets, first identify the foods that are high in sugar, then take action to eliminate them from your diet. Here is a list of foods you should be saying good-bye to:

- Beverages sweetened with sugar, including flavored syrups added to hot beverages
- Frosting, icing, and dessert glazes or syrups
- Fruits in heavy syrups, sweetened applesauce
- Fruit drinks that are not 100% juice
- Gelatin, flavored and sweetened
- Jams, jellies, and preserves made with sugar
- Ketchup, salad dressings, peanut butter, and other spreads with added sugars
- Packaged convenience foods such as cakes, cookies, pies, muffins, cereals, flavored beverages, and frozen vegetables and entrees that contain sucrose, honey, brown sugar, syrups, sorghum, molasses, dextrose, and glucose

Craving Sugar?

You aren't the only one! Nibbling on something sweet may be innocent, but before you know it, you may find yourself wanting more. Sugar cravings may develop a couple of ways. First, concentrated sugar strips your body of chromium and other important minerals needed for glucose metabolism. Mineral deficits often spur the desire for more carbohydrates. Second, candida yeast overgrowth perpetuates the desire for sweet, starchy foods.

Regardless of the cause, you'll know you have an addiction to sweets if you experience headaches, mood swings, and depressed feelings when you stop eating them. Like other addictions, the way to cut cravings is by abstinence. Good old-fashioned willpower is needed to overcome the strong desire for sweets. Here are some tips for satisfying a sweet tooth:

- Sweeten plain ready-to-eat breakfast cereals with fresh or dried fruit instead of sugar.
- Reduce the sugar in baked items by one fourth; bring out the sweetness in foods by adding vanilla, lemon, or almond extracts.
- Eat dried, fresh, or frozen fruit. Try baked apples, cooked fruit, and 100% fruit frozen treats.
- Make your own breading or coating mixes for meats and poultry. Commercially prepared mixes may contain more than 50 percent sugar!
- Eat "sweet" vegetables such as yams, winter squash, and carrots.
- Sweeten baked goods with barley malt, Sucanat, or other alternative sweeteners.
- Replace refined sugar and flour with complex, dense

grains such as barley, oats, quinoa, whole wheat, and so on.

- Make your own soft drink: Add 1/2 cup fruit juice to 1/2 cup club soda.
- Add a cinnamon stick or orange slice to sweeten hot beverages.
- If you have a tendency to binge eat, avoid eating any sugary foods. Even one little piece of candy can create a desire for more sugar.
- Avoid a diet high in salt or animal meats, which often prompt a desire for something sweet.
- If you have a tendency toward low blood sugar, carry an emergency snack with you wherever you go. Pack an organic, 100% dried fruit leather. Although it is a concentrated source of fructose, it provides a healthier option to a candy bar.
- Maintain a balanced blood sugar throughout the day. Don't skip meals. Eat a mixed diet.
- Consider taking dietary supplements used to moderate blood sugar levels, such as chromium and bioflavonoids.

Sugar Substitutes

Sugar substitutes are found most often in drinks, baked goods, yogurts, puddings, and frozen desserts. Some people use sugar substitutes to help them lose weight. While it is true that most sugar substitutes don't provide significant calories, research has proven they do not contribute to long-term weight loss.

Animal studies have shown that saccharin (found in Sweet'N Low) is a tumor promoter in the bladder, lungs, and other organs.[11]

Gold Medal Action

Hooray for Honey!

Honey has been used for centuries to heal wounds, relieve allergies, and soothe sore throats. Besides being a great sweetener for foods and liquids, here are some other features about honey that you might not be aware of:[12]

- It contains oligosaccharides, a preferred food source for beneficial gut bacteria.
- It contains organic acids and enzymes that have potential antibacterial and anti-inflammatory properties.
- It is made of about 70 percent sugar from fructose and glucose. This sugar combination has a milder effect on blood glucose than other carbohydrates.
- It can be used in place of sugar in baking (use slightly less honey and reduce liquid by one fourth).
- Is sweeter and more flavorful than granulated sugar, so you need to use less to get the same sweetening effect.

Aspartame (found in Nutrasweet and Equal) has been linked to neurological disorders.[13] Sucralose, also called Splenda, is the newest approved low-calorie sweetener to grace our consumer market. It's about six hundred times sweeter than sugar, is made from sugar, and is calorie free. Safety studies suggest this is a nontoxic product.[14]

An herbal alternative sweetener called stevia may be a better choice than artificial sweeteners for some diabetics. Stevia contains no calories and has been shown to lower blood sugar levels.[15] Stevia's flavor is quite acceptable, although some patients have reported that it has a mild licorice aftertaste.

Alternative Sweeteners

The following sweeteners offer you an alternative to highly processed sugars and artificial sweeteners. Because they are unrefined, these natural choices have some vitamins and minerals and can provide distinct flavors to your foods or beverages. All of these alternative sweeteners take longer to digest, thus promoting better blood sugar control. Nevertheless, don't be misled by these natural sweeteners. They are highly concentrated sugars. Remember to limit your intake of any sweeteners to about 5 percent of your total caloric intake.

- Brown Rice Syrup: Enzymes are used to break down the rice starch. This syrup contains 50 percent complex carbohydrates and is also available in powdered form. Brown rice syrup is great for baked goods and hot drinks.
- Barley Malt Syrup: Sprouted barley is used to turn grain starches into this sweetener. Products contain about 40 percent complex carbohydrates.
- Date sugar: This pulverized product provides fiber and other nutrients found in dates.
- Fruitsource: This brand name sweetener is a combination of grape juice and brown rice syrup. It is about 80 percent as sweet as sugar and comes in liquid and granulated form.

- Honey: Flavor varies depending on what plant the nectar was collected from. Honey is sweeter than sugar, so you can use less. You can purchase honey in liquid or granulated form.
- Stevia: An herb native to South America, this sweetener has been shown to regulate blood sugar levels. Unrefined stevia tastes like molasses.
- Sucanat: This brand name sweetener blends sugar and molasses back together to make a dry product with restored vitamins and minerals. It creates smooth-textured baked goods.
- Whole Fruit: Fruit purees, dried fruit, and cooked fruit can sweeten cereals, breads, main dishes, and desserts.

— 7 —

Plants To Help You Advance

"Why not go out on a limb? Isn't that where the fruit is?"
— Frank Scully

Good Advice

DO YOU REMEMBER YOUR MOTHER telling you to eat your fruits and vegetables? Well, she was right. The disease-fighting potential of plants has been confirmed in hundreds of population and clinical research studies. The health benefits of fruits and vegetables are so dramatic that the National Cancer Institute, in conjunction with the produce industry, state health departments, and other consumer groups, have begun a five-a-day campaign to educate consumers on the benefits of eating more plants.

Plants and Cancer

Studies show a strong protective association between the consumption of fruits and vegetables and cancers of the bladder, larynx, lung, mouth, pharynx, and stomach. A positive link between fruits and vegetables also exists for resisting cancers of the breast, cervix, endometrium, ovary, pancreas, and thyroid.

The Power of Plants

Many fruits and vegetables contain a variety of compounds called phytochemicals. The amount of phytochemicals in plants varies by growing region, but the kind of phytochemicals present in plants remains consistent. While research is ongoing in the field of plant chemicals, researchers realize we have not yet discovered the full health potential of these powerful plant substances.

Phytochemicals protect plants by acting as a natural pesticide. Phytochemicals protect humans, too. They turn on enzymes in our body to help us detoxify carcinogens and other environmental poisons. In this way and in others, plant components can change the course of cancer by[1,2]

- Inhibiting enzymes responsible for cancer growth,
- Activating protective enzymes that stop cancer from progressing,
- Modifying how carcinogens are detoxified,

- Acting as free radical scavengers,
- Suppressing the abnormal growth of precancerous lesions,
- Stimulating the immune system,
- Decreasing platelet aggregation, and
- Exhibiting antibacterial and antiviral activity.

When More Food Is Better

The National Cancer Institute recommends you consume at least five servings of fruits and vegetables per day. Eighty percent of American children and nearly 70 percent of adults don't even come close to meeting this goal.[3] In fact, the latest surveys show that the average American consumer eats fewer than three servings of fruits and vegetables per day.

As a daily minimum, you should consume at least two servings of fruit and three servings of vegetables each day. Keep in mind that this five-a-day goal is appropriate for someone who requires about 1,200 calories per day. As caloric requirements increase, so should fruit and vegetable intake. For example, if you need 2,000 calories per day, you should shoot for an intake goal of eight to ten servings of produce each day. That may seem like a lot, but for fighting cancer, more produce is better. Researchers at Johns Hopkins Medical Institute found greater levels of antioxidants in individuals who consumed eight to ten servings of fruits and vegetables each day as compared to individuals who ate fewer servings.[4]

On Your Way to Five-a-Day

If you want to provide your body with the best cancer-fighting foods, there is no way around it—you must eat your greens (and your reds, yellows, oranges, and purples!). Maximize the health potential of your fruits and vegetables by following these suggestions:

- Eat vegetables and fruits that have deep, rich colors. The darker a plant is, the greater the phytochemical potential. Sweet potatoes are better than white potatoes. One serving of romaine lettuce contains almost eight times as much vitamin A as a serving of iceberg lettuce. Get the picture?

- Eat a variety of fruits and vegetables each day. Don't limit your vegetable choices to only broccoli and cabbage. While both of these vegetables have outstanding nutritional profiles, they can contribute only a fraction of the important cancer fighting chemicals to your diet. Consuming a mixed bag of plants gives you a well-rounded dose of a variety of phytochemicals and provides an opportunity for the chemicals to work together in a more powerful way.

- Eat whole natural fruits and vegetables. Consume phytochemical-rich plants in their raw or slightly cooked form. Eating uncooked, unprocessed plants contributes enzymes for digestion and provides the highest levels of nutrients. Lightly steamed vegetables retain some of the nutrients lost with other cooking methods. If you can't eat fresh produce, frozen produce is your next best choice. Use canned fruits or vegetables as a last resort. Canned produce has been stripped of fiber-rich peelings, has fewer nutrients, and may contain added sweeteners or sodium.

What's a Serving Size?

The National Cancer Institute offers these serving size guidelines for fruits and vegetables:

- 1 medium fruit or 1/2 cup of small or diced fruit
- 1/2 cup 100% juice
- 1/4 cup dried fruit
- 1/2 cup raw non-leafy or cooked vegetables
- 1 cup raw leafy vegetables
- 1/2 cup cooked beans or peas

As you can see, a serving of fruit or vegetables is reasonable in size. Think about the mixed greens you have at dinner. Chances are that your bowl contains at least two cups, or two servings of salad. Serving sizes for fruits depend a bit more on the amount of carbohydrate each food contains. For example, one medium banana is equal to two fruits, while a medium apple is equal to one fruit. Do you eat only one-half of a banana or drink just four ounces of orange juice in the morning? Probably not. So, you see, getting five-a-day really isn't as difficult as you may have once thought!

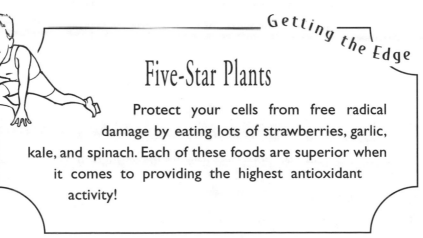

Getting the Edge

Five-Star Plants

Protect your cells from free radical damage by eating lots of strawberries, garlic, kale, and spinach. Each of these foods are superior when it comes to providing the highest antioxidant activity!

Fabulous Phytochemicals
Allylic Sulfide (allicin)

Organic sulfur compounds, found in bulbous plants, protect against carcinogens by increasing enzymes responsible for detoxification.[5] Allicin has demonstrated significant antitumor effects in animal studies for stomach,[6] esophageal, and bladder cancers and may be effective against leukemia.[7] Because of its antibacterial and antiyeast properties, allicin is used to treat *Candida albicans* infections. Food sources include chives, garlic, leeks, onions, scallions, and shallots.

Quick Bites

Leeks make a delicious addition to soups, stews, and egg dishes. They can be steamed or braised and served as a side dish. To prepare, trim away the green tops to within 2 inches of the white part; rinse thoroughly to wash the grit away. Cook 12 to 15 minutes in boiling water. Increase the antioxidant potential of this side dish by seasoning it with basil, rosemary, or thyme.

Anthocyanidins

Anthocyanidins are powerful water-soluble antioxidants that have been found to support cardiovascular function and protect against macular degeneration and cataracts. Antitumor effects using anthocyanidin extracts have been demonstrated on lymphoma cells.[8] Grape seed proanthocyanidin extract has shown cytotoxic activity towards human breast, lung, and stomach cancer cells.[9] Food sources include bilberry, blackberries, cherries, cranberries, currants, eggplant, lentils, plums, raspberries, red cabbage, red grapes, red wine, rhubarb, and strawberries.

Beta Carotene and Carotenoids

Beta carotene, which can be converted to vitamin A in the body, is one of six hundred identified carotenoids. Diets high in beta carotene provide immune protection and antioxidant benefit. One study showed that elderly males who took beta carotene supplements had significantly greater natural killer cell activity than men receiving placebo.[10] Research has demonstrated that beta carotene offers protection against cervical and lung cancers and helps to modulate human prostate cancer cell growth.[11,12] Low levels of beta carotene are found in most upper digestive tract cancers, suggesting a causal relationship with these types of cancer.[13]

Other carotenoids such as alpha carotene, cryptoxanthin, lutein, lycopene, and zeaxanthin also contribute to disease prevention. Several studies have shown that both single and multiple carotenes prevent carcinogens from entering cells and help repair genetic injury.[14,15] By this action carotenes may play a protective role against tumor progression associated with oxidative damage. Lycopenes that provide a reddish tint to tomatoes, watermelon, and pink grapefruit help fend off the occurrence or progression of prostate cancer.[16] Food sources include arugula, broccoli, butternut squash, cantaloupe, carrots, chard, collard greens, daikon, endive, horseradish, kale, mango, mustard greens, nappa cabbage, nectarines, oranges, papaya, peach, peppers, pumpkin, sorrel, spinach, star fruit, tangerine, tomato, turnip greens, and yams.

Capsaicin

Capsaicin is the active component of cayenne pepper. Paprika, which comes from a different variety of this pepper plant, contains canthaxanthin, another powerful antioxidant. Vitamins A and C and a mixture of carotenoids are found in cayenne pepper as well. Capsaicin is used topically by arthritis sufferers as an anti-inflammatory agent and a pain blocker. Research has demonstrated that capsaicin offers protection against gastrointestinal oxidative damage, which implies it may have a role in chemoprevention.[17] Recent studies have also revealed capsaicin has substantial anticarcinogenic activity in human cancers.[18] Food sources include cayenne pepper, chilies, hot red peppers, and paprika.

Catechins

Catechins, or tannins, are chemically active compounds that have been linked to low rates of gastrointestinal cancer. These flavanols are seven times more potent than vitamin E as an antioxidant. They inhibit the activation of carcinogens and have demonstrated anti-inflammatory, probiotic, and antimicrobial properties in human, animal, and test tube studies.[19] Food sources include apple juice, berries, black tea, grapes, green tea, peaches, persimmons, plums, red wine, and strawberries.

Citrus Bioflavonoids

About four hundred flavonoids have been isolated from various fruits and vegetables. Naringin, naringenin, rutin, hesperidin, and quercetin are all citrus flavonoids that prevent cancer-causing hormones from attaching to cells. They also support liver detoxification. Citrus bioflavonoids have anti-allergy and anti-inflammatory benefits as well. In human and animal studies, flavonoids have demonstrated antitumor activity for breast, lung, and prostate cancers.[20-22] Tangeretin, found in tangerines, and hesperetin, found in oranges, protect breast tissue from free radical damage. Additionally, human leukemia cell growth has been slowed by quercetin.[23] Resveratrol, a polyphenol found in citrus fruits, green vegetables, and red grape skin, hinders oral squamous carcinoma and prostate cancer cell growth.[24,25] Food sources of flavonoids include broccoli, black currants, berries, eggplant, grapefruit, kale, kelp, kiwi, lemons, limes, onions, oranges, squash, tangerines, tomatoes, and yams.

Coumarins

Both anti-inflammatory and antioxidant activities are exhibited by coumarins.[26] Coumarin-related compounds such as auraptene and umbelliferone slow the development of esophageal and colon cancer and reduce the spreading ability of melanoma cells.[27,28] Food sources include carrots, grapefruit, lemons, limes, oranges, parsley, and tangerines.

Curcumins

Curcumins protect cells from chromosomal damage. They have been found to be as powerful as vitamin E in reducing the number of abnormal bone marrow cells in radiation-treated experimental animals.[29] Humans at risk for developing cancer of the palate due to reverse smoking who took one gram of turmeric per day had fewer precancerous lesions.[30] Leukemia and colorectal cancer cell growth was inhibited by curcumin administration.[31,32] Food sources include curried foods, turmeric, and mustard.

Ellagic Acid

A flavonoid known to act as a free radical scavenger, ellagic acid may prevent mutation of genes. It is a proven cancer fighter, stopping tumor growth in esophageal and lung cancer animal studies.[33,34] Food sources include apples, blackberries, cranberries, grapes, raspberries, strawberries, and walnuts.

Indoles

Indoles are found in cruciferous vegetables. They reside in the liver and act as detoxifying agents. Indoles offer potent antitumor activity by deactivating estrogen. Based on this mechanism, researchers have inferred that indoles may help prevent cervical cancer.[35] Besides a role in cancer prevention, other studies have shown that indole-3-carbinols cause cancer cells to die.[36]

Food sources include bok choy, broccoli, Brussels sprouts, cabbage, cauliflower, greens, kale, kohlrabi, rutabagas, and turnips.

Gold Medal Action

A recent study revealed that women who consumed at least six servings of spinach, kale, and other leafy greens per week had a nearly 50 percent lower risk of developing ovarian cancer compared to women who consumed fewer than two servings per week.[37]

Isothiocyanates

Isothiocyanates occur in cruciferous and some other kinds of vegetables. These plant chemicals have anticancer properties by inhibiting enzymes involved in cancer activation. Research on animal models has demonstrated this carcinogenic blocking ability on esophageal and lung cancers.[38] Broccoli sprouts have been found to contain up to fifty times the amount of chemoprotective compounds found in broccoli. Animals given sprout extracts developed fewer tumors and had smaller cancer growths that took longer to develop.[39] Food sources include broccoli sprouts, cruciferous vegetables, horseradish, mustard, and radishes.

Monoterpenes

Monoterpenes, found in the essential oils of a variety of plants, inhibit cancer cell growth and help to detoxify carcinogens. These powerful antioxidants have demonstrated efficacy in breast and colon cancer models. Citrus peel consumption (the major source of dietary limonene) has been associated with lowered risk of squamous cell skin cancer.[40] Mice fed a diet containing limonene had a significant reduction in the number of metastatic melanoma nodules.[41] Perillyl alcohol has been shown to regress breast, liver, and pancreatic tumors, and it has potential as an anticancer agent for colon, lung, neuroblastoma, prostate, and skin cancers as well.[42] Dietary geraniol increased survival time of mice with transplanted leukemia cells.[43]

Food sources include basil, broccoli, cabbage, carrots, celery seeds, cherries, grapefruit peel, lemon peel, mint, orange peel, parsley, peppers, squash, tomatoes, and yams.

Phenolic Acids

Phenolic compounds such as chlorogenic, caffeic, and ferulic acids block the formation of nitrosamines.[44] Caffeic acid is an anti-inflammatory agent that has been shown to increase colon cancer cell death.[45] Food sources include broccoli, cabbage, carrots, cherries, citrus fruit, eggplant, grapefruit, oranges, parsley, pears, peppers, prunes, and tomato.

Phthalides

Phthalides are responsible for the characteristic odor of celery. These plant compounds fight cancer by stimulating the production of detoxifying enzymes.[46] Food sources include carrots, celery, and parsley.

Phytoestrogens

Flavonoids such as daidzein and genistein are found in soybeans. They have the most active blocking potential against estrogen receptors in the breast and ovaries. Lignans, coumestans, and saponins are weaker phytoestrogens. Consumption of these plant hormones has been linked to a decreased risk of female cancers. Research has shown that both daidzein and genistein enhance the activation of human natural killer cells.[47] Studies have also demonstrated the ability of isoflavones to prevent the growth of transplanted human breast cancer cells in animals.[48] A recent study has demonstrated the significant antimutagenic activity of saponins.[49] Food sources include bean sprouts, broccoli, cabbage, cucumbers, eggplant, flaxseeds, peppers, soy milk, soybeans, squash, tofu, and whole grains.

Quinones

Members of the rosemary family contain this very active antioxidant. Rosemary extract has demonstrated chemoprotective activity by increasing detoxification and blocking the activation of procarcinogens.[50] Food sources include basil, marjoram, mint, oregano, rosemary, sage, and thyme.

Triterpenoids

Triterpenoids may slow cancer through enzyme inactivation. Human leukemia cell growth has been inhibited by this plant compound.[51] Food sources include grapefruit, lemons, limes, oranges, soybeans, soy milk, tangerines, and tofu.

Self-Assessment:
Are You Eating Your Way to Five-a-Day?

Are your plant choices packed with cancer-fighting phytochemicals, or are you munching on the same old corn and green beans night after night? Answer the questions below to see if you have plant habits that need nurturing:

Dietary Produce Intake Survey

(Circle Yes or No)

1. Do you eat at least five servings of produce each day?   Yes   No
2. Do you eat more fresh than frozen or canned produce?   Yes   No
3. Do you eat vegetables instead of chips or fries?   Yes   No
4. Do you add fruit to your cereal at breakfast?   Yes   No
5. Is fruit juice your beverage of choice at meals?   Yes   No
6. Do you usually order a salad when you dine out?   Yes   No
7. Do you try new kinds of fruits or vegetables?   Yes   No
8. Do you think cost is prohibiting your intake of produce?   Yes   No
9. Do fruits and vegetables take too long to prepare?   Yes   No
10. Are you afraid to eat produce because of the chemicals used on plants?   Yes   No
11. Are you concerned about produce storage issues?   Yes   No

Total: Yes ____   No ____

Survey Interpretation

These questions were designed to provide you with insight as to why you may not be meeting your five-a-day goal. Questions 1 and 2 ask you to analyze your current produce consumption habits. Questions 3 through 6 provide examples of quick and easy dietary strategies to add fruits and vegetables to your meals. Questions 7 through 11 relay common, negative perceptions about produce that may hinder fruit and vegetable consumption.

Putting Plants into Your Diet

Eating more fruits and vegetables isn't difficult, but it does take effort. Develop a routine of eating fruits and vegetables at every meal. Once you get into the habit of eating plants, you'll definitely miss them when you don't eat them.

Look at the following list of suggestions for adding more fruits and vegetables to your diet. Then come up with some of your own strategies to meet your five-a-day!

- Add grated zucchini and carrots to ground turkey, beef, or textured vegetable protein. Shape into burgers or loaf form and grill or bake.
- Dice up colorful peppers and onions and add them to potato wedges. Toss olive oil, chopped garlic cloves, and a quarter teaspoon of thyme. Roast in an oven for about thirty minutes or until the potatoes are tender.
- Replace half the meat in lasagna or spaghetti sauces with sliced or grated vegetables.
- Carry a bag of petite carrots with you to work. Add to a sandwich in place of fries, chips, or potato or macaroni salad.
- Top fish with a citrus chutney or hearty salsa. Add zip to your chicken by adding a cherry sauce; bake cinnamon sprinkled apple wedges with pork chops.
- Dress up homemade or commercial soups by adding canned or frozen vegetables. Just like that, you've added a half serving of vegetables per one cup of soup!

- Mix frozen blueberries or raspberries into pancake or waffle mixes. Top hot or cold cereal with bananas, berries, or peaches.
- Place peeled pear halves in a bowl with one cup of water. Drizzle with lemon juice and microwave for about ten minutes. Discard the water and spoon some Polander's Raspberry All Fruit over each pear.
- Add golden raisins and scallions to curry flavored couscous.
- Thaw and puree frozen fruits. Drizzle over a frozen tofu dessert.
- Try frozen pineapple and blueberry, or raspberry and banana combinations in your fruit smoothies.
- Snack on a healthy trail mix made of dried fruit (cranberries, pineapples, dates or raisins), low-fat granola, and raw almonds.
- Instead of stopping for coffee or ordering tea, drink juice. Buy a six-pack of tomato juice and keep it in the refrigerator for days when eating vegetables become a challenge.
- Mix fresh berries, apple slices, kiwi, or pineapple chunks into plain nonfat yogurt for a sweet treat.
- When dining out, ask for a double helping of the vegetable of the day. Order vegetable filled sandwiches or fajitas. Visit the salad bar and stick with the plain veggies and fresh fruits.

No More Excuses!

Feeling reluctant to eat fruits and vegetables? After reading about all the special chemicals found in produce, it makes no sense

At the Training Table

Fast Snacks

Looking for a quick way to get your five-a-day? These easy, nutritious products are available at your local health food store:

- Dig into Mann's Broccoli Cole Slaw. Shredded carrots, red cabbage, and hearts of broccoli have been mixed to make a crunchy snack right out of the bag. Add a dollop of nonfat yogurt or low-fat mayo and enjoy!

- Cooley's SmoothyPaks are bags of frozen fruit combinations such as apricot–strawberry–papaya and strawberry–mango–pineapple. Just drop the chunks into a blender with yogurt and juice and puree yourself a shake. Sure beats the same old strawberry–banana concoction!

to limit your cancer-fighting potential. Here are some common reasons people won't eat produce. Are any of these excuses keeping you from eating your five-a-day?

- People don't want to try new foods.
- Produce can be expensive.
- It takes too long to eat fruits and vegetables.
- Fruits and vegetables contain dangerous chemicals.
- The shelf life of produce is limited.

If you don't like many vegetables, it is time to expand your horizons. Review the phytochemical listings of specific vegetables and choose one or two that you'd be willing to try. If you don't like fruit, do the same thing. Make a goal to try one new plant every three weeks or so.

Budgeting for Produce

Fresh fruits and vegetables in season can be far cheaper than some packaged snack foods. For example, based on prices at a local grocery store, a large red apple costs 21¢ while a serving of cinnamon twist cake costs 63¢. You can reduce the cost of fruits and vegetables even more. Clip coupons for money off on your brand of canned and frozen fruits and vegetables. If you aren't partial to a particular brand, compare prices of canned and frozen produce and juices and try a less expensive brand. Buy in bulk, especially fruits such as grapefruits and oranges, and vegetables such as carrots and celery. These produce picks tend to have a longer shelf life than bananas, berries, peppers, and cucumbers.

Fast Fruits (and veggies, too!)

In this busy world time is a precious commodity, and yes, it takes more time to peel, cut, chop, and cook fruit and vegetables. Try this experiment with your family. Fill one bowl with peeled and sectioned tangerines and fill another bowl with kiwi. Chances are, the bowl of prepared tangerines will empty first. When you eliminate the preparation time, you are more likely to grab a piece of fruit as part of a quick snack or after-dinner treat. The same principle applies to vegetables. You can buy precut ready-to-eat vegetables and prepared salads. Buy frozen vegetables and pop the bag into the microwave to give yourself an additional serving or two of vegetables at dinnertime.

Many grocery stores also carry precut fruit and vegetable trays. When you are in a crunch for time, use canned and frozen fruit, canned and bottled juices, and dried fruits. Just open the container and eat or drink. Many foods such as raisins, dates, grapes, and cherry tomatoes can be eaten on the spot.

Quick Bites

Pick and Pack Produce!

Stretch Island makes fruit leathers in delectable flavors such as great grape, tangy apricot, and organic apple and cinnamon. Only fruits and natural juices are used; fructose is not added to any of these snacks. Fruit leather fits neatly into your purse or wallet and can't be beat when it comes to a convenient, easy-to-pack form of fruit.

Picking Safe Produce

Small amounts of pesticide residue have been found on some fruits and vegetables. Cancer-causing and neurotoxic chemicals may have been banned for use in the United States, but imported produce still has potential for contamination. If you purchase certified organic produce, you can avoid these chemicals, but you will pay about 30 percent more for these foods.

During the winter, avoid produce from South America or Mexico. These plants have the highest risk of being covered in hazardous chemicals. Wash or soak all produce with a citrus surfactant spray such as Veggi Wash or Fit. This will help rid the produce surface of chemicals and wax coating. Fruits and vegetables that are typically coated with wax include apples, cucumbers, eggplant, grapefruit, melons, oranges, peaches, rutabagas, squash, and tomatoes.

Gold Medal Action

Clean Up Your Act!

Thoroughly wash your fruits and vegetables with a vinegar solution (1/4 cup vinegar to 1 gallon of water) or buy a spray wash designed to clean and remove wax from produce. Remember to wash the outside of melons (even though you don't eat the rind) because when you cut into the fruit, exterior bacteria can enter into the flesh.

Before It's Too Late...

Tossing rotten fruits or vegetables into the garbage feels like dumping dollars down the drain. No one wants to spend money on food that spoils before it's eaten. If you don't have a large family or only cook for yourself, you should shop for both fresh and processed forms of produce. Consume the fresh fruits and vegetables first, then add canned and frozen produce to your meals for the rest of the week. Buy ripe and unripe bananas and tomatoes so that the unripe produce will be available to eat days after the ripe produce has been consumed. Keep fruits and vegetables where you can see them. Apples in a basket placed on your kitchen table is a gentle reminder that healthy snacks are available for the taking.

Juicy News

I think juice should be considered the original fast food. After all, there is no peeling, slicing, dicing, or chewing. Just open, pour, and gulp! Adding juice to a whole foods natural diet is a convenient way to help you meet your daily fruit intake goal. Drinking juice provides variety to your diet and gives your body fluid and nutrients that can support organ function.

If you have difficulty swallowing, a poor appetite, or have been placed on a low-fiber diet because of some gastrointestinal complications, it may be difficult for you to consume the suggested five servings of fruits and vegetables every day. Drinking juice can be a good way to overcome this dietary obstacle.

There are a couple things to remember when you drink juice:

- Always consume juice with a meal or snack that contains protein. Never drink juice alone.
- Look for "100% juice" on labels. Don't pick "sugar water" disguised as ades, cocktails, or juice blends.

While many of us consume a glass or two of juice each day, others spend more time at the kitchen counter, creating phytochemical cocktails for their health. Drinking juice to alter health, called juice therapy, is used for the purpose of detoxification and healing. Learn more about juice therapy in the chapter on detoxification.

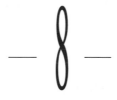

8

Fast Forward with Fiber

"Even if you're on the right track, you'll get run over if you just sit there."
— *Will Rogers*

What Is Fiber?

SOMETIMES KNOWN AS ROUGHAGE, this threadlike complex carbohydrate is a component of fruits, vegetables, and whole grains. Since the body can't absorb food fibers, they don't supply any nutrients or calories. When we eat foods containing fiber, the fiber passes through our gastrointestinal tract. It is precisely this action that gives fiber its health benefits.

What Happens to Fiber When You Cook It?

Cooking doesn't change the amount of fiber in foods. Cooking will, however, decrease the bulk of some vegetables. For example, one cup of raw spinach will equal about one quarter cup when cooked. This is an important point to keep in mind when you compare the fiber content of raw versus cooked foods.

Classifying Fiber

Dietary fibers are categorized as soluble or insoluble according to their physical characteristics and physiological effects on the body. Although fiber works primarily in the gastrointestinal tract, each form of fiber has unique functions and health benefits.

Insoluble fibers (hemicellulose, cellulose, and lignan) are found in crunchy foods such as fruits, vegetables, legumes, wheat bran, seeds, popcorn, brown rice, and whole grain products. Our typical diet is usually much higher in insoluble, rather than soluble, fiber. Because insoluble fibers don't dissolve in water, their physical appearance remains unchanged. Insoluble fiber helps draw water into the colon, resulting in increased stool bulk and regulated bowel movements.

Soluble fibers (gum, pectin, and mucilages) are found in fruits such as apples, oranges, and prunes, and vegetables, seeds, oats, barley, psyllium, rye, and whole grain products. Soluble fibers are softer, thicker, and more gummy in texture than insoluble fibers. Soluble fibers swell in water and can slow the passage of food through the digestive tract. This action helps to regulate cholesterol and blood sugar levels in the body by affecting absorption rates.

Getting the Edge

Good for the Gut

Fructooligosaccharide (FOS), also known as a prebiotic, is a non-digestible carbohydrate that provides food for friendly gut bacteria and promotes a healthy colon. Fructooligosaccharides have prevented the development of colon cancer in genetically predisposed laboratory mice.[1]

Oligosaccharides can be found in smaller amounts in foods such as soybeans, blueberries, and onions. To get a quick dose of oligosaccharides, try a dietary supplement called NutraFlora. It has been used in many clinical studies and is available at health food stores.

Whole Grain Goodness

If you don't eat enough fiber in your diet, you increase your chance of developing high blood cholesterol, hardening of the arteries, hypertension, obesity, gallstones, constipation, gastrointestinal bacterial overgrowth, and certain cancers. Ongoing research has found that dietary fiber offers protection against cancer in a number of ways:[2]

- Whole grain fiber provides a source of fermentable carbohydrates. Fermentation in the colon enhances production of butyrate, a short chain fatty acid. Butyrate has the ability to lower colonic pH and induce colon cancer cell death.
- Whole grains are rich in antioxidants such as phytic acid and flavonoids. These compounds protect cells from free radical damage.
- Whole grains are phytoestrogen rich. Phytoestrogens prevent hormonally based cancers because they partially fit into estrogen receptors, blocking against hormonal stimulation of cancer cells.
- Whole grains mediate blood sugar response. High glucose and insulin levels contribute to immune suppression and cancer cell growth.

How Fiber Fights Cancer

There is a clear association between dietary fiber and colorectal cancer prevention. A combined analysis of thirteen studies showed colorectal cancer rates dropped significantly when the intake of fiber-rich foods increased.[3]

High-fiber foods may have more than one health-promoting factor. Recent studies suggest that other components (folate, calcium, omega-3 fatty acids) found in fiber-rich foods might have equally important chemopreventive actions.[4] For example, the oil found in wheat bran showed a strong ability to stop tumor growth in experimental animals.[5] Phytic acid, another component of wheat bran, has the ability to maintain healthy colon walls and promote colon cancer cell death.[6]

Current studies have shown that dietary fiber can positively impact many forms of cancer. A comparative analysis of twelve studies showed that women who ate a high-fiber diet had less risk for breast cancer than women who ate typical American diets.[7] Breast tumor growth was significantly stunted when animals were fed a high-fiber diet.[8]

Other hormonally based cancers appear to be linked to dietary fiber as well. Prostate cancer cells grew less when animals were fed a diet that contained rye bran.[9] A diet rich in fibrous vegetables appears to contribute to lowered risk of ovarian cancer development.[10]

Consistent findings link low fiber intake to increased risk for pancreatic and endometrial cancers, too.[11,12] In one study, a high-fiber diet showed a possible protective effect for oral, pharyngeal, and esophageal cancers.[13] Apple pectin, a fiber concentrate, was able to block liver metastasis.[14]

How Much Fiber Is Enough?

The National Cancer Institute and many other professional health organizations recommend your diet should contain twenty-five to thirty-five grams of fiber per day. The average American diet contains half of this amount.[15] Because there are different types of fiber in foods, your diet should include a variety of plants in order to get the most health benefits. For example, both soluble and insoluble dietary fibers are needed to maintain healthy levels of gastrointestinal bacteria in our colon.

Getting enough fiber in your diet, even if you eat plants, can be tricky. Most fruits and vegetables contain less than two grams of

Getting the Edge

Fiber Health Facts

Eating fiber can help you maintain health, prevent disease, and control disease processes that occur in the body. Here's what fiber can do for you:

- It speeds up elimination and regulates bowel patterns.
- It decreases inflammatory bowel disease flare-ups.
- It normalizes serum cholesterol levels.
- It stabilizes blood sugar levels.
- It promotes weight loss.
- It decreases risk of breast, colon, esophagus, mouth, ovarian, pharynx, rectum, stomach and prostate cancers.
- It reduces and absorbs carcinogenic toxins.
- It reduces circulating levels of estrogen.

dietary fiber per serving. Refined breads, cereals, grains, and pastas usually contain only one gram of dietary fiber per serving. If you want to pack in fiber, you need to eat more legumes, whole grain breads, and unprocessed flour products.

How Much Fiber Is Too Much?

The American Dietetic Association advises that eating more than fifty to sixty grams of fiber per day can decrease the absorption of calcium, copper, zinc, magnesium, and iron.[16] The risk for nutrient malabsorption apparently doesn't apply to diets moderately high in fiber. When you eat a plant-based diet, you usually can get enough of most of these minerals to offset any risk of poor mineral absorption. This is not the case if you take too many fiber supplements, which don't contain added nutrients.

Eating too much fiber can also cause severe bloating, cramping, or gas. You can reduce your risk of these GI symptoms by slowly increasing the amount of fiber you eat and making sure you drink enough fluid each day. Another key to tolerating fiber is to mix and match your dietary fiber sources. You shouldn't place too much emphasis on one fiber in your diet. Choosing a variety of plants will help you achieve maximum health benefits.

Self-Assessment: Finding Fiber

Put your detective hat on. It's time to test your ability to recognize roughage. This exercise is meant to help you identify foods that are high in fiber and teach you the art of bulking up your diet.

High Fiber Food Selection Quiz

Look at the sample menu below. First, underline the food items that are high in fiber. Then, write high-fiber alternatives next to the food choices that could be improved upon. For suggested substitutions, see Appendix 14.

Sample Menu   High-Fiber Substitutions
Breakfast

Orange juice
Bran flakes
Scrambled egg
White toast

Lowfat milk
Coffee

Lunch

Split pea soup
Roast beef
White rice
Carrots
Coleslaw
French bread
Butter
Baked apple with skin
Water

Dinner

Baked salmon
Boiled new potatoes
Collard greens
Rye rolls
Butter
Mixed fruit cup
Angel food cake
Coffee

How To Increase Your Fiber Intake

Start adding it up! The amount of dietary fiber in common foods is listed in Appendix 15. For packaged goods, read the "Nutrition Facts" panel to determine how many grams of total fiber you are getting with each serving.

The following guidelines suggest the best way to consume fiber:

- Gradually move from low-fiber to high-fiber food items. If you progress too quickly, your digestive tract might rebel. Don't just add high-fiber foods to your diet;

replace low-fiber products. Otherwise, you may gain unwanted pounds and increase blood glucose levels.

- Drink lots of liquid! Six to eight glasses per day will help reduce the gastrointestinal side effects associated with increased fiber intake. Remember, adequate water is necessary to help bulk up the stool for easy passage through the colon.

- Pick up some produce. Eat three or more servings of dark green and deep yellow vegetables each day. Eat vegetables that have edible stems or stalks, such as broccoli. Consume two or more servings of fruit. Eat citrus fruits, melons, or berries to get the additional value of vitamin C. Consume fruits more often than fruit juices. Choose fruits and vegetables with edible skins and seeds. Raw, whole foods will contain the most fiber, but you still can derive fiber from frozen or canned produce. Juice usually contains very little fiber.

- Cooked dried beans should be eaten several times per week and are a perfect alternative to meat. Dried beans and peas may cause some intestinal gas if you aren't used to eating them. Lentils, split peas, and lima beans are most easily digested. Work up to navy, pinto, kidney or black beans, and peas. Try digestive enzymes when you eat beans to reduce bloating and gas.

- Go for the grains. Choose crackers, cereals, and breads that contain whole grains such as wheat, rye, buckwheat, oats, quinoa, millet, or amaranth. Remember to store whole grains in a cool, dry place as they are more perishable than refined grains.

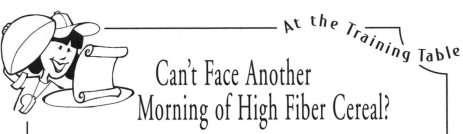

At the Training Table

Can't Face Another Morning of High Fiber Cereal?

Try mixing 1/2 cup of your favorite cereal with 1/2 cup of a high-fiber cereal such as From Kashi to Good Friends or Bran Buds. You'll get at least 14 grams of fiber and get to keep the taste you love!

Gold Medal Action

Cereal Sensation

Two tablespoons of wheat germ sprinkled on cereal adds an extra two grams of fiber and provides six essential vitamins and minerals, including cancer-fighting nutrients such as vitamin E and folate.

Bean Basics

The American Institute for Cancer Research reports that adding beans to a plant-based diet can reduce the risk of cancer. Beans don't seem to get much attention despite the fact that they are low in fat and are excellent sources of protein, dietary fiber, folate, magnesium, iron, and phytochemicals. Additionally, replacing animal foods with beans can help lower the saturated fat in your diet.

Getting the Edge

The Flip Side of Fiber Cereals

Not all high-fiber cereals qualify as health food. A serving of one popular oat bran cereal, for example, contains seven grams of partially hydrogenated fat. Most granolas are notorious for containing unhealthy tropical oils. Read the label before you buy.

Beans can be well tolerated if you follow these simple guidelines:

- Gradually add beans to your diet. Beans are fiber powerhouses, so give your gut a chance to adjust to the extra roughage.

- Cook and rinse beans thoroughly. Don't eat beans that are served al dente or are not completely rinsed off. Discard the liquid from canned beans, too. Uncooked bean starch and indigestible sugars that get into the cooking water can cause gas.

- Add a small amount of fat or a source of protein such as chicken or fish to your beans. A mixed diet will help moderate the inevitable blood sugar surge associated with eating starchy beans.

- Use digestive aids. Health food store digestive enzymes or Beano, an over-the-counter liquid enzyme solution, helps to digest starches that cause gas.

Quick Bites

Heat and Eat Beans

Choosing the best beans may not be as easy as opening up a can. Watch out for added fat and too much sodium by checking the product labels. Some of the healthiest brands include Eden Organic, Heinz Premium Vegetarian, S&W 50% Less Salt, and Westbrae Natural beans.

In the Granary

Most Americans eat only one serving of whole grains per day, choosing instead to load up their plates with refined white breads and pastas.[17]

One of the best ways to increase your fiber intake is to experiment with grains. You're familiar with wheat, rye, corn, and rice. But what about quinoa, millet, and bulgur? These and other grains are delicious alternatives to the same old cereal seeds. Try using the following grains in your recipes for deliciously different and healthy results. You can find these grains in specialty markets, health food stores, and in some grocery stores:

- Amaranth can be used for dishes that call for oats or rice. Amaranth is a rich source of vitamin A, calcium, and potassium. Try pastas made with amaranth; they are an interesting alternative to regular noodles.
- Buckwheat is used as flour in pancake mixes or is roasted and called kasha, which is eaten as a cereal. Soba

noodles are a dense buckwheat pasta. It isn't a true grain, but a relative of the rhubarb plant, and it is very susceptible to rancidity. To avoid waste, buy in small quantities.

- Bulgur is cracked wheat that is boiled, dried out, and ground. Bulgur makes a great side dish, or can be used to fill, stuff, or thicken other foods.

- Millet is probably better known than you think. Millet is sold as birdseed! Couscous is cracked millet. Millet, combined with beans or peas, makes a tasty vegetarian burger. One half cup cooked millet provides over four grams of dietary fiber.

- Quinoa is another nutrient-rich grain, containing protein, fiber, iron, magnesium, and potassium. Quinoa is served as a side dish or may be used in risotto, pilaf, or vegetable stuffings.

Sorghum, spelt, triticale, and kamut (great for those who experience wheat allergies) join a host of other less commonly known grains that are equally delicious.

Getting the Edge

Brown Doesn't Mean Better

Always check the label before you buy bread to make sure the first ingredient is whole wheat flour or 100% whole wheat flour. Many brown breads are made from enriched wheat flour that makes it as nutritionally void as white bread.

Looking for Some Healthy Crackers?

Try munching on these! According to product labels, they all contain whole wheat flour and are low in saturated fat and sodium. The number of crackers per serving size is listed in parentheses.

Product	Calories	Fiber, in grams
Nabisco Deli Style Rye (7)	140	4
Nabisco Garden Herb Triscuits (6)	120	3
Ryvita Dark Rye (3)	105	4
Ry Krisp Natural (4)	120	8
Wasa Fiber Rye (3)	90	6
Wasa Multi Grain (2)	90	4

Ready for Roughage?

- Combine equal parts of a high- and a low-fiber cereal during your transition to a high-fiber diet.
- Add 1/4 cup wheat bran to cooked cereal, applesauce, meatloaf, or blended fruit smoothies.
- Snack on raw vegetables as you prepare meals.
- Top oatmeal or other hot cereals with 2 tablespoons of ground flaxseeds.
- Sprinkle sunflower seeds or peanuts on top of mixed greens.

Glorious Morning Muffins

(Makes 18 muffins)

1 cup crushed bran flakes

1 cup unbleached white flour

1/2 cup whole wheat flour

1/3 cup packed brown sugar

1/2 tsp baking soda

2 tsp baking powder

1 tsp ground cinnamon

1/2 tsp ground nutmeg

1 1/2 cups grated carrots

1 cup raisins

1/2 cup chopped walnuts

1 1/4 cups skim milk

1 egg, beaten

3 Tbs canola oil

Heat oven to 400 degrees. Spray muffin tin with nonstick spray or use paper muffin cups. In a large bowl, combine the dry ingredients. Make a well in the center and add the first three liquid ingredients. Blend together for 50 strokes. Batter should still be lumpy. Gently stir in carrots, raisins, and walnuts. Divide batter among cups. Bake for 25 to 30 minutes, or until the center is done.

At the Training Table

Spicy Rice and Beans

(Serves 6)

- 1 16 oz can black beans, drained
- 1 15 oz can Italian-style chopped tomatoes, undrained
- 1/2 cup chopped green peppers
- 1/2 cup chopped purple onions
- 1 tsp dried oregano
- 1/2 tsp minced garlic
- 1 1/2 cups brown rice

In a medium saucepan, cook brown rice according to package directions. In another saucepan, bring beans, tomatoes, peppers, onions, and spices to a boil. Cover and simmer for 15 minutes. Remove from heat, stir mixture into brown rice and serve.

Fiber Supplements

Thinking about swallowing a pill rather than eating all that fiber? Experts agree that for efficiency and nutrient value, eating fibrous foods are the way to go. The cancer-protective effects of fruits, vegetables, and whole grains are partly due to a variety of plant constituents, not just fiber. While certain kinds of fiber have proved useful in cancer treatment (pectin and psyllium husk), taking purified fiber supplements won't provide the variety you need to achieve maximum health benefits.

If you decide to supplement your diet with fiber pills or powder, make sure you drink plenty of water. Take pills or powders in moderation. Excessive use of fiber supplements can lead to severe gastrointestinal problems and blockages. Bowel obstructions may occur when people on prescription pain medications such as morphine or codeine take psyllium-based supplements. These pain killers increase risk for constipation by slowing down bowel movements,[18] allowing soluble fibers to sludge up in the colon. In this situation, constipation is best relieved by a stimulant laxative and a stool softener. I suggest not using psyllium, found in products such as Metamucil, which is a bulk-forming laxative. Talk to your doctor about a suitable alternative.

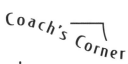

Get Your Fiber Here!

Boosting your fiber intake to 35 grams per day can be easy.

For breakfast
Select a high-fiber cereal (10 grams)
Top with six prunes (3 grams)

For lunch
Heat up a cup of black bean soup (10 grams)
Munch on 6 Triscuit crackers (3 grams)
Add an apple (3 grams)

For dinner
Cook up a cup of brown rice (4 grams)
Add a cup of stir-fried veggies (2 grams)
End with orange wedges (2 grams)

Getting the Edge

Fiber Supplement Watch

Some fiber supplements aren't as healthy as you'd think. Read labels carefully and look for products that don't contain added sugars, artificial sweeteners, or other additives!

Getting the Edge

Fiber Supplements Versus Food

The amount of fiber contained in six fiber capsules is equal to the amount of fiber found in a large orange. Before you invest in costly fiber pills or powders, think of the advantages of eating whole foods. After all, if you eat the orange, you get bioflavonoids and vitamin C thrown in for free.

— 9 —

Step Up to Soy

"When you come to a fork in the road, take it."
— *Yogi Berra*

What Is Soy?

S OY COMES FROM SOYBEANS. A staple of Asian fare, this little bean is used to make a variety of foods from miso soup to textured vegetable protein. The soybean is unique in many ways. It is the only plant that contains high-quality protein. Soybeans have isoflavones, which are plant-like estrogens that produce health benefits.

Health Benefits of Soy

Isoflavones, along with protein, vitamin E, omega-3 fatty acids, saponins, phytosterols, phytates, fiber, and oligosaccharides, appear to work together to contribute to overall health in a number of ways:

- Soy isoflavones are used to treat menopausal symptoms. Phytoestrogens have promoted vaginal health and relieved hot flashes in women who produce very little estrogen.[1]
- Soy may decrease the risk for heart disease by lowering total cholesterol and LDL cholesterol (the bad kind) levels.[2]
- Soy has a low glycemic index, which can help regulate blood sugar levels. Supplemental soy fiber may also slow the absorption rate of sugar.[3]
- Soy, used as a substitute for animal protein, decreases the amount of calcium lost in the urine and indirectly keeps bones strong.[4]
- Soy protein is lactose-free and dairy-free. Products such as soy milk, soy yogurt, and soy cheese offer tasty alternatives for those who are intolerant or allergic to cow's milk.
- Limited research suggests that soy may favorably affect kidney function in diabetics, and in one experimental animal study it slowed kidney damage.[5,6]

Soy Beneficial!

For more than fifteen years, research has focused on the connection between soy consumption and cancer. Considerable evidence from population studies suggests that soy offers protection against several kinds of cancer.

Countries with high soy intake experience substantially lower incidence of breast, prostate, and uterine cancers than in the United States.[7] High consumption of soy products and other legumes were associated with a decreased risk of endometrial cancer.[8] Regular consumption of tofu and other soy foods has been linked to a 66 to 80 percent decreased risk for rectal cancer.[9,10]

Animal and human cell studies have demonstrated that soy isoflavones such as genistein and daidzein have weak estrogenic properties that block the important enzymes that promote the growth of hormone-sensitive tumors.[11]

Phytosterols, a plant compound that is undigested in humans, offers a protective effect in the colon. Animals fed a diet with beta-sitosterol developed half as many colon tumors as controls.[12]

Phytates such as inositol hexaphosphate may squelch free radicals and stop cancer cells from growing.[13] Saponins, another antioxidant found in soybeans, have reduced genetic damage and mutation of normal cells in mammals.[14]

Can Soy Stop Cancer?

While the observed cancer protection benefits may be a result of a mixture of dietary and lifestyle factors in certain populations, research clearly indicates that soy foods have promising anticancer potential for established cancers. Most studies have focused on the isoflavone called genistein.

In test tubes, genistein halted the growth of human prostate, breast, squamous cell, and bladder cancers.[15–19] Additionally, human leukemia cells stopped growing when they were treated with a genistein complex.[20]

Animal studies using soy have produced favorable results as well. Genistein has slowed the growth of melanoma and bladder cancer in laboratory animals.[21,22]

Other cancer-fighting benefits have been linked to genistein. The metastatic properties of cancer cells have decreased with administration of genistein, which has the ability to blunt new blood vessel growth.[23] Genistein has enhanced the effectiveness of Cisplatin and Vincristine treatments on pediatric brain cancers.[24]

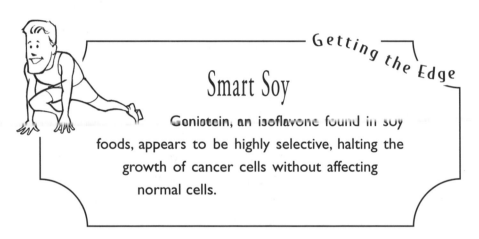

Getting the Edge

Smart Soy

Genistein, an isoflavone found in soy foods, appears to be highly selective, halting the growth of cancer cells without affecting normal cells.

Soy and Estrogen-Dependent Cancers

Genistein's impact on breast cancer cells is contradictory. In test tubes, genistein either stops cancer cells from growing or makes them grow. Animal studies don't seem to offer consistent conclusions either. Some studies reveal that isoflavones can suppress the development of breast cancer cells by blocking receptor sites from circulating estradiol (the natural estrogen that promotes some breast cancers).[25,26] Other animal studies have shown that genistein acts as an estrogen in normal breast tissues and stimulates the growth of estrogen-receptor-positive breast cancer cells.[27]

The million-dollar question remains: Should women diagnosed with estrogen-dependent cancers load up on soy or isoflavones? Unfortunately, it's too early to say for sure whether isoflavones should be used therapeutically in uterine, endometrial, ovarian, and breast cancer patients. More studies are needed to determine whether soy ingestion is safe for any estrogen-dependent cancers.

The American Dietetic Association suggests that to play it safe, women with breast cancer or women using Tamoxifen should completely avoid dietary soy supplements.[28] While soy protein powders or pills contain high doses of genistein and daidzein, food sources of soy contain less concentrated levels of isoflavones and offer a variety of health benefits. For these reasons, healthcare professionals suggest soy foods may be safely consumed in moderation (two to three servings per week) by women with estrogen-sensitive tumors.

Coach's Corner

Soy Safety

If you are on thyroxine (Synthroid), a drug used to regulate thyroid function, avoid taking your medication with meals containing soy. Stay away from isoflavone supplements, too. High doses of soy isolates can act as goitrogens, compounds that may cause an enlargement of the thyroid gland, and may interfere with the activity of thyroid medications.[29]

Soy Supplements

While your first choice should always be whole soy foods, soy supplements can benefit those who don't consume soy every day. There may be toxicity concerns with higher intakes of purified or synthetic soy isoflavones, so it makes sense to model your soy consumption after Asian dietary practices. Currently, the average intake of soy protein per day in the Japanese population has been estimated at about ten grams of soy protein a day.[30] This equates to an intake of about 50 to 60 mg of isoflavones per day. Supplemental soy comes in pill or powder form and can be found in most grocery stores in the vitamin or health food section. The brands I recommend most are Genisoy and Take Care soy protein powders.

Self-Assessment: How Soy Savvy Are You?

In the past, soy foods have been almost exclusively consumed by vegetarians. Now, mainstream consumers are gobbling up soy foods like crazy. Don't you think it's time to join the 26 million Americans who eat soy? Answer the following questions to see how well versed you are on the subject of soy.

Soy Foods Awareness Quiz
(Circle True or False)

1. Soy products are only available in health food stores. True   False
2. There is not much variety in soy foods.   True   False
3. Soy is difficult to cook with.   True   False

4. Soy isoflavones are destroyed by heat.   True   False
5. All soy foods are high in protein.   True   False
6. All soy foods are low in fat.   True   False
7. Soybean oil contains isoflavones.   True   False
8. Veggie burgers are made of soy.   True   False
9. Roasted soy nuts are a healthy snack.   True   False
10. Soy snack bars are a great way to get soy into your diet.
    True   False

Total: Yes _____   No _____

Quiz Interpretation

If you've answered true on any of the above questions, you don't know all you need to know about soy. Questions 1 through 3 allude to common consumer misconceptions about soy foods. Questions 4 through 10 reflect soy food choices that may be less than optimal. Read on to learn the truth about this beneficial bean and experience the joy of soy for yourself.

Shopping for Soy

Look no further than your local market! In an effort to increase consumer exposure to soy foods, soy products are being displayed throughout grocery stores. Tofu, tempeh, veggie dogs, soy deli slices, and soy cheeses can be found in the dairy or organic produce sections. Soy milk appears in the health food specialty aisle, as well as in the dairy case. Textured vegetable protein crumbles, veggie burgers, and breakfast meat alternatives are located in the freezer section. Soy powders may be available in the vitamin or health food section.

Searching for something, but you can't find it? Check with your local health food store. Many proprietors will be happy to place an order for you. Or, place an order yourself by calling one of the health food mail order companies listed in the resource section of this book.

Soy Many Products!

Soybeans are extremely versatile and have been made into a variety of foods. Soybeans by themselves have a very mild flavor and should be combined with other ingredients to help create a flavorful product.

Most soy foods vary in protein and fat content. Tofu and soy milk, for example, come in regular and lite (reduced fat) versions. Texturized vegetable protein and soy protein isolates, unlike other soy products, contain very little fat. Most soy milks contain about seven grams of protein per serving, but this can vary depending on the brand you buy. Flavored soy milk and silken tofu typically contain less

At the Training Table

Hot 'n Spicy Soy Nuts

Soak soybeans overnight in room temperature water. Drain the water. Spread beans evenly over a cookie sheet. Drizzle 2 tablespoons canola oil to evenly coat the beans. Sprinkle with a mixture of garlic salt, onion powder, Cajun spices, or Szechuan pepper blend. Bake at 300 degrees for about one hour. Every 15 minutes or so, shake the pan to ensure even roasting. Enjoy!

protein, so make sure you read the labels to choose the best product for your needs.

Let's take a closer look at all the soy products you can choose from:

Whole Soybeans

Whole soybeans are available in health food stores and super-markets in bags or bulk bins. Dry soybeans expand two to three times when cooked in liquid; they should be soaked to decrease cooking time and enhance the digestibility of the beans. Edamame, green soy beans, are picked before they reach maturity and look like green peas. Soybeans are eaten as a side dish or used in salads and soups. Roasted soybeans, called soy nuts, are a crunchy snack. Read labels carefully to make sure hydrogenated oils were not used in the roasting process.

Soy Milk

Soy milk is a nutty flavored liquid extracted from soybeans. Soy milk comes in a variety of flavors such as chocolate, vanilla, carob, almond, and plain. Read product labels carefully because the protein content varies in different brands of soy milk. Choose lite soy milks because they are lower in fat. You can drink soy milk straight from the carton, pour it over cold cereal, or use it for cooking or baking.

Tofu

Tofu, or soybean curd, is made by curdling fresh, hot soymilk. The curds are generally pressed together to form a solid block. Consistency varies by type. Firm tofu is dense and retains its shape well. It is used in stir-fry recipes, soups, or on the grill. Soft tofu is less dense and used in Oriental soups or in recipes that call for blended tofu. Silken tofu is creamy like custard. It is often pureed or blended and used to make salad dressings, dips, pasta sauces, desserts, and smoothies.

Tempeh

Pronounced "tem-pay," this traditional delight from Indonesia is a cultured soy food made with soybeans and grain. It has a dense, chewy texture and can be added to sandwiches, soup, and casseroles, or it can be grilled and served next to rice. If you don't like tofu because it lacks texture, you might like tempeh.

Miso

Miso is made by combining soybeans, grain, salt, and a mold culture. Miso is used as a condiment to flavor soups, sauces, dressings, and marinades. Make your own miso broth by mixing a tablespoon of miso with one cup of hot water.

Texturized Vegetable Protein

Texturized soy protein is made from compressed soy flour. It comes in granular, flake, or chunk form, and in a variety of flavors. When it is rehydrated with boiling water, texturized soy protein has a grainy texture similar to meat. It is found in commercial products as a meat extender or is pressed into patties to form veggie burgers. Read labels carefully. Some veggie burgers are a combination of grains and vegetables and do not contain soy at all.

Soy Flour

Soy flour is made from roasted soybeans ground into a fine powder. Soy flour is used in commercial baked goods, pastas, pancake mixes, and frozen desserts. When baking, soy flour should be mixed with other flours to ensure a quality product is achieved. In yeast raised products, about 15 percent of the flour used may be

Coach's Corner

All of the soy foods listed below are excellent sources of isoflavones, providing a range of 30 to 50 mg per serving:

1/2 cup cooked mature soybeans

1/2 cup green soybeans

1/2 cup tempeh

1/4 cup texturized soy protein

1/4 cup soy nuts

1/2 cup tofu

1/2 cup soy flour, defatted

1 cup soy milk

soy; in products that are not yeast raised, up to one-quarter cup can be used.

Soybean Oil

Soy oil is the natural oil pressed from soybeans. Soybean oil accounts for nearly 75 percent of our total vegetable oil intake, mostly through processed food products such as mayonnaise, coffee creamers, margarines, sandwich spreads, and salad dressings. Vegetable oils sold in the grocery store are usually 100 percent soybean oil. Soy oil does not contain isoflavones.

Soy Protein Isolates

Concentrated soy proteins are made from defatted soy flour where most of the carbohydrate and fat has been removed. Infant formulas, health food protein powder drinks, and supplements all contain soy protein isolates. You might also find them in commercial shakes, soups, puddings, or baked products. Soy snack bars look healthy, but tend to be high in sugar. Coated flavors may contain palm kernel oil, so check the label before you buy.

Buying and Storing Soy Products

Perishable soy products found in the dairy case or produce section must be refrigerated. Always check the expiration date before purchasing a refrigerated soy product. Once opened, leftover tofu should be rinsed and covered with fresh water for storage. Use the opened tofu within seven days. Aseptically packaged soy milk must also be refrigerated once it is opened. It will stay fresh for about five days. Tempeh can be kept refrigerated for up to ten days, and miso can be stored in the refrigerator for several months. Don't be alarmed when you see mold growing on the surface of fermented soy foods; this is natural for any aged product.

Dry soy products such as meat analogs or texturized soy protein are low in moisture and have a long shelf life. They can be kept in a tightly closed container at room temperature for several months. Once these products are rehydrated, use them within a few days. Like whole grain flours, soy flour should be stored in the refrigerator or freezer to prevent rancidity.

Cooking with Soy

Want to increase your soy intake, while reducing calories, total fat, saturated fat, and cholesterol? Try these suggestions:

- Add chunks of firm tofu to soups and stews.
- Mix crumbled tofu into a meatloaf.

Cooking with Soy	
Instead of	**Try**
I cup milk	I cup fortified soymilk
I cup fruited yogurt	I cup soft silken tofu + blended fruit
I egg	I Tbs soy flour + I Tbs water
I egg	I two-inch square of tofu
I cup ricotta cheese	I cup firm tofu, mashed
2 Tbs flour	I Tbs soy flour
3 oz chunk chicken breast	1/2 cup chicken-flavored texturized soy protein
I Tbs sour cream	I Tbs tofu sour cream
3 oz ground beef	1/2 cup beef-flavored texturized soy protein granules

- Add tofu to cottage cheese for a sandwich spread.
- Marinate tofu in barbecue sauce, grill it, and serve it with crusty Italian bread.
- Blend dried onion soup mix into soft tofu for a great onion dip.
- Add silken tofu to sour cream for a lower-fat baked potato topper.
- Blend tofu with melted chocolate chips and a little sweetener to make chocolate cream pie.
- Pour soy milk over hot or cold breakfast cereal.
- Make rich pancake and waffle mixes with soy milk.
- Replace milk with soy milk in cream soups.

- Create delicious fruit-flavored soy milkshakes.
- Mix sherry wine vinegar, chopped basil, leeks, and parsley with olive oil to make an herbed marinade for tofu.
- Add onion, garlic, or bay leaves to cooked soybeans.
- Throw some soybeans into chilies and soups.
- Use texturized soy protein in recipes that call for ground beef or turkey.
- Add chunks of tempeh to spaghetti sauce or sloppy joes.
- Sauté tempeh with mushrooms, onion, and breadcrumbs and use as a stuffing.

Quick Bites

Tofu Egg Salad

(Serves 4 to 6)

- 12 oz tofu (squeeze in a cheesecloth to remove excess water)
- 2 hard-boiled eggs, chopped
- 2 Tbs canola oil
- 2 Tbs lemon juice
- 1/2 tsp salt
- 2 Tbs minced onion
- 1/4 cup chopped celery

Combine the first five ingredients in a blender and puree for 30 seconds. Fold in onion and celery. Mix well. Serve as a sandwich spread on whole grain toast.

Quick Bites

Splendid Soy Shakes

These frozen concoctions are high in protein and chock full of disease-fighting phytochemicals. Blend the following ingredients at high speed for about a minute and drink up. Each recipe makes one serving.

Purple Passion

1/2 cup silken tofu

1/2 cup unsweetened plain yogurt

3/4 cup unsweetened pineapple juice

1/3 cup frozen blueberries

1/3 cup frozen pineapple wedges

3 to 4 ice cubes

Banana Dreamsicle

1/2 cup silken tofu

1/2 cup unsweetened vanilla yogurt

1 banana

1 cup orange juice

3 to 4 ice cubes

— 10 —

Dietary Supplements — Gaining a Competitive Edge

"The era of nutrient supplements to promote health and reduce illness is here to stay."
— *Journal of the American Medical Association (1997)*

Do You Need Dietary Supplements?

Many conventional physicians answer this question one of two ways. Either they claim that cancer patients do not need vitamins as long as they eat a balanced diet, or they discount the benefit of taking nutritional supplements altogether.

Both of these responses arise from a lack of nutritional knowledge and, unfortunately, leave cancer patients completely in the dark.

We know that most Americans do not eat a healthy diet. That is why multivitamins were invented. They help fill in the gaps left by a less than perfect diet. As a cancer patient, your chances of eating right every day tend to decrease as treatment continues. Additionally, your nutritional and detoxification requirements are much higher than a so-called healthy individual's. Rapid cellular turnover, greater exposure to chemicals and free radical damage, and evidence that up to 80 percent of all cancer patients develop some degree of malnutrition support this fact.[1]

If you don't assimilate enough nutrients to sustain your body's ever-changing state, you can suffer grave consequences. For example, a large study of cancer patients in Finland revealed that many had lower levels of selenium and vitamin E. For those who had low selenium levels, their risk of death from cancer was nearly six times greater than the controls. When both selenium and vitamin E levels were low, the risk of death from cancer increased to more than eleven times that of controls.[2]

By contrast, when you give your body the nutritional components it needs, the benefits can be staggering. In a well-known study conducted by Pauling and Hoffer, 101 advanced cancer patients received large doses of vitamin C and other nutrients. Among the patients who responded well in the supplemented group, the mean survival time was 122 months. Those who did not receive supplements survived less than six months.[3]

Supplements During Treatment

There has been much controversy surrounding the idea of taking antioxidants during radiation and chemotherapy. While a handful of studies have suggested that concurrent administration of oral antioxidants during cancer treatment may be contraindicated, the majority of animal and human studies using dietary supplementation during treatment reveal a variety of benefits.

Extensive studies have shown that dietary antioxidants and other nutritional supplements can prevent, inhibit, or reverse one or more stages of carcinogenesis through a variety of pathways. Considerable data exists showing that oral nutrient supplementation can improve immune system response, detoxify cancer-causing compounds, block the oxidative damage of cells, increase the effectiveness of many cancer therapeutic agents, and decrease adverse treatment side effects.[4] Furthermore, the vast majority of test tube and animal studies have shown that antioxidant administration is not counterproductive to standard cancer treatments.[5]

Rather than counting on one magic pill, it appears that multiple antioxidant vitamin supplements, coupled with diet and lifestyle modifications, can improve the efficacy of standard and experimental cancer therapies.[6]

Here are a few examples of how dietary supplements may help you during cancer treatment:

- Curcumin and ellagic acid prevented chromosomal damage in rodents undergoing radiation.[7]
- Melatonin reduced Cisplatin-induced immunosuppression and increased glutathione levels in human mononuclear cells.[8]
- Vitamin A or beta carotene decreased systemic toxicity while enhancing the antitumor action of local radiation in tumor-bearing mice.[9]
- The combination of nicotinamide and hyperthermia was effective in enhancing radiation-induced cell death.[10]

- Vitamin C improved the antineoplastic (cancer-killing) activity of Adriamycin, Cisplatin, and Piclataxel in human breast cancer cells in vitro.[11]
- N-acetyl cysteine prevented chemotherapy-induced hair loss in animals.[12]
- Glutathione and other sulfur-containing compounds increased the effectiveness of Cisplatin and protected against kidney damage.[13]
- Irradiated mice with breast cancer given niacin showed marked reduction in tumor size compared to controls.[14]
- Humans with colon cancer given beta carotene supplements showed a decreased proliferation of cancer cells.[15]
- Beta carotene inhibited liver cancer cell growth through antioxidant and detoxification actions.[16]

Power Chemo!	
Adriamycin	Genistein, Green tea, Omega-3 fatty acids, Vitamins A, C, and D
5-FU	Aloe, Folate, N-acetylcysteine, Quercetin, Vitamin E
Cytoxan	Aloe, Folate, Quercetin
Taxol	Vitamins A, C, and D
Vincristine	Vitamins A and C
Cisplatin	Vitamins A and C

You may be able to increase the cancer-killing capacity of your treatment! Each supplement has been shown to enhance the effectiveness of the above chemotherapies.[17-29]

- Patients with small cell lung cancer, treated with chemotherapy and antioxidants, lived longer than patients who underwent chemotherapy without antioxidants.[30]

Supplements That Fight Cancer

Several nutrients have surfaced as leading contenders in the race against cancer. The following vitamins, minerals, accessory nutrients, and herbs have been used in research studies or clinical settings to suppress tumors, enhance chemotherapy or radiation, protect cells, assist in detoxification, decrease treatment side effects, and optimize metabolic processes.

Before you rush down to your health food store in search of supplements, it makes sense to seek the advice of a trained nutritional professional who has experience in the field of oncology. While dosage ranges are provided, individual needs can vary considerably based on medical condition, illness history, prescription medication, dietary habits, and lifestyle factors. Because dietary supplements can have pharmacological activity, you should inform all medical providers who are responsible for your care about your vitamin or herbal regimen.

Vitamins
Vitamin A and Carotenoids

Vitamin A and mixed carotenoids work together to promote detoxification, protect cells, stimulate immunity, enhance cell-to-cell communication, and maintain healthy epithelial tissues. Many studies involving vitamin A have focused on the prevention of squamous cell cancers. Vitamin A metabolites and analogs (retinoids) have suppressed head, neck, and lung cancer in animals and have halted the progression of precancerous lesions in humans who were at risk for developing upper digestive tract cancers.[31]

Fast Facts

- The average diet supplies about 5,000 IU of Vitamin A per day.
- Palmitate and acetate forms of vitamin A are readily absorbed; the best supplements contain a half-and-half mixture of retinol and carotenoids.
- Algae and palm oil are the preferred sources for carotenoids. Look for all-trans beta-carotene and 9-cis-beta-carotene on the label.
- Carotenosis, or yellowing of the skin, is caused by a high intake of carotene. It is not toxic.
- Habitual intake of 25,000 IU of vitamin A has been associated with liver damage.
- If you are pregnant, do not take more than 6,000 IU of vitamin A, as higher levels are associated with birth defects.

Dosage

- Vitamin A: 10,000 to 15,000 IU per day.
- Carotenoids: 100,000 to 300,000 IU per day.

The Carotene Controversy

Two separate studies of high-risk groups (smokers and asbestos workers) concluded that beta carotene supplementation promoted cancer growth. However, researchers did not consider that beta carotene readily oxidizes in these toxic environments. Research in China showed that supplementation with beta carotene, vitamin E, and selenium decreased cancer incidence and cancer-related deaths.[32] Based on this and many other studies, it appears the safest way to take beta carotene or other antioxidants is in combination with other antioxidants. For maximum cancer preventive effects, choose a supplement that contains a mixture of carotenoids, not just beta carotene alone.

Thiamin (B1)

Thiamin assists with carbohydrate metabolism and helps to keep the appetite, digestive tract, and nervous system healthy.

Fast Fact

- If you regularly use antacids, you may inactivate thiamin, which requires an acid environment for absorption.

Dosage

- 50 to 100 mg per day

The Trouble with Thiamin

Some clinical and experimental studies have shown that tumor cells may use thiamin to grow, or it may decrease the effectiveness of chemothcrapy.[33,34] However, because thiamin has such a crucial role in energy production, it is needed in appropriate amounts for anyone who experiences rapid cellular turnover. Populations at risk for thiamin deficiency include alcoholics, the elderly, people with gastrointestinal cancers, and those undergoing chemotherapy or radiation. Additionally, it has been determined that prostate cancer risk increases with decreased thiamin intake.[35]

Riboflavin (B₂)

Riboflavin assists with carbohydrate, protein, and fat metabolism and helps to maintain the lining of the mouth and esophagus. It is also essential for the production of glutathione peroxidase, a major cellular protective enzyme. The body's need for vitamin B_2 rises as calorie or activity levels increase. Riboflavin deficiencies may increase the susceptibility of the oral cavity and esophagus to cancer-causing agents.[36]

Fast Facts

- Low dietary levels of riboflavin may produce anemia.
- Riboflavin supplements make the urine a bright yellow color.

Dosage

- 5 to 10 mg per day

Niacin (B₃)

Niacin is necessary for carbohydrate, protein, and fat metabolism, and participates in antioxidant mechanisms and detoxification reactions. Decreased intake of niacin has been linked to esophageal and pharyngeal cancers.[37,38] Niacin has been found to decrease the toxicity of Adriamycin treatment without affecting its antineoplastic activity.[39]

Fast Facts

- Inositol hexaniacinate is the safest form of niacin to take.
- Avoid timed-release niacin; it causes liver toxicity.
- Niacin can impair glucose tolerance. Individuals taking niacin who have difficulty moderating blood sugar levels need to be monitored closely.

Dosage

- 500 to 1,000 mg per day

Pantothenic Acid

Pantothenic acid is important for the proper functioning of the adrenal gland, which is necessary for handling stress. Prolonged stress can reduce the cytotoxicity of natural killer cells and disrupt a healthy gut environment.[40]

Fast Facts

- Correcting a pantothenic acid deficiency can alleviate pain associated with rheumatoid arthritis.
- Pantethine, another form of pantothenic acid, can lower cholesterol, triglyceride, and LDL cholesterol levels.

Dosage

- 250 to 500 mg per day

Vitamin B$_6$

Pyridoxine is needed in the conversion of tryptophan to niacin. It also assists with heme production and the metabolism of carbohydrates, proteins, and fats. B$_6$ deficiencies cause lymphatic tissue to shrink, reduce thymus gland activity, and lower lymphocyte counts.[41]

Pyridoxine is a potent anticancer nutrient. Vitamin B$_6$ has inhibited the growth of melanoma cells in test tubes and animals.[42] Separate studies of cancer patients on Cisplatin and Adriamycin found reduced neuropathy with B$_6$ supplements.[43,44]

Fast Facts

- Pyridoxine has increased the immune-stimulating effects of CoQ10.[45]

- Supplementing over 2,000 mg per day of B_6 can cause neurotoxicity.
- The elderly are at risk for developing B_6 deficiency.
- Low levels of B_6 are indirectly linked to osteoporosis risk.

Dosage

- 50 to 100 mg

Folate

Folic acid plays a role in the development of healthy blood cells, protein metabolism, and immune system response. Deficiencies are usually found with alcohol abuse and malabsorption syndromes.

Folate and other micronutrient deficiencies found in the elderly have been associated with decreased natural killer cell activity.[46] In clinical studies, 10 mg per day of folacin improved cervical dysplasia, a precancerous condition of the cervix.[47] Folate offers protection against methotrexate-induced side effects of the GI tract.

Fast Facts

- Large doses of folic acid (1000 mg) can mask a vitamin B_{12} deficiency which, if undetected, can lead to irreversible nerve damage.
- If you supplement with folate, always add vitamin B_{12}.
- Digestive enzymes containing pancreatic extracts can inhibit folate absorption; take these supplements at different times.

Dosage

- 200 to 400 mcg daily

Vitamin B$_{12}$

Cobalamin works with folate to manufacture red blood cells. B$_{12}$ is essential for proper cell division and is needed for the manufacture of nerve fiber covers. Metabolism of carbohydrate and fat requires adequate amounts of B$_{12}$.

Adequate levels of cobalamin helped prevent DNA damage.[48] A combination of B$_{12}$ and ascorbic acid led to increased survival time of mice implanted with leukemia cells.[49]

Fast Facts

- Cyanocobalamin is commonly found in supplements, but methylcobalamin is a more effective form of B$_{12}$.
- Patients who have had gastrectomies or who are strict vegans are at risk for developing B$_{12}$ deficiency.
- Cobalamin reactivates folate.

Dosage

- 100 to 1,000 mcg per day

Vitamin C

Ascorbic acid helps iron and calcium absorption, fights infection, promotes wound healing, stimulates immunity, acts as a free radical scavenger, and slows cancer cell growth. Vitamin C prevents the formation of nitrosamines.

Fast Facts

- Tobacco smokers need additional vitamin C.
- High doses of ascorbic acid may give false readings in occult blood tests for colon cancer.
- Decreased copper levels have been seen with the intake of two grams of vitamin C per day.

- The best supplemental form is mixed bioflavonoids with vitamin C.
- Chewable ascorbic acid can erode tooth enamel.
- Calcium or sodium ascorbate buffered forms of vitamin C are better tolerated.
- "Bowel tolerance" indicates the amount of vitamin C one can tolerate without experiencing diarrhea and intestinal discomfort.

Dosage

- 250 mg per day to bowel tolerance

Vitamin C Controversy

Recent speculation that vitamin C may protect cancer cells and hinder treatment effectiveness has prompted many physicians to question the safety of taking vitamin C during chemotherapy or radiation.

A handful of studies support this conclusion. Clinical research has proven that ascorbic acid accumulates in cancer cells,[50,51] and test tube studies reveal that vitamin C may act as a pro-oxidant.[52,53] Most studies, however, show no pro-oxidant effects in experimental animals. Furthermore, the role of vitamin C in the prevention and treatment of cancer has been scientifically validated repeatedly. Low levels of ascorbic acid have been linked to increased risk of breast, cervical, pancreatic, colon, lung, stomach, and oral cancers.[54-56] High doses of vitamin C have extended the life of terminal cancer patients by 162 days over controls.[57] Ascorbic acid significantly prolonged the life of animals treated with Adriamycin and may also prevent cardiac toxicity.[58]

It appears vitamin C continues to qualify as a powerful anti-cancer nutrient, effectively preventing cancer, slowing cancer cell growth, and enhancing conventional treatment.

Vitamin D

Vitamin D regulates the metabolism of calcium and phosphorus and has been shown to stop cellular proliferation and DNA synthesis in test tubes.[59] Several studies have demonstrated that vitamin D inhibits the growth of human prostate and colorectal cancer cells.[60,61]

Fast Facts

- Vitamin D_2 is the most common supplement form.
- Calcitriol, a prescription form of vitamin D, is ten times as potent as ergocalciferol.
- Fifteen minutes of sun exposure twice a week may be all that is needed for the body to synthesize adequate levels of vitamin D.

Dosage

- 200 to 400 IU per day

Vitamin E

Vitamin E protects cell membranes and fatty acids from oxidation, helps in the synthesis of DNA and red blood cells, stimulates immune function, and prevents the formation of nitrosamines.

Vitamin E succinate has been found to increase the tumor kill rate without affecting normal cells during radiation therapy.[62] When succinate was combined with vitamin C, selenium, and beta carotene, human melanoma cell growth was halted.[63] Vitamin E, alone or in combination with selenium, reduced the growth of breast and prostate cancer cells.[64,65]

Fast Facts

- 400 IU daily, along with a caffeine-free diet, has reversed fibrocystic breast disease, a risk factor for breast cancer.

- Notify your doctor if you take vitamin E with anticoagulant drugs; the dosage may need to be adjusted.
- People who have had a gastrectomy or a diagnosis of celiac disease are at risk for low levels of vitamin E.
- Even with a good diet, total vitamin E intake rarely exceeds 20 IU. The RDA for natural vitamin E is 22 IU per day.
- The natural form of vitamin E (d-alpha tocopherol) is better utilized by humans.
- Tocotrienol, a relative of tocopherol, may have potent antioxidant and antitumor effects.[66]

Dosage

- 400 to 800 IU per day

Minerals
Calcium

Calcium is responsible for bone health, muscle contraction, and healthy nerves. It may protect against high blood pressure and colon cancer.[67] It has been suggested that excess dietary calcium from milk is a significant risk factor for lymphoma.[68]

Fast Facts

- Dairy products supply 75 percent of the calcium in the diet.
- Diets high in caffeine, alcohol, sugar, protein, sodium, and phosphorus increase calcium excretion.
- Calcium carbonate or citrate forms of calcium are best absorbed. Choose calcium lactate or gluconate if you have hypochlorhydria, ulcers, or other stomach ailments.

- Avoid oyster shell, dolomite, and bone meal sources of calcium because they may contain high levels of lead.
- Calcium absorption is enhanced with vitamin C, magnesium, and vitamin D.
- Supplements should contain twice the amount of calcium as magnesium.
- Dosages over 2,000 mg per day can increase the risk of kidney stone formation.

Dosage

- 500 to 1,500 mg daily

Chromium

Chromium enhances cellular uptake of glucose and indirectly affects blood fat levels. These functions are crucial for supporting immunity, and therefore for controlling cancer cell production. Chromium picolinate has been found to increase macrophage activity.[69]

Fast Facts

- A diet rich in refined sugar and flour can deplete chromium levels.
- Don't take calcium and chromium supplements at the same time. Calcium may reduce absorption of chromium.

Dosage

- 200 to 600 mcg daily

Copper

Copper assists in the formation of hemoglobin and various enzymes, including superoxide dismutase (SOD). SOD acts as a free radical scavenger.

Fast Facts

- Copper gluconate may be gentlest on the system.
- Excessive copper can produce nausea and vomiting.
- Iron deficiency anemia is linked to copper deficiency.
- Your copper needs may be increased if you consume large doses of zinc and vitamin C.

Dosage

- 1.5 to 3 mg per day

Iron

Iron is a component of hemoglobin, which plays an essential role in red blood cell function. People with hereditary hemochromatosis (high levels of iron in the blood) have a high risk of liver cancer and other malignancies.[70,71] Unused iron can be detrimental to cancer patients because it can become a pro-oxidant in the body, causing cellular damage.[72]

- Many people experience some degree of GI upset, constipation, heartburn, or gas with iron supplements. Side effects can be reduced if a small amount of iron is introduced, then gradually increased.
- Diets high in fiber, coffee, tea, calcium, and magnesium supplements, or antacids containing carbonates, may increase your need for iron.
- Vitamin C increases iron absorption.
- Ferrous sulfate, a common form of iron, can interfere with sugar urine tests (Clinistix and Diastix).

Dosage

- For iron deficiency, 60 mg per day

Magnesium

Magnesium is important for nerve impulse transmission and is used in a variety of enzyme systems. Recent studies suggest that a diet rich in magnesium may reduce the risk for breast and prostate cancers.[73,74] Intravenous magnesium has effectively blocked pain in cancer patients who were unresponsive to morphine treatment.[75]

Fast Facts

- Magnesium bound to citrate or fumarate is better absorbed.
- Chronic use of alcohol, antibiotics, and certain diuretics increases magnesium needs.
- People with kidney disease or atrioventricular block heart disease should not take magnesium.

Maximum Dosage

- 1,000 mg per day

Selenium

Selenium maintains healthy muscles and red blood cells. Selenium regulates the immune system and detoxifies the body of heavy metals. Low-selenium diets deprive the body of glutathione peroxidase, which is a cell protector.

Selenium supplementation has increased white blood cell counts and stimulated thymus gland function.[76] Selenium has prevented cancers of the breast, colon, and liver.[77–79] Selenium demonstrated effective antioxidant properties in animals with liver cancer.[80]

Fast Facts

- Soil content determines the selenium content of foods.

- Selenomethionine is extracted from selenium-rich yeast or algae. This form is the least toxic and appears to be the most absorbable.
- Chemotherapy drugs may increase the need for selenium.

Dosage

- 200 to 800 mcg per day

Zinc

Zinc is a component of many enzymes. Zinc is required for protein synthesis, bone health, wound healing, and taste and smell acuity. Low intake of zinc increases risk for esophageal, lung, and melanoma cancers.[81–84]

Fast Facts

- Zinc is absorbed from flesh foods (meats) much better than from non-flesh foods.
- Zinc gluconate is the form used in supplements.
- Excess zinc supplementation may impair immunity.
- Zinc cold lozenges decrease the duration of a cold.
- You may need more zinc if your diet is high in phosphates, fiber, alcohol, or calcium.

Dosage

- 15 to 60 mg per day

Accessory Compounds
Glandulars

Glandulars can be used to support optimal health and immunity. Cancer and cancer treatment can be extremely stressful, leading to adrenal exhaustion and organ strain. Extracts of the adrenal gland help the body adapt to stress. Thymus glandulars have been shown to maintain immune system response during chemotherapy and radiation.[85,86]

Fast Facts

- Support adrenal gland function with adequate intake of potassium, B_6, vitamin C, and magnesium.
- Prevent thymus gland atrophy with adequate intake of carotenoids, vitamin C, vitamin E, zinc, and selenium.
- There are no quality control regulations for glandulars; it is best to choose concentrated and standardized products.

Dosage

For adrenal glandulars, follow label directions; you may wish to start at half the recommended dose and increase only if you do not feel a stimulating effect; for thymus glandulars, 120 mg per day.

Digestive Aids

Digestive enzymes and probiotics can improve impaired digestion and promote a healthy gut environment. Digestive enzymes can reduce a number of GI complaints and should be part of a treatment plan for any gastrointestinal cancer.

Probiotics are health-promoting microbes that help reduce cancer-forming compounds in the colon. Probiotics are linked to reduced colon cancer risk, decreased bladder cancer occurrence, and improved radiation enterocolitis.[87-89]

Fast Facts

- Check expiration dates on labels to make sure the product is still active.
- Choose a digestive enzyme that contains at least these three ingredients: lipase, amylase, and pepsin.
- Fermentable carbohydrates such as fructooligosaccharides (FOS) are called prebiotics. They serve as food for bacteria and should be taken along with probiotics.

Dosage

- For digestive enzymes, 1 to 2 capsules with each meal or snack
- For probiotics, 1 to 10 billion colony-forming units (CFUs) daily.

Amino Acids

Glutathione is a powerful antioxidant, immune stimulator, and regulator of cell division. Glutathione can protect the liver from harmful toxins.[90] Researchers are divided on how well glutathione is absorbed and studies have shown that whey protein or 500 mg of ascorbic acid can be used to sufficiently raise glutathione levels.[91–93] Additionally, animal experiments showed that the concentrates of whey proteins exhibited anticarcinogenic and anticancer activity.[94] For these reasons, vitamin C or whey protein may be the best ways to get additional glutathione into your diet.

N-acetyl cysteine (NAC) is a component of glutathione. Both animal and human studies of NAC have shown it is a potential cancer-fighting agent. NAC, in combination with ascorbic acid, protected against lung cancer development in mice.[95] NAC has also exhibited antiangiogenesis properties (decreased blood supply to tumors).[96]

Dosage

- 500 to 1000 mg per day

Glutamine, another component of glutathione, reduced toxic side effects in colon cancer patients treated with 5FU.[97] Oral glutamine decreased both the severity and duration of mouth sores associated with high-dose bone marrow transplant chemotherapy regimens.[98]

Dosage

During cancer treatment it is 30 gm per day; pretreatment or maintenance dosage is 15 gm per day.

S-Adenosylmethionine (SAM) is an amino acid complex involved in many biochemical reactions, including detoxification processes. Supplemental SAM significantly protected animals against liver cancer when they were exposed to liver carcinogens.[99] SAM should not be taken if you suffer from bipolar depression.

Dosage

- 400 to 1,200 mg per day

Fatty Acids

Eicosapentaenoic acid (EPA) is a recognized cancer chemo-preventive and antimetastatic agent.[100] A mixture of EPA and vitamins C and E enhanced the effectiveness of Cisplatin on cancer suppression.[101] EPA combined with genistein has stopped human breast cancer cells from growing.[102] Animal studies have shown that EPA reduces tumor size.[103] Oral EPA supplements have also been used to stop weight loss in cachetic pancreatic cancer patients.[104] EPA thins the blood, so it should not be taken before or after surgery.

Dosage

- 1,000 to 6,000 mg of essential fatty acids per day

Flaxseed oil, rich in omega-3 fatty acids and alpha-linolenic acid (ALA), demonstrates significant anticancer properties. Dietary intake of ALA halted the growth and spreading capability of breast cancer.[105] ALA has stimulating immunity in animals.[106]

Dosage

- 1,000 to 6,000 mg of essential fatty acids per day

Caprylic acid is an antifungal fatty acid used to treat candida infections. Take enterically coated caprylic acid with meals to enhance absorption.

Dosage

- 1,000 to 3,000 mg daily

Miscellaneous

Modified citrus pectin (MCP), also known as fractionated pectin, comes from the peel and pulp of citrus fruits. MCP blocks the spread of certain cancers, including melanomas, prostate, and colon cancers.[107--109]

Dosage

- 1 to 3 tablespoons daily

CoQ10, an activator of energy within cells, has promising implications for cancer patients. Deficiencies have been established in breast cancer and lymphoma patients.[110] Numerous studies have demonstrated that supplemental CoQ10 can cause partial or full breast cancer remission, even in high-risk, end-stage patients.[111–113] CoQ10 can reduce the toxic side effects from a combined radiation and chemotherapy regimen without altering the effectiveness of Adriamycin.[114,115] CoQ10 has exhibited a strong immune-stimulating effect in one recent study.[116]

Dosage

- 100 to 400 mg per day

Melatonin is a neurohormone that can modulate immunity. Melatonin reduced cytotoxic damage to bone marrow and lymphoid tissues, and stimulated suppressed bone marrow.[117] Animal studies demonstrated melatonin's anticancer effect on lung cancer and hormonally related cancers such as breast, prostate, and ovarian cancers.[118,119] A combination of flaxseed oil and melatonin significantly decreased the number of mammary tumors and the tumor weight in experimental animals.[120] Survival rates increased when melatonin was used with interleukin-2 and interferon cancer treatments.

Dosage

- 5 to 30 mg per day

Herbs

The popularity of herbal medications as adjunctive therapy for cancer has grown in part because of the desire for a more natural approach to health and healing.

Plant extracts that may be commonly used in a clinical or research setting are discussed for their therapeutic benefits to cancer patients. Some plants may have more than one health benefit, but are classified under a particular category based on a primary function.

Antioxidants
Grape Seed Extract

- It is a potent antioxidant and free radical scavenger.[121]
- Grape seed has more antioxidant activity than pine bark.

Suggested Dosage

- 100 to 300 mg daily

Green Tea

- Polyphenols, compounds found in green tea, exhibited greater antioxidant potential than vitamins C and E.[122]
- It blocked human melanoma, colon, prostate, lung cancer cell growth.[123]
- It protected against esophageal cancer.[124]
- Caffeine activates the cancer-fighting potential of compounds found in green tea.

Suggested Dosage

- 3 to 4 cups per day or 300 mg green tea extract.

Detoxifiers
Dandelion

- It is a natural diuretic.
- It has anticancer properties in animals.[125]
- It has been used to treat liver and gallbladder disorders.

Suggested Dosage

- 250 to 500 mg, three times per day

Milk Thistle

- Restored damaged liver cells in irradiated animals.[126]
- Inhibited the growth of prostate cancer cells.[127]
- Halted new blood vessel formation in breast and prostate cancer epithelial cells in test tubes.[128]

Suggested Dosage

- 420 mg daily

Gastrointestinal Supporters

Aloe Vera

- It has antibacterial and antifungal activity and may be used to treat candidiasis.
- It contains saccharides with potent immune-stimulating effects.[129]
- Aloe polymers injected into transplanted sarcomas caused enhanced macrophage attack and sarcoma cell death.[130]

Suggested Dosage

- Limit aloe juice consumption to less than one quart per day

Garlic

- It reduced the risk of stomach and colorectal cancers in high-risk populations.[131]
- It may stop *H. pylori* bacterial infections.[132]
- It inhibited the production of nitrosamines.[133]

- It stimulated macrophages and lymphocytes and protected against chemotherapy and radiation-induced immune suppression.[134]
- Both regular and odorless garlic products have a therapeutic benefit.

Suggested Dosage

- 4,000 mcg allicin or 1 clove fresh garlic daily

Ginger

- It is used to reduce chemotherapy-induced nausea.[135]
- It inhibited human leukemia cell proliferation.[136]
- It reduced GI side effects associated with Cisplatin administration.[137]

Suggested Dosage

- 500 mg as needed

Immune Enhancers
Astragalus

- It contains polysaccharides, which stimulate immunity.
- Increased natural killer cells in patients with systemic lupus erythematosus.[138]
- Reduced the incidence of urinary bladder carcinoma in mice.[139]
- Supported immune system function in animals treated with a cytotoxic drug or radiation.[140]
- Improved the function of T-lymphocytes in cancer patients by 260 percent compared with untreated cells in test tubes.[141]

Suggested Dosage

- 400 mg three times per day

Echinacea

- It "turns on" T-lymphocytes, macrophages, and natural killer cells.
- It has antiviral and antibacterial properties.
- It is used to successfully treat *Candida albicans*.[142]
- Look for products containing *Echinacea purpurea,* currently thought of as the most beneficial part of the plant.
- For long-term use, take it for eight weeks, then stop for one week before resuming again.
- Don't take it if you are suffering from an autoimmune disorder.

Suggested Dosage

- 300 to 900 mg daily

Mushroom Extracts

- It contains beta glucan polysaccharides.
- Lentinan from shiitake mushrooms has little activity if taken orally.
- Numerous studies show that mushroom compounds can stimulate T-lymphocytes, macrophages, and natural killer cells.[143]
- PSK and PSP, both polysaccharide complexes from *Coriolus versicolor,* significantly extended survival rates of patients with stomach, colorectal, oral cavity, lung, and esophageal cancers.[144]
- An in vitro study revealed prostate cancer cells treated with maitake fractions caused a ninety-five percent kill-rate within twenty-four hours of administration.[145]

Suggested Dosage

- As directed

Miscellaneous
Essiac and Flor-essence

- Essiac contains sheep sorrel, burdock, slippery elm, and rhubarb. Flor-essence contains herbs found in Essiac plus watercress, blessed thistle, red clover, and kelp.
- Some of the individual herbs have demonstrated anti-tumor, antioxidant, and antiestrogenic actions, but only anecdotal reports of product efficacy exist. No clinical studies have been published.[146]
- It has reduced GI symptoms in a clinical setting.

Suggested Dosage

- 2 oz tea three times per day, on an empty stomach

Inositol Hexaphosphate (IP-6)

- Inositol supplementation has positively affected brain, breast, colon, leukemia, liver, lung, prostate, and skin cancers.[147–49]
- Research findings suggest it stimulates immunity by acting as an antioxidant and enhancing natural killer cells.[150]
- It may potentiate the actions of radiation and chemotherapy.

Suggested Dosage

- 6,000 to 8,000 mg per day, on an empty stomach

Saw Palmetto

- Reduced prostate enlargement as well as Proscar, the drug of choice for benign prostatic hypertrophy, with fewer side effects.[151]
- It combines with seven other herbs to form PC-SPES, an estrogenic compound that has controlled the progression of prostate cancer.[152]

Suggested Dosage

- 160 mg twice per day

Shark Cartilage

- Failed to slow the spread of cancer or improve the quality of life in a study of forty-seven patients with previously treated advanced cancers of the breast, colon, lung, or prostate.[153]
- Recent studies show shark cartilage halts angiogenesis in animals and humans.[154,155]
- Based on clinical observation, GI upset and intolerance have occurred with shark cartilage intake.

Suggested Dosage

- 1 gram of powder per kilogram of body weight per day

How To Become Supplement Savvy

Supplement sales are booming nationwide. People are fighting chronic disease with dietary supplements in an effort to reclaim their health. More than half of the cancer patients in one recent study used dietary supplements, with two thirds of them taking more than one supplement each day.[156]

If you are among the many Americans taking dietary supplements, you may be frustrated because you know more than your healthcare provider about nutritional therapy. Unless you have a nutritionist in the family, you have probably learned about nutritional supplements on your own. Unfortunately, much of the dietary supplement information available to the public is confusing and misleading. You may be purchasing natural products that make miraculous health claims without substantiated research to back them up. You may be taking the wrong dose or the wrong product altogether for your specific needs. You may be taking supplements at the wrong time, or storing them incorrectly.

Unless you are one hundred percent sure of what you're doing, your first step should not be into a health food store, but into a nutritionist's office. The only way to ensure you are choosing appropriate nutritional formulas is to find a qualified professional who can develop a specific program for you. If you are going to spend your hard-earned money on dietary supplements, you should be confident that you are buying products that are best for you.

Look for a registered dietitian, certified nutrition specialist, or naturopathic physician who has clinical oncology experience. Most individuals who carry these credentials base their recommendations on current scientific findings. The resource listing provides the names of organizations that can help you locate a qualified nutritional professional in your area.

After you have your supplement recommendations in hand, follow these basic guidelines to help you achieve the maximum therapeutic benefit from your supplement program. Keep in mind that dietary supplements won't make up for a lousy diet. Supplements always work better when they are part of a holistic healthcare plan that includes proper dietary habits and lifestyle choices:

- Buy supplements in gelatin capsules. Uncompressed, powdered compounds are usually better absorbed than hard-pressed tablets.
- Look for the letters "USP" on the label. This indicates the product meets the voluntary standards of the U.S. Pharmacopoeia, and it dissolves in a lab test designed to mimic what happens in your gut.
- Avoid supplements that contain fillers, additives, or coal tars. Products that are additive-free will tell you so on the label. Many multivitamins contain sugar substitutes, so read labels carefully.
- Divide your doses over the course of the day to ensure maximum nutrient absorption per dose and decrease the chance of GI intolerance.
- If you develop an upset stomach, rash, or some other adverse reaction, stop taking all supplements. Notify your doctor. Restart your vitamin regimen one supplement at a time. Add a new supplement every two or three days until you determine which supplement bothers you.
- If you have trouble swallowing supplements, try taking them with a thick liquid such as fruit nectar or a fruit smoothie. Chewable, liquid, or powdered forms of vitamins are easy to swallow alternatives to capsules and pills.
- Take all supplements with food, unless otherwise specified. Most nutrients are better absorbed when your digestive tract is processing food. Amino acids, however, should be taken on an empty stomach.
- If you need to limit your supplementation program, begin by taking a multivitamin. From there, add a few antioxidants such as vitamins C and E, then add an

omega-3 fatty acid source. As you are able to add more supplements, review your nutrition action plan for the suggested nutrients best suited for your cancer.

- Fish oil capsules (EPA/DHA) are better tolerated when taken in the middle of a meal. If you suffer from gastroesophageal reflux, you may wish to take flaxseed oil instead. Regurgitation of fish oil is not a pleasant experience!
- Natural vitamins aren't better. Most synthetic vitamins are just as bioavailable to the body as natural vitamins. Vitamin E is the exception; naturally occurring vitamin E (d-alpha tocopherol) is better utilized by the body.
- If you take a multivitamin with iron, take calcium at a different time. High doses of calcium can impair your ability to absorb iron.
- If you take 50 mg of zinc per day, you will need more copper. Zinc tends to decrease the absorption of copper.
- Look for a calcium supplement that contains magnesium and vitamin D. Both help calcium absorption.
- Avoid boron supplements if you have breast or prostate cancers. Boron may increase serum concentrations of estrogen and testosterone.
- Look for standardized herbal products that guarantee product contents. The labels should specify the compounds for which the product is standardized.
- Keep fish oil and other oil-based supplements such as CoQ10 or vitamin E in the refrigerator to ensure freshness.
- Store supplements in a cool, dry, and dark place. Check your product for expiration dates. Avoid the temptation to purchase discounted products that are about to expire.
- Shelf life is shortened when you transfer supplements from the original container to smaller containers.

- Use a magnifying glass to read supplement labels prior to purchasing. Most labels are difficult to read, and you want to make sure you buy exactly what you need!
- Reliable brands include Twin Lab, Carlson, Solgar, Enzymatic Therapy, Nature's Herbs, and Gaia Herbs. For up-to-date information about the quality of supplements,

Coach's Corner

What To Ask Yourself When You Buy a Dietary Supplement

- Are you allergic to any of the ingredients listed on the product label?
- If health claims are made, does the product include an appropriate FDA disclaimer?
- Has the product been laboratory tested for potency, purity, and quality according to U.S. Pharmacopeia (USP) standards?
- Has the bottle or packet been safely sealed?
- Does the product have an expiration date; is it about to expire?
- Is the price consistent with that of other similar products, or if it is more expensive, is there an obvious reason why?
- Will you be able to follow the recommended dosage instructions? If not, you may not achieve therapeutic benefits.

check out the Web site www.consumerlab.com. ConsumerLab provides an independent analysis of supplement quality for common brands of vitamins and herbal supplements. Other sources of information for vitamins and herbal products are listed in the resource section of this book.

What Should You Tell Your Doctor?

Seventy percent of Americans do not tell their physicians that they use some form of complementary medicine, including the use of nutritional supplements.[157] This lack of communication can have serious implications when side effects arise. Doctors who are unaware of a patient's self-treatment regimen may erroneously attribute GI distress, skin rashes, or fever to chemotherapy or radiation and discontinue or delay cancer treatment.

Dietary supplements can have pharmacological, or drug-like, actions. You should always inform your physician of your personal choice to use supplements and supply a detailed list of all supplements you take, including product literature.

Don't be afraid to talk to your doctor about vitamins and herbs. You might be pleasantly surprised at your doctor's response to your supplement regimen. For example, the *Annals of Internal Medicine* reported that when patients told their doctors of their alternative therapy choice, 71 percent received support for its continued use.[158]

Whether your physician approves of your natural therapy approach or not, you stand a better chance of receiving the best medical treatment for your cancer when you share information pertinent to your health. Ultimately, the decision to take supplements is yours.

Getting the Edge

Buyer Beware!

Be wary of anyone who makes supplement recommendations. Are they trying to sell you a product? Can you trust their knowledge? Reliable nutritional advice usually comes from individuals who have nothing to gain by giving it.

— 11 —

Cooling Off

"The art of medicine consists in amusing the patient while nature cures the disease."
— *Voltaire (1694–1778)*

Living in a Toxic World

CHANCES ARE, if you live in this world, your body is inundated with toxins. It is unavoidable. We eat, breathe, and live in a hazardous environment. Toxins can invade our body and linger, sometimes passing on through our genes to other generations. Amazingly, every child born in the United States today has detectable pesticide levels in its tissues.[1]

Toxins can be traced to either environmental or physiological sources. Most prescription or over-the-counter drugs, pollutants such as pesticides or tobacco smoke, and food additives such as bromides and nitrates are examples of environmental contaminants.

Physiological sources of toxins occur as a result of everyday metabolic activity. Parasites, yeast, and other microbes produce waste products that can compromise tissues. Free radicals are highly reactive biochemical toxins that, if not transformed, can damage healthy cells. Even negative thoughts and emotions can increase our toxic burden.

The Toxic Buildup

Your body normally has the capacity to dispose of harmful substances and can miraculously inactivate, remove, or change toxic substances in an attempt to prevent a buildup of waste products. The organs primarily responsible for detoxification include the gastrointestinal tract, kidney, and liver. The lymphatic system and skin also have specific elimination functions. At the cellular level, compounds such as superoxide dismutase (SOD) and glutathione peroxidase act as free radical scavengers and assist in the excretion of potential cancer-causing agents.[2]

With all of these cleansing mechanisms in place, how can toxicity occur? If you have constipation or your immune system is compromised, wastes tend to build up in the body, leak through the intestinal wall, and flow into the liver. The liver is primarily responsible for clearing the body of poisons. If the liver is overtaxed, toxins simply circulate in the blood, taking shelter in the brain, nervous system, and fatty tissues. Healthy cells are injured when exposed to these toxins. Studies have shown that individuals with compromised detoxification systems are the most susceptible to developing a chronic disease such as cancer.

Think about your ability to detoxify. How will you combat the pesticides, hormones, and antibiotics that saturate our food supply? How will your body purge itself of the effects of radiation, chemotherapy, and any prescription drugs that you might have used to diminish treatment side effects?

Gold Medal Action

Benefits of Detoxification

While the obvious advantage of detoxification is clearing the body of disease-producing substances, many people who follow a whole foods diet report other health improvements:

- Increased energy levels
- Better work productivity
- Heightened spiritual awareness
  - Enhanced adaptation to stressful situations
  - Mental clarity

How You Can Safely Detoxify

Any time you drastically change your diet or lifestyle habits, you begin to detoxify your body. This cooling off process can begin immediately. There is no need to wait until the end of your cancer treatment to begin cleansing through dietary change. Of course, advanced forms of detoxification such as colonics or fasting should not be used by anyone going through surgery, chemotherapy, or radiation. Cancer treatments cause your body to undergo many changes, and it is important to stabilize your metabolism to support your body's natural detoxification processes before trying advanced techniques.

If you would like to try colonics or fasting, see the resource section for recommended books that discuss these techniques. Usually the more advanced regimens are developed with the assistance of a qualified healthcare professional. Be mindful that if you are in a weakened state of health, suffer from heart problems, or have lost a significant amount of weight, you probably are not a candidate for these more rigorous detoxification practices.

The Detox Diet

It has been estimated that up to 90 percent of all cancers can be linked to the environment, with diet being the number one contributing factor. When you eat foods that are unadulterated, you help your body clear unwanted pollutants so it can begin healing. A detoxification program isn't going to help much if you aren't making appropriate dietary choices to begin with.

If you follow the nutritional recommendations in this book, you can begin to cleanse your body and enjoy a higher level of health. I think of my program as a race course to healing, which will help you track your dietary progress. You will see a definite connection between the detox diet discussed in this chapter and your nutrition action plan. The point of this chapter is to help you assess and change toxic eating habits.

From the starting line of my race course, food choices are presented at four hurdles. In a progressive fashion, the first three hurdles challenge you to exclude foods from your diet that are highly processed, contain hidden sugars and fats, or are of limited nutritional value. Hurdle four challenges you to eat the best whole foods diet.

Begin by reducing your intake of sugar, caffeine, and alcohol. Move toward a chemical-free diet by refraining from artificial sweeteners, colors, and flavoring agents. Unadulterated foods leave little behind for the liver to clear out.

Read food package labels to identify and dismiss any foods that contain sulfites, nitrates, and phosphates. These additives have been linked to a number of health problems.

Avoid foods made with hydrogenated and partially hydrogenated fats and chemically extracted oils. Processed fats are toxic to our cells, and rancid fats increase the free radicals in the body.

Limit high temperature cooking (grilling or broiling) of meats, which contributes to the formation of potentially cancer-causing chemicals called heterocyclic amines.

Buy organically grown, hormone- and antibiotic-free products. Steer clear of foods that have been genetically engineered or irradiated.

Consume a plant-based diet. Eat more whole grains, seeds, nuts, and legumes. Fiber is essential for healthy gut function, aids in reducing blood glucose and cholesterol levels, and helps to detoxify the body by binding to carcinogenic materials in the colon.

Eat at least five servings of antioxidant-rich fruits and vegetables every day. Bright yellow and deep orange produce contains immune-stimulating carotenoids. Consume cruciferous vegetables several times each week. The indoles in cabbage, broccoli, and other crucifers have potent antitumor activity.

Consuming animal fats, which are a primary source of saturated fats, increases your risk for many kinds of cancer. Reduce saturated fat intake by limiting red meat, pork, and poultry. Eat more fish, especially those rich in omega-3 fatty acids such as salmon, tuna, and mackerel.

Hurdle One
Reduce processed, hydrogenated fats,
and high-sugar foods

Hurdle Two
Reduce hidden sugars, refined flour products,
high-fat dairy products, and risky animal flesh

Hurdle Three
Reduce animal products, avoid canned goods,
and cut back on natural sweeteners

Hurdle Four
Cut back on low-fiber fruits, add organics, soy,
and omega-3 fatty acid fish

Finish Line
Eat more raw, whole, natural foods
without processing and with little cooking

Replace animal products with low-fat soy foods. Eat at least one vegetarian meal each day. Limit dairy products, except for yogurt, which contributes bacteria friendly to the colon.

Drink plenty of purified water to prevent dehydration and toxic buildup. Grain coffee substitutes, herbal teas, natural fruit juices, and purified water are preferable beverage choices. Fluids to avoid include caffeinated beverages, which cause dehydration, and sugar-laden sports drinks, soda pops, and fruit drinks. Alcohol consumption is generally not recommended. Move toward a raw foods diet. Approximately 75 percent of your food selections should come from raw fruits and vegetables and sprouted greens from seeds and whole grains such as buckwheat, alfalfa, sunflower, beans, and nuts. Uncooked foods contain more nutrients and live enzymes that assist digestion. Eating raw foods also promotes an alkaline environment, which is preferable because cancer cells may thrive in acidic conditions.

This diet can be difficult to stick to and may contribute to negative gastrointestinal side effects such as diarrhea, bloating, cramping, and indigestion. These symptoms may be the result of a change from processed, refined foods to raw natural foods or may be your body's natural reaction to the detoxification process.

Juicing

Juicing is more than just adding fresh fruit or vegetable juice to your diet. Drinking large quantities of juice is an effort to provide your body with large amounts of valuable nutrients such as the essential fatty acids, vitamins, minerals, enzymes, and phytochemicals necessary to support a strong immune system and promote elimination of toxins. Unlike commercially processed juices, fresh juice is packed with high-quality nutrients because it has not been subjected to heat during processing.

Here's how to get the most from your juicing regimen:

- Choose an appropriate juicer. Rotary blade juicers are very good at extracting juice and are reasonably priced. Juicers with compressor actions are the best for those who juice several times per day.
- Look for tasty juice recipes. Sometimes, the juicer manufacturer includes a small pamphlet of juice recipes. If not, try experimenting with blends on your own or buy a book on juicing.
- Use organic produce. Plants grown without pesticides and herbicides tend to contain higher levels of nutrients and pose less of a health threat.

Dietary Hurdles for Eating Well

Hurdle One	Hurdle Two	Hurdle Three	Hurdle Four	Hurdle Five
Candy	Fruit Juice Popsicles	Frozen Juices	Fresh Fruit Juice	Purified Water
Soda Pop	Canned Fruit in Heavy Syrup	Commercial Juices	All Fruit Sorbets	Free-Range Meats
Diet Soda Pop	Flavored Seltzers, Teas	Fruit Spreads	Dried Fruits	Fresh Veggies
Jellies & Jams	Sorbet & Sherbet	Grain Sweeteners	Frozen Fruit	Fruit w/Skin
Syrups	Fruit & Juice Alone	Blackstrap Molasses	Herbal Teas	Lentils, Peas & Beans
Popsicles	Raw Sugar	Date Sugar	Whole Grain Bread, Pasta & Cereal	Plain Yogurt
Processed Honey	Sweetened Carob	Raw Honey	Goat's Milk	Buckwheat
Brown & White Sugars	Decaf Tea & Coffee	Unsweetened Carob	Buttermilk	Quinoa
Chocolate	White Rice, Pasta & Bread	Granola	Low-fat Milk	Amaranth
Commercial Baked Goods	Ice Cream & Whipped Cream	Whole Grain Muffins	Tofu & Soy	Raw Nuts & Seeds
Commercial Cereals	High-Fat Cheeses	Plain Cereals	Legumes	Bran
Non-Dairy Creamers	Butter	Low-fat Cheese	No-Added-Fat Nuts	Wild Game
Hydrogenated Oils	Mayonnaise	Whole Milk	Frozen Veggies	
Margarines	Peanuts	Sweetened Yogurt	Organic Eggs	
Artificial Fats	Roasted Seeds & Nuts	Frozen Yogurt	Organic Meats	
Coconut & Palm Oils	Organ Meats	Canola & Olive Oils	Canned Tuna	
Fried Snack Foods	Fried Fish & Poultry	Safflower & Sunflower Oils	Fresh Salmon	
Bacon Bits	Smoked Meats & Fish	Canned Legumes	Sardines	
Beef	Canned Meats	Canned Vegetables		
Processed Cheeses		Eggs		
		Meat & Poultry		
		Frozen & Breaded Fish		

SOURCE: *Product labels*

How Much Juice?

Although some individuals drink quarts of juice, you can achieve healthful results with as little as two cups of juice per day. This can keep you on track if you need to watch your calorie or sugar intake.

- Drink your juice right away. Excessive storage time will strip the juice of valuable nutrients, particularly ascorbic acid and the B vitamins.
- Don't throw out the pulp. Add it to your compost heap; make baby food, or mix a quarter cup of the pulp into a quick bread batter.
- Pack additional nutrients into your juice by adding ground flaxseeds, wheat grass, chlorella, or spirulina.
- Throw in most of the plant. With the exception of citrus rinds, pits, or hard seeds, you should juice all of the plant, including the white pithy part of oranges and grapefruits, stems, soft seeds, and leaves.
- Avoid juicing starchy fruits such as bananas, mangoes, and papayas. They don't juice well.
- Juice plants that have cancer-fighting potential. For example, tomatoes rich in lycopene reduce the risk of prostate cancer; garlic contains allyl sulfides, found to lower the risk of squamous cell cancers; and strawberries, rich in ellagic acid, protect cells from genetic damage.
- Reduce the blood sugar rush caused by drinking juice between meals. Mix a scoop of soy or whey protein powder into the juice or eat a few nuts or seeds with your juice.

At the Training Table

Juicy Juices

Not sure what to throw into your juicer? Try some of these delicious, nutritious combinations:

Apple–Tangerine–Pineapple

Carrot–Pineapple

Apple–Cherry–Grated Ginger Root

Carrot–Pomegranate

Carrot–Spinach–Beet

Tomato–Celery–Tabasco–Lemon

Cucumber–Parsley–Spinach

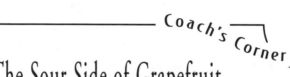

Coach's Corner

The Sour Side of Grapefruit

Certain drugs, including Taxol, Vincristine, and Tamoxifen, can be affected by drinking grapefruit juice or eating grapefruit.

The bioflavonoids found in grapefruit inactivate enzymes responsible for clearing drugs from your body. If you drink grapefruit juice with these medications, you risk serious toxicity if these drugs build up in your system.

When Not To Juice

- During cancer treatment, you can add fresh juice to a whole foods diet as a way of assisting detoxification, but drinking large amounts of juice or fasting on juice is not recommended for individuals undergoing chemotherapy or radiation. Sometimes, a one- to two-day juice cleansing regimen can be followed during the early stages of cancer or as a preventative to recurrence. Talk to a nutritional professional if you want to attempt a juice fast.

- When your immune system is severely compromised, you need to be especially careful about what you eat or drink. If your doctor informs you that your absolute neutrophil count (ANC) is low, you will need to restrict your raw food and juice intake in order to reduce your risk of bacterial infection. While raw fruits and vegetables are not allowed during this time, you can still consume cooked produce.

- If you have difficulty managing your blood sugar, be careful. Fresh juices require minimal digestion, so nutrients are quickly released and integrated into the cells, rapidly raising blood sugar levels. If you have diabetes, you should avoid juice fasts. Drinking juice with a protein meal or adding soy or whey protein powder to your juice can help stabilize blood sugar levels. Although fruit juices tend to contain the most sugar, beet and carrot juice also produce a high glycemic response.

- If you are malnourished, remember that juice provides very few calories and almost no protein. If you have lost a significant amount of weight, or are losing weight, you should limit the amount of juice you drink and avoid juice fasting. Individuals with limited gastrointestinal capacity or who are malnourished should avoid drinking large amounts of juice. It is far more important to meet daily energy needs through solid food so that valuable muscle mass and immune system integrity is not lost.

Detox Supplements

When people have cancer, their cellular protection systems are out of balance due to exposure to chemicals, poor dietary choices, and the debilitating effects of illness. In an effort to counterbalance cellular destruction and assist the body's natural detoxification processes, nutritional supplements can be used in combination with a whole foods diet and a juicing regimen.

Many nutrients are needed to support the function of organs directly involved in whole body cleansing:

- Psyllium husk and other soluble fibers, along with fructooligosaccharides, acidophilus culture, and L-glutamine promote a healthy gastrointestinal tract.
- Support liver health with vitamins A, C, and E, and selenium, zinc, calcium, L-cysteine, and milk thistle.
- Kidney health is supported by vitamins A, C, B_6, and the minerals magnesium and potassium. Dandelion and parsley have natural diuretic properties.

Potent Protectors	
With	**Try**
Adriamycin	CoQ10 + Glutathione, Garlic, L-glutamine, L-carnitine, Melatonin + Vitamin E, N-acetylcysteine
Cytoxan	Glutathione
5-FU	CoQ10, Vitamins B_3, B_6, and C
Mitomycin-C	Vitamins B_3, B_6, and C
Bleomycin	Vitamins B_3, B_6, and C
Methotrexate	Glutamate, Omega-3 fatty acids
Cisplatin	Gingko Biloba, Milk Thistle, Quercetin, Selenium
Vincristine	Milk Thistle

Reduce toxic side effects of chemotherapy by taking nutrients that protect your immune system, heart, intestines, and other organs.[3-17]

Not Feeling Right?

As you begin to make healthy changes to your diet, you might feel worse before you feel better. Depending on what you used to eat, you may actually experience withdrawal symptoms. For example, if you regularly consume coffee or other caffeinated products and quickly eliminate them from your diet, your head might ache, and you might lack energy for a few days.

There is a chance that you could confuse signs of withdrawal with treatment complications, so I have listed some of the symptoms that my patients have experienced during their dietary transitions. Be on the lookout for these withdrawal signs and consider that your feelings of malaise could be caused by your diet, not your disease. Regardless of the cause, always report any new or unusual symptoms to your doctor.

Expect symptoms to last a variable amount of time. After all, the more the body has to detoxify, the longer and more potent a withdrawal can be. Most symptoms should dissipate within a few days. If your symptoms continue, you should seek the advice of your physician immediately.

Keep in mind that you are an individual and not everyone will experience the same kind or degree of the following symptoms:

- Coated tongue or bad breath
- Changes in bowel habits
- General discomfort
- Fatigue
- Frequent urination
- Mental anxiety
- Mental confusion
- Skin rashes or acne
- Taste or smell changes
- Temperature fluctuations (fevers, chills)
- Trouble sleeping

Food Safety

Fruits and vegetables, along with other foods, are highly susceptible to contamination. Soil may contain microbes and irrigation water may harbor harmful bacteria. Food stored improperly can become spoiled and contaminated with mycotoxins and other infectious pathogens. Food-borne illnesses can wreak havoc on your health and well-being. With a little common sense and applied kitchen rules, you can keep yourself out of the contamination zone.

Self-Assessment: How Safe Are You?

Answer the following questions to determine how knowledgeable you are about making sure your food is safe to eat. See Appendix 16 for answers.

Food Safety Quiz
(Circle True or False)

1. Cooking hamburger meat will kill any potentially dangerous bacteria. True False
2. You should devein shrimp before you eat it. True False
3. Cooling a large pot of spaghetti sauce in the refrigerator will reduce the risk of food-borne illness. True False
4. Cold cuts, once opened, should be consumed within three days. True False
5. It is safe to cut a moldy section off of cheese before you eat it. True False
6. You should always taste test your cooking. True False
7. Brown spots on leaf lettuce are harmless. True False
8. You can eat a food that has passed its "sell by" date. True False
9. If you buy organic produce, you don't need to wash it. True False
10. Adding a raw egg to your blended soy shake is a good way to get more protein. True False

Total: Yes _____ No _____

Safety First

How to keep your foods safe and reduce your risk of bacterial infection:

- Wash your hands thoroughly before and after handling food, especially fresh fruits and vegetables and raw meats, poultry, and fish.
- Wash fruits or vegetables with a produce wash, even if they are organic.
- Clean cutting boards with soap and water after cutting raw poultry or seafood.
- Discard the tops and outer leaves of leafy vegetables such as lettuce and cabbage.
- Store produce on a shelf above raw meat in the refrigerator to avoid dripping meat juices.
- Thaw frozen foods in the refrigerator or defrost in the microwave.
- Thoroughly cook all meats, poultry, fish, and eggs. Precook meats before grilling.
- Don't allow cooked foods to cool at room temperature. Refrigerate them while they are still hot.
- Choose pasteurized honey and dairy products.

Toxic Food Additives

Food additives are added to processed foods to extend storage life and to improve taste, nutritional value, color, or texture. Some food additives have been connected to health problems and increased cancer risk. In general, you will want to limit the amount of processed foods you eat (and thereby, reduce your intake of food additives).

Avoid the Following Additives

- MSG (monosodium glutamate)
  A substance found in spice flavorings, it can be added to hydrolyzed vegetable protein (HVP), a soy product. MSG has been associated with neurological disorders.

- Aluminum Additives
  This heavy metal, linked to Alzheimer's disease, can be found in food packaging, pickles, flours, cheese, chewing gums, and baking powder.

- Nitrates and Nitrites
  These additives combine with stomach acid to form nitrosamines, a cancer-causing agent. They are found in processed meats such as bacon, hot dogs, pepperoni, and sausage.

- Sulfites
  A substance found in salad bars, wine, and seafood. Linked to asthma attacks, diarrhea, nausea, and anaphylactic shock.

- Potassium Bromate
  Found in white flour, this chemical rapidly breaks down to form cancer-causing bromides.

- Fat Replacements
  Olestra and Simplesse are compounds used to lower the fat and calorie content of snack foods. Consumption has led to a risk of malabsorption of fat soluble vitamins and diarrhea.

- Artificial Colors
  Hazardous food colorings are widely used in candy, desserts, and gelatins. The Food and Drug Administration claims that food coloring doesn't increase cancer risk, but animal studies suggest artificial colorings may be

linked to various cancers. If you attempt to avoid these empty calorie foods and eat a whole foods diet, you should be able to avoid most artificial colorings.

- Artificial Sweeteners
  Animal studies have shown that saccharin (found in Sweet'N Low) is a tumor promoter in the bladder, lung, and other organs.[18] Aspartame (found in Nutrasweet and Equal) has been linked to neurological disorders.[19]
- Risky Food Products
  Peanuts may contain aflatoxins, which are cancer-causing substances made by a fungus that grows inside of the nut.[20] Cottonseed oil contains toxic natural ingredients and has been linked to reduced red blood cell integrity and impaired liver and kidney function.[21]

Environmental Pollutants Linked to Cancer

You can support your body's efforts to eliminate toxic waste by limiting your exposure to chemicals and environmental pollutants. Heterocyclic amines (HCAs) develop when fish, chicken, or red meats are pan-fried. Polycyclic aromatic hydrocarbons (PAHs) form when fat drips onto hot coals, creating smoke that rises and deposits on the outside of grilled meats. More carcinogenic compounds are formed when fatty cuts of meat are cooked. Both chemicals raise the risk of cancer. The Iowa's Women's Health Study found that women who consistently ate well-done red meat had about five times the risk of breast cancer compared to women who ate their meats rare or medium.[22]

How To Limit Your Exposure to HCAs and PAHs

- Do not consume grilled meats every day. Instead, bake, broil, or stew meats.

- Choose the least fatty cuts of meat. Eat more fish and chicken and less beef and pork.
- Mix textured vegetable protein into your ground beef or turkey to cut the fat.
- Trim fat from meats prior to cooking and discard any charred parts.
- Precook meats in the microwave for about sixty to ninety seconds.
- Thaw meat before putting it on the grill. Frozen meat usually chars on the outside while the inside remains frozen.
- Marinate your meat before you grill it to help set up a barrier to prevent the formation of HCAs.
- Don't eat the skin or liquid drippings from meat.
- Eat foods rich in linoleic acid such as soybeans, walnuts, pumpkin seeds, and flaxseeds. In preliminary studies, high doses of linoleic acid appear to inhibit cancer caused by PAHs.[23]
- Eat foods rich in citrus bioflavonoids such as oranges, grapefruits, and tangerines. The bioflavonoids naringin, naringenin, and rutein offer protection against HCAs.[24]
- Polychlorinated biphenyls (PCBs) were used in electrical devices until the mid 1970s, when it was determined that they caused liver cancer and reproductive problems in animals. Unfortunately, they still contaminate our water supply. Freshwater fish from the Great Lakes region and other industrial waterways contribute the highest levels of dietary PCBs.[25] You may wish to limit your intake of fish caught from industrial waterways in Michigan, New York, and Maryland.

- Pesticides are sprayed on plants in order to increase crop yield. Melons, berries, and grapes appear to have the highest levels of pesticide contamination. Watch for imported produce from South America or Mexico during the winter months. Some pesticides used in these countries have been linked to cancer and nerve damage. Choose organic produce or use a produce spray wash to remove exterior pesticides.

A Nontoxic Lifestyle

You can promote detoxification by making some concerted lifestyle choices. For example, if you use tobacco products, stop now. Limit your exposure to secondhand smoke. Sidestream smoke contains more carbon monoxide than inhaled smoke.

Avoid alcohol, which is metabolized to acetaldehyde, a carcinogenic compound. Alcohol also increases the production of free

Gold Medal Action

Is It Really Organic?

Finally! The U.S. Department of Agriculture has passed a nationwide standard for organic foods. Before this, rules varied from state to state, which made it difficult for consumers to feel confident about their organic purchases. Effective February 2001, this standard ensures that only foods that comply with organic criteria can display the "USDA Organic" seal.

Detox Your Home

There are all kinds of things you can do to reduce exposure to harmful chemicals!

- Remove the plastic bags from dry-cleaned items and air out your clothes before you bring them into your house.
- Make sure your lawn care service uses natural, instead of synthetic, herbicides and pesticides.
- Avoid aerosol sprays, which contain methylene chloride, a suspected cancer-causing compound.
- Always transfer leftover food from plastic containers into glass containers prior to heating in the microwave.

radicals, inhibits the breakdown of other toxins by competing for detoxification enzymes, and impairs nutrient metabolism. In animal studies, administering alcohol increased cell proliferation in mouth, esophagus, rectal, and breast cancers.[27, 28]

Physical activity helps the body to sweat out toxins. Exercise can help you maintain a healthy weight and increase your energy level. Spending time in a sauna can help to facilitate the cleansing of heavy metals and fat-soluble chemicals.[29]

Regular washing and dry-brushing the skin removes dead cells and invigorates tissues. Massage therapy, deep breathing regimens, and meditation reduce stress, stimulate elimination, and promote relaxation.

Recombinant bovine growth hormone (rBGH) is used to make dairy cows produce more milk. While the FDA claims it is safe for consumption, research suggests that rBGH-treated milk may promote certain cancers. rBGH may contain very high levels of IGF-1, the insulin-like growth factor that has been linked to prostate, colon, and breast cancers.[26] If you consume dairy foods, choose organic, hormone-free products. Horizon and Organic Valley are two companies that don't use antibiotics, hormones, pesticides, or herbicides.

Section III

Go!

— 12 —

Nutrition Action Plans

"The undertaking of a new action brings new strength."
— *Evenius*

Which Plan Is Right for You?

Follow the nutrition action plan designed for your primary cancer diagnosis. Your primary cancer site is where your cancer originated. Cancer cells can spread and form new tumors in the lymph nodes, liver, lungs, bones, or brain, but these new tumors have the same kind of abnormal cells and the same name as the primary tumor. For example, if breast cancer spreads to the lungs, the cancer cells in the lungs are breast cancer cells. The disease is metastatic breast cancer; it is not lung cancer. In this case, you would follow the nutrition action plan for breast cancer. It is essential that you know your primary cancer diagnosis before beginning this nutritional program. Contact your physician if you need clarification about your diagnosis.

If you have a cancer not covered in a specific action plan, or you don't know the primary site of your cancer, follow the guidelines for "Other Cancers."

Getting a Head Start

It's time to put into action what you've learned in the first two sections of this book. Getting started on a new diet can seem overwhelming when you're not sure where to begin. It takes time to pull it all together.

In an effort to reduce your learning curve, each nutrition action plan has several features. If you are a big picture kind of person, the general dietary recommendations may help you the most. The quick reference guide to eating is great for those who need a fast review of the dietary recommendations for their particular cancer. I've also devised a sample meal plan of what a typical day's meals might look like and a food selection guide to provide do's and don'ts at a glance. You may wish to laminate some of this information and post it on your refrigerator or carry it in your bag or briefcase when you dine from home.

Building Momentum

As you will see, after you have made one dietary adjustment, it becomes easier to meet a number of your nutritional goals. For example, when you eat more soy, you will find you eat less animal protein, thereby automatically reducing the amount of saturated fat you consume. By making small changes, you are building momentum in the direction of positive change. One change will lead to another until you are eating an optimal diet.

Checking Your Progress

After you have followed your nutrition action plan for a while, you may find it helpful to periodically complete a food record and see how your diet measures up against your suggested nutrition action plan. There are two good reasons for doing this:

- If you have veered off course, you will be able to pinpoint where you have gone astray. Reevaluate your dietary habits by completing the chapter surveys; they can help you determine where you need improvement.
- By reevaluating your dietary habits on a regular basis, you ensure long-term success.

Proceed to the nutrition action plan that applies to your specific cancer. (See the Table of Contents, page viii.)

Nutrition Action Plan for Bladder Cancer

The Mediterranean diet, a diet rich in grains and produce, has been associated with lowering the risk of bladder cancer. A whole foods, plant-based diet is essential for anyone who wants to eat to beat bladder cancer. Proper nutrition can rebuild cells, stimulate immune system function, protect against chemical and environmental toxins, and promote total body wellness. Here's how you can take action to beat bladder cancer, one step at a time:

Step One: Stabilize Your Weight

If you've lost more than a few pounds, you should take immediate action to prevent further weight loss. As little as a 5-percent weight loss can dramatically reduce your ability to cope with treatment side effects and can lead to malnutrition, a complication that

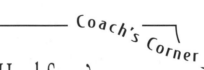

Need a Head Start?

Here are some changes that you can make to your diet NOW that will help you get on the fast track to health! For this week:

1. Eat two servings of broccoli or other cruciferous vegetables.
2. Try a veggie burger.
3. Eat two servings of fish.
4. Eat whole grain bread or rolls.
5. Eat a beans and rice meal.

causes 40 percent of deaths in cancer patients. Don't risk delayed treatment and give cancer a chance to progress while you wait to regain your ability to tolerate treatment! Chapter 2 provides nutritional support recommendations to help you maintain your weight and prevent malnutrition.

Step Two: Lose Weight If You Need To

The American Institute for Cancer Research recommends limiting weight gain to eleven pounds during adulthood. Excessive weight can elevate serum levels of insulin-like growth factor (IGF-1), which can cause cancer cells to grow and spread. Studies also suggest that higher levels of cancer-causing chemicals might be stored in excess fat tissue or that extra calories provide fuel for increased cell proliferation. Often changing what you eat can prompt weight loss; this jump-start to a leaner figure can be a strong motivational factor for continued adherence to a more healthful diet. Don't forget the other part of the weight maintenance equation: Physical activity can help increase muscle mass and burn calories.

As you adjust to new eating habits, your new energy requirements will be established as your body composition changes. Talk with a registered dietitian who can help you design a meal plan for realistic and safe weight loss. Avoid strict or fad diets in an attempt to lose weight. Quick weight loss deprives the body of valuable nutrients needed for growth and repair, and can reduce the fighting capacity of your immune system.

Step Three: Maintain a Healthy Gut

Radiation treatment for bladder cancer can disrupt bowel function, causing diarrhea and cramping. If your gastrointestinal tract doesn't work very well, you won't be able to utilize all the nutrients you consume. Eating small, frequent meals and taking digestive enzymes can aid digestion. To achieve a balance of beneficial bacteria in the intestines, eat yogurt or take a probiotic supplement on a regular basis. Additional information on gastrointestinal health can be found in Chapter 3.

Step Four: Eat Five-a-Day

Consume at least five servings of produce each day. Numerous studies have reported a positive association between consuming

Gold Medal Action

Get the Phyto-Advantage!

Eat a variety of fruits and vegetables and pile your plate high with powerful phytochemicals to stop bladder cancer in its tracks! Your best plant choices contain carotenoids, citrus bioflavonoids, indoles, and phenols:

- Fruits: Black currants, cantaloupe, cherries, cranberries, grapefruit, kiwi, lemons, limes, mangoes, nectarines, oranges, papayas, peaches, pears, prunes, pumpkin, raspberries, star fruit, strawberries, tangerines
- Vegetables: Arugula, bok choy, broccoli, Brussels sprouts, butternut squash, cabbage, carrots, cauliflower, chard, collard greens, daikon radish, eggplant, endive, horseradish, kale, kelp, kohlrabi, mustard greens, onions, red peppers, rutabagas, sorrel, spinach, squash, tomatoes, turnips, turnip greens, yams

produce and preventing bladder cancer. Nature has packed cancer-fighting phytochemicals into almost every kind of fruit and vegetable. Choose raw produce when possible, which provides more vitamins and minerals and has active plant enzymes. Chapter 7 shows you how easy it is to meet your daily produce goal.

Step Five: Cut the Fat

Limit fat to 25 percent of your total calories. In several case-control studies, total fat intake was related to bladder cancer. Eating too much fat or the wrong kinds of fat has been associated with inflammatory conditions, suppressed immunity, and cancer cell growth. Chapter 5 provides guidelines for avoiding unhealthy fats and balancing your diet with healthy fats. At least 15 percent of your daily calories (60 percent of your total fat allowance) should come from fats that contain monounsaturated and omega-3 fatty acids.

Step Six: Eat Soy

Consume an average of two servings of soy foods daily. Soy, which doesn't contain saturated fat, is a high-protein alternative to animal foods that has been found to reduce metastatic properties, increase cell death, and reduce proliferation of bladder tumors. Mice with transplanted bladder cancer cells given genistein developed smaller tumors than controls. A diet high in soy foods may contribute to decreased incidence of invasive transitional cell bladder cancers. See Chapter 9 to learn more about how soy foods can fit into your diet.

Step Seven: Add Roughage

Consume at least twenty-five grams of fiber each day. Fiber acts to detoxify the body by removing cancer-causing secondary bile acids and cholesterol through the stool. Whole grains and minimally processed starches should supply most of your energy. Chapter 8 details how to eat a variety of plant foods to ensure that you get a mixture of soluble and insoluble fibers.

Step Eight: Cut the Sweets

Limit refined sugar and flour intake to less than 10 percent of total calories. Sugar, as well as other highly processed carbohydrates, can raise blood sugar levels, creating an environment favorable for cancer cell growth and immune suppression. Chapter 6 offers suggestions for cutting the sugar from your diet and provides recommendations for stabilizing blood sugar levels.

Step Nine: Drink Up

A nationwide food consumption survey found that chronic mild dehydration was commonplace among Americans. To be well hydrated and flush your system of toxins, you should consume at least twelve cups of fluid per day if you are a man, nine cups of fluid per day if you are a woman. Drink reverse osmosis treated or distilled water. Consume green tea, which provides powerful antioxidant benefits. You may wish to avoid chlorinated water, which has been associated with increased risk of bladder cancer in several population studies. Bladder cancer risk may be associated with excessive consumption (more than five cups per day) of coffee.

Step Ten: Adopt Healthy Habits

See Chapter 1 for suggestions about a healthier lifestyle. If you smoke, stop now. Continuing to smoke can reduce the benefit of natural therapies while increasing your risk for other diseases. Avoid foods that contain antibiotics, hormones, artificial sweeteners, colorings, or harmful additives. High nitrate levels found in drinking water were associated with increased bladder cancer risk. Eat organically grown produce or use a commercial fruit and vegetable wash to remove pesticides and waxes. Follow the food safety guidelines in Chapter 11 to reduce your risk of contracting a food-borne illness.

Step Eleven: Supplement Your Diet

The following nutritional supplements have demonstrated effectiveness or may have potential value in the treatment of bladder cancer. Consult with a healthcare professional to determine whether you have specific daily requirements for these or other dietary supplements:

- Multivitamin, without iron
- Mixed carotenoids, 15 to 60 mg
- Vitamin C with bioflavonoids, 1,000 to 6,000 mg
- Vitamin E, 400 to 1,000 IU
- Selenium, 200 to 800 mcg
- EPA/DHA (fish oil), 1,000 to 6,000 mg
- Cod-liver oil, 1 to 2 Tbs
- Isolated soy protein powder, 50 to 100 mg isoflavones
- Zinc, 25 to 50 mg
- Copper, 1.5 to 3 mg
- Vitamin B_6, 50 to 100 mg
- Shiitake (LEM), 3 to 9 gm
- CoQ10, 100 to 400 mg
- N-acetylcysteine (NAC), 250 to 500 mg
- Quercetin, 600 to 1,200 mg
- Garlic, 1 clove (equals 4,000 mcg allicin)
- Gingko biloba, 120 to 240 mg standardized for 24 percent flavone glycosides
- Milk thistle, 200 to 400 mg

Quick Reference Guide to Eating Right

Consume Less	Consume More
Total fat (No more than 25 percent of your total calories)	Fruits and vegetables (5 to 9 servings per day)
Deep fat fried foods	Total dietary fiber intake (25 grams per day)
Margarine, shortening, and vegetable oils from corn, safflower, and soybeans	Whole grains (2 or more servings per day)
Red meat (No more than 1 serving per week)	Legumes (1/2 cup per day)
High-fat milk or cheese	Yogurt (3 servings per week)
Smoked or processed meats	Free-range animal products
Sugar, candy, desserts, or beverages containing sugar (No more than 10 percent of your total calories)	Soy foods (2 servings per day)
White bread, rice, and pasta	Cold water fish (3 servings per week)
Salt	Extra virgin olive oil
Alcohol	Green tea (3 to 4 cups per day)
	Purified water (9 to 12 cups per day)

Sample Meal Plan

Eating healthy can be nutritious and delicious! The following sample meal plan provides approximately 1,855 calories, 259 grams of carbohydrate (56%), 88 grams of protein (19%), 52 grams of fat (25%), and 31 grams of dietary fiber. A registered dietitian can help you adjust the portion sizes of this meal plan to meet your individual nutritional needs.

Breakfast

Orange segments	1 medium
Cream of wheat	1 cup
Multigrain toast	1 slice
Butter	1 tsp
Lite soy milk	1 cup
Green tea	1 cup
Purified water	1 cup

Lunch

Tempeh	3 1/2 oz
Whole wheat pasta and bean salad	1 cup
Cauliflower and broccoli, steamed	1 cup
Cantaloupe wedge	1/4 melon
Carrot juice	1 cup
Purified water	1 cup

Dinner

Tuna fillet	4 oz
Brown rice pilaf	1 cup
Brussels sprouts	1 cup
Tossed greens	2 cups
Italian salad dressing	1 tsp
Grapes	15
Green tea	1 cup
Purified water	2 cups

Snack

Yogurt, plain, low fat	1 cup
Sliced, fresh peaches	1 cup
Herbal tea	1 cup
Purified water	1 cup

Food Selection Guide for Bladder Cancer

Beverages

Choose More Often

Soy milk, fruit or vegetable juices, herbal teas, green tea, purified water

Choose Less Often

Cow's milk, buttermilk, nonfat dry milk, malts, shakes, frozen yogurt drinks, carbonated beverages, fruit-flavored drinks, caffeinated coffees and teas

Breads, Cereals & Starches

Choose More Often

All whole grain bread or yeast products, baked goods and pasta made with oats, barley, quinoa, amaranth, millet, bulgur, rye, buckwheat, brown rice, wheat bran, wheat germ

Choose Less Often

Refined flours and cereals, quick breads, muffins, waffles, biscuits, pancakes, doughnuts, sweet rolls, pastries, corn bread, fritters, jams, jellies, marshmallows, molasses, honey, white sugar, syrup, hard candies

Desserts

Choose More Often

Fruit or soy desserts

Choose Less Often

Dairy desserts such as ice cream, pudding, flan, cheesecake; desserts made with whole milk, cream, lard, vegetable oils, coconut, chocolate

Eggs
Choose More Often
Hormone-free eggs limited to one per day, egg substitute
Choose Less Often
Eggs prepared with milk or cheese, fried eggs

Fats
Choose More Often
Butter, limited to 2 tsp per day, I Can't Believe It's Not Butter spray, PAM spray, olive, canola, sesame, and flax oils, avocado
Choose Less Often
Margarine, partially or fully hydrogenated fats, lard, shortening, all other vegetable oils such as sunflower, peanut, soybean, safflower, coconut, palm and cottonseed.

Fruits & Vegetables
Choose More Often
All fresh or frozen produce; emphasize blackberries, black currants, cantaloupe, cherries, cranberries, currants, grapefruit, kiwi, lemons, limes, mangoes, nectarines, oranges, papayas, peaches, plums, pumpkin, raspberries, red grapes, rhubarb, star fruit, strawberries, tangerines, arugula, bok choy, broccoli, Brussels sprouts, butternut squash, cabbage, carrots, cauliflower, chard, chives, collard greens, daikon radish, eggplant, endive, garlic, horseradish, kale, kohlrabi, leeks, mustard greens, onions, red cabbage, red peppers, rutabagas, scallions, shallots, sorrel, spinach, squash, tomatoes, turnips, turnip greens, yams
Choose Less Often
Commercially dried fruits containing sulfites, canned produce, vegetables in mayonnaise, vegetable oil, dressings, or covered in cheese

Meats, Fish & Other Protein

Choose More Often

Remove all visible fat before cooking; bake, broil, roast, stir-fry, grill, or steam lean meat, poultry, pork, and fish; choose often soy, salmon, tuna, mackerel, sardines packed in water; if you eat cheese, choose low-fat cheeses such as mozzarella, ricotta, cottage, Swiss, provolone; eat low-fat, plain yogurt; choose flax, sesame, and pumpkin seeds; choose chestnuts, almonds, walnuts, Brazil nuts; emphasize legumes.

Choose Less Often

All fried meats, poultry, or fish; fatty meats, nitrate containing meats such as sausage, bacon, hot dog, pepperoni, Canadian bacon, lunch meats; avoid meats in oil; limit cheeses, milk, peanut butter made with hydrogenated oils or additives, most other seeds and nuts such as sunflower, macadamia, pistachios, cashews, peanuts

Condiments

Choose More Often

Sea salt, salt, pepper, herbs and spices, lemon juice, relish, vinegar, ketchup, olives, salsa, parsley, garlic

Choose Less Often

Monosodium glutamate (MSG), artificial sweeteners, and artificial flavorings

Nutrition Action Plan for Breast Cancer

The incidence of breast cancer varies greatly around the world; these differences can be attributed in part to diet. Nutritional factors can influence the risk for breast cancer as well as the prognosis following diagnosis and treatment. A whole foods, plant-based diet is essential for anyone who wants to eat to beat breast cancer. Proper nutrition can rebuild cells, stimulate immune system function, protect against chemical and environmental toxins, and promote total body wellness. Here's how you can take action to beat cancer, one step at a time:

Step One: Stabilize Your Weight

If you've lost more than a few pounds, you should take immediate action to prevent further weight loss. As little as a 5-percent

Coach's Corner

Need a Head Start?

Here are some changes that you can make to your diet NOW that will help you get on the fast track to health! For this week:

1. Eat a yellow or orange fruit and vegetable every day.
2. Don't eat cheese.
3. Try a tofu fruit smoothie.
4. Eat a breakfast cereal that contains more than 10 grams of dietary fiber per serving.
5. Eat three vegetarian meals.

weight loss can dramatically reduce your ability to cope with treatment side effects and can lead to malnutrition, a complication that causes 40 percent of deaths in cancer patients. Don't risk delayed treatment and give cancer a chance to progress while you wait to regain your ability to tolerate treatment! Chapter 2 provides nutritional support recommendations to help you maintain your weight and prevent malnutrition.

Step Two: Lose Weight If You Need To

You may be able to decrease breast cancer recurrence by eating less fat! Diets high in calories and fat appear to increase the recurrence rate of breast cancer patients. Furthermore, postmenopausal women who were less overweight had better breast cancer survival rates. Some studies suggest that male breast cancer risk is also associated with obesity, although other studies do not link dietary factors with breast cancer in men. Excessive weight can elevate serum levels of insulin-like growth factor (IGF-1), which can cause cancer cells to grow and spread. Studies also suggest that higher levels of cancer-causing chemicals might be stored in excess fat tissue or that extra calories provide fuel for increased cell proliferation. The American Institute for Cancer Research recommends limiting weight gain to eleven pounds during adulthood. Often, changing what you eat can prompt weight loss; this jump-start to a leaner figure can be a strong motivational factor for continued adherence to a more healthful diet. Don't forget the other part of the weight maintenance equation. Physical activity can help increase muscle mass and burn calories.

As you adjust to new eating habits, your new energy requirements will be established as your body composition changes. Talk with a registered dietitian who can help you design a meal plan for realistic and safe weight loss. Avoid strict or fad diets in an attempt to lose weight. Quick weight loss deprives the body of valuable nutrients needed for growth and repair, and can reduce the fighting capacity of your immune system.

Step Three: Maintain a Healthy Gut

If your gastrointestinal tract doesn't work very well, you won't be able to utilize all the nutrients you consume. Eating small, frequent meals and taking digestive enzymes can aid digestion. To achieve a balance of beneficial bacteria in the intestines, eat yogurt or take a probiotic supplement on a regular basis. Researchers suggest that consuming fermented milk products, such as yogurt and buttermilk, may protect against breast cancer. Additional information on gastrointestinal health can be obtained in Chapter 3.

Step Four: Eat Five-a-Day

Consume at least five servings of produce each day. Numerous studies have reported a positive association between consuming produce and preventing breast cancer. Nature has packed cancer fighting phytochemicals into almost every kind of fruit and vegetable. Choose raw produce when possible, which provides more vitamins and minerals and has active plant enzymes. Chapter 7 will show you how easy it is to meet your daily produce goal.

Step Five: Cut the Fat

Limit fat to 20 percent of your total calories. Eating too much fat or the wrong kinds of fat has been associated with inflammatory conditions, suppressing the immune system, and breast cancer cell growth. High-fat diets rich in polyunsaturated fatty acids can stimulate breast cancer development and may promote metastasis. Fish and flax oil, sources of omega-3 fatty acids, may slow tumor growth and reduce the metastatic properties of breast cancer cells. Breast cancer patients with metastasis to the brain had increased survival times

Get the Phyto-Advantage!

Pile your plate high with powerful phyto-chemicals shown to stop breast cancer in its tracks! Your best plant choices contain allylic sulfides, anthocyanidins, carotenoids, catechins, citrus bioflavonoids, coumarins, curcumin, ellagic acid, indoles, and monoterpenes:

• Fruits: Blackberries, black currants, cantaloupe, cherries, cranberries, currants, grapes, grapefruit, kiwi, lemons, limes, mangoes, nectarines, oranges, papayas, peaches, persimmons, plums, pumpkin, raspberries, red grapes, rhubarb, star fruit, strawberries, tangerines

• Vegetables: Arugula, bok choy, broccoli, Brussels sprouts, butternut squash, cabbage, carrots, cauliflower, chard, chives, collard greens, daikon radish, eggplant, endive, garlic, horseradish, kale, kelp, kohlrabi, leeks, mustard greens, onions, red cabbage, red peppers, rutabagas, scallions (green onions), shallots, sorrel, spinach, squash, tomatoes, turnips, turnip greens, yams

when treated with radiation, omega-3 fatty acids, and bioflavonoids. Chapter 5 provides guidelines for avoiding unhealthy fats and balancing your diet with healthy fats. At least 15 percent of your daily calories (75 percent of your total fat allowance) should come from fats that contain monounsaturated and omega-3 fatty acids.

Step Six: Eat Soy

Consume several servings of soy foods per week. Soy has demonstrated effectiveness in slowing tumor growth and limiting the metastatic properties of breast cancer cells; however, conflicting research suggests that soy may stimulate the growth of estrogen-sensitive breast cancer cells. The American Dietetic Association suggests that women diagnosed with estrogen-receptor-positive breast cancer or women using Tamoxifen should completely avoid dietary soy supplements, which contain high doses of plant estrogens. Food sources of soy, which contain less concentrated levels of isoflavones, may be safely consumed in moderation (two to three servings per week) by women with any type of breast cancer. See Chapter 9 to learn more about how soy foods can fit into your diet.

Step Seven: Add Roughage

Consume between twenty-five and thirty-five grams of fiber each day. Fiber acts to detoxify the body by removing cancer-causing secondary bile acids, excess estrogens, and cholesterol through the stool. Breast cancer risk decreases as fiber consumption increases. Wheat bran has inhibited the growth of breast cancer cells in test tube and animal studies. Flaxseeds are rich in lignans, a form of fiber that has antiestrogenic characteristics. The majority of your diet should consist of whole grains, minimally processed grains, and plenty of legumes. Chapter 8 details how to put a variety of soluble and insoluble fibers in your diet.

Step Eight: Cut the Sweets

Limit refined sugar and flour intake to less than 10 percent of total calories. Sugar, as well as other highly processed carbohydrates, can raise blood sugar levels, creating an environment favorable for cancer cell growth and immune suppression. Chapter 6 offers suggestions for cutting the sugar from your diet and provides recommendations for stabilizing blood sugar levels.

Step Nine: Drink Up

A nationwide food consumption survey found that chronic mild dehydration was commonplace among Americans. To be well hydrated and flush your system of toxins, you should consume at least twelve cups of fluid per day if you are a man, nine cups of fluid per day if you are a woman. Drink reverse osmosis treated or distilled water. Consume green tea, which provides powerful antioxidant benefits and has been shown to inhibit the growth of human breast cancer cells. Avoid alcohol. Several studies have observed a risk of breast cancer associated with alcohol consumption.

Step Ten: Adopt Healthy Habits

See Chapter 1 for suggestions about a healthier lifestyle. If you smoke, stop now. Continuing to smoke can reduce the benefit of natural therapies and increase your risk for other diseases. Avoid foods that contain antibiotics, hormones, artificial sweeteners, colorings, or harmful additives. Eat organically grown produce or use a commercial fruit and vegetable wash to remove pesticides and waxes. Pesticide residues are thought to play a major role in breast cancer development. DDT, DDE, PCB, PCP, and chlordane have been shown to suppress immunity and alter hormone levels. Reduce consumption of well-done meats. When grilled or cooked at high temperatures, meat forms potent carcinogens harmful to breast tissue. Follow the food safety guidelines in Chapter 11 to reduce your risk of contracting a food-borne illness.

Step Eleven: Supplement Your Diet

The following nutritional supplements have demonstrated effectiveness or may have potential value in the treatment of breast cancer.

Consult with a healthcare professional to determine whether you have specific daily requirements for these or other dietary supplements:

- Multivitamin, without iron and boron
- Mixed carotenoids, 15 to 60 mg
- Vitamin C with bioflavonoids, 1,000 to 6,000 mg
- Vitamin E, 400 to 1,000 IU
- Selenium, 200 to 800 mcg
- EPA/DHA (fish oil), 1,000 to 6,000 mg
- Melatonin, 20 mg
- Calcium D-glucarate, 500 mg
- IP-6, 800 to 7,200 mg
- Inositol, 200 to 1,800 mg
- CoQ10, 100 to 400 mg
- Grape seed PCO extract, 150 to 300 mg
- Quercetin, 600 to 1,200 mg
- Garlic, 1 clove (equals 4,000 mcg allicin)
- Milk thistle, 200 to 400 mg

Sample Meal Plan

Eating healthy can be nutritious and delicious! The following sample meal plan provides approximately 1,625 calories, 242 grams of carbohydrate (60%), 81 grams of protein (20%), 37 grams of fat (20%), and 39 grams of fiber. A registered dietitian can help you adjust the portion sizes of this meal plan to meet your individual nutritional needs.

Quick Reference Guide to Eating Right

Consume Less	Consume More
Total fat (No more than 20 percent of your total calories)	Fruits and vegetables (5 to 9 servings per day)
Deep fat fried foods	Total dietary fiber intake (25 to 35 grams per day)
Charred or well-done meats	Whole grains (2 or more servings per day)
Margarine, shortening, and vegetable oils from corn, safflower, and soybeans	Legumes (1/2 cup per day)
Red meat (No more than 1 serving per week)	Yogurt (2 to 3 servings per week)
High-fat milk or cheese	Free-range animal products
Smoked or processed meats	Soy foods (2 to 3 servings per week)
Sugar, candy, desserts, or beverages containing sugar (No more than 10 percent of your total calories)	Cold water fish (3 servings per week)
White bread, rice, and pasta	Seaweed (dulse, kombu, wakime)
Salt	Flaxseeds (1 to 2 tablespoons per day)
Alcohol	Curried foods
	Extra virgin olive oil
	Green tea (3 to 4 cups per day)
	Purified water (9 to 12 cups per day)

Breakfast

Orange and banana slices	1 cup
Bran cereal	1/3 cup
Whole grain toast	1/2 medium
Boiled egg	1 large
Butter	1 tsp
Soy milk	1 cup
Green tea	1 cup
Purified water	1 cup

Lunch

Black bean soup	1 cup
Whole grain crackers	6 each
Mixed greens salad	1 cup
Herb vinaigrette	1 tsp
Cantaloupe	1/4 melon
Green tea	1 cup
Purified water	1 cup

Dinner

Steamed salmon fillet	4 oz
Curried wild rice	1 cup
Broccoli, steamed	1 cup
Dinner roll	1 small
Green tea	1 cup
Purified water	2 cups

Snack

Yogurt, plain, low fat	8 oz
Sliced strawberries	1 cup
Almonds, raw	1 oz
Herbal tea	1 cup
Purified water	1 cup

Food Selection Guide for Breast Cancer

Beverages

Choose More Often

Soy milk, fruit or vegetable juices, herbal teas, green tea, purified water

Choose Less Often

Cow's milk, buttermilk, nonfat dry milk, malts, shakes, frozen yogurt drinks, carbonated beverages, fruit-flavored drinks, caffeinated coffees and teas

Breads, Cereals & Starches

Choose More Often

All whole grain bread or yeast products, baked goods or pasta made with oats, barley, quinoa, amaranth, millet, bulgur, rye, buckwheat, brown rice, wheat bran, wheat germ

Choose Less Often

Refined flours and cereals, quick breads, muffins, waffles, biscuits, pancakes, doughnuts, sweet rolls, pastries, corn bread, fritters, jams, jellies, marshmallows, molasses, honey, white sugar, syrup, hard candies

Desserts

Choose More Often

Fruit or soy desserts

Choose Less Often

Dairy desserts such as ice cream, pudding, flan, cheesecake; desserts made with whole milk, cream, lard, vegetable oils, coconut, chocolate

Eggs
Choose More Often
Hormone-free eggs limited to one per day, egg substitute
Choose Less Often
Eggs prepared with milk or cheese, fried eggs

Fats
Choose More Often
Butter, limited to 2 tsp per day, I Can't Believe It's Not Butter spray, PAM spray, olive, canola, sesame and flax oils, avocado
Choose Less Often
Margarine, partially or fully hydrogenated fats, lard, shortening, all other vegetable oils such as sunflower, peanut, soybean, safflower, coconut, palm, and cottonseed

Fruits & Vegetables
Choose More Often
All fresh or frozen produce; emphasize blackberries, black currants, cantaloupe, cherries, cranberries, currants, grapes, grapefruit, kiwi, lemons, limes, mangoes, nectarines, oranges, papayas, peaches, persimmons, plums, pumpkin, raspberries, red grapes, rhubarb, star fruit, strawberries, tangerines, arugula, bok choy, broccoli, Brussels sprouts, butternut squash, cabbage, carrots, cauliflower, chard, chives, collard greens, daikon radish, eggplant, endive, garlic, horseradish, kale, kelp, kohlrabi, leeks, mustard greens, onions, red cabbage, red peppers, rutabagas, scallions, seaweed, shallots, sorrel, spinach, squash, tomatoes, turnips, turnip greens, yams
Choose Less Often
Commercially dried fruits containing sulfites, canned produce, vegetables in mayonnaise, vegetable oil, dressings, or covered in cheese

Meats, Fish & Other Protein

Choose More Often

Remove all visible fat before cooking; bake, roast, stew, stir-fry, boil, or steam lean meat, poultry, pork, and fish; choose often soy, salmon, tuna, mackerel, sardines packed in water; if you eat cheese, choose low-fat cheeses such as mozzarella, ricotta, cottage, Swiss, provolone; eat low-fat, plain yogurt; choose flax, sesame, and pumpkin seeds; choose chestnuts, almonds, walnuts, Brazil nuts; emphasize legumes and curried foods

Choose Less Often

All fried meats, poultry or fish, fatty meats, nitrate-containing meats such as sausage, bacon, hot dog, luncheon meats; limit well-done meats; avoid meats in oil; limit cheeses, milk, peanut butter made with hydrogenated oils or additives, most other seeds and nuts such as sunflower, macadamia, pistachios, cashews, peanuts

Condiments

Choose More Often

Sea salt, salt, pepper, herbs and spices, lemon juice, relish, vinegar, ketchup, olives, salsa; emphasize basil, celery seeds, citrus peels, garlic, onion, mint, mustard, parsley, and turmeric

Choose Less Often

Monosodium glutamate (MSG), artificial sweeteners, and artificial flavorings

Nutrition Action Plan for Colorectal Cancer

According to population study estimates, up to 80 percent of colorectal cancer can be linked to diet. A whole foods, plant-based diet is essential for anyone who wants to eat to beat cancer. Proper nutrition can rebuild cells, stimulate immune system function, protect against chemical and environmental toxins, and promote total body wellness. Here's how you can take action to beat colorectal cancer, one step at a time:

Step One: Stabilize Your Weight

If you've lost more than a few pounds, you should take immediate action to prevent further weight loss. As little as a 5-percent weight loss can dramatically reduce your ability to cope with treatment side effects and can lead to malnutrition, a complication that causes 40 percent of deaths in cancer patients. Don't risk delayed

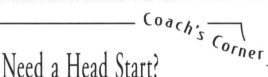

Coach's Corner

Need a Head Start?

Here are some changes that you can make to your diet NOW that will help you get on the fast track to health! For this week:

1. Eat cabbage or other cruciferous vegetables every day.
2. Don't eat red meat.
3. Try a glass of lite soy milk.
4. Skip dessert.
5. Eat two servings of nonfat plain yogurt.

treatment and give cancer a chance to progress while you wait to regain your ability to tolerate treatment! Chapter 2 provides nutritional support recommendations to help you maintain your weight and prevent malnutrition.

Step Two: Lose Weight If You Need To

The American Institute for Cancer Research recommends limiting weight gain to eleven pounds during adulthood. Excessive weight can elevate serum levels of insulin-like growth factor (IGF-1), which can cause colon cancer cells to grow and spread. Studies also suggest that higher levels of cancer-causing chemicals might be stored in excess fat tissue or that extra calories provide fuel for increased cell proliferation. Often, changing what you eat can prompt weight loss; this jumpstart to a leaner figure can be a strong motivational factor for continued adherence to a more healthful diet. Don't forget the other part of the weight maintenance equation. In addition to increasing muscle mass and burning calories, physical activity can also decrease the risk of colon cancer by lowering levels of prostaglandins that accelerate colon cell proliferation, while raising other prostaglandins that speed the movement of cancer-causing agents through the colon.

As you adjust to new eating habits, your new energy requirements will be established as your body composition changes. Talk with a registered dietitian who can help you design a meal plan for realistic and safe weight loss. Avoid strict or fad diets in an attempt to lose weight. Quick weight loss deprives the body of valuable nutrients needed for growth and repair, and can reduce the fighting capacity of your immune system.

Step Three: Maintain a Healthy Gut

Treatments for colorectal cancer often cause gastrointestinal tract dysfunction, and the cancer itself can contribute to bacterial dysbiosis. If your gut doesn't work very well, you won't be able to utilize all the nutrients you consume. Eating smaller meals and taking digestive enzymes can aid digestion. To achieve a balance of beneficial bacteria in the intestines, eat yogurt or take a probiotic supplement on a regular basis. Probiotics are health-promoting microbes that help reduce cancer-forming compounds in the colon. Additional information on gastrointestinal health can be obtained in Chapter 3.

Step Four: Eat Five-a-Day

Consume at least five servings of produce each day. Numerous studies have reported a positive association between consuming produce and preventing colorectal cancer. Nature has packed cancer-fighting phytochemicals into almost every kind of fruit and vegetable. Choose raw produce when possible, which provides more vitamins and minerals and has active plant enzymes. Chapter 7 will show you how easy it is to meet your daily produce goal.

Step Five: Cut the Fat

Limit fat to 20 percent of your total calories. A large number of studies have shown that colorectal tumor growth increases with the consumption of total fat and with saturated fat. Excessive fat causes increased production of bile acids, which can be converted to secondary bile acids in the colon wall. These toxic bile acids can stimulate cell division and promote the growth of colorectal tumors. Eating too much fat or the wrong kinds of fat has also been associated with inflammatory conditions and suppressed immune systems. Chapter 5 provides guidelines for avoiding unhealthy fats and balancing your diet with healthy fats. At least 15 percent of your daily calories (75 percent of your total fat allowance) should come from fats that contain monounsaturated and omega-3 fatty acids.

Gold Medal Action

Get the Phyto-Advantage!

Pile your plate high with powerful phyto-chemicals to stop colorectal cancer in its tracks! Your best plant choices contain allylic sulfides, anthocyanidins, carotenoids, catechins, citrus bioflavonoids, curcumins, ellagic acid, indoles, isothiocyanates, monoterpenes, and polyphenols:

• Fruit: Apples, black currants, blackberries, canta-loupe, cherries, cranberries, currants, grapes, grapefruit, kiwi, lemons, limes, mangoes, nectarines, oranges, papayas, peaches, raspberries, red grapes, rhubarb, star fruit, straw-berries, tangerines

• Vegetables: Arugula, bok choy, broccoli, broccoli sprouts, Brussels sprouts, butternut squash, cabbage, car-rots, cauliflower, chard, chives, collard greens, daikon radish, eggplant, endive, garlic, horseradish, kale, kelp, kohlrabi, leeks, lentils, mustard, mustard greens, onions, radishes, red cabbage, red peppers, rutabagas, scallions (green onions), shallots, sorrel, spinach, squash, tomatoes, turnips, turnip greens, yams

Step Six: Avoid Red Meat

The link between red meat consumption and colorectal cancer may be explained by the presence of dietary heme in red meat, which exposes the colon wall to irritants, and by the formation of hetero-cyclic amines, naturally occurring toxins that develop when meat is cooked. An international study reported a possible correlation between cholesterol and colon cancer mortality. Avoid processed, highly salted, or nitrate-containing meats, which may contribute to colorectal cancer. Soy, a high-protein alternative to animal foods, has been found to slow tumor growth and limit the metastatic properties of colorectal cancer cells. Other legumes (lentils, peas) are rich in folate, a nutrient essential for accurate colon cell division. Refer to Chapters 4 and 9 for suggestions about how to replace beef in your diet with complementary grain proteins and soy foods.

Step Seven: Eat Low-Fat Dairy Products

Populations that consume more dairy products have reported fewer deaths associated with colon and rectal cancers. Researchers speculate that nutrients found in dairy foods, such as calcium, vitamin D, conjugated linoleic acid, and butyrate may contribute to a reduced risk of developing colon tumors by binding excessive bile acids or reducing colon cell proliferation and differentiation. Choose hormone-free, skim, or nonfat milk, cheese, and yogurt products. If you aren't sure about the fat content of a cheese, remember this rule of thumb: White cheeses are usually lower in fat than yellow cheeses.

Step Eight: Cut the Sweets

Limit refined sugar and flour intake to less than 10 percent of your total calories. Refined sugar, especially sucrose (table sugar), has been linked to colorectal cancer in a number of studies. Highly processed carbohydrates can raise blood sugar levels and create an environment favorable for cancer cell growth and suppressing the immune system. Chapter 6 offers suggestions for cutting the sugar from your diet and provides recommendations for stabilizing blood sugar levels. Most research suggests that diets high in fiber can help prevent colon cancer. Whole grains contain fiber, vitamin E, and phytates, which protect the colon by removing cancer-causing secondary bile acids and cholesterol through the stool, and by decreasing free radical formation. Chapter 8 provides information on how to get more whole grains into your diet.

Step Nine: Drink Up

A nationwide food consumption survey found that chronic mild dehydration was commonplace among Americans. To be well hydrated and flush your system of toxins, you should consume at least twelve cups of fluid per day if you are a man, nine cups of fluid per day if you are a woman. Drink reverse osmosis treated or distilled water. Consume green tea, which provides powerful antioxidant benefits. Limit consumption of chlorinated water, which may be associated with increased risk of rectal cancer. Avoid alcohol, which has been found to stimulate cell proliferation in the rectum, leading to an increased risk of colorectal cancer.

Step Ten: Adopt Healthy Habits

See Chapter 1 for suggestions about a healthier lifestyle. If you smoke, stop now. Continuing to smoke can reduce the benefit of natural therapies and increase your risk for other diseases. Avoid foods that contain antibiotics, hormones, artificial sweeteners, colorings, or harmful additives such as nitrates or nitrites. When grilled or cooked at high temperatures, meat forms potent carcinogens harmful to colon tissue. Eat organically grown produce or use a commercial fruit and vegetable wash to remove pesticides and waxes. Follow the food safety guidelines in Chapter 11 to reduce your risk of contracting a food-borne illness.

Step Eleven: Supplement Your Diet

The following nutritional supplements have demonstrated effectiveness or may have potential value in the treatment of colorectal cancer. Consult with a healthcare professional to determine whether you have specific daily requirements for these or other dietary supplements:

- Multivitamin, without iron
- Mixed carotenoids, 15 to 60 mg
- Vitamin C with bioflavonoids, 1,000 to 6,000 mg
- Vitamin E, 400 to 1,000 IU
- Selenium, 200 to 800 mcg
- EPA (fish oil), 1,000 to 6,000 mg
- Isolated soy protein powder, 50 to 100 mg isoflavones
- Probiotic, 1 to 10 billion live cells
- Digestive enzymes
- Calcium, 500 to 1,500 mg
- Vitamin D, 100 to 400 IU
- Folic acid, 400 to 1,200 mcg
- Vitamin B$_{12}$, 400 to 1,200 mcg
- Curcuma root, 500 to 1,500 mg
- Modified citrus pectin, 1 to 3 Tbs
- IP-6, 800 to 7,200 mg
- Inositol, 200 to 1,800 mg
- *Coriolus versicolor* (PSK/PSP)
- CoQ10, 100 to 400 mg
- N-acetylcysteine (NAC), 250 to 500 mg
- Quercetin, 600 to 1,200 mg

Sample Meal Plan

Eating healthy can be nutritious and delicious! The following sample meal plan provides approximately 1,880 calories, 280 grams of carbohydrate (59%), 98 grams of protein (21%), 41 grams of fat (20%), and 35 grams of fiber. A registered dietitian can help you adjust the portion sizes of this meal plan to meet your individual nutritional needs.

Quick Reference Guide to Eating Right

Consume Less	Consume More
Total fat (No more than 20 percent of your total calories)	Fruits and vegetables (5 to 9 servings per day)
Deep fat fried foods	Total dietary fiber intake (25 grams per day)
Margarine, shortening, and vegetable oils from corn, safflower, and soybeans	Whole grains (2 or more servings per day)
Cholesterol	Low-fat dairy products
Red meat	Legumes (1/2 cup per day)
Charred or well-done meats	Yogurt (3 servings per week)
High-fat milk or cheese	Free-range lean poultry (2 servings per week)
Smoked or processed meats	Soy foods (2 servings per day)
Sugar, candy, desserts, or beverages containing sugar (No more than 10 percent of your total calories)	Cold water fish (3 servings per week)
White bread, rice, and pasta	Seaweed (dulse, kombu, wakime)
Salt	Curried foods
Alcohol	Extra virgin olive oil
	Green tea (3 to 4 cups per day)
	Purified water (9 to 12 cups per day)

Breakfast

Orange and banana slices	1/2 cup
Amaranth flakes	1 cup
Rye toast	2 slices
Butter	1 tsp
Skim milk	1 cup
Green tea	1 cup
Purified water	1 cup

Lunch

Black bean soup	2 cups
Whole grain crackers	10 each
Carrot, scallion relish	1/2 cup
Cantaloupe	1/4 melon
Green tea	1 cup
Purified water	1 cup

Dinner

Baked cod	4 oz
Curried wild rice medley	1 cup
Broccoli, steamed	1 cup
Raw spinach and radish salad	2 cups
Herb vinaigrette	2 tsp
Fresh peach	1 medium
Green tea	1 cup
Purified water	2 cups

Snack

Yogurt, plain, low fat	4 oz
Sliced strawberries	1/2 cup
Almonds, raw	1 oz
Herbal tea	1 cup
Purified water	1 cup

Food Selection Guide for Colorectal Cancer

Beverages

Choose More Often

Soy milk, fruit or vegetable juices, herbal teas, green tea, purified water

Choose Less Often

Cow's milk, buttermilk, nonfat dry milk, malts, shakes, frozen yogurt drinks, carbonated beverages, fruit-flavored drinks, caffeinated coffees and teas

Breads, Cereals & Starches

Choose More Often

All whole grain bread or yeast products, baked goods or pasta made with oats, barley, quinoa, amaranth, millet, bulgur, rye, buckwheat, brown rice, wheat bran, wheat germ

Choose Less Often

Refined flours and cereals, quick breads, muffins, waffles, biscuits, pancakes, doughnuts, sweet rolls, pastries, corn bread, fritters, jams, jellies, marshmallows, molasses, honey, white sugar, syrup, hard candies

Desserts

Choose More Often

Fruit or soy desserts on an occasional basis

Choose Less Often

Dairy desserts such as ice cream, pudding, flan, cheesecake; desserts made with whole milk, cream, lard, vegetable oils, coconut, chocolate

Eggs

Choose More Often

Hormone-free eggs, limited to three per week, or egg substitutes

Choose Less Often

Eggs prepared with milk or cheese, fried eggs

Fats

Choose More Often

Butter, limited to 2 tsp per day, I Can't Believe It's Not Butter spray, PAM spray, olive, canola, sesame, and flax oils, avocado

Choose Less Often

Margarine, partially or fully hydrogenated fats, lard, shortening, all other vegetable oils such as sunflower, peanut, soybean, safflower, coconut, palm, and cottonseed

Fruits & Vegetables

Choose More Often

All fresh or frozen produce; emphasize apples, blackberries, currants, cantaloupe, cherries, cranberries, grapes, grapefruit, kiwi, lemons, limes, mangoes, nectarines, oranges, papayas, peaches, plums, pumpkin, raspberries, red grapes, rhubarb, star fruit, strawberries, tangerines, arugula, bok choy, broccoli, broccoli sprouts, Brussels sprouts, butternut squash, cabbage, carrots, cauliflower, chard, chives, collard greens, daikon radish, eggplant, endive, garlic, horseradish, kale, kelp, kohlrabi, leeks, lentils, mustard greens, onions, red cabbage, red peppers, rutabagas, sauerkraut, scallions, seaweed, shallots, sorrel, spinach, squash, tomatoes, turnips, turnip greens, yams

Choose Less Often

Commercially dried fruits containing sulfites, canned produce, vegetables in mayonnaise, vegetable oil, dressings, or covered in cheese

Meats, Fish & Other Protein

Choose More Often

Remove all visible fat before cooking; bake, stew, roast, stir-fry, boil, or steam lean poultry and fish; choose often soy, salmon, tuna, mackerel, sardines packed in water; eat nonfat cheese, yogurt, and milk; choose walnuts, almonds, chestnuts, Brazil nuts; emphasize legumes and curried foods

Choose Less Often

All fried meats, poultry or fish, fatty or smoked meats, nitrate-containing meats such as sausage, pepperoni, hot dogs, luncheon meats; limit well-done meats; limit shellfish; avoid cheese, milk, peanut butter made with hydrogenated oils or additives, most other seeds and nuts such as sunflower, macadamia, pistachios, cashews, peanuts

Condiments

Choose More Often

Pepper, herbs and spices, lemon juice, relish, ketchup, olives, salsa; emphasize basil, horseradish, celery seeds, garlic, onion, mint, mustard, turmeric, and citrus peels

Choose Less Often

Salt, monosodium glutamate, artificial sweeteners, and artificial flavorings

Nutrition Action Plan for Upper Digestive Tract Cancer

Research findings suggest that similar dietary risk factors appear to be linked to head and neck, esophageal, and gastric (stomach) cancers. A whole foods, plant-based diet is essential for anyone who wants to eat to beat upper digestive tract cancer. Proper nutrition can rebuild cells, stimulate immune system function, protect against chemical and environmental toxins, and promote total body wellness. Here's how you can take action to beat cancer, one step at a time:

Step One: Maintain Appropriate Body Weight

Radiation treatment to the oral cavity can create thickening of saliva, poor appetite, or taste alterations, all of which can cause unintentional weight loss. If you've lost more than a few pounds,

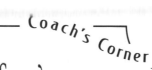
Coach's Corner

Need a Head Start?

Here are some changes that you can make to your diet NOW that will help you get on the fast track to health! For this week:

1. Eat a yellow or orange fruit and vegetable every day.
2. Avoid salty snack foods.
3. Don't eat processed meats.
4. Try a fruit and yogurt smoothie.
5. Eat three servings of beans.

you should take immediate action to prevent further weight loss. As little as a 5-percent weight loss can dramatically reduce your ability to cope with treatment side effects and can lead to malnutrition, a complication that causes 40 percent of deaths in cancer patients. Don't risk delayed treatment and give cancer a chance to progress while you wait to regain your ability to tolerate treatment! Chapter 2 provides nutritional support recommendations to help you maintain your weight and prevent malnutrition. It is particularly important to have a nutritional support plan prior to surgical treatment of the upper digestive tract.

Step Two: Lose Weight If You Need To

Excess body weight has been linked to an increased risk of esophageal and stomach cancer. Excessive weight can elevate serum levels of insulin-like growth factor (IGF-1), which can cause cancer cells to grow and spread. Studies also suggest that higher levels of cancer-causing chemicals might be stored in excess fat tissue or that extra calories provide fuel for increased cell proliferation. The American Institute for Cancer Research recommends limiting weight gain to eleven pounds during adulthood. Often, changing what you eat can prompt weight loss; this jump-start to a leaner figure can be a strong motivational factor for continued adherence to a more healthful diet. Don't forget the other part of the weight maintenance equation: Physical activity can help increase muscle mass and burn calories.

Avoid strict or fad diets in an attempt to lose weight. Quick weight loss deprives the body of valuable nutrients needed for growth and repair, and can reduce the fighting capacity of your immune system. As you adjust to new eating habits and recover from treatment, your new energy needs will be established as your body composition changes. Talk with a registered dietitian who can help you design a meal plan for an optimal weight during and after your treatment.

Get the Phyto-Advantage!

Pile your plate high with powerful phyto-chemicals to stop cancer in its tracks! Your best plant choices contain allylic sulfides, carotenoids, catechins, citrus bioflavonoids, coumarins, curcumins, ellagic acid, indoles, isothiocyanates, and phenols:

- Fruits: Apples, black currants, blackberries, cantaloupe, cranberries, currants, grapes, grapefruit, kiwi, lemons, limes, mangoes, nectarines, oranges, papayas, peaches, raspberries, star fruit, strawberries, tangerines

- Vegetables: Arugula, bok choy, broccoli, broccoli sprouts, Brussels sprouts, butternut squash, cabbage, carrots, cauliflower, chard, chives, collard greens, daikon radish, endive, garlic, horseradish, kale, kelp, kohlrabi, leeks, lentils, mustard, mustard greens, onions, radishes, red cabbage, red peppers, rutabagas, scallions (green onions), shallots, sorrel, spinach, squash, tomatoes, turnips, turnip greens, yams

Step Three: Maintain a Healthy Gut

Treatment side effects such as painful swallowing, dry throat, and indigestion occur frequently with upper digestive tract cancer. Esophageal or gastric surgery may require an antireflux or post-gastrectomy diet. If your gastrointestinal tract doesn't work very well, you won't be able to utilize all the nutrients you consume. Eating small, frequent meals and taking digestive enzymes can aid digestion. Irregular meals and binge eating have been associated with increased risk of stomach cancer. To achieve a balance of beneficial bacteria in the intestines, eat yogurt or take a probiotic supplement on a regular basis. Additional information on gastrointestinal health can be obtained in Chapter 3.

Step Four: Eat Five-a-Day

Consume at least five servings of produce each day. Numerous studies have reported a positive association between consuming produce and preventing upper digestive tract cancer. One study reported that by adding one serving per day of fruit or vegetable, risk of oral cancer risk was cut in half. Nature has packed cancer-fighting phytochemicals into almost every kind of fruit and vegetable. Choose raw produce when possible, which provides more vitamins and minerals and has active plant enzymes. Raw vegetable intake has been associated with a decreased risk of esophageal, stomach, and thyroid cancer. Avoid pickled and salted vegetables. Chapter 7 will show you how easy it is to meet your daily produce goal.

Step Five: Cut the Fat

Limit fat to 25 percent of your total calories. Eating too much fat or the wrong kinds of fat has been associated with inflammatory conditions, suppressed immune system function, and cancer cell growth. Saturated fats seem to promote tumors of the digestive tract, while omega-3 fatty acids have a protective effect. Researchers report that consumption of red meat, for example, is strongly associated with cancer of the oral cavity, pharynx, larynx, and esophagus. Chapter 5 provides guidelines for avoiding unhealthy fats and balancing your diet with healthy fats. At least 15 percent of your daily calories (60 percent of your total fat allowance) should come from fats that contain monounsaturated and omega-3 fatty acids.

Step Six: Eat Soy

Consume an average of two servings of soy foods daily. Soy, which doesn't contain saturated fat, is a high-protein alternative to animal foods that has been found to slow tumor growth and limit the metastatic properties of various cancer cells. Genistein, an isoflavone found in soybeans, was able to stop the proliferation of squamous cell cancers of the head and neck. Other legumes have been able to suppress the growth of stomach tumors.

A combined analysis of fourteen published studies found that fermented soy products such as miso and soy sauce might increase stomach cancer risk. However, none of these studies allowed for the effects of salt, which is positively associated with upper digestive cancer. Until further research is able to determine the exact effect of soy foods on upper digestive tract cancer, it is prudent to avoid fermented soy products. Instead, choose unfermented soy foods such as soy milk, tofu, and soybeans. See Chapter 9 to learn more about how soy foods can fit into your diet.

Step Seven: Limit Salt Intake

Globally, there is a strong and consistent association between salt or salted food intake and the risk of upper digestive tract cancer. Consuming salty snacks more than twice a month increased the risk of stomach cancer by 80 percent, according to one study. Salted meat, a potential source of nitrosamines, was associated with an increased risk for esophageal cancer. Pickled and salted vegetables should be avoided.

Step Eight: Add Roughage

Consume at least twenty-five grams of fiber each day. Fiber acts to detoxify the body by removing cancer-causing secondary bile acids and cholesterol through the stool. Whole grains and minimally processed starches should supply most of your energy. Chapter 8 details how to eat a variety of plant foods to ensure that you get a mixture of soluble and insoluble fibers.

Step Nine: Cut the Sweets

Limit refined sugar and flour intake to less than 10 percent of your total calories. Sugar, as well as other highly processed carbohydrates, can raise blood sugar levels, creating an environment favorable for cancer cell growth and suppressed immune system function. Chapter 6 offers suggestions for cutting the sugar from your diet and provides recommendations for stabilizing blood sugar levels.

Step Ten: Drink Up

A nationwide food consumption survey found that chronic mild dehydration was commonplace among Americans. To be well hydrated and flush your system of toxins, you should consume at least twelve cups of fluid per day if you are a man, nine cups of fluid per day if you are a woman. Drink reverse osmosis treated or distilled water. Consume green tea, which provides powerful antioxidant benefits. Avoid scalding hot coffee or tea, as drinking very hot beverages has been associated with an increased risk of esophageal cancer. Avoid alcohol, which has been positively associated with an increased risk of mouth, pharyngeal, and esophageal cancer, and is possibly linked to stomach cancer.

Step Eleven: Adopt Healthy Habits

See Chapter 1 for suggestions about a healthier lifestyle. If you smoke, stop now. Cigarette smoking is strongly associated with upper digestive cancer. Continuing to smoke can reduce the benefit of natural therapies and increase your risk for other diseases. Avoid foods that contain antibiotics, hormones, artificial sweeteners, colorings, or harmful additives. Eat organically grown produce or use a commercial fruit and vegetable wash to remove pesticides and waxes. When grilled or cooked at high temperatures, meat forms potent carcinogens that may increase the risk of stomach cancer. Follow the food safety guidelines in Chapter 11 to reduce your risk of contracting a food-borne illness.

Step Twelve: Supplement Your Diet

The following nutritional supplements have demonstrated effectiveness or may have potential value in the treatment of upper digestive cancer. Consult with a healthcare professional to determine whether you have specific daily requirements for these or other dietary supplements:

- Multivitamin, without iron
- Mixed carotenoids, 15 to 60 mg
- Vitamin C with bioflavonoids, 1,000 to 6,000 mg
- Vitamin E, 400 to 1,000 IU
- Selenium, 200 to 800 mcg
- EPA/DHA (fish oil), 1,000 to 6,000 mg
- Isolated soy protein powder, 50 to 100 mg isoflavones
- Zinc, 15 to 30 mg
- Copper, 1.5 to 3 mg
- Quercetin, 600 to 1,200 mg
- Probiotic, 1 to 10 billion live cells
- Digestive enzymes
- *Coriolus versicolor* (PSK/PSP)
- Gingko biloba, 120 to 240 mg standardized for 24 percent flavone glycosides
- Milk thistle, 200 to 400 mg

Quick Reference Guide to Eating Right

Consume Less	Consume More
Total fat (No more than 25 percent of your total calories)	Fruits and vegetables (5 to 9 servings per day)
Margarine, shortening, and vegetable oils from corn, safflower, and soybeans	Total dietary fiber intake (25 grams per day)
Deep fat fried foods	Whole grains (2 or more servings per day)
Red meat (No more than 1 serving per week)	Legumes (1/2 cup per day)
High-fat milk or cheese	Yogurt (3 servings per week)
Smoked or processed meats	Free-range animal products
Charred or well-done meats	Unfermented soy foods (2 servings per day)
Fermented soy products	Cold water fish (3 servings per week)
Sugar, candy, desserts, or beverages containing sugar (No more than 10 percent of your total calories)	Extra virgin olive oil
White bread, rice, and pasta	Seaweed (dulse, kombu, wakime)
Salt or salty foods	Green tea (3 to 4 cups per day)
Alcohol	Purified water (9 to 12 cups per day)

Sample Meal Plan

Eating healthy can be nutritious and delicious! The following sample meal plan provides approximately 1,850 calories, 256 grams of carbohydrate (55%), 89 grams of protein (20%), 52 grams of fat (25%), and 28 grams of dietary fiber. A registered dietitian can help you adjust the portion sizes of this meal plan to meet your individual nutritional needs.

Breakfast

Peach, sliced	1 medium
Wheat bran cereal	3/4 cup
Multi-grain toast	1 slice
Butter	1 tsp
Lite soy milk	1 cup
Green tea	1 cup
Purified water	1 cup

Lunch

Cooked soybeans	1/2 cup
Chicken breast	3 1/2 oz
Garlic couscous	1/2 cup
Carrots and broccoli, steamed	1 cup
Strawberries	1 cup
Vegetable juice	1 cup
Purified water	1 cup

Dinner

Salmon fillet	4 oz
Baked sweet potato	1 large
Stewed tomatoes	1 cup
Mixed greens salad	2 cups
Italian salad dressing	1 tsp
Apple slices	1 medium, sliced
Green tea	1 cup
Purified water	2 cups

Snack

Yogurt, plain, low fat	1 cup
Mango and papaya, cubed	1 cup
Herbal tea	1 cup
Purified water	1 cup

Food Selection Guide
for Upper Digestive Tract Cancer

Beverages

Choose More Often

Soy milk, fruit or vegetable juices, warm herbal or green teas, purified water

Choose Less Often

Cow's milk, buttermilk, nonfat dry milk, malts, shakes, frozen yogurt drinks, carbonated beverages, fruit-flavored drinks, caffeinated coffees and teas

Breads, Cereals & Starches

Choose More Often

All whole grain bread or yeast products, baked goods or pasta made with oats, barley, quinoa, amaranth, millet, bulgur, rye, buckwheat, brown rice, wheat bran, wheat germ

Choose Less Often

Refined flours and cereals, quick breads, muffins, waffles, biscuits, pancakes, doughnuts, sweet rolls, pastries, corn bread, fritters, jams, jellies, marshmallows, molasses, honey, white sugar, syrup, hard candies

Desserts

Choose More Often

Fruit or soy desserts

Choose Less Often

Dairy desserts such as ice cream, pudding, flan, cheesecake; desserts made with whole milk, cream, lard, vegetable oils, coconut, chocolate

Eggs

Choose More Often
Hormone-free eggs limited to one per day, egg substitute

Choose Less Often
Eggs prepared with milk or cheese, fried eggs

Fats

Choose More Often
Butter, limited to 2 tsp per day, I Can't Believe It's Not Butter spray, PAM spray, olive, canola, sesame, and flax oils, avocado

Choose Less Often
Margarine, partially or fully hydrogenated fats, lard, shortening, all other vegetable oils such as sunflower, peanut, soybean, safflower, coconut, palm, and cottonseed

Fruits & Vegetables

Choose More Often
All fresh or frozen produce; emphasize blackberries, black currants, cantaloupe, apples, cranberries, currants, grapes, grapefruit, kiwi, lemons, limes, mangoes, nectarines, oranges, papayas, peaches, raspberries, star fruit, strawberries, tangerines, arugula, bok choy, broccoli, Brussels sprouts, butternut squash, cabbage, carrots, cauliflower, chard, chives, collard greens, daikon radish, endive, garlic, kale, kohlrabi, leeks, mustard greens, onions, red cabbage, red peppers, rutabagas, scallions, seaweed, shallots, sorrel, spinach, squash, tomatoes, turnips, turnip greens, yams

Choose Less Often
Commercially dried fruits containing sulfites, canned produce, vegetables in mayonnaise, vegetable oil, dressings, or covered in cheese; avoid pickled vegetables, chilies

Meats, Fish & Other Protein

Choose More Often

Remove all visible fat before cooking; bake, roast, stir-fry, or steam lean meat, poultry, pork, and fish; choose often soy, salmon, tuna, mackerel; if you eat cheese, choose low-fat cheeses such as mozzarella, ricotta, cottage, Swiss, provolone; eat low-fat plain yogurt; choose flax, sesame, and pumpkin seeds, unsalted chestnuts, almonds, walnuts, Brazil nuts; emphasize legumes

Choose Less Often

All fried meats, poultry or fish, fatty meats, nitrate-containing meats such sausage, bacon, hot dog, luncheon meats; limit grilled meats; avoid meats in oil; limit cheese, milk, peanut butter made with hydrogenated oils or additives, most other seeds and nuts such as sunflower, macadamia, pistachios, cashews, peanuts

Condiments

Choose More Often

Pepper, herbs and spices, lemon juice, relish, ketchup, olives, garlic, onion, parsley, and celery seeds

Choose Less Often

Monosodium glutamate (MSG), salt, garlic salt, onion salt, soy sauce, chili powder, hot salsa, artificial sweeteners, and artificial flavorings

Nutrition Action Plan for Gynecological Cancer

Research findings suggest that similar dietary risk factors appear to be linked to ovarian and uterine cancers. A limited number of studies reveal that nutritional implications also exist for endometrial, cervical, and vulvar cancers. A whole foods, plant-based diet is beneficial for anyone who wants to eat to beat gynecological cancer. Proper nutrition can rebuild cells, stimulate immune system function, protect against chemical and environmental toxins, and promote total body wellness. Here's how you can take action to beat cancer, one step at a time:

Step One: Stabilize Your Weight

If you've lost more than a few pounds, you should take immediate action to prevent further weight loss. As little as a 5-percent weight

Coach's Corner

Need a Head Start?

Here are some changes that you can make to your diet NOW that will help you get on the fast track to health! For this week:

1. Eat a yellow or orange fruit and vegetable every day.
2. Eat two servings of fish.
3. Try a veggie burger.
4. Don't eat cheese.
5. Eat a breakfast cereal that contains more than 10 grams of dietary fiber per serving.

loss can dramatically reduce your ability to cope with treatment side effects and can lead to malnutrition, a complication that causes 40 percent of deaths in cancer patients. Don't risk delayed treatment and give cancer a chance to progress while you wait to regain your ability to tolerate treatment! Chapter 2 provides nutritional support recommendations to help you maintain your weight and prevent malnutrition.

Step Two: Lose Weight If You Need To

Excessive weight can elevate serum levels of insulin-like growth factor (IGF-1) and estrogen, which can prompt hormone-based cancer cells to grow and spread. Body size and fat have been found to be associated with an increased risk of endometrial cancer. Furthermore, a recent study revealed that leaner endometrial carcinoma patients survived longer than patients who had more body fat. The American Institute for Cancer Research recommends limiting weight gain to eleven pounds during adulthood. Often, changing what you eat can prompt weight loss; this jump-start to a leaner figure can be a strong motivational factor for continued adherence to a more healthful diet. Don't forget the other part of the weight maintenance equation: Physical activity can help increase muscle mass and burn calories.

As you adjust to new eating habits, your new energy requirements will be established based on your changing body composition. Talk with a registered dietitian who can help you design a meal plan for realistic and safe weight loss. Avoid strict or fad diets in an attempt to lose weight. Quick weight loss deprives the body of valuable nutrients needed for growth and repair, and can reduce the fighting capacity of your immune system.

Step Three: Maintain a Healthy Gut

Radiation to the pelvic area can cause GI complications such as diarrhea, ulcers, and narrowing of the bowels. If your gastrointestinal tract doesn't work very well, you won't be able to utilize all the nutrients you consume. Eating small, frequent meals and taking digestive enzymes can aid digestion. To achieve a balance of beneficial bacteria in the intestines, take a probiotic supplement on a regular basis. Additional information on gastrointestinal health can be obtained in Chapter 3.

Step Four: Eat Five-a-Day

Consume at least five servings of produce each day. Numerous studies have reported a positive relationship between consuming produce and preventing gynecological cancers. For example, one study revealed that the risk for vulvar cancer decreased with increased intake of dark yellow and orange vegetables. Nature has packed cancer-fighting phytochemicals into almost every kind of fruit and vegetable. Choose raw produce when possible, which provides more vitamins and minerals and has active plant enzymes. Chapter 7 will show you how easy it is to meet your daily produce goal.

Step Five: Cut the Fat

Limit fat to 25 percent of your total calories. Eating too much fat or the wrong kinds of fat has been associated with inflammatory conditions, suppressed immunity, and certain gynecological cancers. Based on population studies, diets rich in saturated fat appear to be linked to endometrial and ovarian cancers. Fish and flax oil, sources of omega-3 fatty acids, may slow tumor growth and reduce the metastatic properties of cancer cells. Eicosapentaenoic acid (EPA), found in salmon oil, exhibited powerful cytotoxic action on human cervical carcinoma cells in test tubes. Chapter 5 provides guidelines for avoiding unhealthy fats and balancing your diet with healthy fats. At least 15 percent of your daily calories (60 percent of your total fat allowance) should come from fats that contain monounsaturated and omega-3 fatty acids.

Gold Medal Action

Get the Phyto-Advantage!

Pile your plate high with powerful phyto-chemicals to stop gynecological cancers in their tracks! Your best plant choices contain allylic sulfides, carotenoids, citrus bioflavonoids, and indoles:

- Fruits: Black currants, cantaloupe, cranberries, grapefruit, kiwi, lemons, limes, mangoes, nectarines, oranges, papayas, peaches, pumpkin, raspberries, star fruit, strawberries, tangerines
- Vegetables: Arugula, bok choy, broccoli, Brussels sprouts, butternut squash, cabbage, carrots, cauliflower, chard, chives, collard greens, daikon radish, eggplant, endive, garlic, horseradish, kale, kelp, kohlrabi, leeks, mustard greens, onions, red peppers, rutabagas, scallions (green onions), shallots, sorrel, spinach, squash, tomatoes, turnips, turnip greens, yams

Step Six: Eat Soy

Consume several servings of soy foods per week. Soy has slowed tumor growth and limited the metastatic properties of many kinds of cancer. A study conducted at the University of Hawaii revealed that diets high in soy and other legumes protect against endometrial cancer. Until more research can be conducted, however, it is prudent for women with hormone-based cancers to follow soy intake guidelines established for estrogen-receptor-positive breast cancer. Specifically, women diagnosed with estrogen-sensitive cancers or women using Tamoxifen should completely avoid dietary soy supplements, which contain high doses of plant estrogens. Food sources of soy, which contain less concentrated levels of isoflavones, may be safely consumed in moderation (two to three servings per week). See Chapter 9 to learn more about how soy foods can fit into your diet.

Step Seven: Add Roughage

Consume between twenty-five and thirty-five grams of fiber each day. Fiber acts to detoxify the body by removing cancer-causing secondary bile acids, excess estrogens, and cholesterol through the stool. Flaxseeds are rich in lignans, a form of fiber that has antiestrogenic characteristics. Most of your diet should consist of whole grains, minimally processed grains, and plenty of legumes. A population study conducted in Poland showed that frequent consumption of legumes was associated with a significantly decreased risk of ovarian cancer. Chapter 8 explains how to put a variety of soluble and insoluble fibers in your diet.

Step Eight: Restrict Dairy Intake

Some studies reveal that consuming whole-fat dairy products may increase gynecological cancer risk, so always choose low-fat dairy products. If you have ovarian cancer, you may wish to avoid dairy foods altogether. Research suggests that women with ovarian cancer may have certain genetic or biochemical traits that make galactose, the sugar found in milk and other dairy products, toxic to ovarian germ cells. Animal studies have shown that once these germ cells are destroyed, ovarian cancer cells grow.

Step Nine: Cut the Sweets

Limit refined sugar and flour intake to less than 10 percent of your total calories. Sugar and other highly processed carbohydrates can raise blood sugar levels, creating an environment favorable for cancer cell growth and suppressed immunity. Chapter 6 offers suggestions for removing the sugar from your diet and provides recommendations for stabilizing blood sugar levels.

Step Ten: Drink Up

A nationwide food consumption survey found that chronic mild dehydration was commonplace among Americans. To be well hydrated and flush your system of toxins, women should consume at least nine cups of fluid per day. Drink reverse osmosis treated or distilled water. Limit consumption of chlorinated water, which may be associated with increased risk of ovarian and uterine cancer. Consume green tea, which provides powerful antioxidant benefits.

Step Eleven: Adopt Healthy Habits

See Chapter 1 for suggestions about a healthier lifestyle. If you smoke, stop now. Continuing to smoke can lessen the benefit of natural therapies and increase your risk for other diseases. Avoid foods that contain antibiotics, hormones, artificial sweeteners, colorings, or harmful additives. Eat organically grown produce or use a commercial fruit and vegetable wash to remove pesticides and waxes. DDT, DDE, PCB, PCP, and chlordane are chemicals that have been shown to suppress immunity and alter hormone levels. Follow the food safety guidelines in Chapter 11 to reduce your risk of contracting a food-borne illness.

Step Twelve: Supplement Your Diet

The following nutritional supplements have demonstrated effectiveness or may have potential value in the treatment of gynecological cancer. Consult with a healthcare professional to determine whether you have specific daily requirements for these or other dietary supplements:

- Multivitamin, without iron and boron
- Mixed carotenoids, 15 to 60 mg
- Vitamin C with bioflavonoids, 1,000 to 6,000 mg
- Vitamin E, 400 to 1,000 IU
- Selenium, 200 to 800 mcg
- EPA/DHA (fish oil), 1,000 to 6,000 mg
- Cod-liver oil, 1 to 2 Tbs
- Melatonin, 20 mg
- CoQ10, 100 to 400 mg
- Quercetin, 600 to 1,200 mg
- Folic acid, 2.5 to 10 mg
- Vitamin B_{12}, 1 mg
- Calcium citrate, 500 to 1,500 mg
- Probiotic, 1 to 10 billion live cells
- *Coriolus versicolor* (PSK/PSP)
- Gingko biloba, 120 to 240 mg standardized for 24 percent flavone glycosides
- Milk thistle, 200 to 400 mg

Sample Meal Plan

Eating healthy can be nutritious and delicious! The following sample meal plan provides approximately 1,517 calories, 218 grams of carbohydrate (57%), 78 grams of protein (21%), 37 grams of fat (22%), and 28 grams of fiber. A registered dietitian can help you adjust the portion sizes of this meal plan to meet your individual nutritional needs.

Quick Reference Guide to Eating Right

Consume Less	Consume More
Total fat (No more than 25 percent of your total calories)	Fruits and vegetables (5 to 9 servings per day)
Margarine, shortening, and vegetable oils from corn, safflower, and soybeans	Total dietary fiber (25 to 35 grams per day)
Deep fat fried foods	Whole grains (2 or more servings per day)
Red meat (No more than 1 serving per week)	Legumes (1/2 cup per day)
Dairy foods	Free-range animal products
Smoked or processed meats	Soy foods (2 to 3 servings per week)
Sugar, candy, desserts, or beverages containing sugar (No more than 10 percent of your total calories)	Cold water fish (3 servings per week)
White bread, rice, and pasta	Seaweed (dulse, kombu, wakime)
Alcohol	Flaxseeds (1 to 2 tablespoons per day)
	Extra virgin olive oil
	Green tea (3 to 4 cups per day)
	Purified water (9 to 12 cups per day)

Breakfast

Cantaloupe and pineapple, cubed	1 cup
Whole grain toast	1/2 medium
Boiled egg	1 large
Butter	1 tsp
Soy milk	1 cup
Green tea	1 cup
Purified water	1 cup

Lunch

Navy bean chili	1 cup
Whole grain bread stick	1 each
Mixed greens salad	1 cup
Herb vinaigrette	1 tsp
Cantaloupe	1/4 melon
Green tea	1 cup
Purified water	1 cup

Dinner

Steamed cod fillet	4 oz
Baked yam	1 medium
Broccoli and red pepper medley	1 cup
Dinner roll	1 small
Green tea	1 cup
Purified water	2 cups

Snack

Kiwi	2 medium
Almonds, raw	1 oz
Herbal tea	1 cup
Purified water	1 cup

Food Selection Guide for Gynecological Cancer

Beverages

Choose More Often

Soy milk, fruit or vegetable juices, herbal teas, green tea, purified water

Choose Less Often

Cow's milk, buttermilk, nonfat dry milk, malts, shakes, frozen yogurt drinks, carbonated beverages, fruit-flavored drinks, caffeinated coffees and teas

Breads, Cereals & Starches

Choose More Often

All whole grain bread or yeast products, baked goods or pasta made with oats, barley, quinoa, amaranth, millet, bulgur, rye, buckwheat, brown rice, wheat bran, wheat germ

Choose Less Often

Refined flours and cereals, quick breads, muffins, waffles, biscuits, pancakes, doughnuts, sweet rolls, pastries, corn bread, fritters, jams, jellies, marshmallows, molasses, honey, white sugar, syrup, hard candies

Desserts

Choose More Often

Fruit or soy desserts

Choose Less Often

Dairy desserts such as ice cream, pudding, flan, cheesecake; desserts made with whole milk, cream, lard, vegetable oils, coconut, chocolate

Eggs

Choose More Often

Hormone-free eggs limited to one per day, egg substitute

Choose Less Often

Eggs prepared with milk or cheese, fried eggs

Fats

Choose More Often

Butter, limited to 2 tsp per day, I Can't Believe It's Not Butter spray, PAM spray, olive, canola, sesame, and flax oils, avocado

Choose Less Often

Margarines, partially or fully hydrogenated fats, lard, shortening, all other vegetable oils such as sunflower, peanut, soybean, safflower, coconut, palm, and cottonseed

Fruits & Vegetables

Choose More Often

All fresh or frozen produce; emphasize black currants, cantaloupe, grapefruit, kiwi, lemons, limes, mangoes, nectarines, oranges, papayas, peaches, pumpkin, raspberries, star fruit, tangerines, arugula, bok choy, broccoli, Brussels sprouts, butternut squash, cabbage, carrots, cauliflower, chard, chives, collard greens, daikon radish, eggplant, endive, garlic, horseradish, kale, kelp, kohlrabi, leeks, mustard greens, onions, red peppers, rutabagas, scallions, seaweed, shallots, sorrel, spinach, squash, tomatoes, turnips, turnip greens, yams

Choose Less Often

Commercially dried fruits containing sulfites, canned produce, vegetables in mayonnaise, vegetable oil, dressings, or covered in cheese

Meats, Fish & Other Protein

Choose More Often

Remove all visible fat before cooking; bake, roast, stir-fry, or steam lean meat, poultry, pork, and fish; choose often soy, salmon, tuna, mackerel, sardines packed in water; limit or avoid all dairy; if you eat cheese, choose low-fat mozzarella, ricotta, cottage, Swiss, provolone, and eat low-fat plain yogurt; choose flax, sesame, and pumpkin seeds; choose chestnuts, almonds, walnuts, Brazil nuts; emphasize legumes

Choose Less Often

All fried meats, poultry or fish fatty meats, nitrate-containing meats such as sausage, bacon, hot dog, luncheon meats; limit grilling of meats; avoid meats in oil; limit cheeses, milk, peanut butter made with hydrogenated oils or additives, most other seeds and nuts such as sunflower, macadamia, pistachios, cashews, peanuts

Condiments

Choose More Often

Sea salt, salt, pepper, herbs and spices, lemon juice, relish, vinegar, ketchup, olives, onion, garlic, and salsa

Choose Less Often

Monosodium glutamate (MSG), artificial sweeteners, and artificial flavorings

Nutrition Action Plan for Leukemia

Research findings suggest that a whole foods, plant-based diet is essential for anyone with lymphocytic or myeloid leukemia. Proper nutrition can rebuild cells, stimulate immune system function, protect against chemical and environmental toxins, and promote total body wellness. Here's how you can take action to beat leukemia, one step at a time:

Step One: Maintain an Optimal Weight

If leukemia cells migrate and collect in your digestive tract, you may experience a loss of appetite and other gastrointestinal dysfunction, which can contribute to weight loss. If you've lost more than a few pounds, you should take immediate action to prevent further weight loss. As little as a 5-percent weight loss can dramatically reduce your ability to cope with treatment side effects

Coach's Corner

Need a Head Start?

Here are some changes that you can make to your diet NOW that will help you get on the fast track to health! For this week:

1. Eat a fruit and vegetable at every lunch and dinner.
2. Drink a glass of lite soy milk.
3. Don't eat red meat.
4. Eat whole grain bread or rolls.
5. Drink green tea.

and can lead to malnutrition, a complication that causes 40 percent of deaths in cancer patients. Don't risk delayed treatment and give cancer a chance to progress while you wait to regain your ability to tolerate treatment! It's important that you obtain adequate levels of nutrients to counteract the weakness and fatigue that often accompanies abnormal levels of red blood cells in people with leukemia. Proper nutrition will help you rebuild healthy cells and restore immune system function. Your new energy requirements will be established as your body composition changes. Talk with a registered dietitian who can help you design a meal plan for realistic weight management. Chapter 2 provides nutritional support recommendations to help you maintain your weight and prevent malnutrition.

Step Two: Maintain a Healthy Gut

If your gastrointestinal tract doesn't work very well, you won't be able to utilize all the nutrients you consume. Eating small, frequent meals and taking digestive enzymes can aid digestion. To achieve a balance of beneficial bacteria in the intestines, eat yogurt or take a probiotic supplement on a regular basis. Additional information on gastrointestinal health can be obtained in Chapter 3.

Step Three: Eat Five-a-Day

Consume at least five servings of produce each day. Several studies have reported a positive association between consuming produce and preventing leukemia. Nature has packed cancer-fighting phytochemicals into almost every kind of fruit and vegetable. Choose raw produce when possible, which provides more vitamins and minerals and has active plant enzymes. Chapter 7 will show you how easy it is to meet your daily produce goal.

Get the Phyto-Advantage!

Pile your plate high with powerful phyto-chemicals to stop leukemia in its tracks! Your best plant choices contain carotenoids, citrus bioflavonoids, coumarins, curcumins, and monoterpenes:

- **Fruits:** Black currants, cantaloupe, cherries, cranberries, grapefruit, kiwi, lemons, limes, mangoes, nectarines, oranges, papayas, peaches, pumpkin, raspberries, star fruit, strawberries, tangerines
- **Vegetables:** Arugula, broccoli, butternut squash, cabbage, carrots, chard, collard greens, daikon radish, endive, horseradish, kale, kelp, mustard greens, onions, red peppers, sorrel, spinach, squash, tomatoes, turnip greens, yams

Step Four: Cut the Fat

Limit fat to 25 percent of your total calories. Eating too much fat or the wrong kinds of fat has been associated with inflammatory conditions, suppressed immunity, and cancer cell growth. Eat lean versions of meat and dairy products. Chapter 5 provides guidelines for avoiding unhealthy fats and balancing your diet with healthy fats. At least 15 percent of your daily calories (60 percent of your total fat allowance) should come from fats that contain monounsaturated and omega-3 fatty acids.

Step Five: Eat Soy

Consume at least one serving of soy per day. Soy, which does not contain saturated fat, is a high-protein alternative to animal foods that has been found to slow tumor growth and limit the metastatic properties of various cancer cells. Genistein and daidzein, isoflavones found in soybeans, reduced proliferation rates and caused cellular death of three types of leukemia cells. See Chapter 9 to learn more about how soy foods can fit into your diet.

Step Six: Add Roughage

Consume at least twenty-five grams of fiber each day. Fiber acts to detoxify the body by removing cancer-causing secondary bile acids and cholesterol through the stool. Whole grains and minimally processed starches should supply most of your energy needs. Chapter 8 details how to eat a variety of plant foods to ensure that you get a mixture of soluble and insoluble fibers.

Step Seven: Cut the Sweets

Limit refined sugar and flour intake to less than 10 percent of your total calories. Sugar and other highly processed carbohydrates can raise blood sugar levels, creating an environment favorable for cancer cell growth and suppressed immunity. Chapter 6 offers suggestions for cutting the sugar from your diet and provides recommendations for stabilizing blood sugar levels.

Step Eight: Drink Up

A nationwide food consumption survey found that chronic mild dehydration was commonplace among Americans. To be well hydrated and flush your system of toxins, you should consume at least twelve cups of fluid per day if you are a man, nine cups of fluid per day if you are a woman. Drink reverse osmosis treated or distilled water. Consume green tea, which provides powerful antioxidant benefits and has inhibited tumor growth in several animal studies.

Step Nine: Adopt Healthy Habits

See Chapter 1 for suggestions about a healthier lifestyle. If you smoke, stop now. Continuing to smoke can reduce the benefit of natural therapies and increase your risk for other diseases. Avoid foods that contain antibiotics, hormones, artificial sweeteners, colorings, or harmful additives. Eat organically grown produce or use a commercial fruit and vegetable wash to remove pesticides and waxes. Follow the food safety guidelines in Chapter 11 to reduce your risk of contracting a food-borne illness.

Step Ten: Supplement Your Diet

The following nutritional supplements have demonstrated effectiveness or may have potential value in the treatment of leukemia. Consult with a healthcare professional to determine whether you have specific daily requirements for these or other dietary supplements:

- Multivitamin, with or without iron
- Mixed carotenoids, 15 to 60 mg
- Vitamin C with bioflavonoids, 1,000 to 6,000 mg
- Vitamin E, 400 to 1,000 IU
- Selenium, 200 to 800 mcg
- EPA/DHA (fish oil), 1,000 to 6,000 mg
- Cod-liver oil, 1 to 2 Tbs
- Isolated soy protein powder, 50 to 100 mg isoflavones
- Curcuma root, 500 to 1,500 mg
- Quercetin, 600 to 1,200 mg
- B complex
- Milk thistle, 200 to 400 mg

Quick Reference Guide to Eating Right

Consume Less	Consume More
Total fat (No more than 25 percent of your total calories)	Fruits and vegetables (5 to 9 servings per day)
Margarine, shortening, and vegetable oils from corn, safflower, and soybeans	Total dietary fiber (25 grams per day)
Deep fat fried foods	Whole grains (2 or more servings per day)
Red meat (No more than 1 serving per week)	Legumes (1/2 cup per day)
High-fat milk or cheese	Yogurt (3 servings per week)
Smoked or processed meats	Free-range animal products
Sugar, candy, desserts, or beverages containing sugar (No more than 10 percent of your total calories)	Soy foods (2 servings per day)
White bread, rice, and pasta	Cold water fish (3 servings per week)
Salt	Seaweed (dulse, kombu, wakime)
Alcohol	Curried foods
	Extra virgin olive oil
	Green tea (3 to 4 cups per day)
	Purified water (9 to 12 cups per day)

Sample Meal Plan

Eating healthy can be nutritious and delicious! The following sample meal plan provides approximately 1,802 calories, 252 grams of carbohydrate (56%), 86 grams of protein (19%), 50 grams of fat (25%), and 32 grams of dietary fiber. A registered dietitian can help you adjust the portion sizes of this meal plan to meet your individual nutritional needs.

Breakfast

Red grapefruit	1/2 medium
Oatmeal, cooked	1 cup
Multi-grain toast	1 slice
Butter	1 tsp
Lite soy milk	1 cup
Green tea	1 cup
Purified water	1 cup

Lunch

Cooked kidney beans	1/2 cup
Chicken tenderloin	3 1/2 oz
Brown rice	1/2 cup
Carrots and broccoli, steamed	1 cup
Cantaloupe wedge	1/4 melon
Vegetable juice	1 cup
Purified water	1 cup

Dinner

Salmon fillet	4 oz
Boiled new potatoes	1 large
Stewed tomatoes	1 cup
Raw spinach and radish salad	2 cups
Italian salad dressing	1 tsp
Apple slices	1 medium, sliced
Green tea	1 cup
Purified water	2 cups

Snack

Yogurt, plain, low fat	1 cup
Sliced strawberries	1 cup
Herbal tea	1 cup
Purified water	1 cup

Food Selection Guide for Leukemia

Beverages

Choose More Often

Soy milk, fruit or vegetable juices, herbal teas, green tea, purified water

Choose Less Often

Cow's milk, buttermilk, nonfat dry milk, malts, shakes, frozen yogurt drinks, carbonated beverages, fruit-flavored drinks, caffeinated coffees and teas

Breads, Cereals & Starches

Choose More Often

All whole grain bread or yeast products; baked goods or pasta made with oats, barley, quinoa, amaranth, millet, bulgur, rye, buckwheat, brown rice, wheat bran, wheat germ

Choose Less Often

Refined flours and cereals, quick breads, muffins, waffles, biscuits, pancakes, doughnuts, sweet rolls, pastries, corn bread, fritters, jams, jellies, marshmallows, molasses, honey, white sugar, syrup, hard candies

Desserts

Choose More Often

Fruit or soy desserts

Choose Less Often

Dairy desserts such as ice cream, pudding, flan, cheesecake; desserts made with whole milk, cream, lard, vegetable oils, coconut, chocolate

Eggs

Choose More Often
Hormone-free eggs limited to one per day, egg substitute

Choose Less Often
Eggs prepared with milk or cheese, fried eggs

Fats

Choose More Often
Butter, limited to 2 tsp per day, I Can't Believe It's Not Butter spray, PAM spray, olive, canola, sesame, and flax oils, avocado

Choose Less Often
Margarines, partially or fully hydrogenated fats, lard, shortening, all other vegetable oils such as sunflower, peanut, soybean, safflower, coconut, palm, and cottonseed

Fruits & Vegetables

Choose More Often
All fresh or frozen produce; emphasize black currants, cantaloupe, cherries, cranberries, grapefruit, kiwi, lemons, limes, mangoes, nectarines, oranges, papayas, peaches, pumpkin, raspberries, star fruit, strawberries, tangerines, arugula, broccoli, butternut squash, carrots, chard, collard greens, daikon radish, endive, horseradish, kale, kelp, mustard greens, onions, red cabbage, red peppers, seaweed, sorrel, spinach, squash, tomatoes, turnip greens, yams

Choose Less Often
Commercially dried fruits containing sulfites, canned produce, vegetables in mayonnaise or vegetable oil, dressings, or covered in cheese

Meats, Fish & Other Protein
Choose More Often

Remove all visible fat before cooking; bake, broil, roast, stir-fry, grill, or steam lean meat, poultry, pork, and fish; choose often soy, salmon, tuna, mackerel, sardines packed in water; if you eat cheese, choose low-fat cheeses such as mozzarella, ricotta, cottage, Swiss, provolone; eat low-fat plain yogurt; choose flax, sesame, and pumpkin seeds; choose chestnuts, almonds, walnuts, Brazil nuts; emphasize legumes and curried foods

Choose Less Often

All fried meats, poultry or fish; fatty meats, nitrate-containing meats like sausage, bacon, hot dog, pepperoni, Canadian bacon, lunch meats; avoid meats in oil; limit cheese, milk, peanut butter made with hydrogenated oils or additives, most other seeds and nuts such as sunflower, macadamia, pistachios, cashews, peanuts

Condiments
Choose More Often

Sea salt, salt, pepper, herbs and spices, lemon juice, relish, vinegar, ketchup, olives, salsa; emphasize citrus peels, celery seed, basil, parsley, mint, mustard, ginger, and turmeric

Choose Less Often

Monosodium glutamate (MSG), artificial sweeteners, and artificial flavorings

Nutrition Action Plan for Lung Cancer

Lung cancer is the leading cause of death for men and women in the U.S., according to the American Cancer Society. Researchers have found that tobacco use and poor dietary habits are associated with lung cancer. A whole foods, plant-based diet rich in phytochemicals is essential for anyone who wants to beat cancer. Proper nutrition can rebuild cells, stimulate immune system function, protect against chemical and environmental toxins, and promote total body wellness. Here's how you can take action to beat lung cancer, one step at a time:

Step One: Stabilize Your Weight

Usually, a diagnosis of lung cancer is linked to an undernourished state. Many newly diagnosed lung cancer patients have at least one abnormal nutritional parameter, leading to poorer survival rates. If you've lost more than a few pounds or are hypermetabolic due to

Coach's Corner

Need a Head Start?

Here are some changes that you can make to your diet NOW that will help you get on the fast track to health! For this week:

1. Eat a fruit and vegetable at every lunch and dinner.
2. Try a fruit and soy smoothie.
3. Eat two servings of fish.
4. Eat less than two eggs.
5. Drink green tea.

cancer cachexia, you should take immediate action to prevent further weight loss. As little as a 5-percent weight loss can dramatically reduce your ability to cope with treatment side effects and can lead to severe malnutrition, a complication that causes 40 percent of deaths in cancer patients. Don't risk delayed treatment and give cancer a chance to progress while you wait to regain your ability to tolerate treatment! Chapter 2 provides nutritional support recommendations to help you maintain your weight and prevent malnutrition.

Step Two: Lose Weight If You Need To

A new study published in the *American Journal of Epidemiology* revealed that being overweight is tied to lung cancer risk. This study was the first to link obesity with lung cancer. Excessive weight may elevate serum levels of insulin like growth factor (IGF-1), which can cause cancer cells to grow and spread. Studies also suggest that higher levels of cancer-causing chemicals might be stored in excess fat tissue or that extra calories provide fuel for increased cell proliferation.

The American Institute for Cancer Research recommends limiting weight gain to eleven pounds during adulthood. Often, changing what you eat can prompt weight loss; this jump-start to a leaner figure can be a strong motivational factor for continued adherence to a more healthful diet. Don't forget the other part of the weight maintenance equation: Physical activity can help increase muscle mass and burn calories.

As you adjust to new eating habits, your new energy requirements will be established as your body composition changes. Talk with a registered dietitian who can help you design a meal plan for realistic and safe weight loss. Avoid strict or fad diets in an attempt to lose weight. Quick weight loss deprives the body of valuable nutrients needed for growth and repair, and can reduce the fighting capacity of your immune system.

Step Three: Maintain a Healthy Gut

Complications of the gastrointestinal tract such as heartburn, increased mucus production, and throat irritation are common in patients receiving chest radiation. If your gastrointestinal tract does not work very well, you won't be able to utilize all the nutrients you consume. To achieve a balance of beneficial bacteria in the intestines, eat yogurt or take a probiotic supplement on a regular basis. Eating small, frequent meals and taking enzymes can aid absorption of nutrients. Digestive enzymes also have anticancer action. Bromelain, an enzyme found in pineapple, demonstrated antimetastatic properties in laboratory animals with implanted lung cancer cells. Additional information on gastrointestinal health and natural first aid for treatment side effects can be obtained in Chapter 3.

Step Four: Eat Five-a-Day

Consume at least five servings of produce each day. Numerous studies have reported a positive association between consuming produce and preventing lung cancer. Nature has packed cancer-fighting phytochemicals into almost every kind of fruit and vegetable. Choose raw produce when possible, which provides more vitamins and minerals and has active plant enzymes. Chapter 7 will show you how easy it is to meet your daily produce goal.

Step Five: Cut the Fat

Limit fat to 25 percent of total calories. Dietary fat can alter inflammatory conditions, immune system function, and impact lung cancer. Eating high-fat foods, especially those containing saturated fats and polyunsaturated fats, appears to be linked to lung cancer risk. Diets high in eggs and other cholesterol-rich foods possibly increase the risk of lung cancer. Healthy fats, such as omega-3 fatty acids, were found to suppress the growth of lung cancer tumors.

Get the Phyto-Advantage!

Pile your plate high with powerful phytochemicals to stop lung cancer in its tracks! Your best plant choices contain allylic sulfides, carotenoids, citrus bioflavonoids, coumarins, curcumin, ellagic acid, indoles, and isothiocyanates:

• Fruits: Black currants, cantaloupe, cranberries, grapefruit, grapes, kiwi, lemons, limes, mangoes, nectarines, oranges, papayas, peaches, pumpkin, raspberries, star fruit, strawberries, tangerines

• Vegetables: Arugula, bok choy, broccoli, broccoli sprouts, Brussels sprouts, butternut squash, cabbage, carrots, cauliflower, chard, chives, collard greens, daikon radish, eggplant, endive, garlic, horseradish, kale, kelp, kohlrabi, leeks, mustard greens, onions, radishes, red peppers, rutabagas, scallions (green onions), shallots, sorrel, spinach, squash, tomatoes, turnips, turnip greens, yams

Chapter 5 provides guidelines for avoiding unhealthy fats and balancing your diet with healthy fats. At least 15 percent of your daily calories (60 percent of your total fat allowance) should come from fats that contain monounsaturated and omega-3 fatty acids.

Step Six: Eat Soy

Consume an average of two servings of soy foods daily. Soy, which doesn't contain saturated fat, is a high-protein alternative to animal foods that has slowed tumor growth and limited the metastatic properties of various cancer cells. Researchers found that the soy isoflavone genistein was able to induce lung cancer cell death. See Chapter 9 to learn more about how soy foods can fit into your diet.

Step Seven: Add Roughage

Consume at least twenty-five grams of fiber each day. Fiber acts to detoxify the body by removing cancer-causing secondary bile acids, excess estrogens, and cholesterol through the stool. Whole grains and minimally processed starches should supply most of your energy needs. Chapter 8 details how to eat a variety of plant foods to ensure that you get a mixture of soluble and insoluble fibers.

Step Eight: Cut the Sweets

Limit refined sugar and flour intake to less than 10 percent of your total calories. Sugar, as well as other highly processed carbohydrates, can raise blood sugar levels, creating an environment favorable for cancer cell growth and suppressed immunity. Chapter 6 offers suggestions for cutting the sugar from your diet and provides recommendations for stabilizing blood sugar levels.

Step Nine: Drink Up

A nationwide food consumption survey found that chronic mild dehydration was commonplace among Americans. To be well hydrated and flush your system of toxins, you should consume at least twelve cups of fluid per day if you are a man, nine cups of fluid per day if you are a woman. Drink reverse osmosis treated or distilled water. Some studies show drinking green and black tea offer a protective effect against lung cancer. Limit or avoid alcohol. There may be a possible link between moderate alcohol consumption and lung cancer risk.

Step Ten: Adopt Healthy Habits

If you smoke, stop now. Continuing to smoke can reduce the benefit of natural therapies and increase your risk for other diseases. See Chapter 1 for suggestions about a healthier lifestyle. Avoid foods that contain antibiotics, hormones, artificial sweeteners, colorings, or harmful additives. Eat organically grown produce or use a commercial fruit and vegetable wash to remove pesticides and waxes. When grilled or cooked at high temperatures, meat forms potent carcinogens that may be harmful to lung tissue. Follow the food safety guidelines in Chapter 11 to reduce your risk of contracting a food-borne illness.

Step Eleven: Supplement Your Diet

The following nutritional supplements have demonstrated effectiveness or may have potential value in the treatment of lung cancer. Consult with a healthcare professional to determine whether you have specific daily requirements for these or other dietary supplements:

- Multivitamin, without iron
- Mixed carotenoids, 15 to 60 mg
- Vitamin C with bioflavonoids, 1,000 to 6,000 mg
- Vitamin E, 400 to 1,000 IU
- Selenium, 200 to 800 mcg
- EPA/DHA (fish oil), 1,000 to 6,000 mg
- Cod-liver oil, 1 to 2 Tbs
- Isolated soy protein powder, 50 to 100 mg isoflavones
- Melatonin, 20 mg
- Curcuma root, 500 to 1,500 mg
- N-acetylcysteine (NAC), 250 to 500 mg
- Quercetin, 600 to 1,200 mg

- Bromelain, 1,000 to 3,000 mg
- CoQ10, 100 to 400 mg
- *Coriolus versicolor* (PSK/PSP)
- Gingko biloba, 120 to 240 mg standardized for 24 percent flavone glycosides
- Milk thistle, 200 to 400 mg
- Zinc, 15 to 30 mg

Quick Reference Guide to Eating Right

Consume Less	Consume More
Total fat (No more than 25 percent of your total calories)	Fruits and vegetables (5 to 9 servings per day)
Margarine, shortening, and vegetable oils from corn, safflower, and soybeans	Total dietary fiber (25 grams per day)
Deep fat fried foods	Whole grains (2 or more servings per day)
Red meat (No more than I serving per week)	Legumes (1/2 cup per day)
Eggs (Limited to three per week)	Yogurt (3 servings per week)
High-fat milk or cheese	Free-range animal products
Smoked or processed meats	Soy foods (2 servings per day)
Charred or well-done meats	Cold water fish (3 servings per week)
Sugar, candy, desserts, or beverages containing sugar (No more than 10 percent of your total calories)	Seaweed (dulse, kombu, wakime)
White bread, rice, and pasta	Extra virgin olive oil
Salt	Green tea (3 to 4 cups per day)
Alcohol	Purified water (9 to 12 cups per day)

Sample Meal Plan

Eating healthy can be nutritious and delicious! The following sample meal plan provides approximately 1,855 calories, 259 grams of carbohydrate (56%), 88 grams of protein (19%), 52 grams of fat (25%), and 31 grams of dietary fiber. A registered dietitian can help you adjust the portion sizes of this meal plan to meet your individual nutritional needs.

Breakfast

Pineapple juice	4 oz
Oatmeal, cooked	1 cup
Multi-grain toast	1 slice
Butter	1 tsp
Lite soy milk	1 cup
Green tea	1 cup
Purified water	1 cup

Lunch

Stir-fried tofu	3 1/2 oz
Whole wheat pasta and bean salad	1 cup
Cauliflower and broccoli, steamed	1 cup
Cantaloupe wedge	1/4 melon
Carrot juice	1 cup
Purified water	1 cup

Dinner

Salmon fillet	4 oz
Brown rice pilaf	1 cup
Steamed spinach	1 cup
Tossed greens	2 cups

Italian salad dressing	1 tsp
Grapes	15
Green tea	1 cup
Purified water	2 cups

Snack

Yogurt, plain, low fat	1 cup
Sliced strawberries	1 cup
Herbal tea	1 cup
Purified water	1 cup

Food Selection Guide for Lung Cancer

Beverages

Choose More Often

Soy milk, fruit or vegetable juices, herbal teas, green tea, purified water

Choose Less Often

Cow's milk, buttermilk, nonfat dry milk, malts, shakes, frozen yogurt drinks, carbonated beverages, fruit-flavored drinks, caffeinated coffees and teas

Breads, Cereals & Starches

Choose More Often

All whole grain bread or yeast products; baked goods or pasta made with oats, barley, quinoa, amaranth, millet, bulgur, rye, buckwheat, brown rice, wheat bran, wheat germ

Choose Less Often

Refined flours and cereals, quick breads, muffins, waffles, biscuits, pancakes, doughnuts, sweet rolls, pastries, cornbread, fritters, jams, jellies, marshmallows, molasses, honey, white sugar, syrup, hard candies

Desserts

Choose More Often

Fruit or soy desserts

Choose Less Often

Dairy desserts such as ice cream, pudding, flan, cheesecake; desserts made with whole milk, cream, lard, vegetable oils, coconut, chocolate

Eggs

Choose More Often

Hormone-free eggs limited to three per week, egg substitute

Choose Less Often

Eggs prepared with milk or cheese, fried eggs

Fats

Choose More Often

Butter, limited to 2 tsp per day, I Can't Believe It's Not Butter spray, PAM spray, olive, canola, sesame, and flax oils, avocado

Choose Less Often

Margarine, partially or fully hydrogenated fats, lard, shortening, all other vegetable oils such as sunflower, peanut, soybean, safflower, coconut, palm, and cottonseed

Fruits & Vegetables

Choose More Often

All fresh or frozen produce; emphasize black currants, cantaloupe, cranberries, grapefruit, grapes, kiwi, lemons, limes, mangoes, nectarines, oranges, papayas, peaches, pumpkin, raspberries, star fruit, strawberries, tangerines, arugula, bok choy, broccoli, broccoli sprouts, Brussels sprouts, butternut squash, cabbage, carrots, cauliflower, chard, chives, collard greens, daikon radish, eggplant, endive, garlic, horseradish, kale, kelp, kohlrabi, leeks, mustard greens, onions, radishes, red peppers, rutabagas, scallions, seaweed, shallots, sorrel, spinach, squash, tomatoes, turnips, turnip greens, yams

Choose Less Often

Commercially dried fruits containing sulfites, canned produce, vegetables in mayonnaise, vegetable oil, dressings, or covered in cheese

Meats, Fish & Other Protein

Choose More Often

Remove all visible fat before cooking; bake, broil, roast, stir-fry, grill, or steam lean meat, poultry, pork, and fish; choose often soy, salmon, tuna, mackerel, sardines packed in water; if you eat cheese, choose low-fat cheeses such as mozzarella, ricotta, cottage, Swiss, provolone; eat low-fat plain yogurt; choose flax, sesame, and pumpkin seeds; choose chestnuts, almonds, walnuts, Brazil nuts; emphasize legumes and curried foods

Choose Less Often

All fried meats, poultry or fish, fatty meats, nitrate-containing meats such as sausage, bacon, hot dog, pepperoni, Canadian bacon, lunch meats; avoid meats in oil; limit cheese, milk, peanut butter made with hydrogenated oils or additives, most other seeds and nuts such as sunflower, macadamia, pistachios, cashews, peanuts

Condiments

Choose More Often

Sea salt, salt, pepper, herbs and spices, lemon juice, relish, vinegar, ketchup, olives, salsa; emphasize parsley, turmeric, mustard, garlic, onion, and horseradish

Choose Less Often

Monosodium glutamate (MSG), artificial sweeteners, and artificial flavorings

Nutrition Action Plan for Melanoma

A whole foods, plant-based diet is essential for anyone who wants to eat to beat cancer. Proper nutrition can rebuild cells, stimulate immune system function, protect against chemical and environmental toxins, and promote total body wellness. Here's how you can take action to beat melanoma, the most serious cancer of the skin, one step at a time:

Step One: Maintain an Optimal Weight

Treatment side effects can affect appetite, which may contribute to weight loss. If you've lost more than a few pounds, you should take immediate action to prevent further weight loss. As little as a 5-percent weight loss can dramatically reduce your ability to cope with treatment side effects and can lead to malnutrition, a complication that causes 40 percent of deaths in cancer

Coach's Corner

Need a Head Start?

Here are some changes that you can make to your diet NOW that will help you get on the fast track to health! For this week:

1. Eat a yellow or orange fruit and vegetable every day.
2. Try a soy burger.
3. Don't eat red meat.
4. Eat two servings of fish.
5. Eat three vegetarian meals.

patients. Don't risk delayed treatment and give cancer a chance to progress while you wait to regain your ability to tolerate treatment! Proper nutrition will help you rebuild healthy cells and restore immune system function. Chapter 2 provides nutritional support recommendations to help you maintain your weight and prevent malnutrition.

Often, changing what you eat can prompt weight loss. If you need to lose some weight in order to achieve an optimal weight, this jump-start to a leaner figure can be a strong motivational factor for continued adherence to a more healthful diet. Don't forget the other part of the weight maintenance equation. Physical activity can help increase muscle mass and burn calories. Your new energy requirements will be established based on your changing body composition. Talk with a registered dietitian who can help you establish a meal plan for realistic weight management.

Step Two: Maintain a Healthy Gut

Depending on the treatment you receive, your digestive function may be compromised. If your gastrointestinal tract doesn't work very well, you won't utilize all the nutrients you consume. Eating small, frequent meals and taking digestive enzymes can aid digestion. To achieve a balance of beneficial bacteria in the intestines, eat yogurt or take a probiotic supplement on a regular basis. Additional information on gastrointestinal health can be obtained in Chapter 3.

Step Three: Eat Five-a-Day

Consume at least five servings of produce each day. Numerous studies have reported a positive association between consuming produce and preventing melanoma. Nature has packed cancer-fighting phytochemicals into almost every kind of fruit and vegetable.

Choose raw produce when possible, which provides more vitamins and minerals and has active plant enzymes. Chapter 7 will show you how easy it is to meet your daily produce goal.

Gold Medal Action

Get the Phyto-Advantage!

Pile your plate high with powerful phyto-chemicals to stop melanoma in its tracks! Your best plant choices contain allylic sulfides, carotenoids, citrus bioflavonoids, coumarins, curcumins and monoterpenes:

- Fruits: Blackberries, cantaloupe, cherries, cranberries, grapefruit, kiwi, lemons, limes, mangoes, nectarines, oranges, papayas, peaches, pumpkin, raspberries, star fruit, strawberries, tangerines
- Vegetables: Arugula, broccoli, butternut squash, cabbage, carrots, chard, chives, collard greens, daikon radish, eggplant, endive, garlic, horseradish, kale, kelp, leeks, onions, red peppers, scallions (green onions), shallots, sorrel, spinach, squash, tomatoes, turnip greens, yams

Step Four: Cut the Fat

Limit fat to 25 percent of your total calories. Eating too much fat or the wrong kinds of fat has been associated with inflammatory conditions, suppressed immunity, and cancer cell growth. Polyunsaturated fats appear to enhance the growth of melanoma cells, whereas omega-3 fatty acids were found to suppress the growth of melanoma. In vitro, EPA was able to stop melanoma cells from spreading. Chapter 5 provides guidelines for avoiding unhealthy fats and balancing your diet with healthy fats. At least 15 percent of your daily calories (60 percent of your total fat allowance) should come from fats that contain monounsaturated and omega-3 fatty acids.

Step Five: Go Vegetarian

Several studies suggest restricting animal foods may have anti-cancer benefit for melanoma patients. Dietary restriction of tyrosine and phenylalanine, two amino acids found primarily in animal foods, lowered activation factors responsible for melanoma cell growth. Foods high in tyrosine and phenylalanine include cheddar and cottage cheese, mackerel, beef, and poultry. Soybeans are also quite high in tyrosine and phenylalanine, but foods made from soybeans contain much smaller amounts of these amino acids. Soy powder appears to be helpful as well. Animals studies have shown diets supplemented with soy protein isolates reduced melanoma cell growth and metastasis to the lung. You can find the amino acid content of foods listed in a food composition book, or contact a registered dietitian for a list of foods highest in phenylalanine and tyrosine. See Chapter 9 to see how soy foods can fit into your diet.

Step Six: Add Roughage

Consume at least twenty-five grams of fiber each day. Fiber acts to detoxify the body by removing cancer-causing secondary bile acids and cholesterol through the stool. Whole grains and minimally processed starches should supply most of your energy. Chapter 8 details how to eat a variety of plant foods to ensure that you get a mixture of soluble and insoluble fibers.

Step Seven: Cut the Sweets

Limit refined sugar and flour intake to less than 10 percent of your total calories. Sugar and other highly processed carbohydrates can raise blood sugar levels, creating an environment favorable for cancer cell growth and suppressed immunity. Chapter 6 offers suggestions for cutting the sugar from your diet and provides recommendations for stabilizing blood sugar levels.

Step Eight: Drink Up

A nationwide food consumption survey found that chronic mild dehydration was commonplace among Americans. To be well hydrated and flush your system of toxins, you should consume at least twelve cups of fluid per day if you are a man, nine cups of fluid per day if you are a woman. Drink reverse osmosis treated or distilled water. Consume green tea, which provides powerful antioxidant benefits.

Step Nine: Adopt Healthy Habits

See Chapter 1 for suggestions about a healthier lifestyle. Apply sunscreen when you spend time outdoors. If you smoke, stop now. Continuing to smoke can reduce the benefit of natural therapies and increase your risk for other diseases. Avoid foods that contain antibiotics, hormones, artificial sweeteners, colorings, or harmful additives. Eat organically grown produce or use a commercial fruit and vegetable wash to remove pesticides and waxes. Follow the food safety guidelines in Chapter 11 to reduce your risk of contracting a food-borne illness.

Step Ten: Supplement Your Diet

The following nutritional supplements have demonstrated effectiveness or may have potential value in the treatment of melanoma. Consult with a healthcare professional to determine whether you have specific daily requirements for these or other dietary supplements:

- Multivitamin, without iron
- Mixed carotenoids, 15 to 60 mg
- Vitamin C with bioflavonoids, 1,000 to 6,000 mg
- Vitamin E, 400 to 1,000 IU
- Selenium, 200 to 800 mcg
- EPA/DHA (fish oil), 1,000 to 6,000 mg
- Isolated soy protein powder, 50 to 100 mg isoflavones
- Vitamin B_6, 50 mg
- Boswellia, standardized 37.5 percent boswellic acids, 400 to 1,200 mg
- Quercetin, 660 to 1,200 mg
- Cod-liver oil, 1 to 2 Tbs
- *Panax ginseng,* standardized 4 to 7 percent ginsenosides, 100 to 200 mg
- Licorice, 250 to 500 mg

Sample Meal Plan

Eating healthy can be nutritious and delicious! The following sample meal plan provides approximately 1,855 calories, 259 grams of carbohydrate (56%), 88 grams of protein (19%), 52 grams of fat (25%), and 27 grams of dietary fiber. A registered dietitian can help you adjust the portion sizes of this meal plan to meet your individual nutritional needs.

Quick Reference Guide to Eating Right

Consume Less	Consume More
Total fat (No more than 25 percent of your total calories)	Fruits and vegetables (5 to 9 servings per day)
Margarine, shortening, and vegetable oils from corn, safflower, and soybeans	Total dietary fiber (25 grams per day)
Deep fat fried foods	Whole grains (2 or more servings per day)
Meat	Legumes (1/2 cup per day)
Dairy	Yogurt (3 servings per week)
Smoked or processed meats	Free-range animal products
Sugar, candy, desserts, or beverages containing sugar (No more than 10 percent of your total calories)	Soy foods (2 servings per day)
White bread, rice, and pasta	Curried foods
Salt	Cold water fish (3 servings per week)
Alcohol	Extra virgin olive oil
	Green tea (3 to 4 cups per day)
	Purified water (9 to 12 cups per day)

Breakfast

Raisins	2 tablespoons
Oatmeal	1 cup
Multi-grain toast	1 slice
Butter	1 tsp
Lite soy milk	1 cup
Green tea	1 cup
Purified water	1 cup

Lunch

Tempeh	3 1/2 oz
Couscous and bean salad	1 cup
Olive oil	1 tsp
Eggplant	1/2 medium
Cantaloupe wedge	1/4 melon
Vegetable juice	1 cup
Purified water	1 cup

Dinner

Tuna fillet	4 oz
Brown rice pilaf	1 cup
Collard greens	1 cup
Tomato slices	1 medium
Mango and papaya medley	1/2 cup
Green tea	1 cup
Purified water	2 cups

Snack

Yogurt, plain, low fat	1 cup
Sliced fresh peaches	1 cup
Herbal tea	1 cup
Purified water	1 cup

Food Selection Guide for Melanoma

Beverages

Choose More Often

Soy milk, fruit or vegetable juices, herbal teas, green tea, purified water

Choose Less Often

Cow's milk, buttermilk, nonfat dry milk, malts, shakes, frozen yogurt drinks, carbonated beverages, fruit-flavored drinks, caffeinated coffees and teas

Breads, Cereals & Starches

Choose More Often

All whole grain bread or yeast products, baked goods or pasta made with oats, barley, quinoa, amaranth, millet, bulgur, rye, buckwheat, brown rice, wheat bran, wheat germ

Choose Less Often

Refined flours and cereals, quick breads, muffins, waffles, biscuits, pancakes, doughnuts, sweet rolls, pastries, corn bread, fritters, jams, jellies, marshmallows, molasses, honey, white sugar, syrup, hard candies

Desserts

Choose More Often

Fruit or soy desserts

Choose Less Often

Dairy desserts such as ice cream, pudding, flan, cheesecake; desserts made with whole milk, cream, lard, vegetable oils, coconut, chocolate

Eggs

Choose More Often

Hormone-free eggs limited to one per day, egg substitute

Choose Less Often

Eggs prepared with milk or cheese, fried eggs

Fats

Choose More Often

Butter, limited to 2 tsp per day, I Can't Believe It's Not Butter spray, PAM spray, olive, canola, sesame and flax oils, avocado

Choose Less Often

Margarine, partially or fully hydrogenated fats, lard, shortening, all other vegetable oils such as sunflower, peanut, soybean, safflower, coconut, palm, and cottonseed

Fruits & Vegetables

Choose More Often

All fresh or frozen produce; emphasize blackberries, cantaloupe, cherries, cranberries, grapefruit, kiwi, lemons, limes, mangoes, nectarines, oranges, papayas, peaches, pumpkin, raspberries, star fruit, strawberries, tangerines, arugula, broccoli, butternut squash, cabbage, carrots, chard, chives, collard greens, daikon radish, eggplant, endive, garlic, horseradish, kale, kelp, leeks, onions, red peppers, scallions, shallots, sorrel, spinach, squash, tomatoes, turnip greens, yams

Choose Less Often

Commercially dried fruits containing sulfites, canned produce, vegetables in mayonnaise, vegetable oil, dressings, or covered in cheese

Meats, Fish & Other Protein

Choose More Often

Remove all visible fat before cooking; bake, broil, roast, stir-fry, grill, or steam lean meat, poultry, pork, and fish; choose often soy, salmon, tuna, sardines packed in water; if you eat cheese, choose low-fat cheeses such as mozzarella, ricotta, Swiss, provolone; eat low-fat plain yogurt; choose flax, sesame, and pumpkin seeds; choose chestnuts, almonds, walnuts, Brazil nuts; emphasize legumes and curried foods

Choose Less Often

All fried meats, poultry or fish, fatty meats, nitrate-containing meats such as sausage, bacon, hot dog, pepperoni, Canadian bacon, lunch meats; avoid meats in oil; limit cheese, milk, peanut butter made with hydrogenated oil or additives, most other seeds and nuts such as sunflower, macadamia, pistachios, cashews, peanuts

Condiments

Choose More Often

Sea salt, salt, pepper, herbs and spices, lemon juice, relish, vinegar, ketchup, olives, salsa; emphasize basil, celery seed, citrus peels, garlic, mint, mustard, onion, parsley, and turmeric

Choose Less Often

Monosodium glutamate (MSG), artificial sweeteners, and artificial flavorings

Nutrition Action Plan for Non-Hodgkin's Lymphoma

A whole foods, plant-based diet can rebuild cells and stimulate immunity. These are important factors for non-Hodgkin's lymphoma, which occurs more frequently in individuals with a compromised immune system. Non-Hodgkin's lymphoma is the fifth most common cancer in the United States, yet there is limited information on the association between diet and this disease. Population studies suggest certain nutritional factors can protect against chemical and environmental toxins, reduce lymphoma risk, and stop lymphoma cells from growing. Here's how you can take action to beat cancer of the lymph glands, one step at a time:

Step One: Stabilize Your Weight

If you've lost more than a few pounds, you should take immediate action to prevent further weight loss. As little as a 5-percent weight loss can dramatically reduce your ability to cope with treatment side

Coach's Corner

Need a Head Start?

Here are some changes that you can make to your diet NOW that will help you get on the fast track to health! For this week:

1. Eat a fruit and vegetable at every lunch and dinner.
2. Try a soy burger.
3. Eat two servings of fish.
4. Drink green tea.
5. Buy organic foods or use a commercial produce wash.

effects and can lead to malnutrition, a complication that causes 40 percent of deaths in cancer patients. Don't risk delayed treatment and give cancer a chance to progress while you wait to regain your ability to tolerate treatment! Chapter 2 provides nutritional support recommendations to help you maintain your weight and prevent malnutrition.

Step Two: Lose Weight If You Need To

The American Institute for Cancer Research recommends limiting weight gain to eleven pounds during adulthood. Excessive weight can elevate serum levels of insulin-like growth factor (IGF-1), which can cause cancer cells to grow and spread. Studies also suggest that higher levels of cancer-causing chemicals might be stored in excess fat tissue or that extra calories provide fuel for increased cell proliferation. Restricting calories has been shown to be beneficial. For example, a low-calorie diet increased lymphocyte and macrophage activity and stopped the growth of lymphoma in animals. Often, changing what you eat can prompt weight loss; this jump-start to a leaner figure can be a strong motivational factor for continued adherence to a more healthful diet. Don't forget the other part of the weight maintenance equation: Physical activity can help increase muscle mass and burn calories.

As you adjust to new eating habits, your new energy requirements will be established as your body composition changes. Talk with a registered dietitian who can help you design a meal plan for realistic and safe weight loss. Avoid strict or fad diets in an attempt to lose weight. Quick weight loss deprives the body of valuable nutrients needed for growth and repair, and can reduce the fighting capacity of your immune system.

Step Three: Maintain a Healthy Gut

If your gastrointestinal tract doesn't work very well, you won't be able to utilize all the nutrients you consume. Eating small, frequent meals and taking digestive enzymes can aid digestion. To achieve a balance of beneficial bacteria in the intestines, eat yogurt or take a probiotic supplement on a regular basis. Additional information on gastrointestinal health can be obtained in Chapter 3.

Step Four: Eat Five-a-Day

Consume at least five servings of produce each day. Several studies have reported a positive association between consuming produce and preventing lymphoma. Nature has packed cancer-fighting

Gold Medal Action

Get the Phyto-Advantage!

Pile your plate high with powerful phytochemicals to stop lymphoma in its tracks! Your best plant choices contain anthocyanadins, carotenes, citrus bioflavonoids, curcumin, and indoles:

• Fruits: Blackberries, black currants, cantaloupe, cherries, cranberries, currants, grapefruit, kiwi, lemons, limes, mangoes, nectarines, oranges, papayas, peaches, plums, pumpkin, raspberries, red grapes, rhubarb, star fruit, strawberries, tangerines

• Vegetables: Arugula, bok choy, broccoli, Brussels sprouts, butternut squash, cabbage, carrots, cauliflower, chard, collard greens, daikon radish, eggplant, endive, horseradish, kale, kohlrabi, lentils, mustard greens, onions, red peppers, rutabagas, sorrel, spinach, squash, tomatoes, turnips, turnip greens, yams

phytochemicals into almost every kind of fruit and vegetable. Choose raw produce when possible, which provides more vitamins and minerals and has active plant enzymes. Chapter 7 will show you how easy it is to meet your daily produce goal.

Step Five: Cut the Fat

Limit fat to 25 percent of your total calories. Eating too much fat or the wrong kinds of fat has been associated with inflammatory conditions, suppressed immunity, and cancer cell growth. Intake of animal fats and unhealthy trans-fatty acids (found in hydrogenated foods) were found to be associated with an increased risk of non-Hodgkin's lymphoma. Animals with lymphoma who were treated with fish oil, arginine, and Adriamycin had fewer recurrences and lived longer than controls. Chapter 5 provides guidelines for avoiding unhealthy fats and balancing your diet with healthy fats. At least 15 percent of your daily calories (60 percent of your total fat allowance) should come from fats that contain monounsaturated and omega-3 fatty acids.

Step Six: Eat Soy

Consume an average of two servings of soy foods daily. Soy, which doesn't contain saturated fat, is a high-protein alternative to animal foods that has been found to slow tumor growth and limit the metastatic properties of various cancer cells. Soy, added to a restricted calorie diet, improved immunity in animals with lymphoma. See Chapter 9 to learn more about how soy foods can fit into your diet.

Step Seven: Add Roughage

Consume at least twenty-five grams of fiber each day. Fiber acts to detoxify the body by removing cancer-causing secondary bile acids and cholesterol through the stool. Whole grains and minimally processed starches should supply most of your energy. Chapter 8 details how to eat a variety of plant foods to ensure that you get a mixture of soluble and insoluble fibers.

Step Eight: Cut the Sweets

Limit refined sugar and flour intake to less than 10 percent of your total calories. Sugar, as well as other highly processed carbohydrates, can raise blood sugar levels, creating an environment favorable for cancer cell growth and suppressed immunity. Chapter 6 offers suggestions for cutting the sugar from your diet and provides recommendations for stabilizing blood sugar levels.

Step Nine: Drink Up

A nationwide food consumption survey found that chronic mild dehydration was commonplace among Americans. To be well hydrated and flush your system of toxins, you should consume at least twelve cups of fluid per day if you are a man, nine cups of fluid per day if you are a woman. Drink reverse osmosis treated or distilled water. Consume green tea, which provides powerful antioxidant benefits and has been able to induce apoptosis (death) in human lymphoma cells. Nitrate contamination in drinking water has been associated with non-Hodgkin's lymphoma risk.

Step Ten: Adopt Healthy Habits

See Chapter 1 for suggestions about a healthier lifestyle. If you smoke, stop now. Continuing to smoke can reduce the benefit of natural therapies and increase your risk for other diseases. Avoid foods that contain antibiotics, hormones, artificial sweeteners, colorings, or harmful additives such as nitrates. Eat organically grown produce or use a commercial fruit and vegetable wash to remove pesticides and waxes. Pesticide residues should be avoided, as certain herbicides have been shown to increase mortality and incidence rates of lymphoma. When grilled or cooked at high temperatures, meat forms potent carcinogens that are associated with an increased risk of lymphoma. Follow the food safety guidelines in Chapter 11 to reduce your risk of contracting a food-borne illness.

Step Eleven: Supplement Your Diet

The following nutritional supplements have demonstrated effectiveness or may have potential value in the treatment of non-Hodgkin's lymphoma. Consult with a healthcare professional to determine whether you have specific daily requirements for these or other dietary supplements:

- Multivitamin, without iron
- Mixed carotenoids, 15 to 60 mg
- Vitamin C with bioflavonoids, 1,000 to 6,000 mg
- Vitamin E, 400 to 1,000 IU
- Selenium, 200 to 800 mcg
- EPA/DHA (fish oil), 1,000 to 6,000 mg
- Isolated soy protein powder, 50 to 100 mg isoflavones
- Curcuma root, 500 to 1,500 mg
- N-acetylcysteine (NAC), 250 to 500 mg
- CoQ10, 100 to 400 mg
- Garlic, 1 clove (equals 4,000 mcg allicin)
- Milk thistle, 200 to 400 mg

Quick Reference Guide to Eating Right

Consume Less	Consume More
Total fat (No more than 25 percent of your total calories)	Fruits and vegetables (5 to 9 servings per day)
Deep fat fried foods	Total dietary fiber (25 grams per day)
Margarine, shortening, and vegetable oils from corn, safflower, and soybeans	Whole grains (2 or more servings per day)
Hydrogenated or partially hydrogenated fats	Legumes (1/2 cup per day)
Red meat (No more than 1 serving per week)	Yogurt (3 servings per week)
Charred or well-done meats	Free-range animal products
High-fat milk or cheese	Organic foods
Smoked or processed meats	Soy foods (2 servings per day)
Sugar, candy, desserts, or beverages containing sugar (No more than 10 percent of your total calories)	Curried foods
White bread, rice, and pasta	Cold water fish (3 servings per week)
Salt	Extra virgin olive oil
Alcohol	Green tea (3 to 4 cups per day)
Restrict Calorie Intake	Purified water (9 to 12 cups per day)

Sample Meal Plan

Eating healthy can be nutritious and delicious! The following sample meal plan provides approximately 1,802 calories, 251 grams of carbohydrate (55%), 92 grams of protein (20%), 53 grams of fat (25%), and 30 grams of dietary fiber. A registered dietitian can help you adjust the portion sizes of this meal plan to meet your individual nutritional needs.

Breakfast

Red grapefruit	1/2 medium
Buckwheat pancakes	3- to 4-inch cakes
Butter	1 tsp
Lite soy milk	1 cup
Green tea	1 cup
Purified water	1 cup

Lunch

Whole wheat, pasta, chicken and bean bake	2 cups
Carrots and broccoli, steamed	1 cup
Cantaloupe wedge	1/4 melon
Vegetable juice	1 cup
Purified water	1 cup

Dinner

Salmon fillet	4 oz
Wild rice	2/3 cup
Stewed tomatoes	1 cup
Mixed greens salad	2 cups
Italian salad dressing	1 tsp
Tangerine	1 medium
Green tea	1 cup
Purified water	2 cups

Snack

Yogurt, plain, low fat	1 cup
Berry medley	1 cup
Herbal tea	1 cup
Purified water	1 cup

Food Selection Guide for Non-Hodgkin's Lymphoma
Beverages
Choose More Often
Soy milk, fruit or vegetable juices, herbal teas, green tea, purified water
Choose Less Often
Cow's milk, buttermilk, nonfat dry milk, malts, shakes, frozen yogurt drinks, carbonated beverages, fruit-flavored drinks, caffeinated coffees and teas

Breads, Cereals & Starches
Choose More Often
All whole grain bread or yeast products, baked goods or pasta made with oats, barley, quinoa, amaranth, millet, bulgur, rye, buckwheat, brown rice, wheat bran, wheat germ
Choose Less Often
Refined flours and cereals, quick breads, muffins, waffles, biscuits, pancakes, doughnuts, sweet rolls, pastries, corn bread, fritters, jams, jellies, marshmallows, molasses, honey, white sugar, syrup, hard candies

Desserts
Choose More Often
Fruit or soy desserts
Choose Less Often
Dairy desserts such as ice cream, pudding, flan, cheesecake; desserts made with whole milk, cream, lard, vegetable oils, coconut, chocolate

Eggs

Choose More Often

Hormone-free eggs limited to one per day, egg substitute

Choose Less Often

Eggs prepared with milk or cheese, fried eggs

Fats

Choose More Often

Butter, limited to 2 tsp per day, I Can't Believe It's Not Butter spray, PAM spray, olive, canola, sesame and flax oils, avocado

Choose Less Often

Margarine, partially or fully hydrogenated fats, lard, shortening, all other vegetable oils such as sunflower, peanut, soybean, safflower, coconut, palm, and cottonseed

Fruits & Vegetables

Choose More Often

All fresh or frozen produce; emphasize blackberries, cantaloupe, cherries, cranberries, grapefruit, kiwi, lemons, limes, mangoes, nectarines, oranges, papayas, peaches, pumpkin, raspberries, star fruit, strawberries, tangerines, arugula, broccoli, butternut squash, cabbage, carrots, chard, chives, collard greens, daikon radish, eggplant, endive, garlic, horseradish, kale, kelp, leeks, onions, red peppers, scallions, shallots, sorrel, spinach, squash, tomatoes, turnip greens, yams

Choose Less Often

Commercially dried fruits containing sulfites, canned produce, vegetables in mayonnaise, vegetable oil, dressings, or covered in cheese

Meats, Fish & Other Protein

Choose More Often

Remove all visible fat before cooking; bake, broil, roast, stir-fry, grill, or steam lean meat, poultry, pork, and fish; choose often soy, salmon, tuna, sardines packed in water; if you eat cheese, choose low-fat cheeses such as mozzarella, ricotta, Swiss, provolone; eat low-fat plain yogurt; choose flax, sesame, and pumpkin seeds; choose chestnuts, almonds, walnuts, Brazil nuts; emphasize legumes and curried foods

Choose Less Often

All fried meats, poultry or fish, fatty meats, nitrate-containing meats such as sausage, bacon, hot dog, pepperoni, Canadian bacon, lunch meats; avoid meats in oil; limit cheese, milk, peanut butter made with hydrogenated oil or additives, most other seeds and nuts such as sunflower, macadamia, pistachios, cashews, peanuts

Condiments

Choose More Often

Sea salt, salt, pepper, herbs and spices, lemon juice, relish, vinegar, ketchup, olives, salsa; emphasize basil, celery seed, citrus peels, garlic, mint, mustard, onion, parsley, and turmeric

Choose Less Often

Monosodium glutamate (MSG), artificial sweeteners, and artificial flavorings

Nutrition Action Plan for Pancreatic Cancer

Nutritional therapy can positively influence the outcome of pancreatic cancer. In one small study, patients with inoperable pancreatic cancer, stage II through stage IV, were treated with large doses of enzymes, supplements, detox procedures, and organic foods. At the end of one year, 81 percent of the patients were alive, compared to the national average of a 25-percent survival rate at one year.

A whole foods, plant-based diet is essential for anyone who wants to eat to beat cancer. Proper nutrition can rebuild cells, stimulate immune system function, protect against chemical and environmental toxins, and promote total body wellness. Here's how you can take action to beat pancreatic cancer, one step at a time:

Step One: Maintain an Optimal Weight

Because pancreatic cancer is often diagnosed at a late stage, you may have lost a substantial amount of weight before you knew you

Coach's Corner

Need a Head Start?

Here are some changes that you can make to your diet NOW that will help you get on the fast track to health! For this week:

1. Take digestive enzymes with every meal or snack.
2. Eat a fruit and vegetable at every lunch and dinner.
3. Try a fruit and soy smoothie.
4. Don't eat red meat.
5. Skip dessert.

had cancer. Even if you are overweight, you should take immediate action to prevent further weight loss. As little as a 5-percent weight loss can dramatically reduce your ability to cope with treatment side effects and can lead to malnutrition, a complication that causes 40 percent of deaths in cancer patients. Don't risk delayed treatment and give cancer a chance to progress while you wait to regain your ability to tolerate treatment! Oral nutritional supplements containing fish oil, a source of omega-3 fatty acids, were able to reverse cachexia and promote weight gain in patients with advanced pancreatic cancer. Chapter 2 provides nutritional support recommendations to help you maintain your weight and prevent malnutrition.

Your new energy requirements will be established as your body composition changes. Talk with a registered dietitian who can help you design a meal plan for realistic weight management. It is important that you obtain adequate levels of nutrients for rebuilding healthy cells and immune system function.

Step Two: Maintain a Healthy Gut

Cancer of the pancreas and its treatment may cause a reduction in digestive enzyme levels, leading to poor digestion. If your gastrointestinal tract doesn't work very well, you won't be able to utilize all the nutrients you consume. Eating small, frequent meals and taking digestive enzymes are critical to support digestion. Your doctor may have prescribed Pancrease or Pancreatin, digestive enzyme replacements. To achieve a balance of beneficial bacteria in the intestines, eat yogurt or take a probiotic supplement on a regular basis. Additional information on gastrointestinal health can be obtained in Chapter 3.

Step Three: Eat Five-a-Day

Consume at least five servings of produce each day. Several studies have reported a positive association between consuming produce and preventing pancreatic cancer. Nature has packed cancer-fighting phytochemicals into almost every kind of fruit and vegetable. If tolerated, choose raw produce, which provides more vitamins and minerals and has active plant enzymes. Chapter 7 will show you how easy it is to meet your daily produce goal.

Gold Medal Action
Get the Phyto-Advantage!

Pile your plate high with powerful phyto-chemicals to stop pancreatic cancer in its tracks! Your best plant choices contain carotenoids, citrus bio-flavonoids, indoles, monoterpenes, and phenols:

• Fruits: Blackberries, black currants, cantaloupe, cherries, cranberries, grapefruit, kiwi, lemons, limes, mangoes, nectarines, oranges, papayas, peaches, pears, prunes, pumpkin, raspberries, star fruit, strawberries, tangerines

• Vegetables: Arugula, broccoli, Brussels sprouts, butternut squash, cabbage, carrots, cauliflower, chard, collard greens, daikon radish, eggplant, endive, horseradish, kale, kelp, mustard greens, red peppers, rutabagas, sorrel, spinach, squash, tomatoes, turnip greens, yams

Step Four: Cut the Fat

Limit fat to 25 percent of your total calories. Animal studies show that dietary fat influences pancreatic tumor development. Analysis of twenty-two countries showed that diets high in total and saturated fats contributed to pancreatic cancer mortality. High intakes of polyunsaturated fats were found to enhance pancreatic tumor promotion, while omega-3 fatty acids inhibited tumor growth. Dietary cholesterol was found to be a risk factor for pancreatic cancer. Eating too much fat or the wrong kinds of fat has also been associated with inflammatory conditions and suppressed immunity. Chapter 5 provides guidelines for avoiding unhealthy fats and balancing your diet with healthy fats. At least 15 percent of your daily calories (60 percent of your total fat allowance) should come from fats that contain monounsaturated and omega-3 fatty acids.

Step Five: Cut the Sweets

Cancer of the pancreas and its treatment may interfere with insulin production, making it difficult to maintain proper blood sugar levels. Limit refined sugar and flour intake to less than 10 percent of total calories. Sugar and other highly processed carbohydrates can raise blood sugar levels, creating an environment favorable for cancer cell growth and suppressed immunity. Chapter 6 offers suggestions for cutting the sugar from your diet and provides recommendations for stabilizing blood sugar levels.

Step Six: Eat Legumes

Consume an average of one serving of legumes (beans, peas, and lentils) per day. Soy, which doesn't contain saturated fat, is a high-protein alternative to animal foods that has been found to slow tumor growth and limit the metastatic properties of various cancer cells. L-canaline, a component of legumes, demonstrated anticancer activity against human pancreatic cancer cells in vitro. See Chapter 9 to learn more about how soy foods can fit into your diet.

Step Seven: Add Roughage

Consume at least twenty-five grams of fiber each day. Fiber acts to detoxify the body by removing cancer-causing secondary bile acids and cholesterol through the stool. Whole grains and minimally processed starches, which don't raise blood sugar levels as quickly, should supply most of your energy. Population studies suggest a low-fiber diet may be linked to pancreatic cancer risk. Chapter 8 details how to eat a variety of plant foods to ensure that you get a mixture of soluble and insoluble fibers.

Step Eight: Drink Up

A nationwide food consumption survey found that chronic mild dehydration was commonplace among Americans. To be well hydrated and flush your system of toxins, you should consume at least twelve cups of fluid per day if you are a man, nine cups of fluid per day if you are a woman. Drink reverse osmosis treated or distilled water. Consume green tea, which provides powerful antioxidant benefits. There may be a correlation between coffee consumption and pancreatic cancer risk. Avoid alcohol.

Step Nine: Adopt Healthy Habits

See Chapter 1 for suggestions about a healthier lifestyle. If you smoke, stop now. Continuing to smoke can reduce the benefit of natural therapies and increase your risk for other diseases. Avoid foods that contain antibiotics, hormones, artificial sweeteners, colorings, or harmful additives. Eat organically grown produce or use a commercial fruit and vegetable wash to remove pesticides and waxes. Pesticide residues, DDT, DDE, and PCBs are thought to play a role in pancreatic cancer development. Follow the food safety guidelines in Chapter 11 to reduce your risk of contracting a food-borne illness.

Step Ten: Supplement Your Diet

The following nutritional supplements have demonstrated effectiveness or may have potential value in the treatment of pancreatic cancer. Consult with a healthcare professional to determine whether you have specific daily requirements for these or other dietary supplements:

- Multivitamin, without iron
- Mixed carotenoids, 15 to 60 mg
- Vitamin C with bioflavonoids, 1,000 to 6,000 mg
- Vitamin E, 400 to 1,000 IU
- Selenium, 200 to 800 mcg
- B complex
- EPA/DHA (fish oil), 1,000 to 6,000 mg
- Digestive enzymes
- Chromium picolinate, 200 to 400 mcg
- CoQ10, 100 to 400 mg
- N-acetylcysteine (NAC), 250 to 500 mg
- Quercetin, 600 to 1,200 mg

Sample Meal Plan

Eating healthy can be nutritious and delicious! The following sample meal plan provides approximately 1,804 calories, 256 grams of carbohydrate (58%), 96 grams of protein (22%), 44 grams of fat (22%), and 29 grams of dietary fiber. A registered dietitian can help you adjust the portion sizes of this meal plan to meet your individual nutritional needs.

Quick Reference Guide to Eating Right

Consume Less	Consume More
Total fat (No more than 25 percent of your total calories)	Fruits and vegetables (5 to 9 servings per day)
Deep fat fried foods	Total dietary fiber (25 grams per day)
Margarine, shortening, and vegetable oils from corn, safflower, and soybeans	Whole grains (2 or more servings per day)
Red meat (No more than 1 serving per week)	Legumes (1/2 cup per day)
High-fat milk or cheese	Yogurt (3 servings per week)
Eggs	Free-range and organic products
Smoked or processed meats	Soy foods
Sugar, candy, desserts, or beverages containing sugar (No more than 10 percent of your total calories)	Curried foods
White bread, rice, and pasta	Cold water fish (3 servings per week)
Salt	Extra virgin olive oil
Coffee	Green tea (3 to 4 cups per day)
Alcohol	Purified water (9 to 12 cups per day)

Breakfast

Orange segments	1 medium
Oatmeal, cooked	1 cup
Multi-grain toast	1 slice
Butter	2 tsp
Lite soy milk	1 cup
Green tea	1 cup
Purified water	1 cup

Lunch

Vegetarian baked beans	1/2 cup
Veggie burger	1 each
Whole wheat bun	1 each
Carrots and broccoli, steamed	1 cup
Pear slices and raspberries	1/2 cup
Vegetable juice	1 cup
Purified water	1 cup

Dinner

Steamed cod fillet	4 oz
Sweet potato	1 large
Stewed tomatoes	1 cup
Raw spinach and radish salad	2 cups
Italian salad dressing	2 tsp
Kiwi	1 medium
Green tea	1 cup
Purified water	2 cups

Snack

Yogurt, plain, low fat	1 cup
Sliced strawberries	1 cup
Walnuts	1 oz
Herbal tea	1 cup
Purified water	1 cup

Food Selection Guide for Pancreatic Cancer

Beverages

Choose More Often

Soy milk, fruit or vegetable juices, herbal teas, green tea, purified water

Choose Less Often

Cow's milk, buttermilk, nonfat dry milk, malts, shakes, frozen yogurt drinks, carbonated beverages, fruit-flavored drinks, coffees and teas

Breads, Cereals & Starches

Choose More Often

All whole grain bread or yeast products, baked goods or pasta made with oats, barley, quinoa, amaranth, millet, bulgur, rye, buckwheat, brown rice, wheat bran, wheat germ

Choose Less Often

Refined flours and cereals, quick breads, muffins, waffles, biscuits, pancakes, doughnuts, sweet rolls, pastries, corn bread, fritters, jams, jellies, marshmallows, molasses, honey, white sugar, syrup, hard candies

Desserts

Choose More Often

Fruit or soy desserts

Choose Less Often

Dairy desserts such as ice cream, pudding, flan, cheesecake; desserts made with whole milk, cream, lard, vegetable oils, coconut, chocolate

Eggs

Choose More Often

Hormone-free eggs limited to two per week or egg substitute

Choose Less Often

Eggs prepared with milk or cheese, fried eggs

Fats

Choose More Often

Butter, limited to 1 tsp per day, I Can't Believe It's Not Butter spray, PAM spray, olive, canola, sesame, and flax oils, avocado

Choose Less Often

Margarine, partially or fully hydrogenated fats, lard, shortening, all other vegetable oils such as sunflower, peanut, soybean, safflower, coconut, palm, and cottonseed

Fruits & Vegetables

Choose More Often

All fresh or frozen produce; emphasize blackberries, black currants, cantaloupe, cherries, cranberries, grapefruit, kiwi, lemons, limes, mangoes, nectarines, oranges, papayas, peaches, pears, prunes, pumpkin, raspberries, star fruit, strawberries, tangerines, arugula, broccoli, Brussels sprouts, butternut squash, cabbage, carrots, cauliflower, chard, collard greens, daikon radish, eggplant, endive, horseradish, kale, kelp, mustard greens, red peppers, rutabagas, sorrel, spinach, squash, tomatoes, turnip greens, yams

Choose Less Often

Commercially dried fruits containing sulfites, canned produce, vegetables in mayonnaise, vegetable oil, dressings, or covered in cheese

Meats, Fish & Other Protein

Choose More Often

Remove all visible fat before cooking; bake, broil, roast, stir-fry, grill, or steam lean meat, poultry, pork, and fish; choose often soy, salmon, tuna, mackerel, sardines packed in water; if you eat cheese, choose low-fat cheeses such as mozzarella, ricotta, cottage, Swiss, provolone; eat low-fat plain yogurt; choose flax, sesame, and pumpkin seeds; choose chestnuts, almonds, walnuts, Brazil nuts; emphasize legumes

Choose Less Often

All fried meats, poultry or fish, fatty meats, nitrate-containing meats such as sausage, bacon, hot dog, pepperoni, Canadian bacon, lunch meats; avoid meats in oil; limit cheese, milk, peanut butter made with hydrogenated oils or additives, most other seeds and nuts such as sunflower, macadamia, pistachios, cashews, peanuts

Condiments

Choose More Often

Sea salt, salt, pepper, herbs and spices, lemon juice, relish, vinegar, ketchup, olives, salsa; emphasize basil, citrus peels, celery seeds, mint, and parsley

Choose Less Often

Monosodium glutamate (MSG), artificial sweeteners, and artificial flavorings

Nutrition Action Plan for Prostate Cancer

A whole foods, plant-based diet is essential for anyone who wants to eat to beat cancer. Current evidence suggests that too much fat, saturated fat, animal protein, and certain dairy products are positively associated with prostate cancer, particularly in the advanced stages. Here's how you can take action to beat prostate cancer, one step at a time:

Step One: Stabilize Your Weight

If you've lost more than a few pounds, you should take immediate action to prevent further weight loss. As little as a 5-percent weight loss can dramatically reduce your ability to cope with treatment side effects and can lead to malnutrition, a complication that causes 40 percent of deaths in cancer patients. Don't risk delayed treatment and give cancer a chance to progress while you wait to regain your ability to tolerate

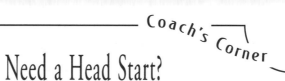

Coach's Corner

Need a Head Start?

Here are some changes that you can make to your diet NOW that will help you get on the fast track to health! For this week:

1. Drink a glass of tomato or mixed vegetable juice every day.
2. Try a veggie burger.
3. Eat two servings of fish.
4. Don't eat cheese.
5. Eat a beans and rice meal.

treatment! Chapter 2 provides nutritional support recommendations to help you maintain your weight and prevent malnutrition.

Step Two: Lose Weight If You Need To

Current evidence suggests there may be a link between body size and prostate cancer. The American Institute for Cancer Research recommends limiting weight gain to eleven pounds during adulthood. Excessive weight can elevate serum levels of insulin-like growth factor (IGF-1), which may cause prostate cancer to spread. Studies also suggest that higher levels of cancer-causing chemicals might be stored in excess fat tissue or that extra calories provide fuel for increased cell proliferation. Often, changing what you eat can prompt weight loss; this jump-start to a leaner figure can be a strong motivational factor for continued adherence to a more healthful diet. Don't forget the other part of the weight maintenance equation: Physical activity can help increase muscle mass and burn calories.

As you adjust to new eating habits, your new energy requirements will be established as your body composition changes. Talk with a registered dietitian who can help you design a meal plan for realistic and safe weight loss. Avoid strict or fad diets in an attempt to lose weight. Quick weight loss deprives the body of valuable nutrients needed for growth and repair, and can reduce the fighting capacity of your immune system.

Step Three: Maintain a Healthy Gut

If your gastrointestinal tract doesn't work very well, you won't be able to utilize all the nutrients you consume. Eating small, frequent meals and taking digestive enzymes can aid digestion. To achieve a balance of beneficial bacteria in the intestines, take a probiotic supplement on a regular basis. Additional information on gastrointestinal health can be obtained in Chapter 3.

Step Four: Eat Five-a-Day.

Consume at least five servings of produce each day. Numerous studies have reported a positive association between consuming produce and preventing prostate cancer. Nature has packed cancer-fighting phytochemicals into almost every kind of fruit and vegetable. Choose raw produce when possible, which provides more vitamins and minerals and has active plant enzymes. Chapter 7 will show you how easy it is to meet your daily produce goal.

Gold Medal Action

Get the Phyto-Advantage!

Pile your plate high with powerful phytochemicals to stop prostate cancer in its tracks! Your best plant choices contain allylic sulfides, beta-sitosterols, carotenoids, citrus bioflavonoids, curcumin, indoles, lycopenes, and polyphenols:

- **Fruits:** Black currants, cantaloupe, grapefruit, guava, kiwi, lemons, limes, mangoes, nectarines, oranges, papayas, peaches, pumpkin, red grapefruit, star fruit, tangerines, watermelon
- **Vegetables:** Arugula, bok choy, broccoli, Brussels sprouts, butternut squash, cabbage, carrots, cauliflower, chard, chives, collard greens, cucumber, daikon radish, endive, garlic, horseradish, kale, kohlrabi, leeks, mustard, mustard greens, onions, peanuts, pumpkin seeds, red cabbage, red peppers, rutabagas, scallions, shallots, sorrel, soy beans, spinach, summer squash, tomatoes, turnips, turnip greens, yams, winter squash

Step Five: Cut the Fat

Limit fat to 20 percent of your total calories. Diets high in total, saturated, and animal fats increase the risk of prostate cancer and have been associated with inflammatory conditions, suppressed immunity, and general cancer cell growth. Several studies have shown that a low-fat diet may help keep early prostate cancer from metastasizing. Chapter 5 provides guidelines for avoiding unhealthy fats and balancing your diet with healthy fats. At least 15 percent of your daily calories (75 percent of your total fat allowance) should come from olive oil and omega-3 fatty acid food sources.

Step Six: Eat Soy

Consume an average of two servings of soy foods daily. Soy, which doesn't contain saturated fat, is a high-protein alternative to animal foods. Countries with high soy intake experience substantially lower incidence of prostate cancers than the United States. Soy has inhibited the formation of new blood vessels and slowed prostate cancer cell growth. See Chapter 9 to learn more about how soy foods can fit into your diet.

Step Seven: Limit Dairy

Population studies consistently show a positive link between prostate cancer and diets high in milk and cheese. Dairy products, along with meats, contribute certain dietary factors that may decrease 1,25 dihydroxyvitamin D, a cell differentiator, leading to accelerated prostate cancer development.

Step Eight: Add Roughage

Consume between twenty-five and thirty-five grams of fiber each day. Fiber acts to detoxify the body by removing cancer-causing secondary bile acids and cholesterol through the stool. Whole grains and minimally processed starches should supply most of your energy needs. Legumes (peas, beans, and lentils) are a rich source of fiber and are particularly beneficial for prostate cancer. Chapter 8 details how to eat a variety of plant foods to ensure that you get a mixture of soluble and insoluble fibers.

Step Nine: Cut the Sweets

Limit refined sugar and flour intake to less than 10 percent of total calories. Sugar and other highly processed carbohydrates can raise blood sugar levels, creating an environment favorable for cancer cell growth and suppressed immunity. Chapter 6 offers suggestions for cutting the sugar from your diet and provides recommendations for stabilizing blood sugar levels.

Step Ten: Drink Up

A nationwide food consumption survey found that chronic mild dehydration was commonplace among Americans. To be well hydrated and flush your system of toxins, men should consume at least twelve cups of fluid per day. Drink reverse osmosis treated or distilled water. Consume green tea, which provides powerful antioxidant benefits.

Step Eleven: Adopt Healthy Habits

See Chapter 1 for suggestions about a healthier lifestyle. If you smoke, stop now. Continuing to smoke can reduce the benefit of natural therapies and increase your risk for other diseases. Avoid foods that contain antibiotics, hormones, artificial sweeteners, colorings, or harmful additives. Eat organically grown produce or use a commercial fruit and vegetable wash to remove pesticides and waxes. Follow the food safety guidelines in Chapter 11 to reduce your risk of contracting a food-borne illness.

Step Twelve: Supplement Your Diet

The following nutritional supplements have demonstrated effectiveness or may have potential value in the treatment of prostate cancer. Consult with a healthcare professional to determine whether you have specific daily requirements for these or other dietary supplements:

- Multivitamin, without iron or boron
- Mixed carotenoids, 15 to 60 mg
- Vitamin C with bioflavonoids, 1,000 to 6,000 mg
- Vitamin E, 400 to 1,000 IU
- Selenium, 200 to 800 mcg
- EPA/DHA (fish oil), 1,000 to 6,000 mg
- Isolated soy protein powder, 50 to 100 mg isoflavones
- Probiotic, 1 to 10 billion live cells
- Zinc, 20 to 50 mg
- Quercetin, 600 to 1,200 mg
- Citrus pectin, 1 to 3 Tbs
- Curcuma root, 500 to 1,500 mg
- Melatonin, 20 mg
- PC-SPES, 6 tablets
- IP-6, 800 to 7,200 mg
- Inositol, 200 to 1,800 mg
- Maitake, 3 to 7 gm

Quick Reference Guide to Eating Right	
Consume Less	**Consume More**
Total fat (No more than 20 percent of your total calories)	Fruits and vegetables (5 to 9 servings per day)
Deep fat fried foods	Total dietary fiber (25 grams per day)
Margarine, shortening, and vegetable oils from corn, safflower, and soybeans	Whole grains (2 or more servings per day)
Red meat (No more than 1 serving per week)	Legumes (1/2 cup per day)
Dairy foods	Free-range animal products
Smoked or processed meats	Soy foods (2 servings per day)
Sugar, candy, desserts, or beverages containing sugar (No more than 10 percent of your total calories)	Curried foods
White bread, rice, and pasta	Cold water fish (3 servings per week)
Salt	Extra virgin olive oil
Alcohol	Green tea (3 to 4 cups per day)
	Purified water (9 to 12 cups per day)

Sample Meal Plan

Eating healthy can be nutritious and delicious! The following sample meal plan provides approximately 1,880 calories, 279 grams of carbohydrate (60%), 94 grams of protein (20%), 43 grams of fat (20%), and 32 grams of fiber. A registered dietitian can help you adjust the portion sizes of this meal plan to meet your individual nutritional needs.

Breakfast

Red grapefruit	1/2 medium
Bran cereal	1/2 cup
Multi-grain toast	2 slices
Butter	1 tsp
Lite soy milk	1 cup
Green tea	1 cup
Purified water	1 cup

Lunch

Vegetarian baked beans	1/2 cup
Veggie burger	1 each
Whole grain bun	1 bun
Carrot, green pepper relish	1 each
Onions, sliced	1/2 cup
Watermelon, cubed	1 cup
Vegetable juice	1 cup
Purified water	1 cup

Dinner

Grilled tuna steak	4 oz
Boiled new potatoes	1 large
Stewed tomatoes	1 cup
Raw spinach and radish salad	2 cups
Herb vinaigrette	1 tsp
Orange and banana slices	1 medium, 1/2 medium
Green tea	1 cup
Purified water	2 cups

Snack

Sliced strawberries	1 cup
Pumpkin seeds, dried	1 oz
Herbal tea	1 cup
Purified water	1 cup

Food Selection Guide for Prostate Cancer

Beverages

Choose More Often

Soy milk, fruit or vegetable juices, herbal teas, green tea, purified water

Choose Less Often

Cow's milk, buttermilk, nonfat dry milk, malts, shakes, frozen yogurt drinks, carbonated beverages, fruit-flavored drinks, caffeinated coffees and teas

Breads, Cereals & Starches

Choose More Often

All whole grain bread or yeast products, baked goods or pasta made with oats, barley, quinoa, amaranth, millet, bulgur, rye, buckwheat, brown rice, wheat bran, wheat germ

Choose Less Often

Refined flours and cereals, quick breads, muffins, waffles, biscuits, pancakes, doughnuts, sweet rolls, pastries, corn bread, fritters, jams, jellies, marshmallows, molasses, honey, white sugar, syrup, hard candies

Desserts

Choose More Often

Fruit or soy desserts

Choose Less Often

Dairy desserts such as ice cream, pudding, flan, cheesecake; desserts made with whole milk, cream, lard, vegetable oils, coconut, chocolate

Eggs

Choose More Often

Hormone-free eggs limited to one per day, egg substitute

Choose Less Often

Eggs prepared with milk or cheese, fried eggs

Fats

Choose More Often

Butter, limited to 2 tsp per day, I Can't Believe It's Not Butter spray, PAM spray, olive oil, avocado

Choose Less Often

Margarine, partially or fully hydrogenated fats, lard, shortening, all other vegetable oils such as canola, flax, sunflower, peanut, soybean, safflower, coconut, palm, and cottonseed

Fruits & Vegetables

Choose More Often

All fresh or frozen produce; emphasize black currants, cantaloupe, grapefruit, guava, kiwi, lemons, limes, mangoes, nectarines, oranges, papayas, peaches, pumpkin, red grapefruit, star fruit, tangerines, watermelon, arugula, bok choy, broccoli, Brussels sprouts, butternut squash, cabbage, carrots, cauliflower, chard, chives, collard greens, cucumber, daikon radish, endive, garlic, horseradish, kale, kohlrabi, leeks, mustard, mustard greens, onions, pumpkin seeds, red cabbage, red peppers, rutabagas, scallions, shallots, sorrel, soy beans, spinach, summer squash, tomatoes, turmeric, turnips, turnip greens, yams, winter squash

Choose Less Often

Commercially dried fruits containing sulfites, canned produce, vegetables in mayonnaise, vegetable oil, dressings, or covered in cheese

Meats, Fish & Other Protein
Choose More Often

Remove all visible fat before cooking; bake, broil, roast, stir-fry, grill, or steam lean meat, poultry, pork, and fish; choose often soy, salmon, tuna, mackerel, sardines packed in water; if you eat cheese, choose low-fat cheeses such as mozzarella, ricotta, cottage, Swiss, provolone; eat low-fat plain yogurt; choose flax, sesame, and pumpkin seeds; choose chestnuts, almonds, Brazil nuts; emphasize legumes, curried foods

Choose Less Often

All fried meats, poultry or fish, fatty meats, nitrate-containing meats such as sausage, bacon, hot dog, pepperoni, Canadian bacon, lunch meats; avoid meats in oil; avoid cheeses, milk, peanut butter made with hydrogenated oils or additives; most other seeds and nuts such as sunflower, macadamia, pistachios, cashews, peanuts

Condiments
Choose More Often

Sea salt, salt, pepper, herbs and spices, lemon juice, relish, vinegar, ketchup, olives; emphasize garlic, onion, salsa, and turmeric

Choose Less Often

Monosodium glutamate (MSG), artificial sweeteners, and artificial flavorings

Nutrition Action Plan for Other Cancers

A whole foods, plant-based diet is essential for anyone who wants to eat to beat cancer. Proper nutrition can rebuild cells, stimulate immune system function, protect against chemical and environmental toxins, and promote total body wellness. Here's how you can take action to beat or prevent cancer, one step at a time:

Step One: Stabilize Your Weight

If you've lost more than a few pounds, you should take immediate action to prevent further weight loss. As little as a 5-percent weight loss can dramatically reduce your ability to cope with treatment side effects and can lead to malnutrition, a complication that causes 40 percent of deaths in cancer patients. Don't risk delayed treatment and give cancer a chance to progress while you wait to regain your ability to tolerate treatment! Chapter 2 provides

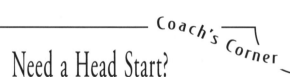

Coach's Corner

Need a Head Start?

Here are some changes that you can make to your diet NOW that will help you get on the fast track to health! For this week:

1. Eat a fruit and vegetable at every lunch and dinner.
2. Try a veggie burger.
3. Don't eat red meat.
4. Eat a breakfast cereal that contains more than ten grams of dietary fiber per serving.
5. Eat a beans and rice meal.

nutritional support recommendations to help you maintain your weight and prevent malnutrition.

Step Two: Lose Weight If You Need To

The American Institute for Cancer Research recommends limiting weight gain to eleven pounds during adulthood. Excessive weight can elevate serum levels of insulin-like growth factor (IGF-1), which can cause cancer cells to grow and spread. Studies also suggest that higher levels of cancer-causing chemicals might be stored in excess fat tissue or that extra calories provide fuel for increased cell proliferation. Often, changing what you eat can prompt weight loss; this jump-start to a leaner figure can be a strong motivational factor for continued adherence to a more healthful diet. Don't forget the other part of the weight maintenance equation: Physical activity can help increase muscle mass and burn calories.

As you adjust to new eating habits, your new energy requirements will be established as your body composition changes. Talk with a registered dietitian who can help you design a meal plan for realistic and safe weight loss. Avoid strict or fad diets in an attempt to lose weight. Quick weight loss deprives the body of valuable nutrients needed for growth and repair, and can reduce the fighting capacity of your immune system.

Step Three: Maintain a Healthy Gut

If your gastrointestinal tract doesn't work very well, you won't be able to utilize all the nutrients you consume. Eating small, frequent meals and taking digestive enzymes can aid digestion. To achieve a balance of beneficial bacteria in the intestines, eat yogurt or take a probiotic supplement on a regular basis. Additional information on gastrointestinal health can be obtained in Chapter 3.

Step Four: Eat Five-a-Day

Consume at least five servings of produce each day. Hundreds of studies have reported a positive association between consuming produce and preventing cancer. Nature has packed cancer-fighting phytochemicals into almost every kind of fruit and vegetable. Choose raw produce when possible, which provides more vitamins and minerals and has active plant enzymes. Chapter 7 will show you how easy it is to meet your daily produce goal.

Gold Medal Action

Get the Phyto-Advantage!

Pile your plate high with powerful phytochemicals to stop cancer in its tracks! Your best plant choices contain allylic sulfides, anthocyanidins, carotenoids, citrus bioflavonoids, and indoles:

• Fruits: Blackberries, black currants, cantaloupe, cherries, cranberries, currants, grapefruit, kiwi, lemons, limes, mangoes, nectarines, oranges, papayas, peaches, plums, pumpkin, raspberries, red grapes, rhubarb, star fruit, strawberries, tangerines

• Vegetables: Arugula, bok choy, broccoli, Brussels sprouts, butternut squash, cabbage, carrots, cauliflower, chard, chives, collard greens, daikon radish, eggplant, endive, garlic, horseradish, kale, kohlrabi, leeks, mustard greens, onions, red cabbage, red peppers, rutabagas, scallions (green onions), shallots, sorrel, spinach, squash, tomatoes, turnips, turnip greens, yams

Step Five: Cut the Fat

Limit fat to 25 percent of your total calories. Eating too much fat or the wrong kinds of fat has been associated with inflammatory conditions, suppressed immunity, and cancer cell growth. Chapter 5 provides guidelines for avoiding unhealthy fats and balancing your diet with healthy fats. At least 15 percent of your daily calories (60 percent of your total fat allowance) should come from fats that contain monounsaturated and omega-3 fatty acids.

Step Six: Eat Soy

Consume an average of two servings of soy foods daily. Soy, which doesn't contain saturated fat, is a high-protein alternative to animal foods that has been found to slow tumor growth and limit the metastatic properties of various cancer cells. See Chapter 9 to learn more about how soy foods can fit into your diet.

Step Seven: Add Roughage

Consume at least twenty-five grams of fiber each day. Fiber acts to detoxify the body by removing cancer-causing secondary bile acids, excess estrogens, and cholesterol through the stool. Whole grains and minimally processed starches should supply most of your energy. Chapter 8 details how to eat a variety of plant foods to ensure that you get a mixture of soluble and insoluble fibers.

Step Eight: Cut the Sweets

Limit refined sugar and flour intake to less than 10 percent of your total calories. Sugar and other highly processed carbohydrates can raise blood sugar levels, creating an environment favorable for cancer cell growth and suppressed immunity. Chapter 6 offers suggestions for cutting the sugar from your diet and provides recommendations for stabilizing blood sugar levels.

Step Nine: Drink Up

A nationwide food consumption survey found that chronic mild dehydration was commonplace among Americans. To be well hydrated and flush your system of toxins, you should consume at least twelve cups of fluid per day if you are a man, nine cups of fluid per day if you are a woman. Drink reverse osmosis treated or distilled water. Consume green tea, which provides powerful antioxidant benefits.

Step Ten: Adopt Healthy Habits

See Chapter 1 for suggestions about a healthier lifestyle. If you smoke, stop now. Continuing to smoke can reduce the benefit of natural therapies and increase your risk for other diseases. Avoid foods that contain antibiotics, hormones, artificial sweeteners, colorings, or harmful additives. Eat organically grown produce or use a commercial fruit and vegetable wash to remove pesticides and waxes. Follow the food safety guidelines in Chapter 11 to reduce your risk of contracting a food-borne illness.

Step Eleven: Supplement Your Diet

The following nutritional supplements have demonstrated effectiveness or may have potential value in the treatment of cancer. Consult with a healthcare professional to determine whether you have specific daily requirements for these or other dietary supplements:

- Multivitamin, without iron
- Mixed carotenoids, 15 to 60 mg
- Vitamin C with bioflavonoids, 1,000 to 6,000 mg
- Vitamin E, 400 to 1,000 IU
- Selenium, 200 to 800 mcg
- EPA/DHA (fish oil), 1,000 to 6,000 mg
- Isolated soy protein powder, 50 to 100 mg isoflavones

Quick Reference Guide to Eating Right

Consume Less	Consume More
Total fat (No more than 25 percent of your total calories)	Fruits and vegetables (5 to 9 servings per day)
Deep fat fried foods	Total dietary fiber (25 grams per day)
Margarine, shortening, and vegetable oils from corn, safflower, and soybeans	Whole grains (2 or more servings per day)
Red meat (No more than 1 serving per week)	Legumes (1/2 cup per day)
High-fat milk or cheese	Yogurt (3 servings per week)
Smoked or processed meats	Free-range animal products
Sugar, candy, desserts, or beverages containing sugar (No more than 10 percent of your total calories)	Soy foods (2 servings per day)
White bread, rice, and pasta	Cold water fish (3 servings per week)
Salt	Extra virgin olive oil
Alcohol	Green tea (3 to 4 cups per day)
	Purified water (9 to 12 cups per day)

Sample Meal Plan

Eating healthy can be nutritious and delicious! The following sample meal plan provides approximately 1,802 calories, 252 grams of carbohydrate (56%), 86 grams of protein (19%), 50 grams of fat (25%), and 32 grams of dietary fiber. A registered dietitian can help you adjust the portion sizes of this meal plan to meet your individual nutritional needs.

Breakfast

Red grapefruit	1/2 medium
Oatmeal, cooked	1 cup
Multi-grain toast	1 slice
Butter	1 tsp
Lite soy milk	1 cup
Green tea	1 cup
Purified water	1 cup

Lunch

Cooked kidney beans	1/2 cup
Chicken tenderloin	3 1/2 oz
Brown rice	1/2 cup
Carrots and broccoli, steamed	1 cup
Cantaloupe wedge	1/4 melon
Vegetable juice	1 cup
Purified water	1 cup

Dinner

Salmon fillet	4 oz
Boiled new potatoes	1 large
Stewed tomatoes	1 cup
Raw spinach and radish salad	2 cups
Italian salad dressing	1 tsp
Apple slices	1 medium, sliced
Green tea	1 cup
Purified water	2 cups

Snack

Yogurt, plain, low fat	1 cup
Sliced strawberries	1 cup
Herbal tea	1 cup
Purified water	1 cup

Food Selection Guide for Other Cancers

Beverages

Choose More Often

Soy milk, fruit or vegetable juices, herbal teas, green tea, purified water

Choose Less Often

Cow's milk, buttermilk, nonfat dry milk, malts, shakes, frozen yogurt drinks, carbonated beverages, fruit-flavored drinks, caffeinated coffees and teas

Breads, Cereals & Starches

Choose More Often

All whole grain bread or yeast products, baked goods or pasta made with oats, barley, quinoa, amaranth, millet, bulgur, rye, buckwheat brown rice, wheat bran, wheat germ

Choose Less Often

Refined flours and cereals, quick breads, muffins, waffles, biscuits, pancakes, doughnuts, sweet rolls, pastries, corn bread, fritters, jams, jellies, marshmallows, molasses, honey, white sugar, syrup, hard candies

Desserts

Choose More Often

Fruit or soy desserts

Choose Less Often

Dairy desserts such as ice cream, pudding, flan, cheesecake; desserts made with whole milk, cream, lard, vegetable oils, coconut, chocolate

Eggs

Choose More Often

Hormone-free eggs limited to one per day, egg substitute

Choose Less Often

Eggs prepared with milk or cheese, fried eggs

Fats

Choose More Often

Butter, limited to 2 tsp per day, I Can't Believe It's Not Butter spray, PAM spray, olive, canola, sesame, and flax oils, avocado

Choose Less Often

Margarine, partially or fully hydrogenated fats, lard, shortening, all other vegetable oils such as sunflower, peanut, soybean, safflower, coconut, palm, and cottonseed

Fruits & Vegetables

Choose More Often

All fresh or frozen produce; emphasize blackberries, black currants, cantaloupe, cherries, cranberries, currants, grapefruit, kiwi, lemons, limes, mangoes, nectarines, oranges, papayas, peaches, plums, pumpkin, raspberries, red grapes, rhubarb, star fruit, strawberries, tangerines, arugula, bok choy, broccoli, Brussels sprouts, butternut squash, cabbage, carrots, cauliflower, chard, chives, collard greens, daikon radish, eggplant, endive, garlic, horseradish, kale, kohlrabi, leeks, mustard greens, onions, red cabbage, red peppers, rutabagas, scallions, shallots, sorrel, spinach, squash, tomatoes, turnips, turnip greens, yams

Choose Less Often

Commercially dried fruits containing sulfites, canned produce, vegetables in mayonnaise, vegetable oil, dressings, or covered in cheese

Meats, Fish & Other Protein
Choose More Often

Remove all visible fat before cooking; bake, broil, roast, stir-fry, grill, or steam lean meat, poultry, pork, and fish; choose often: soy, salmon, tuna, mackerel, sardines packed in water; if you eat cheese, choose low-fat cheeses such as mozzarella, ricotta, cottage, Swiss, provolone; eat low-fat plain yogurt, and flax, sesame, and pumpkin seeds; choose chestnuts, almonds, walnuts, Brazil nuts; emphasize legumes

Choose Less Often

All fried meats, poultry or fish, fatty meats, nitrate-containing meats such as sausage, bacon, hot dog, pepperoni, Canadian bacon, lunch meats; avoid meats in oil; limit cheese, milk, peanut butter made with hydrogenated oils or additives, most other seeds and nuts such as sunflower, macadamia pistachios, cashews, peanuts

Condiments
Choose More Often

Sea salt, salt, pepper, herbs and spices, lemon juice, relish, vinegar, ketchup, olives, salsa, garlic, and onion

Choose Less Often

Monosodium glutamate (MSG), artificial sweeteners, and artificial flavorings

Appendices

Appendix 1

Ideal body weight range chart for adults. If you fall below your ideal weight range, you are considered underweight; if you fall above your ideal weight range, you are considered overweight.*

Height	Women's Ideal Weight Range	Men's Ideal Weight Range
4'10"	87 - 105	
4'11"	88 - 108	
5'0"	90 - 110	
5'1"	94 - 116	
5'2"	99 - 121	106 - 130
5'3"	103 - 127	112 - 136
5'4"	108 - 132	117 - 143
5'5"	112 - 138	123 - 149
5'6"	117 - 143	128 - 156
5'7"	121 - 149	133 - 163
5'8"	126 - 154	139 - 169
5'9"	130 - 160	144 - 176
5'10"	135 - 165	150 - 182
5'11"	139 - 171	155 - 189
6'0"	144 - 176	160 - 196
6'1"		166 - 202
6'2"		171 - 209
6'3"		176 - 216
6'4"		182 - 222
6'5"		187 - 229

* *Using the Hamwi Method(7)*

Appendix 2

Percent Weight Change Worksheet

If you have a calculator and want to figure out whether the weight you have lost is increasing your risk for complications due to malnutrition, here is an equation to help you.

Percent weight loss can be calculated by the following formula:

(Usual Weight – Current Weight) / Usual Weight x 100) = % Weight Change

Enter Your Numbers

Usual Weight _____ - Current Weight _____ = _____

Divide this number by your Usual Weight = _____

Multiply times 100 = _____ (% Weight Change)

Patient Profile Example

Sally has been diagnosed with metastatic breast cancer. She currently weighs 135 pounds and is 5'9" tall. She used to weigh 160 pounds, so she has lost 25 pounds since her treatments began. She has a history of migraine headaches, which seem worse after the Adriamycin treatment. These headaches have made it difficult for Sally to function normally and have left her with no appetite for several days each month. In addition, Sally experiences frequent bouts of nausea for weeks after her chemotherapy infusions.

Plugging those numbers into the weight loss equation, you will find that Sally has lost a little less than 16 percent of her usual body weight.

Usual weight = 160   Current weight = 135

[(160 – 135) / 160] x 100 = 16 percent weight change

This much weight change presents a significant risk for developing health complications that reduce Sally's chances of recovery. Sally needs to meet with a nutritionist right away to stabilize her weight and think of ways to provide her body with adequate nutrients, which are essential for rebuilding.

Appendix 3

Calorie and Protein Requirements Worksheet

Determine your calorie and protein requirements* by completing the worksheet below:

Calories

Step 1. Calculate your base requirements.

Females: Current weight x 10 = _____

Males: Current weight x 11 = _____

Step 2. Add in energy calories for physical activity.

Activity Level	Adjusted Requirements
Sedentary	Add 20% to base requirements
Light activity	Add 30% to base requirements
Moderate activity	Add 40% to base requirements
Very active	Add 50% to base requirements

Step 3: Adjust calories for weight gain or loss goal.

Weight gain	Add 500 to base requirements
Weight loss	Subtract 500 from base requirements

Example: Female, 64", 175 lbs, light activity level

Step 1:   175 x 10 = 1750 calories

Step 2:   1750 x.30 = 525; 1750 + 525 = 2275 calories

Step 3:   2275 - 500 = 1775 calories required per day for safe weight loss.

Protein

Step 1: Find your ideal body weight on the chart in Appendix 1.

Step 2: Divide your ideal body weight by 2.2 to arrive at estimated protein needs.

Example: Female, 64", 175 lb, light activity level

Step 1:   Ideal body weight = 120 pounds

Step 2:   120 / 2.2 = 55 grams of protein per day

* Calculated values are meant to provide estimated energy and protein needs. The values do not take into account individual medical complications, weight loss history, and so forth. Please consult a nutritionist if you have any questions about your calorie and protein requirements.

Appendix 4
Sample Laboratory Report

Complete Blood Count

Test	Result	Units	Normals
WBC	4.6	K/UL	3.9 - 11.1
RBC	4.52	M/UL	4.2 - 5.7
Hgb	13.6	G/DL	13.2 - 16.9
Hct	40.2	%	38.5 - 49.0
MCV	88.8	FL	80.0 - 99.0
MCH	26.8 L	PG	27.0 - 35.0
MCHC	33.8	G/DL	27.0 - 35.0
PLT	237	K/DL	160 - 400
MPV	8.1	FL	8.0 - 12.0
RDW	13.1	%	11.0 - 14.0
SEGS	69 H	%	45 - 61

Comprehensive Metabolic Panel

Test	Result	Units	Normals
Glu	88	MG/DL	65 - 109
BUN	16	MG/DL	5 - 26
Creat	1.3	MG/DL	0.6 - 1.5
TP	7.3	G/DL	6.0 - 8.5
Alb	4.1	G/DL	3.5 - 5.5
Calcium	9.0	MG/DL	8.8 - 10.5
T Bili	0.5	MG/DL	0.1 - 1.2
SGOT	19	IU/L	15 - 37
SGPT	36	U/L	30 - 65
Alk Phos	123	U/L	50 - 136
TG	209 H	MG/DL	30 - 200
Chol	222 H	MG/DL	120 - 200

Appendix 5
Food Record Sheets

Name:_____

Date:_____

Food Eaten (include servings sizes/amounts):

Breakfast

Snack

Noon meal

Snack

Evening meal

Snack

Appendix 6
Common Side Effects Associated with Chemotherapy

Adriamycin: Hair loss, nausea, vomiting, anemia, risk of infection, mouth sores, discolored urine, skin darkening

Altretamine (Hexalen): Nausea, vomiting, dizziness and fatigue, anemia, risk of infection, hair loss, neuropathy

Asparaginase: Nausea, vomiting, loss of appetite, changes in blood clotting factors (increased risk of bleeding or increased risk of blood clots), liver function changes

Bleomycin: Fever, chills, skin rash, loss of appetite, mouth sores, nails darker or ridged

Busulphan: Anemia, risk of infection, skin darkening

Capecitabine (Xeloda): Nausea, vomiting, mouth sores, diarrhea, loss of appetite, red palms and soles (called palmar plantar syndrome), fatigue, increased tear production

Carboplatin: Anemia, risk of infection, nausea, vomiting, loss of appetite

Carmustine: Nausea, vomiting, anemia, risk of infection

Cisplatin: Nausea, vomiting, kidney function changes

Cyclophosphamide: Anemia, risk of infection, nausea, vomiting, loss of appetite, bladder irritation

Cytarabine: Anemia, risk of infection, nausea, vomiting, diarrhea, loss of appetite, increased levels of uric acid, gritty eyes

Dacarbazine: Nausea, vomiting, anemia, risk of infection, loss of appetite

Daunorubicin: Nausea, vomiting, hair loss, anemia, risk of infection, mouth sores, pink-red urine color, sensitivity to the sun

Epirubicin: Hair loss, nausea, vomiting, anemia, risk of infection, mouth sores, pink-red urine color, skin rash

Etoposide: Anemia, risk of infection, hair loss, nausea, vomiting

Fluorouracil (5-FU): Nausea, vomiting, mouth sores, diarrhea, gritty eyes, blurred vision, skin darkening, anemia, risk of infection

Gemcitabine (Gemzar): Anemia, risk of infection, nausea, vomiting, loss of appetite, liver function changes, kidney function changes, skin rash, flu-like symptoms

Idarubicin: Anemia, risk of infection, nausea, vomiting, mouth sores, hair loss, pink-red urine color

Ifosfamide: Anemia, risk of infection, nausea, vomiting, hair loss, bladder irritation, nails may become ridged

Irinotecan (Camptosar): Increased sweating and salivation, delayed diarrhea, nausea, vomiting, loss of appetite, anemia, risk of infection, fatigue and weakness, hair loss

Lomustine: Nausea, vomiting, anemia, risk of infection

Mercaptopurine: Anemia, risk of infection, liver function changes

Methotrexate: Anemia, risk of infection, taste changes, mouth sores, diarrhea, skin darkening, kidney function changes, gritty eyes

Mitomycin: Anemia, risk of infection, loss of appetite

Paclitaxel (Taxol): Anemia, risk of infection, mouth sores, diarrhea, hair loss, joint and muscle pain, itchy rash, neuropathy, headaches, nausea, vomiting

Procarbazine: Anemia, risk of infection, nausea, vomiting, flu-like symptoms

Streptozocin: Nausea, vomiting, hair loss, liver function changes, kidney function changes

Taxotere: Anemia, risk of infection, nausea, vomiting, mouth sores, diarrhea, hair loss, skin rash, red palms and soles (palmar plantar syndrome), neuropathy, fatigue, fluid retention

Thiotepa: Anemia, risk of infection, nausea, vomiting

Topotecan (Hycamtin): Anemia, risk of infection, nausea, vomiting, loss of appetite, hair loss

Vinblastine: Anemia, risk of infection, skin rash

Vincristine: Abdominal cramps, constipation, neuropathy

Vindesine: Anemia, risk of infection, abdominal cramps, constipation, neuropathy

Vinorelbine (Navelbine): Anemia, risk of infection, constipation, diarrhea, neuropathy

Appendix 7

Post GI Surgery Diet

Diet Principles

1. Eat hot and cold foods slowly to avoid stimulating peristalsis.

2. Limit milk to two cups per day.

3. Avoid cheeses made with herbs, seeds, or spices. Mild cheddar and cottage cheeses are allowed. Yogurt with allowed fruit is to be counted as part of the milk allowance.

4. Choose fruit such as ripe bananas, grapefruit, baked apples (without skin), cooked or canned fruit without seeds, cherries, white grapes, plums, apple-sauce, peaches, apricots, and mandarin oranges. All fruit juices are allowed. Avoid prune juice if it has a laxative effect on you. Avoid raisins.

5. Choose fresh, cooked, canned, or frozen vegetables such as lettuce, celery, beets, asparagus, green beans, squash, tomatoes without seeds, and veg-etable juices. Avoid foods that may lead to gut distention such as dried beans, peas, and legumes, cauliflower, broccoli, cabbage, onions, and garlic.

6. Avoid high-fiber cereals and breads in an effort to cut down the amount of residue in the colon. Choose white potatoes, rice, and pasta.

7. Avoid tough gristled meat, smoked meat or fish, corned beef, hotdogs, luncheon meats, and sausage.

8. Avoid desserts containing coconuts, nuts, spices or fruits.

9. Avoid pepper, mustard, nuts, olives, pickles, popcorn, spices, and seeds such as caraway, sesame, celery, and poppy.

10. Limit visible fat to three teaspoons per day. Avoid all fried foods.

Appendix 8
Low-Fat Diet for Fat Malabsorption

Diet Principles

1. Limit visible fat (butter, margarine, mayonnaise) to three teaspoons per day.

2. Avoid red meat. Choose lean fish, poultry, and no-fat dairy products.

3. Limit eggs to four per week.

4. Prepare all foods without any added fat. Use cooking oil spray to coat pans.

5. Avoid quick breads, muffins, biscuits, pancakes, corn bread, sweet rolls, and doughnuts. Choose whole grain breads, melba toast, pretzels, saltines, and rye wafers.

6. Avoid fried potatoes, potato chips, and snack chips. Pasta, rice, baked snack chips, and potatoes prepared without added fat are allowed.

7. Avoid avocados. All other fruits are allowed.

8. Avoid vegetables made with cheese or cream sauces. All other vegetables are allowed.

9. Avoid soups that are cream based. Soups made with skim milk or broth are allowed.

10. Avoid nuts and olives.

Appendix 9

Antiesophageal Reflux Diet

Diet Principles

1. Limit caffeine-containing foods or beverages such as coffee, tea, selected soft drinks, cocoa, chocolate, chocolate drinks, etc.

2. Based on tolerance, you may wish to avoid foods and beverages that contain citric acid such as tomatoes, grapefruit, oranges, lemons, limes, tangerines, etc.

3. Limit deep fat fried foods, high-fat meats, dairy products such as cream soups or sauces, whole milk, whipped cream, and high-fat foods such as butter, margarine, gravies, pastries, etc.

4. Avoid alcoholic beverages.

5. Based on tolerance, you may wish to avoid black or red pepper, peppermint, and spearmint oils.

6. Do not lie down immediately after a meal. You may wish to elevate the head of your bed with a 4-inch block to avoid nighttime reflux.

Appendix 10
Protein Content of Selected Foods

1/2 cup cooked soybeans	10 gm
1/2 cup cooked navy, pinto, kidney beans	8 gm
2 Tbs powdered soy protein	6 gm
2 Tbs nonfat dry milk	3 gm
2 Tbs wheat germ	3 gm
1 Tbs tahini	3 gm
1 Tbs peanut butter	5 gm
1 oz almonds	6 gm
1 oz peanuts	7 gm
1/4 cup soy nuts, roasted	16 gm
1 oz sunflower seeds	6 gm
1 large egg	6 gm
4 oz lite tofu	13 gm
1/2 cup prepared textured vegetable protein	11 gm
3 oz cooked skinless poultry breast	27 gm
3 oz lean ground beef	21 gm
3 oz tuna, water packed	18 gm
3 oz baked cod or other white fish	22 gm
1/4 cup nonfat or low-fat cottage cheese	8 gm
1 oz nonfat or low-fat cheese	6 gm
8 oz nonfat or low-fat yogurt	10 gm
8 oz skim milk	8 gm
8 oz soy milk	8 gm
8 oz rice milk	1 gm

Sources: Product labels, United States Department of Agriculture Nutrient Data Laboratory

(www.nal.usda.gov/fnic/foodcomp)

Appendix 11
Daily Fat Gram Allowance Worksheet

Step 1. Determine your calorie requirement. _____
(Ask a dietitian to calculate it or do it yourself using the worksheet in Appendix 3.)

Step 2. Multiply your answer in step 1 by the decimal version of the fat allowance given in the nutrition action plan for your specific cancer.
For a 20 percent fat diet, use .20
For a 25 percent fat diet, use .25
For a 30 percent fat diet, use .30

Step 3. Write the result here: _____

Step 4. Divide the result by 9
(The number of calories per gram of fat).

Step 5. Write the new amount here. _____
This is the amount of fat, in grams, you should eat per day.

Example:

If you require 2,000 calories on a twenty percent fat diet, an average of 400 of those calories should come from fats (2,000 multiplied by .20). This places your goal at 44 grams of fat per day (400 divided by 9).

Appendix 12

Counting Fat Grams

Foods not listed below contain negligible amounts of fat, or will have a product label that will specify fat grams.

Food	Grams of Fat
Meat, Fish, Poultry & Eggs (3 oz portions unless otherwise specified)	
London broil	15
Rib eye steak	13
Roast	8
Flounder	1
Haddock	1
Lamb chop	16
Salmon	5
Tuna fish	1
Shrimp	1
Chicken breast, no skin	3
Chicken drumstick, no skin, 1 avg	2
Turkey, light meat, no skin	3
Turkey, dark meat, no skin	6
Egg, 1 large	5
Milk and Dairy Products (8 oz unless otherwise specified)	
Milk, whole	8
Milk, 2%	5
Milk, 1%	3
Milk, skim	0
Buttermilk	2
Half and half, 1 Tbs	2
American cheese, 1 oz	9
Cheddar, 1 oz	9
Cottage cheese, creamed	9
Cottage cheese, 1%	2
Cream cheese, 1 oz	10
Mozzarella, part skim, 1 oz	5
Parmesan, 1 Tbs	2
Swiss, 1 oz	8

Yogurt, plain	7
Yogurt, plain, nonfat	0

Grains

Bagel, 1	2
English muffin, 1	1
Whole wheat bread, 1 slice	1
Oatmeal, 2/3 cup, cooked	2
Pasta, 1 cup, cooked	1
Pancakes, 4" plain	2
Waffles, 7" plain	8
French toast, 1 slice	7

Beans, Nuts & Seeds

Cashews, 1/4 cup	16
Coconut, flaked, 1/4 cup	6
Peanuts, 1/4 cup	17
Peanut butter, 1 Tbs	8
Pistachios, 1/4 cup	14
Sesame seeds, 1/4 cup	21
Tahini (sesame butter), 1 Tbs	7
Tofu, 1/2 cup	6
Tofu light, 1/2 cup	1
Walnuts, 1/4 cup	18

Spreads & Oils

Avocado, 1/2 medium	15
Butter, 1 tsp	4
Margarine, 1 tsp	4
Vegetable oil, 1 Tbs	14
Vegetable spray 2.5-second spray	1

Salad Dressings (1 Tbs serving size)

Blue cheese	8
French	9
Italian	7
Thousand Island	6

Sources: Product labels, United States Department of Agriculture Nutrient Data Laboratory (www.nal.usda.gov/fnic/foodcomp) and Handbook 8.

Appendix 13
Recipe Modifications for Lowering Fat Content

By reducing an ingredient, or substituting one ingredient for another, you can alter recipes to reduce calories, total fat, saturated fat, and cholesterol.

Here are some tips for cutting fat without compromising flavor:

Ingredient	Quantity	Substitute Modification
Whole egg	1	1/4 cup egg substitute or 1 egg white plus 1tsp olive or canola oil or 2 egg whites
Shortening	1 cup	3/4 cup canola oil
Whole milk	1 cup	1 cup skim milk
Sour cream	1 cup	1 cup plain yogurt or 1 cup blended low-fat cottage cheese plus 1 Tbs lemon juice
Regular cheese	1 oz	1 oz part skim cheese
Salad dressing	1 tsp	1 Tbs low-calorie salad dressing
Cream soups	1 can	1 cup homemade skim milk white sauce and celery, mushrooms, or chicken bouillon
Vegetable oil	1 cup	2/3 cup unsweetened applesauce plus 1/3 cup canola oil

Appendix 14
Answers to Dining Out Quiz

Sample Menu	High-Fiber Substitutions
Breakfast	
Orange juice	Orange segments
Bran flakes	
Scrambled egg	
White toast	Whole wheat toast
Low-fat milk	
Coffee	
Lunch	
Split pea soup	
Roast beef	
White rice	Brown rice
Carrots	
Coleslaw	
French bread	Pumpernickel rolls
Butter	
Baked apple with skin	
Water	
Dinner	
Baked salmon	
Boiled new potatoes	Baked potato with skin
Collard greens	
Rye rolls	
Butter	
Mixed fruit cup	
Angel food cake	Oatmeal raisin cookie
Coffee	

Appendix 15
Fiber Content of Selected Foods

Food	Amount	Grams of Fiber
Fruit		
Apple (with skin)	1 medium	3.0
Dried figs	2	3.5
Orange	1 medium	3.1
Pear (with skin)	1 medium	4.3
Prunes	3	1.8
Raisins (seedless)	1/4 cup	1.9
Grapes	20	1.0
Strawberries	1 cup	3.9
Raspberries	1 cup	8.0
Vegetables		
Broccoli	1/2 cup	2.7
Brussels sprouts	1/2 cup	3.4
Baked potato (with skin)	1 medium	3.6
Spinach	1/2 cup	2.0
Corn	2/3 cup	1.5
Sweet potato	1/2 medium	1.7
Carrots (raw)	1 medium	2.9
Romaine lettuce	1 cup	1.1
Tomato (raw)	1 medium	1.6
Legumes		
Baked beans	1/2 cup	9.8
Kidney beans	1/2 cup	7.3
Lima beans	1/2 cup	3.6
Green peas	1/2 cup	2.8
Lentils	1/2 cup	3.7

Peanuts	1/4 cup	2.9
Almonds, with skin	15	5.6

Breads, Grains, Cereals and Pasta

Pumpernickel bread	1 slice	1.9
Brown rice (cooked)	1/2 cup	1.7
Bulgur (cooked)	1 cup	8.0
Whole wheat bread	1 slice	1.9
Spaghetti (cooked)	1 cup	2.2
Pasta, whole wheat (cooked)	1 cup	6.0
All Bran	1/3 cup	8.5
Bran Chex	2/3 cup	4.6
Bran flakes	3/4 cup	5.3
Oatmeal (regular cook)	3/4 cup	2.0
Shredded wheat	2/3 cup	3.0
Raisin bran	3/4 cup	4.8
Wheat germ	1/4 cup	7.8

SOURCES: Product labels, United States Department of Agriculture Nutrient Data Laboratory (www.nal.usda.gov/fnic/foodcomp) and Handbook 8.

Appendix 16

How Safe Are You? Food Safety Quiz Answers

1. It is safe to eat a medium rare hamburger. False

Ground beef is particularly susceptible to bacterial contamination if not cooked
to an internal temperature of 160 degrees. Any ground meats should be
cooked until well done.

2. You should devein shrimp before you eat it. False

The thin, dark line that runs down the spine of shrimp is actually the intestine.
Proper cooking of shrimp will render the bacteria within the intestine harmless.

**3. Cooling a large pot of spaghetti sauce in the refrigerator will reduce the risk
of food-borne illness. False**

The food in the center of a deep pot may not reach a safe temperature fast
enough. It is safer to pour the sauce into shallow containers and then refrigerate them.

4. Purplish blotches on cold cuts are not a food safety concern. False

For all meats, discoloration is cause for concern. Brown, green, or purple
blotches are all signs of microbial attack.

5. It is safe to cut a moldy section off of cheese. True

It is safe to trim away mold from hard cheeses, but soft cheeses that show evidence of mold should be discarded.

6. It is okay to taste test while cooking. False

Taste testing while cooking is not recommended because the ingredients in the
foods you are tasting may not be thoroughly cooked.

7. Brown spots on leaf lettuce are harmless. True

When the cell walls of lettuce break down, rust spots develop. These are harmless blotches that should be trimmed away prior to serving.

8. You can eat a food that has passed its "sell by" date. True

Foods that have a "sell by" date on the label typically have a short shelf life, such
as milk or bread. If stored properly, most foods are safe to eat for a few days
beyond this date.

9. If you buy organic produce, you don't need to wash it. False

While organic produce may not have pesticide residues, it can harbor soil
microbes.

**10. Mixing a raw egg into your blended soy shake is a good way to get more
protein. False**

Consuming anything made with a raw egg increases your risk of salmonella poi-
soning.

Endnotes

Chapter 1 Notes

1. Zeze, K. et al. Factors influencing depression of natural killer activity and its prevention in esophageal cancer patients. *Nippon Geka Gakkai Zasshi* (Japanese) 90(1): 22-33, Jan 1989.

2. Nakayama, Y. et al. Varied effects of thoracic irradiation on peripheral lymphocyte subsets in lung cancer patients. *Intern Med* 34(10): 959–65, Oct 1995.

3. Beitsch, P. et al. Natural immunity in breast cancer patients during neoadjuvant chemotherapy and after surgery. *Surg Oncol* 3(4): 211–9, Aug 1994.

4. Greer, S. Psychological response to cancer and survival. *Psychol Med* 21(1): 43–9, Feb 1991.

5. Kabat-Zinn, J. An outpatient program in behavioral medicine for chronic pain patients based on the practice of mindfulness meditation: theoretical considerations and preliminary results. *Gen Hosp Psychiatry* 4(1): 33–47, Apr 1982.

6. Sims, S. Slow stroke back massage for cancer patients. *Nursing Times* 82(47): 47–50, 1986.

7. Rutledge, D.N. et al. Changes in well-being of women cancer survivors following a survivor weekend experience. *Oncol Nurs Forum* 28(1): 85–91, Jan/Feb 2001.

8. Raleigh, E.D. Sources of hope in chronic illness. *Oncol Nurs Forum* 19: 443–8, 1992.

9. Hassed, C. How humour keeps you well. *Aust Fam Physician* 30(1): 25–8, Jan 2001.

10. Shephard, R.J. et al. Associations between physical activity and susceptibility to cancer: possible mechanisms. *Sports Med* 26(5): 293–315, Nov 1998.

11. Bacaua, R.F. et al. Effect of a moderate intensity exercise training protocol on the metabolism of macrophages and lymphocytes of tumour-bearing rats. *Cell Biochem Funct* 18(4): 249–58, Dec 2000.

12. Woods, J.A. Exercise and resistance to neoplasia. *Can J Physiol Pharmacol* 76(5): 581–8, May 1998.

13. Koenig, H.G. Psychoneuroimmunology and the faith factor. *J Gend Specif Med* 3(5): 37–44, Jul/Aug 2000.

14. Meisenhelder, J.B. et al. Prayer and health outcomes in church lay leaders. *West J Nurs Res* 22(6): 706–16, Oct 2000.

15. Koenig, H.G. et al. Religion and coping with serious medical illness. *Ann Pharmacother* 35(3):352–9, Mar 2001.

16. Easton, K.L. et al. The roles of the pastor in the interdisciplinary rehabilitation team. *Rehabil Nurs* 25(1): 10–2, Jan/Feb 2000.

17. Chandra, S. et al. Nutrition, immune response and outcome. *Prog Food Nutr Sci* 10(1–2): 1–65, 1986.

Chapter 2 Notes

1. Grant, J.P. Proper use and recognized role of TPN in the cancer patient. *Nutrition* 6(4): Suppl, 6S–7S, 10S, Jul/Aug 1990.

2. Edington, J. et al. Outcomes of undernutrition in patients in the community with cancer or cardiovascular disease. *Proc Nutr Soc* 58(3): 655–61, Aug 1999.

3. Kern,K. et al. Cancer cachexia. *J Parenteral Enteral Nutrition* 12(3): 286–98, May/Jun 1988.

4. Delmore, G. Assessment of nutritional status in cancer patients: widely neglected? *Support Care Center* 5(5): 376–80, Sep 97.

5. DeWys, W.D. et al. Prognostic effect of weight loss prior to chemotherapy in cancer patients. *Am J Med* 69: 491–497, 1980.

6. Grant, A. and DeHoog, S. *Nutritional Assessment and Support*, 3rd edition (Seattle, 1985).

7. Lund E.K. et al. Oral ferrous sulfate supplements increase the free radical-generating capacity of feces from healthy volunteers. *Am J Clin Nutr* 69(2): 250–5, Feb 1999.

8. Pennington, J.A. et al. Total diet study: estimated dietary intakes of nutritional elements, 1982–1991. *Int J Vitam Nutr Res* 66(4): 350–62, 1996.

9. Simopoulos, A. Overview of nutritional status in the United States, *Prog Clin Biol Res* 67: 237–47, 1981.

10. Windham, C. et al. Consistency of nutrient consumption patterns in the United States. *J Am Diet Assoc* 78(6): 587–95, Jun 1981.

11. Von Roenn, J.H. Randomized trials of megestrol acetate for AIDS-associated anorexia and cachexia, *Oncology* 51(S1): 19–24, Oct 1994.

12. Buntzel, J. et al. Value of megestrol acetate in treatment of cachexia in head–neck tumors. *Laryngorhinootologie* 74(8): 504–7, Aug 1995.

13. Beal, J.E. et al. Dronabinol as a treatment for anorexia associated with weight loss in patients with AIDS. *J Pain Symptom Manage* 10(2): 89–97, Feb 1995.

14. Bozzetti, F. et al. Perioperative total parenteral nutrition in malnourished, gastrointestinal cancer patients: A randomized, clinical trial. *Journal of Parenteral and Enteral Nutrition* 24(1): 7–14, Jan–Feb 2000.

15. Celaya, P.S. et al. Nutritional management of oncologic patients. *Nutr Hosp* 14S(2): 43S–52S, May 1999.

16. Nitenberg, G. and Raynard B. Nutritional support of the cancer patient: issues and dilemmas. *Crit Rev Oncol Hematol* 34(3): 137–68, Jun 2000.

17. Galban, C. et al. An immune-enhancing enteral diet reduces mortality rate and episodes of bacteremia in septic intensive care unit patients. *Crit Care Med* 28(3): 643–8, Mar 2000.

Chapter 3 Notes

1. Pool-Zobel, B.L. et al. Lactobacillus- and bifidobacterium-mediated antigenotoxicity in the colon of rats. *Nutr Cancer* 26(3): 365–80, 1996.

2. Viscoli, C. et al. Candidemia in cancer patients: a prospective, multicenter surveillance study by the IFIG. *Clin Infect Dis* 28(5): 1071–9, May 1999.

3. Abe, F, et al. Experimental candidiasis in liver injury. *Mycopathologia* 110(1): 37–42, Oct 1987.

4. Potter, J.D. et al. Colon cancer: A review of the epidemiology. *Epidemiol Rev* 15(2): 499–545, 1993.

5. Keeling, W.F. et al. Gastrointestinal transit during mild exercise. *J Appl Physiol* 63(3): 978–81, Sep 1987.

6. Desser, L. et al. Induction of tumor necrosis factor in human peripheral-blood mononuclear cells by proteolytic enyzmes. *Oncology* 47(6): 475–77, 1990.

7. Funk-Archeluta, M. et al. A soy-derived antiapoptotic fraction decreases methotrexate toxicity in the gastrointestinal tract of the rat. *Nutr Cancer* 29(3): 217–21, 1997.

8. McRorie, J. et al. Effects of olestra and sorbitol consumption on objective measures of diarrhea: impact of stool viscosity on common gastrointestinal symptoms. *Regul Toxicol Pharmacol* 31(1): 59–67, Feb 2000.

9. El-Omar, E.M. et al. Increased prevalence of precancerous changes in relatives of gastric cancer patients: critical role of H. pylori. *Gastroenterology* 118(1): 22–30, Jan 2000.

10. Freys, S.M. et al. Epidemiology and pathophysiology of Barrett esophagus. *Zentralbl Chir* 125(5): 406–13, 2000.

11. Jokinen, J. et al. Celiac sprue in patients with chronic oral mucosal symptoms. *J Clin Gastroenterol* 26(1): 23–6, Jan 1998.

12. Griffith, R.S. et al. Success of L-lysine therapy in frequently recurrent herpes simplex infection. *Dermatologica* 175: 183–90, 1987.

13. Fischer-Rasmussen, W. et al. Ginger treatment of hyperemesis gravidarum. *Eur J Obstet Gynecol Reprod Bio* 38, 19–24, 1990.

14. Prasad, A.S. et al. Trace elements in head and neck cancer patients: zinc status and immunologic functions. *Otolaryngol Head Neck Surg* 16(6:1): 624–9, Jun 1997.

15. Fong, L.Y. et al. Nitrosobenzylmethylamine, zinc deficiency and oesophageal cancer. *IARC Sci Publ* 19: 503–13, 1978.

16. Bakan, N. et al. Serum zinc and angiotensin-converting enzyme levels in patients with lung cancer. *Biofactors* 1(2): 177–8, Jul 1988.

17. Miller, A.L. Therapeutic considerations of L-glutamine: a review of the literature. *Altern Med Rev* 4(4): 239–48, Aug 1999.

18. Kimata, M. et al. Effects of luteolin, quercetin and baicalein on immunoglobulin E-mediated mediator release from human cultured mast cells. *Clin Exp Allergy* 30(4): 501–8, Apr 2000.

Chapter 4 Notes

1. *McDonald's Nutrition Facts* (630) 623–6198.
2. *Auntie Anne's Nutrition Facts* (717) 442–4766.

Chapter 5 Notes

1. Anand, R.S. et al. Rise in amount of total fat and number of calories consumed by Americans. *The FASEB Journal* 11(3): A183.

2. Pedersen, B.K. et al. Training and natural immunity: effects of diets rich in fat or carbohydrate. *Eur J Appl Physiol* 82(1–2): 98–102, May 2000.

3. Ng, E. et al. Risk factors for breast carcinoma in Singaporean Chinese women. *Cancer* 80: 725–731, 1997.

4. Schoen, R. E. et al. Increased blood glucose and insulin, body size, and incident colorectal cancer. *J Natl Cancer Inst* 91(13): 1147–54, Jul 1999.

5. Goodman, M.T. et al. Diet, body size, physical activity and the risk of endometrial cancer. *Cancer Res* 57(22): 5077–85, Nov 1997.

6. Hartz, A. J. et al. The association of girth measurements with disease in 32,856 women. *Am J Epidemiol.* 119, 71–80, 1984.

7. Lindblad, P. et al. The role of obesity and weight fluctuations in the etiology of renal cell cancer. *Cancer Epidemiol Biomarkers Prev* 3: 361–639, 1994.

8. Kesteloot, H. et al. Dairy fat, saturated animal fat, and cancer risk. *Prev Med* 20(2): 226–36, Mar 1991.

9. Bruemmer, B. et al. Nutrient intake in relation to bladder cancer among middle-aged men and women. *Am J Epidemiol* 144: 485–495, 1996.

10. Goodman, M.T. et al. Diet, body size, physical activity and the risk of endometrial cancer. *Cancer Res* 57(22): 5077–85, Nov 1997.

11. Hankin, J.H. et al. Attributable risk of breast, prostate and lung cancer in Hawaii due to saturated fat. *Cancer Causes Control* 3(1): 17–23, Jan 1992.

12. Peters, R.K. et al. Diet and colon cancer in Los Angeles County, California. *Cancer Causes Control* 3: 457–73, 1992.

13. Goodman, M.T. et al. Diet, body size, physical activity and the risk of endometrial cancer. *Cancer Res* 57(22): 5077–85, Nov 1997.

14. Sinha, R. et al. Fried, well-done red meat and risk of lung cancer in women. *Cancer Causes Control* 9(6): 621–30, Dec 1998.

15. Ogawa, T. et al. Promoting effects of both dietary cholesterol and cholestyramine on pancreatic carcinogenesis initiated by N-nitrosobis(2-oxopropyl)amin in Syrian golden hamsters. *Carcinogenesis* 13(11): 2047–52, Nov 1992.

16. Goodman, M.T. et al. Diet, body size, physical activity and the risk of endometrial cancer. *Cancer Res* 57(22): 5077–85, Nov 1997.

17. Connolly, J.M. et al. Effects of dietary fatty acids on DU145 human prostate cancer cell growth in athymic nude mice. *Nutr Cancer* 29(2): 114–119, 1997.

18. Rose, D.P. Dietary fat, fatty acids and breast cancer. *Breast Cancer* 4(1): 7–16, Mar 1997.

19. Mukutmoni-Norris, M. et al. Modulation of murine mammary tumor vasculature by dietary n-3 fatty acids in fish oil. *Cancer Lett* 150(1): 101–9, Mar 2000.

20. de Pablo, MA. Modulatory effects of dietary lipids on immune system functions. *Immunol Cell Biol* 78(1): 31–9, Feb 2000.

21. Furukawa, K. et al. Effects of soybean oil emulsion and EPA on stress response and immune function after a severely stressful operation. *Ann Surg* 229(2): 255–61, 1999.

22. Fritsche, K.L. Effects of dietary alpha linolenic acid on growth, metastasis, fatty acid profile and prostaglandin production of two murine mammary adenocarcinomas. *J Nutr* 120(12): 1601–9, Dec 1990.

23. Klein, V. et al. Low alpha-linolenic acid content of adipose breast tissue is associated with an increased risk of breast cancer. *Eur J Cancer* 36(3): 335–40, Feb 2000.

24. Owen, R.W. et al. Phenolic compounds and squalene in olive oils: the concentration and antioxidant potential of total phenols, simple phenols, secoiridoids, lignans and squalene. *Food Chem Toxicol* 38(8): 647–59, Aug 2000.

25. Owen, R.W. et al. The antioxidant/anticancer potential of phenolic compounds isolated from olive oil. *Eur J Cancer* 36(10): 1235–47, Jun 2000.

26. Bartoli, R. et al. Effect of olive oil on early and late events of colon carcinogenesis in rats. *Gut* 46(2): 191–9, Feb 2000.

27. Awad, A.B. et al. Peanuts as a source of beta-sitosterol, a sterol with anticancer properties. *Nutr Cancer* 36(2): 238–41, 2000.

28. Sanders, T.H. et al. Occurrence of resveratrol in edible peanuts. *J Agric Food Chem* 48(4): 1243–6, Apr 2000.

29. Freitas, V.P. et al. Occurrence of aflatoxins B1, B2, G1, and G2 in peanuts and their products marketed in the region of Campinas, Brazil in 1995 and 1996. *Food Addit Contam* 15(7): 807–11, Oct 1998.

30. Colin-Negrete, J. et al. Effect of whole cottonseed on serum constituents, fragility of erythrocyte cells and reproduction of growing Holstein heifers. *J Dairy Sci* 79(11): 2016–23, Nov 1996.

31. Allison, D.B. et al. Estimates intakes of trans fatty and other fatty acids in the U.S. population. *J Amer Diet Assoc* 99(2): 166–174, Feb 1999.

32. Katan, M.B. Trans fatty acids and plasma lipoproteins. *Nutr Rev* 58(6): 188–191, Jun 2000.

33. Allison, D.B. et al. Estimates intakes of trans fatty and other fatty acids in the U.S. population. *J Amer Diet Assoc* 99(2): 166–174, Feb 1999.

34. Reprinted with permission, *Tufts University Health & Nutrition Letter*, Feb 2000, telephone 1 800 274-7581.

35. Yanez, E. et al. Fat substitutes in human diet. *Arch Latinoam Nutr* 49(2): 101–5, Jun 1999.

Chapter 6 Notes

1. Favero, A. et al. Energy sources and risk of cancer of the breast and colorectum in Italy. *Adv Exp Med Biol* 472: 51–5, 1999.

2. Baghurst, P.A. A case-control study of diet and cancer of the pancreas. *Am J Epidemidol* 134: 167–79, 1991.

3. Kneller, R.W. et al. A cohort study of stomach cancer in a high-risk American population. *Cancer* 68: 672–8, 1991.

4. Rothkopf, M. Fuel utilization in neoplastic disease: implications for the use of nutritional support in cancer patients. *Nutrition* 6(4S): 14S–16S, Jul–Aug 1990.

5. Bruce, W.R. et al. Mechanisms linking diet and colorectal cancer: the possible role of insulin resistance. *Nutr. Cancer* 37(1): 19–26, 2000.

6. Kruis, W. et al. Effect of diets low and high in refined sugars on gut transit, bile acid metabolism, and bacterial fermentation. *Gut* 32, 367–71, 1991.

7. Foster, M.P. et al. Humoral and cell-mediated immunity in mice with genetic deficiencies of prolactin, growth hormone, insulin-like growth factor-I, and thyroid hormone. *Clin Immunol* 96(2): 140–9, Aug 2000.

8. Alvarez Gasca, M.A. et al. Fungal agents isolated from cancer patients. *Rev latinoam Microbiol* 40(1–2): 15–24, Jan–Jun 1998.

9. Jenkins, D. Lente carbohydrate: a newer approach to the management of diabetes. *Diabetes Care* 5: 634 9, 1982.

10. Reprinted with permission, *Tufts University Health & Nutrition Letter* 3, March 2000, telephone 1 800 274 7591.

11. Reuber, M.D. Carcinogenicity of saccharin. *Envion. Health Perspect* 25: 173–200, Aug 1978.

12. Reprinted with permission from *Environmental Nutrition* 8, Sep 2000, 52 Riverside Drive, Suite 15A, New York, NY 10024. For subscription information: 1 800 829-5384.

13. Robbins, P.I. et al. Aspartame and symptoms of carpal tunnel syndrome. *J Occup Envir Med* 41(6): 418, Jun 1999.

14. *Splenda, The Facts* (pamphlet) McNeil Speciality Products Company

15. Curi, R. et al. Effect of Stevia rebaudiana on glucose tolerance in normal adult humans. *Braz J Med Biol Res* 19(6): 771–4, 1986.

Chapter 7 Notes

1. Abdulla, M. et al. Role of diet modification in cancer prevention. *Biofactors* 12(1–4): 45–51, 2000.

2. Wargovich, M.J. Experimental evidence for cancer preventive elements in foods. *Cancer Lett* 114: 11–7, Mar 1997.

3. Ames, B.N. Micronutrient deficiencies. A major cause of DNA damage. *Ann NY Acad Sci* 889: 87–106, 1999.

4. Miller, E.R. et al. Effect of dietary patterns on measurement of lipid peroxidation. *Circulation* 98(22): 2390–5, Dec 1998.

5. Sparnins, V.L. et al. Effects of organosulfur compounds from garlic and onions on benzapyrene-induced neoplasia and glutathione S-transferase activity in the mouse. *Carcinogenesis* 9(1): 131–4, Jan 1988.

6. Nagabhushan, M. et al. Anticarcinogenic action of diallyl sulfide in hamster buccal pouch and forestomach. *Cancer Lett* 6: 207–216, 1992.

7. Caldes, G. A potential antileukemic substance present in Allium ascalonicum. *Planta Medica* 23: 90–100, 1973.

8. Koide, T. et al. Antitumor effect of hydrolyzed anthocyanin from grape rinds and red rice. *Cancer Biother Radiopharm* 11(4): 273–7, Aug 1996.

9. Bagchi, D. et al. Free radicals and grape seed proanthocyanidin extract: importance in human health and disease prevention. *Toxicology* 148(2–3): 187–97, Aug 2000.

10. Santa, M.S. et al. Beta carotene-induced enhancement of NK cell activity in elderly men: an investigation of the role of cytokines. *Am J Clin Nutr* 68(1): 164–70, Jul 1998.

11. Herrero, R. et al. A case-control study of nutrient status and invasive cervical cancer. I. Dietary indicators. *Am J Epidemiol* 134(11): 1335–46, Dec 1991.

12. Comstock, G.W. et al. The risk of developing lung cancer associated with antioxidants in the blood. *Cancer Epidemiol Biomarkers Prev* 6(11): 907–16, Nov 1997.

13. Nomura, A.M. et al. Serum micronutrients and upper aerodigestive tract cancer. *Cancer Epidemiol Biomarkers Prev* 6(6): 407–12, Jun 1997.

14. Matos, H.R. et al. Protective effect of lycopene on lipid peroxidation and oxidative DNA damage in cell culture. *Arch Biochem Biophys* 383(1): 56–9, Nov 2000.

15. Kim, H.P. et al. Zeaxanthin dipalmitate from Lycium chinense has hepatoprotective activity. *Res Commun Mol Pathol Pharmacol* 97(3): 301–14, Sep 1997.

16. Gann, P.H. et al. Lower prostate cancer risk in men with elevated plasma lycopene levels: results of a prospective analysis. *Cancer Res* 59(6): 1225–30, Mar 1999.

17. Park, J.S. et al. Capsaicin protects against ethanol-induced oxidative injury in the gastric mucosa of rats. *Life Sci* 67(25): 3087–93, Nov 2000.

18. Surh, Y.J. et al. Chemoprotective properties of some pungent ingredients present in red pepper and ginger. *Mutat Res* 402(1–2): 259–67, 1998.

19. Giovannelli, L. et al. Effect of complex polyphenols and tannins from red wine on DNA oxidative damage of rat colon mucosa in vivo. *Eur J Nutr* 39(5): 207–12, Oct 2000.

20. Zand, R.S. et al. Steroid hormone activity of flavonoids and related compounds. *Breast Cancer Res Treat* 62(1): 35–49, Jul 2000.

21. Bai, F. et al. Promoter activation and following induction of the p21/WAF1 gene by flavone is involved in G1 phase arrest in A549 lung adenocarcinoma cells. *FEBS Lett* 437(1–2): 61–4, Oct 1998.

22. Hayashi, A. et al. Effects of daily oral administration of quercetin chalcone and modified citrus pectin. *Altern Med Rev* 5(6): 546–52, Dec 2000.

23. Uddin, S. et al. Quercetin, a bioflavonoid, inhibits the DNA synthesis of human leukemia cells. *Biochem Mo Biol Int* 36(3): 545–50, Jul 1995.

24. ElAttar, T.M. et al. Modulating effect of resveratrol and quercetin on oral cancer cell growth and proliferation. *Anticancer Drugs* 10(2): 187–93, Feb 1999.

25. Kampa, M. et al. Wine antioxidant polyphenols inhibit the proliferation of human prostate cancer cell lines. *Nutr Cancer* 37(2): 223–33, 2000.

26. Hadjipavlou-Litina, D.J. New diaminoether coumarinic derivatives with anti-inflammatory activity. *Arzneimittelforschung* 50(7): 631–5, Jul 2000.

27. Kawabata, K. et al. Suppression of N-nitrosomethylbenzylamine-induced rat esophageal tumorigenesis by dietary feeding of auraptene. *J Exp Clin Cancer Res* 19(1): 45–52, Mar 2000.

28. Tanaka, T. et al. Suppressing effects of dietary supplementation of the organoselenium 1,-4-phenylenebis(methylene) selenocyanate and the citrus antioxidant auraptene on lung metastasis on melanoma cells in mice. *Cancer Res* 60(14): 3713–6, Jul 2000.

29. Thresiamma, K.C. et al. Protective effect of curcumin, ellagic acid and bixin on radiation induced genotoxicity. *J Exp Clin Cancer Res* 17(4): 431–4, Dec 1998.

30. Krishnaswamy, K. et al. Bioactive phytochemicals with emphasis on dietary practices. *Indian J Med Res* 108: 167–81, 1998.

31. Mahmound, N.N. et al. Plant phenolics decrease intestinal tumors in an animal model of familial adenomatous polyposis. *Carcinogenesis* 21(5): 921–7, May 2000.

32. Conney, A.H. et al. Some perspectives on dietary inhibition of carcinogenesis: studies with curcumin and tea. *Proc Soc Exp Biol Med* 216(2): 234–45, Nov 1997.

33. Stoner, G.D. et al. Isothiocyanates and freeze-dried strawberries as inhibitors of esophageal cancer. *Toxicol Sci* 52(2S): 95–100, Dec 1999.

34. Khanduja, K.L. et al. Prevention of N-nitrosodiethylamine-induced lung tumorigenesis by ellagic acid and quercetin in mice. *Food Chem Toxicol* 37(4): 313–8, Apr 1999.

35. Yuan, F. et al. Anti-estrogenic activities of indole-3-carbinol in cervical cells: implication for prevention of cervical cancer. *Anticancer Res* 19(3A): 1673–80, 1999.

36. Rahman, K.M. et al. Translocation of Bax to mitochondria induces apoptotic cell death in indole-3-carbinol (I3C) treated breast cancer cells. *Oncogene* 19(50): 5764–71, Nov 2000.

37. Kushi, L.H. et al. Prospective study of diet and ovarian cancer. *Amer J Epidem* 149(1): 21–31, Jan 1999.

38. Hecht, S.S. et al. Inhibition of carcinogenesis by isothiocyanates. *Drug Metab Rev* 32(3–4): 395–411, Aug 2000.

39. Fahey, J.W. et al. Broccoli sprouts: an exceptionally rich source of inducers of enzymes that protect against chemical carcinogens. *Proc Natl Acad Sci* (USA) 94(19): 10367–72, Sep 1997.

40. Hakim, I.A. et al. Citrus peel use is associated with reduced risk of squamous cell carcinoma of the skin. *Nutr Cancer* 37(2): 161–8, 2000.

41. Benson, P.J. et al. Inhibition of experimental pulmonary metastasis of B16F10 mouse melanoma by limonene, a naturally occurring monoterpene. *Proc Annu Meet Am Assoc Cancer Res* 1996.

42. Belanger, J.T. Perillyl alcohol: applications in oncology. *Altern Med Rev* 3(6): 448–57, Dec 1998.

43. Shoff, S.M. et al. Concentration-dependent increase of murine P388 and B16 population doubling time by the acyclic monoterpene geraniol. *Cancer Res* 51(1): 37–42, Jan 1991.

44. Kuroiloi, T. et al. Potential nitrite scavengers as inhibitors of the formation of N-nitrosamines in solution and tobacco matrix systems. *J Agric Food Chem* 48(9): 4381–8, Sep 2000.

45. Mahmoud, N.N. et al. Plant phenolics decrease intestinal tumors in an animal model of familial adenomatous polyposis. *Carcinogenesis* 21(5): 921–7, May 2000.

46. Zheng, G.Q. et al. Chemoprevention of benzo[a]pyrene-induced forestomach cancer in mice by natural phthalides from celery seed oil. *Nutr Cancer* 19(1): 77–86, 1993.

47. Zhang, Y. et al. Daidzein and genistein glucuronides in vitro are weakly estrogenic and activate human natural killer cells at nutritionally relevant concentrations. *J Nutr* 129(2): 399–405, Feb 1999.

48. Constantinou, A.I. et al. Genistein induces maturation of cultured human breast cancer cells and prevents tumor growth in nude mice. *Am J Clin Nutr* 68(6S): 1426S–30S, Dec 1998.

49. Berhow, M.A. et al. Characterization and antimutagenic activity of soybean saponins. *Mutat Res* 448(1): 11–22, 2000.

50. Offord, E.A. et al. Dual mechanisms involved in the chemoprotective effects of oltipraz and rosemary extract. *Proc Annu Meet Am Assoc Cancer Res* 38: A2473, 1997.

51. Ito, Y. et al. The novel triterpenoid 2-cyano-3, 12-dioxoolean-1, 9-dien-28-oic acid induces apoptosis of human myeloid leukemia cells by a caspase-8-dependent mechanism. *Cell Growth Differ* 11(5): 261-7, May 2000.

Chapter 8 Notes

1. Fabrice, P. et al. Short chain FOS reduce the occurrence of colon tumors and develop gut associated lymphoid tissue in Min Mice. *Cancer Research* 57: 225-228, 1997.

2. Slavin, J.L. Mechanisms for the impact of whole grain foods on cancer risk. *J Am Coll Nutr* 19(3S): 300S–307S, Jun 2000.

3. Howe, G.R. et al. Dietary intake of fiber and decreased risk of cancers of the colon and rectum: evidence from the combined analysis of 13 case controlled studies. *J Natl Cancer Inst* 84: 1887–1896, 1992.

4. Mason, J.B. et al. Nutritional strategies in the prevention of colorectal cancer. *Curr Gastroenterol Rep* 1(4): 341–53, Aug 1999.

5. Reddy, B.S. et al. Preventive potential of wheat bran fractions against experimental colon carcinogenesis: implications for human colon cancer prevention. *Cancer Res* 60(17): 4792–7, Sep 2000.

6. Phytic acid in wheat bran affects colon morphology, cell differentiation and apoptosis. *Carcinogenesis* 21(8): 1547–52, Aug 2000.

7. Howe, G.R. et al. Dietary factors and risk of breast cancer: combined analysis of 12 case-control studies. *J Natl Cancer Inst* 82: 561–9, 1990.

8. Taper, H.S. et al. Influence of inulin and oligofructose on breast cancer and tumor growth. *J Nutr* 129(7S): 1488S–91S, Jul 1999.

9. Bylund, A. et al. Rye bran and soy protein delay growth and increase apoptosis of human LNCaP prostate adenocarcinoma in nude mice. *Prostate* 42(4): 304–14, Mar 2000.

10. Risch, H.A. et al. Dietary fat intake and risk of epithelial ovarian cancer. *J Natl Cancer* 86(18): 1409–15, Sep 1994.

11. Howe, G.R. et al. Nutrition and pancreatic cancer. *Cancer Causes Control* 7(1): 69–82, Jan 1996.

12. McCann, S.E. et al. Diet in the epidemiology of endometrial cancer in western New York. *Cancer Causes Control* 11(10): 965–74, Dec 2000.

13. Soler, M. et al. Fiber intake and the risk of oral, pharyngeal and esophageal cancer. *Int J Cancer* 91(3): 283–7, Feb 2001.

14. Tazawa, K. et al. Dietary fiber inhibits the incidence of hepatic metastasis with the anti-oxidant activity and portal scavenging functions. *Hum Cell* 12(4): 189–96, Dec 1999.

15. Slavin, J.L. Implication of dietary modifications. *Am J Med* 106(1A): 46S–49S, Jan 1999.

16. ADA Reports. Position of the American Dietetic Association: Health implications of dietary fiber. *J Am Diet Assoc* 88: 216, 1988.

17. Kantor, L.S. et al. Choose a variety of grains daily, especially whole grains: a challenge for consumers. *J Nutr* 131 (2S–1): 473S–86S, Feb 2001.

18. Canty, S.L. Constipation as a side effect of opiods. *Oncol Nurs Forum* 21(4): 739–45, May 1994.

Chapter 9 Notes

1. Murkies, A.L. et al. Dietary flour supplementation decreases post menopausal hot flashes: effect of soy and wheat. *Maturitas* 221: 189–195, 1995.

2. Anderson. J.W. et al. Meta-analysis of the effects of soy protein intake on serum lipids. *New Engl J Med* 333: 276–282, 1995.

3. Lo, G.S. et al. Soy fiber improves lipid and carbohydrate metabolism in primary hyperlipidemic subjects. *Atherosclerosis* 62: 239–48, 1986.

4. Arjimandi, B.H. et al. Dietary soy bean protein prevents bone loss in an ovariectomized rat model of osteoporosis. *J Nutr* 126: 161–167, 1996.

5. Anderson, J.W. et al. Effects of soy protein on renal function and proteinuria in patients with type 2 diabetes. *Am J Clin Nutr* 68(6S): 1347S–1353S, Dec 1998.

6. Williams, A.J. et al. Metabolic consequences of differing protein diets in experimental renal disease. *Eur J Clin Invest* 17(2): 117–22, Apr 1987.

7. Messina, M.J. et al. Soy intake and cancer risk: a review of the in vitro and in vivo data. *Nutr Cancer* 21(2): 113–31, 1994.

8. Goodman, M.T. et al. Association of soy and fiber consumption with the risk of endometrial cancer. *Am J Epidemiol* 146(4): 294–306, Aug 1997.

9. Berhow, M.A. et al. Characterization and antimutagenic activity of soy bean saponins. *Mutat Res* 448(1): 11–22, 2000.

10. Rao, A.V. et al. The role of dietary phytosterols in colon carcinogenesis. *Nutr Cancer* 18: 43–52, 1992.

11. Messina, M.J. Legumes and soybeans: overview of their nutritional profile and health effects. *Am J Clin Nutr* 70–(3S): 439S–450S, Sep 1999.

12. Hu, J. et al. Diet and cancer of the colon and rectum: case control study in China. *Int J Epidemiol* 20: 362–7, 1991.

13. Shamsuddin, A.M. et al. Novel anti-cancer functions of IP6: growth inhibition and differentiation of human mammary cancer cell lines in vitro. *Anticancer Res* 16(6A): 3287–3292, 1996.

14. Watanabe, Y. et al. A case control study of cancer of the rectum and the colon. *Nippon Shokakibyo Gakkai Zasshi* 81, 185–194, 1984.

15. Peterson, G. et al. Genistein and biochanin A inhibit the growth of human prostate cancer cells but not epidermal growth factor receptor tyrosine autophosphorylation. *Prostate* 22: 335–45, 1993.

16. Peterson, G. et al. Genistein inhibition of the growth of human breast cancer cells: independence from estrogen receptors and the multi-drug resistance gene. *Biochem Biophys Res Commun* 179(1): 661–7, 1991.

17. Zava, D.T. et al. Estrogenic and antiproliferative properties of genistein and other flavonoids in human breast cancer cells in vitro. *Nutr Cancer* 27(1): 31–40, 1997.

18. Alhasan, S.A. et al. Genistein-induced cell cycle arrest and apoptosis in a head and neck squamous cell carcinoma cell line. *Nutr Cancer* 34(1): 12–19, 1999.

19. Zhou, J.R. et al. Inhibition of murine bladder tumorigenesis by soy isoflavones via alterations in the cell cycle, apoptosis and angiogenesis. *Cancer Res* 59(23): 5231–5236, 1998.

20. Polkowski, K. et al. Anticancer activity of genistein-piperazine complex. In vitro study with HL-60 cells. *Acta Pol Pharm* 57(3): 223–32, May/Jun 2000.

21. Record, I.R. et al. Genistein inhibits growth of B16 melanoma cells in vivo and in vitro and promotes differentiation in vitro. *Int J Cancer* 72(5): 860–4, Sep 1997.

22. Su, S.J. et al. The potential of soy bean foods as a chemoprevention approach for human urinary tract cancer. *Clin Cancer Res* 6(1): 230–6, Jan 2000.

23. Fotsis, T. et al. Genistein, a dietary-derived inhibitor of in vitro angiogenesis. *Proc Natl Acad Sci* (USA) 90: 2690–94, 1993.

24. Khoshyomn, S. et al. Synergistic action of genistein and cisplatin on growth inhibition and cytotoxicity of human medulloblastoma cells. *Pediatr Neurosurg* 33(3): 123–31, Sep 2000.

25. Shao, Z.M. et al. Genistein's "ER dependent and independent" actions are mediated through ER pathways in ER positive breast carcinoma cell lines. *Anticancer Res* 20(4): 2409–16, Jul/Aug 2000.

26. Hsieh, C.Y. et al. Estrogenic effects of genistein on the growth of estrogen receptor-positive human breast cancer (MCF-7) cells in vitro and in vivo. *Cancer Res* 58(17): 3833–8, Sep 1998.

27. Shao, Z.M. et al. Genistein inhibits proliferation similarly in estrogen receptor-positive and negative human breast carcinoma cell lines characterized by P21WAF1/CIP1 induction, G2/M arrest, and apoptosis. *J Cell Biochem* 69(1): 44–54, Apr 1998.

28. Position of the American Dietetic Association and Dietitians of Canada: Women's health and nutrition. *J Am Diet Assoc* 99(6): 738–75, Jun 1999.

29. Divi, R.L. et al. Anti-thyroid isoflavones from soybean: isolation, characterization and mechanisms of action. *Biochem Pharmacol* 54(10): 1087–96, Nov 1997.

30. Nagata, C. et al. Decreased serum total cholesterol concentration is associated with high intake of soy products in Japanese men and women. *J Nutr* 128(2): 209–13, Feb 1998.

Chapter 10 Notes

1. Kern, K. et al. Cancer cachexia. *J Parenteral Enteral Nutrition* 12(3): 286–98, May/Jun 1988.

2. Salonen, J.T. et al. Risk of cancer in relation to serum concentrations of selenium and vitamins A and E: matched case-control analysis of prospective data. *Br Med J* (Clin Res Ed) 290(6466): 417–20, Feb 1985.

3. Hoffer, A. et al. Hardin Jones biostatistical analysis of mortality data of cancer patients. *J Orthomolecular Med* 5(3): 143–54, 1990.

4. Conklin, K.A. Dietary antioxidants during cancer chemotherapy: impact on chemotherapeutic effectiveness and development of side effects. *Nutr Cancer* 37(1): 1–18, 2000.

5. Lamson, D.W. et al. Antioxidants and cancer therapy II: quick reference guide. *Altern Med Rev* 5(2): 152–63, Apr 2000.

6. Prasad, K.N. et al. High doses of multiple antioxidant vitamins: essential ingredients in improving the efficacy of standard cancer therapy. *J Am Coll Nutr* 18(1): 13–25, Feb 1999.

7. Thresiamma, K.C. et al. Protective effect of curcumin, ellagic acid and bixin on radiation induced genotoxicity. *J Exp Clin Cancer Res* 17(4): 431–4, Dec 1998.

8. Hassan, M.I. et al. Cis-platinum-induced immunosuppression: relationship to melatonin in human peripheral blood mononuclear cells. *Clin Biochem* 32(8): 621–6, Nov 1999.

9. Seifter, E. et al. Morbidity and mortality reduction by supplemental vitamin A or beta carotene in CBA mice given total-body gamma-radiation. *J Natl Cancer Inst* 73(5): 1167–77, Nov 1984.

10. Ogawa, A. et al. Effect of a combination of mild-temperature hyperthermia and nicotinamide on the radiation response of experimental tumors. *Radiat Res* 153(3): 327–31, Mar 2000.

11. Kurbacher, C.M. et al. Ascorbic acid (vitamin C) improves the antineoplastic activity of doxorubicin, cisplatin, and paclitaxel in human breast carcinoma cells in vitro. *Cancer Lett* 103(2):183–9, Jun 1996.

12. D'Agostini, F. et al. Inhibition by oral N-acetylcysteine of doxorubicin-induced clastogenicity and alopecia, and prevention of primary tumors and lung micrometastases in mice. *Int J Oncol* 13(2): 217–24, Aug 1998.

13. Satoh, M. et al. Renal toxicity caused by cisplatinum in glutathione-depleted metallothionein-null mice. *Biochem Pharmaco* 60(11): 1729–34, Dec 2000.

14. Jonsson, G.G. et al. Radiosensitization effects of nicotinamide on malignant and normal mouse tissue. *Cancer Res* 45(8): 3609–14, Aug 1985.

15. Phillips, R.W. et al. Beta-carotene inhibits rectal mucosal ornithine decarboxylase activity in colon cancer patients. *Cancer Res* 53(16): 3723–5, Aug 1993.

16. Bishayee, A. et al. Further evidence for chemopreventative potential of beta carotene against experimental carcinogenesis. *Nutr Cancer* 37(1): 89–98, 2000.

17. Uckun, F.M. et al. In vivo toxicity, pharmacokinetics and anticancer activity of Genistein linked to recombinant human epidermal growth factor. *Clin Cancer Res* 4(5): 1125–34, May 1998.

18. Sadzuka, Y. et al. Efficacies of tea components on doxorubicin induced antitumor activity and reversal of multidrug resistance. *Toxicol Lett* 114(1–3): 155–62, Apr 2000.

19. Germain, E. et al. Dietary n-3 polyunsaturated fatty acids and oxidants increase rat mammary tumor sensitivity to epirubicin without change in cardiac toxicity. *Lipids* 34: S223, 1999.

20. Kurbacher, C.M. et al. Ascorbic acid (vitamin C) improves the antineoplastic activity of doxorubicin, cisplatin and paclitaxel in human breast carcinoma cells in vitro. *Cancer Lett* 103(2): 183–9, Jun 1996.

21. Wang, Q. et al. 1,25-Dihydroxyvitamin D3 and all-trans-retinoic acid sensitize breast cancer cells to chemotherapy induced cell death. *Cancer Res* 60(7): 2040–8, Apr 2000.

22. Gribel, N.V. et al. Antimetastatic properties of aloe juice. *Vopr Onkol* (Russia) 32(12): 38–40, 1986.

23. Branda, R.F. et al. Repletion of folate deficiency enhances effectiveness of 5-FU and cytoxan. *Blood* 92(7): 2471–6, Oct 1998.

24. Busch, D.B. et al. Quercetin increases effectiveness of cytoxan. *Environ Mutagen* 8(3): 393–9, 1986.

25. Liu, J. et al. All-trans retinoic acid modulates fas expression and enhances chemosensitivity of human medulloblastoma cells. *Int J Mol Med* 5(2): 145–9, Feb 2000.

26. Adeyemo, D. et al. Antioxidants enhance the susceptibility of colon carcinoma cells to 5-fluorouracil by augmenting the induction of the bax protein. *Cancer Lett* 164(1): 77–84, Mar 2001.

27. Koide, T. et al. Influence of flavonoids on cell cycle phase as analyzed by flow-cytometry. *Cancer Biother Radiopharm* 12(2): 111–5, Apr 1997.

28. Leung, M.F. et al. The differentiating effect of retinoic acid and vincristine on acute myeloid leukemia. *J Hematother* 8(3): 275–9, Jun 1999.

29. Song, E.J. et al. Potentiation of growth inhibition due to vincristine by ascorbic acid in a resistant human non-small cell lung cancer cell line. *Eur J Pharmacol* 292(2): 119–25, Jan 1995.

30. Jaakkola, K. et al. Treatment with antioxidant and other nutrients in combination with chemotherapy and irradiation in patients with small-cell lung cancer. *Anticancer Res* 12(3): 599–606, May/Jun 1992.

31. Lotan R. Retinoids and chemoprevention of aerodigestive tract cancers. *Cancer Metastasis Rev* 16(3–4): 349–56, Sep/Dec 1997.

32. Blot, W.J. Nutrition intervention trials in Linxian, China: Supplementation with specific vitamin/mineral combinations, cancer incidence, and disease-specific mortality in the general population. *J Nat Canc Inst* 85: 1483–91, 1993.

33. Cascante, M. Role of thiamin (vitamin B-1) and transketolase in tumor cell proliferation. *Nutr Cancer* 36(2): 150–4, 2000.

34. Boros, L.G. et al. Thiamin supplementation to cancer patients: a double edged sword. *Anticancer Res* 18(1B): 595–602, Jan/Feb 1998.

35. Day, B. et al. Relationship between dietary nutrients intakes and human prostate cancer. *Wei Sheng Yan Jiu* 26(2):122–5, Mar 1997.

36. Munoz, N. et al. Effect of riboflavin, retinol, and zinc on the micronuclei of buccal mucosa and of esophagus. *J Nat Cancer Inst* 79: 687–91, 1987.

37. Franceschi, S. et al. Role of macronutrients, vitamins and minerals in the etiology of squamous-cell carcinoma of the esophagus. *Int J Cancer* 86(5): 626–31, Jun 2000.

38. Negri, E. et al. Selected micronutrients and oral and pharyngeal cancer. *Int J Cancer* 86(1): 122–7, Apr 2000.

39. Schmitt-Graff, A. et al. Prevention of adriamycin cardiotoxicity by niacin, isocitrate or N-acetylcysteine in mice. A morphological study. *Pathol Res Pract* 181(2): 168–74, May 1986.

40. Kelly, G.S. Nutritional and botanical interventions to assist with the adaptation to stress. *Altern Med Rev* 4(4): 249–65, Aug 1999.

41. Beisel, W. et al. Single-nutrient effects of immunologic functions. *JAMA* 245: 53–58, 1981.

42. DiSorbo, D.M. et al. In vivo and in vitro inhibition of B16 melanoma growth by vitamin B$_6$. *Nutr Cancer* 7(1–2): 43–52, 1985.

43. Wiernik, P.H. et al. Hexamethylmelamine and low or moderate dose cisplatin with or without pyridoxine for treatment of advanced ovarian carcinoma: a study of the Eastern Cooperative Oncology Group. *Cancer Invest* 10(1): 1–9, 1992.

44. Vail, D.M. et al. Efficacy of pyridoxine to ameliorate the cutaneous toxicity associated with doxorubicin containing pegylated (Stealth) liposomes: a randomized, double-blind clinical trial using a canine model. *Clin Cancer Res* 4(6): 1567–71, Jun 1998.

45. Folkers, K. et al. The activities of coenzyme Q10 and vitamin B$_6$ for immune responses. *Biochem Biophys Res Commun* 193(1): 88–92, May 1993.

46. Ravaglia, G. et al. Effect of micronutrient status on natural killer cell immune function in healthy free-living subjects aged >/=90 y. *Am J Clin Nutr* 71(2): 590–8, Feb 2000.

47. Butterworth, C. et al. Improvement in cervical dysplasia associated with folic acid therapy in users of oral contraceptives. *Am J Clin Nutr* 35: 73–82, 1982.

48. Duthie, S.J. et al. DNA stability and genomic methylation status in colonocytes isolated from methyl-donor-deficient rats. *Eur J Nutr* 39(3): 106–11, Jun 2000.

49. Poydock, M.E. Effect of combined ascorbic acid and B-12 on survival of mice with implanted Ehrlich carcinoma and L1210 leukemia. *Am J Clin Nutr* 54(6S): 1261S–1265S, Dec 1991.

50. Agus, D.B. et al. Stromal cell oxidation: a mechanism by which tumors obtain vitamin C. *Cancer Res* 59(18): 4555–8, Sep 1999.

51. Vera, J.C. et al. Human HL-60 myeloid leukemia cells transport dehydroascorbic acid via the glucose transporters and accumulate reduced ascorbic acid. *Blood* 84(5): 1628–34, Sep 1994.

52. Podmore, I.D. et al. Vitamin C exhibits pro-oxidant properties. *Nature* 392(6676): 559, Apr 1998.

53. Podmore, I.D. et al. Does Vitamin C have a pro-oxidant effect? (letter): *Nature* 395: 232, 1998.

54. Howe, G.R. et al. Dietary factors and risk of breast cancer. Combined analysis of 12-case control studies. *J Natl Cancer Inst* 82: 561–569, 1990.

55. Romney, S. et al. Plasma vitamin C and uterine cervical dysplasia. *Am J Ob Gyn* 151: 978–80, 1985.

56. Block, G. Vitamin C and cancer prevention: The epidemiological evidence. *Am J Clin Nutr* 53: 270S–282S, 1991.

57. Cameron, E. et al. Innovation vs. quality control. An unpublishable clinical trial of supplemental ascorbate in incurable cancer. *Med Hypothesis* 36: 185–9, 1991.

58. Shimpo K. et al. Ascorbic acid and adriamycin toxicity. *Am J Clin Nutr* 54(6S): 1298S–1301S, Dec 1991.

59. Sorenson, S. et al. Effects of vitamin D_3 on keratinocyte proliferation and differentiation in vitro. *Skin Pharmacol* 10: 144–52, 1997.

60. Schwartz, G.G. et al. Calcitriol inhibits the invasiveness of human prostate cancer cells. *Cancer Epidemiol Biomarkers Prev* 6: 727–32, 1997.

61. Shabahang, M. et al. Growth inhibition of HT-29 human colon cancer cells by analogues of 1,25-dihydroxyvitamin D3. *Cancer Res* 54: 4057–64, 1994.

62. Jha, M.N. et al. Vitamin E (d-alpha-tocopheryl succinate) decreases mitotic accumulation in gamma-irradiated human tumor, but not in normal, cells. *Nutr Cancer* 35(2): 189–94, 1999.

63. Prasad, K.N. et al Modification of the effect of tamoxifen, cis-platin, DTIC, and interferon-alpha 2b on human melanoma cells in culture by a mixture of vitamins. *Nutr Cancer* 22(3): 233–45, 1994.

64. Takada, H. et al. Inhibition of 7,12-dimethylbanz{a}anthracene-induced lipid peroxidation and mammary tumor development in rats by vitamin E in conjunction with selenium. *Nut Cancer* 17: 115–22, 1992.

65. Sigounas, G. et al. S-Allylmercaptocysteine inhibits cell proliferation and reduces the viability of erthroleukemia, breast and prostate cancer cell lines. *Nutr Cancer* 27: 186–91, 1997.

66. Theriault, A. et al. Tocotrienol: a review of its therapeutic potential. *Clin Biochem* 32(5): 309–19, Jul 1999.

67. Rozen, P. et al. Calcium supplements interact significantly with long-term diet while suppressing rectal epithelial proliferation of adenoma patients. *Cancer* 91(4): 833–40, Feb 2001.

68. Grant, W.B. Ecological study of dietary and smoking links to lymphoma. *Altern Med Rev* 5(6): 563–72, Dec 2000.

69. Lee, D.N. et al. Chromium-induced glucose uptake, superoxide anion production, and phagocytosis in cultured pulmonary alveolar macrophages of weanling pigs. *Biol Trace Elem Res* 77(1): 53–64, Oct 2000.

70. Fracanzani, A.L. et al. Increased cancer risk in a cohort of 230 patients with hereditary hemochromatosis in comparison to matched control patients with non-iron-related chronic liver disease. *Hepatology* 33(3): 647–51, Mar 2001.

71. Poljak-Blazi M. The role of iron in neoplasms. *Lijec Vjesn* 122(9–10): 234–8, Sep/Oct 2000.

72. Lund E.K. et al. Oral ferrous sulfate supplements increase the free radical-generating capacity of feces from healthy volunteers. *Am J Clin Nutr* 69(2): 250–5, Feb 1999.

73. Yang, C.Y. et al. Calcium and magnesium in drinking water and the risk of death from breast cancer. *J Toxicol Environ Health A* 60(4): 231–41, Jun 2000.

74. Yang, C.Y. et al. Calcium and magnesium in drinking water and risk of death from prostate cancer. *J Toxicol Environ Health A* 60(1): 17–26, may 2000.

75. Crosby, V. et al. The safety and efficacy of a single dose (500 mg or 1 g) of intravenous magnesium sulfate in neuropathic pain poorly responsive to strong opioid analgesics in patients with cancer. *J Pain Symptom Manage* 19(1): 35–9, Jan 2000.

76. Kiremidjian-Schumacher, L. et al. Supplementation with selenium and human immune cell functions; II, Effect on cytotoxic lymphocytes and natural killer cells. *Biol Trace Elem Res* 41: 115–27, 1994.

77. Chigbrow, M. et al. Inhibition of mitotic cyclin B and cdc2 kinase activity by selenomethionine in synchronized colon cancer cells. *Anticancer Drugs* 12(1): 43–50, Jan 2001.

78. Davis, C.D. et al. Dietary selenium and arsenic affect DNA methylation in vitro in Caco-2 cells and in vivo in rat liver and colon. *J Nutr* 130(12): 2903–9, Dec 2000.

79. Dias, M.F. et al. Chemoprevention of DMBA-induced mammary tumors in rats by a combined regimen of alpha-tocopherol, selenium and ascorbic acid. *Breast J* 6(1): 14–19, Jan 2000.

80. Thirunavukkarasu, C. et al. Effect of selenium on N-nitrosodiethylamine-induced multistage hepatocarcinogenesis with reference to lipid peroxidation and enzymic antioxidants. *Cell Biochem Funct* 19(1): 27–35, Mar 2001.

81. Baruh, D.H. Esophageal cancer and microelements. *J Am Coll Nutr* 8(2): 99–107, Apr 1989.

82. Allen, J.I. et al. Association between urinary zinc excretion and lymphocyte dysfunction in patients with lung cancer. *Am J Med* 79(2): 209–15, Aug 1985.

83. Kirkpatrick, C.S. et al. Case-control study of malignant melanoma in Washington State. II. Diet, alcohol, and obesity. *Am J Epidemiol* 139(9): 869–80, May 1994.

84. Bain, C. et al. Diet and melanoma. An exploratory case-control study. *Ann Epidemiol* 3(3): 235–8, May 1993.

85. Kouttab, N.M. et al. Thymomodulin: Biological properties and clinical applications. *Med Oncology and Tumor Pharmaco* 6. 5–9, 1989.

86. Kang, S.D. et al. The effects of calf-thymus extract on recovery of bone marrow function in anticancer chemotherapy. *New Med J* (Korea) 28, 11–15, 1985.

87. McIntosh, G.H. et al. A probiotic strain of *L. acidophilus* reduces DMH-induced large intestinal tumors in male Sprague-Dawley rats. *Nutr Cancer* 35(2): 153–9, 1999.

88. Aso, Y. et al. Preventative effect of *L. casei* preparation on the recurrence of superficial bladder cancer in a double-blind trial. *Eur Urol* 27: 104–9, 1995.

89. Kocian, J. Lactobacilli in the treatment of dyspepsia due to dysmicrobia of various causes. *Vnitr Lek* 40(2): 79–83, Feb 1994.

90. Grattagliano, I. et al. Effect of oral glutathione monoethyl ester and glutathione on circulating and hepatic sulfhydrils in the rat. *Pharmacol Toxicol* 75(6): 343–7, Dec 1994.

91. Witschi, A. et al. The systemic availability of oral glutathione. *Eur J Clin Pharmacol* 43: 667–669, 1992.

92. Deleve, L.D. Dacarbazine toxicity in murine liver cells: a model of hepatic endothelial injury and glutathione defense. *J Pharmacol Exp Ther* 268(3): 1261–70, Mar 1994.

93. Micke, P. et al. Oral supplementation with whey proteins increases plasma glutathione levels of HIV-infected patients. *Eur J Clin Invest* 31(2): 171–8, Feb 2001.

94. Bounous, G. Whey protein concentrate (WPC) and glutathione modulation in cancer treatment. *Anticancer Res* 20(6C): 4785–92, Nov/Dec 2000.

95. D'Agostini, F. et al. Interactions between N-acetylcysteine and ascorbic acid in modulating mutagenesis and carcinogenesis. *Int J Cancer* 88(5): 702–7, Dec 2000.

96. Aluigi, M.G. et al. Antiapoptotic and antigenotoxic effects of N-acetylcysteine in human cells of endothelial origin. *Anticancer Res* 20(5A): 3183–7, Sep/Oct 2000.

97. Daniele, B. et al. Oral glutamine in the prevention of fluorouracil induced intestinal toxicity: a double blind, placebo controlled, randomized trial. *Gut* 48(1): 28–33, Jan 2001.

98. Cockerham, M.B. et al. Oral glutamine for the prevention of oral mucositis associated with high-dose paclitaxel and melphalan for autologous bone marrow transplantation. *Ann Pharmacother* 34(3): 300–3, Mar 2000.

99. Simile, M.M. et al. Persistent chemopreventive effect of S-adenosyl-L-methionine on the development of liver putative preneoplastic lesions induced by thiobenzamide in diethylnitrosamine-initiated rats. *Carcinogenesis* 17(7): 1533–7, Jul 1996.

100. Iigo, M. et al. Inhibitory effects of docosahexaenoic acid on colon carcinoma 26 metastasis to the lung. *Br J Cancer* 75(5): 650–5, 1997.

101. Yam, D. et al. EPA: supportive effect of omega-3 PUFA in chemotherapy. *Cancer Chemother Pharmacol* 47(1): 34–40, 2001.

102. Nakagawa. H. et al. Effects of genistein and synergistic action in combination with eicosapentaenoic acid on the growth of breast cancer cell lines. *J Cancer Res Clin Oncol* 126(8): 448–54, Aug 2000.

103. Palakurthi, S.S. et al. Inhibition of translation initiation mediates the anticancer effect of the n-3 polyunsaturated fatty acid eicosapentaenoic acid. *Cancer Res* 60(11): 2919–25, Jun 2000.

104. Wigmore, S.J. et al. Effect of oral eicosapentaenoic acid on weight loss in patients with pancreatic cancer. *Nutr Cancer* 36(2): 177–84, 2000.

105. Fritsche, K.L. et al. Effect of dietary alpha-linolenic acid on growth, metastasis, fatty acid profile and prostaglandin production of two murine mammary adenocarcinomas. *J Nutr* 120: 1601–9, 1990.

106. Benquet, C. et al. Modulation of exercise-induced immunosuppression by dietary polyunsaturated fatty acids in mice. *J Toxicol Env Health* 43: 225–37, 1994.

107. Pienta, K.J. et al. Inhibition of spontaneous metastasis in a rat prostate cancer model by oral administration of modified citrus pectin. *J Natl Cancer Inst* 87(5): 348–53, Mar 1995.

108. Inohara, H. et al. Effects of natural complex carbohydrate (citrus pectin) on murine melanoma cell properties related to galectin-3 functions. *Glycoconj J* 11(6): 527–32, Dec 1994.

109. Hayashi, A. et al. Effects of daily oral administration of quercetin chalcone and modified citrus pectin. *Altern Med Rev* 5(6): 546–52, Dec 2000.

110. Folkers, K. et al. Activities of vitamin Q10 in animal models and a serious deficiency in patients with cancer. *Biochem Biophys Res Commun* 234(2): 296–9, May 1997.

111. Lockwood, K. et al. Progress on therapy of breast cancer with vitamin Q10 and the regression of metastases. *Biochem Biophys Res Commun* 212(1): 172–7, Jul 1995.

112. Lockwood, K. et al. Partial and complete regression of breast cancer in patients in relation to dosage of coenzyme Q10. *Biochem Biophys Res Commun* 199(3): 1504–8, Mar 1994.

113. Lockwood, K. et al. Apparent partial remission of breast cancer in 'high risk' patients supplemented with nutritional antioxidants, essential fatty acids and coenzyme Q10. *Mol Aspects Med* 15S: 231S–40S, 1994.

114. Takimoto, M. et al. Protective effect of CoQ 10 administration on cardial toxicity in FAC therapy. *Gan To Kagaku Ryoho* (Japanese) 9(1): 116–21, Jan 1982.

115. Shaeffer, J. et al. Coenzyme Q10 and adriamycin toxicity in mice. *Res Commun Chem Pathol Pharmacol* 29(2): 309–15, Aug 1998.

116. Kokawa, T. et al. Coenzyme Q10 in cancer chemotherapy — experimental studies on augmentation of the effects of masked compounds, especially in the combined chemotherapy with immunopotentiators. *Gan To Kagaku Ryoho* (Japan) 10(3): 768–74, Mar 1983.

117. Anwar, M.M. et al. Potential protective effects of melatonin on bone marrow of rats exposed to cytotoxic drugs. *Comp Biochem Physiol A Mol Integr Physiol* 119(2): 493–501, Feb 1998.

118. Bartsch, H. et al. Effect of melatonin and pineal extracts on human ovarian and mammary tumor cells in a chemosensitivity assay. *Life Sci* 67(24): 2953–60, Nov 2000.

119. Marelli, M.M. et al. Growth-inhibitory activity of melatonin on human androgen-independent DU 145 prostate cancer cells. *Prostate* 45(3): 238–44, Nov 2000.

120. Rao, G.N. et al. Effect of melatonin and linolenic acid on mammary cancer in transgenic mice with c-neu breast cancer oncogene. *Breast Cancer Res Treat* 64(3): 287–96, Dec 2000.

121. Shao, Z.H. et al. Grape seed proanthocyanidins reduce oxidant stress in cardiomyocytes. *Acad Emer Med* 8(5): 562, May 2001.

122. Ho, C. et al. Antioxidative effect of polyphenol extract prepared from various Chinese teas. *Prev Med* 21: 520–5, 1992.

123. Valcic, S. et al. Inhibitory effect of six green tea catechins and caffeine on the growth of four selected human tumor cell lines. *Anticancer Drugs* 7(4): 461–8, Jun 1996.

124. Gao, Y.T. et al. Reduced risk of esophageal cancer associated with green tea consumption. *J Natl Cancer Inst* 86: 855–8, 1994.

125. Baba, K. Antitumor activity of hot water extract of dandelion, Taraxacum officinale-correlation between anti-tumor activity and timing of administration. *Yakugaku Zasshi* (Japan) 101(6): 538–43, Jun 1981.

126. Kropacova, K. et al. Protective and therapeutic effect of silymarin on the development of latent liver damage. *Radiats Biol Radioecol* 38(3): 411–5, May/Jun 1998.

127. Bhatia, N. et al. Detrimental effect of cancer preventive phytochemicals silymarin, genistein and epigallocatechin 3-gallate on epigenetic events in human prostate carcinoma DU145 cells. *Prostate* 46(2): 98–107, Feb 2001.

128. Jiang, C. et al. Anti-angiogenic potential of a cancer chemopreventive flavonoid antioxidant, silymarin: inhibition of key attributes of vascular endothelial cells and angiogenic cytokine secretion by cancer epithelial cells. *Biochem Biophys Res Commun* 276(1): 371–8, Sep 2000.

129. Djeraba, A. et al. In vivo macrophage activation in chickens with Acemannan, a complex carbohydrate extracted from Aloe vera. *Int J Immunopharmacol* 22(5): 365–72, May 2000.

130. Peng, S.Y. et al. Decreased mortality of Norman murine sarcoma in mice treated with the immunomodulator, Acemannan. *Mol Biother* 3(2): 79–87, Jun 1991.

131. Fleischauer, A.T. et al. Garlic consumption and cancer prevention: meta-analyses of colorectal and stomach cancers. *Am J Clin Nutr* 72(4): 1047–52, Oct 2000.

132. Sivam, G.P. Protection against *Helicobacter pylori* and other bacterial infections by garlic. *J Nutr* 131(3): 1106S–8S, Mar 2001.

133. Shenoy, N.R. et al. Inhibitory effect of diet related sulphydryl compounds on the formation of carcinogenic nitrosamines. *Cancer Lett* 65(3): 227–32, Aug 1992.

134. Lamm, D.L. et al. The potential application of *Allium sativum* (garlic) for the treatment of bladder cancer. *Urol Clin North Am* 27(1): 157–62, xi, Feb 2000.

135. Hamilton, K.K. Case problem: presenting conventional and complementary approaches for relieving nausea in a breast cancer patient undergoing chemotherapy. *J Am Diet Assoc* 100(2): 259, Feb 2000.

136. Lee, E. et al. Induction of apoptosis in HL-60 cells by pungent vanilloids, [6]-gingerol and [6]-paradol. *Cancer Lett* 134(2): 163–8, Dec 1998.

137. Sharma, S.S. et al. Reversal of cisplatin-induced delay in gastric emptying in rats by ginger (*Zingiber officinale*). *J Ethnopharmacol* 62(1): 49–55, Aug 1998.

138. Zhao, X.Z. Effects of *Astragalus membranaceus* and *Tripterygium hypoglancum* on natural killer cell activity of peripheral blood mononuclear in systemic lupus erythematosus. *Zhongguo Zhong Xi Yi Jie He Za Zhi* (China) 12(11): 669–71, 645, Nov 1992.

139. Kurashige, S. et al. Effects of astragali radix extract on carcinogenesis, cytokine production, and cytotoxicity in mice treated with a carcinogen, N-butyl-N'-butanolnitrosoamine.*Cancer Invest* 17(1): 30–5, 1999.

140. Zhao, K.S. et al. Enhancement of the immune response in mice by *Astragalus membranaceus* extracts. *Immunopharmacology* 20(3): 225–33, Nov/Dec 1990.

141. Chu, D.T. et al. Immunotherapy with Chinese medicinal herbs immune restoration of local xenogeneic graft-versus-host reaction in cancer patients by fractionated *Astragalus membranaceus* in vitro. *J Clin Lab Immunol* 25(3): 19–23, 1988.

142. Wildfeuer, A. et al. The effects of plant preparations on cellular functions in body defense. *Arzneimittelforschung* (German) 44(3): 361–6, Mar 1994.

143. Ooi, V.E. et al. Immunomodulation and anti-cancer activity of polysaccharide-protein complexes. *Curr Med Chem* 7(7): 715–29, Jul 2000.

144. Kidd, P.M. The use of mushroom glucans and proteoglycans in cancer treatment. *Altern Med Rev* 5(1): 4–27, Feb 2000.

145. Fullerton, S.A. et al. Induction of apoptosis in human prostatic cancer cells with beta-glucan (Maitake mushroom polysaccharide). *Mol Urol* 4(1): 7–13, Spring 2000.

146. Tamayo, C. et al. The chemistry and biological activity of herbs used in Flor-Essence herbal tonic and Essiac. *Phytother Res* 14(1): 1–14, Feb 2000.

147. Ishikawa, T. et al. Inhibition of skin cancer by IP6 in vivo: initiation-promotion model. *Anticancer Res* 19(5A): 3749–52, Sep/Oct 1999.

148. Shamsuddin, A.M. et al. Mammary tumor inhibition by IP6: a review. *Anticancer Res* 19(5A): 3671–4, Sep/Oct 1999.

149. Vucenik, I. et al. IP6 in treatment of liver cancer. I. IP6 inhibits growth and reverses transformed phenotype in HepG2 human liver cancer cell line. *Anticancer Res* 18(6A): 4083–90, Nov/Dec 1998.

150. Shamsuddin, A.M. Metabolism and cellular functions of IP6: a review. *Anticancer Res* 19(5A): 3733–6, Sep/Oct 1999.

151. Marks, L.S. Tissue effects of saw palmetto and finasteride: use of biopsy cores for in situ quantification of prostatic androgens. *Urology* 57(5): 999–1005, May 2001.

152. Pirani, J.F. The effects of phytotherapeutic agents on prostate cancer: an overview of recent clinical trials of PC spes. *Urology* 58(2S): 36-8, Aug 2001.

153. Miller, D.R. et al. Phase I/II trial of the safety and efficacy of shark cartilage in the treatment of advanced cancer. *J Clin Oncol* 16(11): 3649–55, Nov 1998.

154. Gonzalez, R.P. et al. Demonstration of inhibitory effect of oral shark cartilage on basic fibroblast growth factor-induced angiogenesis in the rabbit cornea. *Biol Pharm Bull* 24(2): 151–4, Feb 2001.

155. Berbari, P. et al. Antiangiogenic effects of the oral administration of liquid cartilage extract in humans. *J Surg Res* 89(2): 197, Apr 2000.

156. Sandler, R.S. et al. Use of vitamins, minerals, and nutritional supplements by participants in a chemo-prevention trial. *Cancer* 91(5): 1040–5, Mar 2001.

157. Crock, R.D. et al. Confronting the communication gap between conventional and alternative medicine: a survey of physicians' attitudes. *Altern Ther Health Med* 5(2): 61–6, Mar 1995.

158. *Prescription for Health*. PhytoPharmica Natural Medicines, 5, Jan 2000.

Chapter 11 Notes

1. Zavon, M.R. et al. Chlorinated hydrocarbons insecticide content of the neonate, *Annals NY Acad Sciences* 160, 196–200, Jun 1969.

2. Lall, S.B. et al. Role of nutrition in toxic injury. *Indian J Exp Biol* 37(2): 109–16, Feb 1999.

3. Shinozawa, S. et al. Effect of biological membrane stabilizing drugs on adriamycin-induced toxicity and microsomal lipid peroxidation in mice. *Gan To Kagaku Ryoho* 23(1): 93–8, Jan 1996.

4. Dwivedi, C. et al. Effects of oil-soluble organosulfur compounds from garlic on doxorubicin-induced lipid peroxidation. *Anticancer Drugs* 9(3): 291–4, Mar 1998.

5. Tavares, D.C. et al. Protective effects of the amino acid glutamine and of ascorbic acid against chromosomal damaged induced by doxorubicin in mammalian cells. *Teratog Carcinog Mutagen* 18(4): 153–61, 1998.

6. Sayed-Ahmed, M.M. et al. Propionyl-L-carnitine as potential protective agent against adriamycin-induced impairment of fatty acid beta-oxidation in isolated heart mitochondria. *Pharmacol Res* 41(2): 143–50, Feb 2000.

7. Wahab, M.H. et al. Modulatory effects of melatonin and vitamin E on doxorubicin-induced cardiotoxicity in Ehrlich ascites carcinoma-bearing mice. *Tumori* 86(2): 157–62, Mar/Apr 2000.

8. D'Agostini, F. et al. Inhibition by oral N-acetylcysteine of doxorubicin-induced clastogenicity and alopecia, and prevention of primary tumors and lung micrometastases in mice. *Int J Oncol* 13(2): 217–24, Aug 1998.

9. Zhao, Z.Z. et al. A study of vitamin inhibition on the mutagenicity of the antineoplastic drugs. *Zhonghua Yu Fang Yi Xue Za Zhi* (China) 26(5): 291–3, Sep 1992.

10. Fukaya, H. et al. Experimental studies of the protective effect of ginkgo biloba extract (GBE) on cisplatin-induced toxicity in rats. *Nippon Jibiinkoka Gakkai Kaiho* (Japan) 102(7): 907 17, Jul 1999.

11. Sonnenbichler, J. et al. Stimulatory effects of silibinin and silicristin from the milk thistle Silybum marianum on kidney cells. *J Pharmacol Exp Ther* 290(3): 1375–83, Sep 1999.

12. Coletta Francescato, H.D. et al. Effect of oral selenium administration on cisplatin induced nephrotoxicity in rats. *Pharmacol Res* 43(1): 77–82, Jan 2001.

13. Kuhlmann, M.K. et al. Reduction of cisplatin toxicity in cultured renal tubular cells by the bioflavonoid quercetin. *Arch Toxicol* 72(8): 536–40, Jul/Aug 1998.

14. Di Re F. et al. High-dose cisplatin and cyclophosphamide with glutathione in the treatment of advanced ovarian cancer. *Ann Oncol* 4(1): 55–61, Jan 1993.

15. Takimoto, M. et al. Protective effect of CoQ10 administration on cardial toxicity in FAC therapy. *Gan To Kagaku Ryoho* (Japanese) 9(1): 116–21, Jan 1982.

16. Lin, C.M. et al. Effect of dietary glutamate on chemotherapy induced immunosuppression. *Nutrition* 15(9): 687–96, Sep 1999.

17. Horie, T. et al. Docosahexaenoic acid exhibits a potent protection of small intestine from methotrexate-induced damage in mice. *Life Sci* 62(15): 1333–8, 1998.

18. Reuber, M.D. Carcinogenicity of saccharin. *Environ Health Perspect* 25: 173–200, Aug 1978.

19. Robbins, P.I. et al. Aspartame and symptoms of carpal tunnel syndrome. *J Occup Environ Med* 41(6): 418, Jun 1999.

20. Freitas, V.P. et al. Occurrence of aflatoxins B1, B2, G1, and G2 in peanuts and their products marketed in the region of Campinas, Brazil in 1995 and 1996. *Food Addit Contam* 15(7): 807–11, Oct 1998.

21. Colin-Negrete, J. et al. Effect of whole cottonseed on serum constituents, fragility of erythrocyte cells and reproduction of growing Holstein heifers. *J Dairy Sci* 79(11): 2016–23, Nov 1996.

22. Zheng, W. et al. Well-done meat intake and the risk of breast cancer. *J Nat Cancer Inst* 90(22): 1724–9, Nov 1998.

23. Ha, Y.L et al. Anticarcinogens from fried ground beef: heat-altered derivatives of linoleic acid. *Carcinogenesis* 8(12): 1881–7, Dec 1987.

24. Bear, W.L. et al. Effects of citrus bioflavonoids on the mutagenicity of heterocyclic amines and on cytochrome P450 1A2 activity. *Anticancer Res* 20(5B): 3609–14, Sep 2000.

25. Laden, F. et al. Predictors of plasma concentrations of DDE and PCBs in a group of U.S. women. *Environ Health Perspect* 107(1): 75–81, Jan 1999.

26. Smith, G.D. et al. Cancer and insulin-like growth factor-1. A potential mechanism linking the environment with cancer risk. *BMJ* 321(7265): 847–8, Oct 2000.

27. Simanowski, U. et al. Effect of alcohol on gastrointestinal cell regeneration as a possible mechanism in alcohol-associated carcinogenesis. *Alcohol* 12: 111–115, 1995.

28. Singletary, K. et al. Ethanol consumption and DMBA-induced mammary carcinogenesis in rats. *Nutr Cancer* 16: 13–23, 1991.

29. Pizzorno, J.E. et al. Detoxification: A naturopathic perspective. *Natural Medicine Journal* 1(4): 6–17, May 1998.

Chapter 12 Notes
Bladder Cancer Nutrition Action Plan

Cantor, K.P. et al. Drinking water source and chlorination byproducts. I. Risk of bladder cancer. *Epidemiology* 9(1): 7–8, Jan 1998.

Freedman, D.M. et al. Bladder cancer and drinking water: a population-based case-control study in Washington County, Maryland (United States). *Cancer Causes Control* 8(5): 738–44, Sep 1997.

Kamat, A.M. et al. Chemoprevention of urological cancer. *J Urol* 161(6): 1748–60, Jun 1999.

Koivusalo, M. et al. Drinking water mutagenicity and urinary tract cancers: a population-based case-control study in Finland. *Am J Epidemiol* 148(7): 704–12, Oct 1998.

Kurashige, S. et al. Effects of Lentinus edodes, Grifola frondosa and Pleurotus ostreatus administration on cancer outbreak, and activities of macrophages and lymphocytes in mice treated with a carcinogen, N-butyl-N-butanolnitrosoamine. *Immunopharmacol Immunotoxicol* 19(2): 175–83, May 1997.

La Vecchia, C. et al. Nutrition and bladder cancer. *Cancer Causes Control* 7(1): 95–100, Jan 1996.

Lamm, D.L. et al. Megadose vitamins in bladder cancer: a double-blind clinical trial. *J Urol* 151(1): 21–6, Jan 1994.

Michaud, D.S. et al. Fruit and vegetable intake and incidence of bladder cancer in a male prospective cohort. *J Natl Cancer Inst* 91(7): 605–13, Apr 1999.

Nagano, J. et al. Bladder cancer incidence in relation to vegetable and fruit consumption: a prospective study of atomic-bomb survivors. *Int J Cancer* 86(1): 132–8, Apr 2000.

Peluso, M. et al. White blood cell DNA adducts and fruit and vegetable consumption in bladder cancer. *Carcinogenesis* 21(2): 183–7, Feb 2000.

Shibata, A. et al. Intake of vegetables, fruits, beta-carotene, vitamin C and vitamin supplements and cancer incidence among the elderly: a prospective study. *Br J Cancer* 66(4): 673–9, Oct 1992.

Su, S.J. et al. The potential of soybean foods as a chemoprevention approach for human urinary tract cancer. *Clin Cancer Res* 6(1): 230–6, Jan 2000.

Theodorescu, D. et al. Inhibition of human bladder cancer cell motility by genistein is dependent on epidermal growth factor receptor but not p21ras gene expression. *Int J Cancer* 78(6): 775–82, Dec 1998.

Weyer, P.J. et al. Municipal drinking water nitrate level and cancer risk in older women: the Iowa Women's Health Study. *Epidemiology* 12(3): 327–38, May 2001.

Zhou, J. et al. Dietary soy products inhibit the growth of transplanted murine bladder carcinoma in mice (Meeting abstract). *Proc Annu Meet Am Assoc Cancer Res* 38: A746, 1997.

Zhou, J.R et al. Inhibition of murine bladder tumorigenesis by soy isoflavones via alterations in cell cycle, apoptosis and angiogenesis. *Cancer Res* 58(22): 5231–8, Nov 1998.

Breast Cancer Nutrition Action Plan

Bagchi, D. et al. Free radicals and grape seed proanthocyanidin extract: importance in human health and disease prevention. *Toxicology* 148(2–3): 187–97, Aug 2000.

Bardon, S. et al. Monoterpenes inhibit cell growth, cell cycle progression, and cyclin D1 gene expression in human breast cancer cell lines. *Nutr Cancer* 32(1): 1–7, 1998.

Belanger, J.T. Perillyl alcohol: applications in oncology. *Altern Med Rev* 3(6): 448–57, Dec 1998.

Challier, B. et al. Garlic, onion and cereal fiber as protective factors for breast cancer: a French case-control study. *Eur J Epidemiol* 14(8): 737–47, Dec 1998.

Chew, B.P. et al. A comparison of the anticancer activities of dietary beta-carotene canthaxanthin and astaxanthin in mice in vivo. *Anticancer Res* 19(3A): 1849–53, May/Jun 1999.

Dixon-Shanies, D. et al. Growth inhibition of human breast cancer cells by herbs and phytoestrogens. *Oncol Rep* 6(6): 1383–7, Nov/Dec 1999.

Falck, F. et al. Pesticides and polychlorinated biphenyl residues in human breast lipids and their relation to breast cancer. *Arch Environ Health* 47: 143–6, 1992.

Funahashi, H. et al. Wakame seaweed suppresses the proliferation of 7,12-dimethylbenz(a)-anthracene-induced mammary tumors in rats. *Jpn J Cancer Res* 90(9): 922–7, Sep 1999.

Gramaglia, A. et al. Increased survival in brain metastatic patients treated with stereotactic radiotherapy, omega three fatty acids and bioflavonoids. *Anticancer Res* 19(6C): 5583–6, Nov/Dec 1999.

Guthrie, N. et al. Inhibition of mammary cancer by citrus flavonoids. *Adv Exp Med Biol* 439: 227–36, 1998.

██████, █ ███ ██ ██ █████ ██████ ███ █████ █████ ███████ (██████ █████), ██████ ██████ ███████ ██(█), ███ ███, May 1998.

Hubbard, N.E. et al. Reduction of murine mammary tumor metastasis by conjugated linoleic acid. *Cancer Lett* 150(1): 93–100, Mar 2000.

Inano, H. et al. Potent preventive action of curcumin on radiation-induced initiation of mammary tumorigenesis in rats. *Carcinogenesis* 21(10): 1835–41, Oct 2000.

Lash, T.L. et al. Alcohol drinking and risk of breast cancer. *Breast J* 6(6): 396-9, Nov 2000.

Mukutmoni-Norris, M. et al. Modulation of murine mammary tumor vasculature by dietary n-3 fatty acids in fish oil. *Cancer Lett* 150(1): 101–9, Mar 2000.

Nakagawa, H. et al. Effects of genistein and synergistic action in combination with EPA on the growth of breast cancer cell lines. *J Cancer Res Clin Oncol* 126(8): 448–54, Aug 2000.

Nakagawa, H. et al. Resveratrol inhibits human breast cancer cell growth and may mitigate the effect of linoleic acid, a potent breast cancer sell stimulator. *J Cancer Res Clin Oncol* 127(4): 258–64, Apr 2001.

Pena-Rosas, J.P. et al. Wheat bran and breast cancer: revisiting the estrogen hypothesis. *Arch Latinoam Nutr* (Spain) 49(4): 309 17, Dec 1999.

Portakal, O. et al. CoQ10 concentrations and antioxidant status in tissues of breast cancer patients. *Clin Biochem* 33(4): 279–84, Jun 2000.

Position of the American Dietetic Association and Dietitians of Canada: Women's health and nutrition. *J Am Diet Assoc* 99(6): 738–75, Jun 1999.

Rahman, K.M. et al. Translocation of Bax to mitochondria induces apoptotic cell death in indole-3-carbinol (I3C) treated breast cancer cells. *Oncogene* 19(50): 5764–71, Nov 2000.

Rao, G.N. et al. Effect of melatonin and linolenic acid on mammary cancer in transgenic mice with c-neu breast cancer oncogene. *Breast Cancer Res Treat* 64(3): 287–96, Dec 2000.

Rodgers, E.H. et al. The effect of flavonoids, quercetin, myricetin and epicatechin on the growth and enzyme activities of MCF7 human breast cancer cells. *Chem Biol Interact* 116(3): 213–28, Nov 1998.

Rose, D.P. Dietary fat, fatty acids and breast cancer. *Breast Cancer* 4(1): 7–16, Mar 1997.

Rosenblatt, K.A. et al. The relationship between diet and breast cancer in men (United States). *Cancer Causes Control* 10(2): 107–13, Apr 1999.

Saxe, G.A. et al. Diet and risk for breast cancer recurrence and survival. *Breast Cancer Res Treat* 53(3): 241–53, Feb 1999.

Shamsuddin, A.M. et al. Mammary tumor inhibition by IP6: a review. *Anticancer Res* 19(5A): 3671–4, Sep/Oct 1999.

Shamsuddin, A.M. et al. Novel anti-cancer function of IP-6: Growth inhibition and differentiation of human mammary cancer cell lines in vitro. *Anticancer Res* 16: 3287–92, 1996.

Stellman, S.D. et al. Breast cancer risk in relation to adipose concentrations of organochlorine pesticides and polychlorinated biphenyls in Long Island, New York. *Cancer Epidemiol Biomarkers Prev* 9(11): 1241–9, Nov 2000.

Teas, J. et al. Dietary seaweed and mammary carcinogenesis in rats. *Cancer Res* 44(7): 2758–61, Jul 1984.

Valcic, S. et al. Inhibitory effect of six green tea catechins and caffeine on the growth of four selected human tumor cell lines. *Anticancer Drugs* 7(4): 461–8, Jun 1996.

van't Veer, P. et al. Consumption of fermented milk products and breast cancer: a case-control study in the Netherlands. *Cancer Res* 49(14): 4020–3, Jul 1989.

Walaszek, Z. et al. Metabolism, uptake, and excretion of a D-glucaric acid salt and its potential use in cancer prevention. *Cancer Detection Prev* 21, 178–90, 1997.

Willett, W.C. Dietary fat and breast cancer. *Toxicol Sci* 52(2) Suppl: 127–46, Dec 1999.

Zhang, S. et al. Better breast cancer survival for post menopausal women who are less overweight and eat less fat. The Iowa Women's Health Study. *Cancer* 76(2): 275–83, Jul 1995.

Zheng, W. et al. Well-done meat intake and the risk of breast cancer. *J Natl Canc Inst* 90: 1724–9, 1998.

Colorectal Cancer Nutrition Action Plan

Azuma, N. et al. Preventive effect of soybean resistant proteins against experimental tumorigenesis in rat colon. *J Nutr Sci Vitaminol* (Tokyo) 46(1): 23–9, Feb 2000.

Bingham, S.A. Diet and colorectal cancer prevention. *Biochem Soc Trans* 28(2): 12–6, Feb 2000.

Bingham, S.A. et al. Does increased endogenous formation of N-nitroso compounds in the human colon explain the association between red meat and colon cancer? *Carcinogenesis* 17(3): 515–23, Mar 1996.

Bruce, W.R. et al. Mechanisms linking diet and colorectal cancer: the possible role of insulin resistance. *Nutr Cancer* 37(1): 19–26, 2000.

Chol, S.W. et al. Folate and carcinogenesis: An integrated scheme. (Review) *J Nutr* 130, 129–32, Feb 2000.

Dashwood, R.H. Early detection and prevention of colorectal cancer (Review). *Oncol Rep* 6(2): 277–81, Mar/Apr 1999.

Davis, P.A. et al. Whole almonds and almond fractions reduce aberrant crypt foci in a rat model of colon carcinogenesis. *Cancer Lett* 165(1): 27–33, Apr 2001.

de Deckere, E.A. Possible beneficial effect of fish and fish n-3 polyunsaturated fatty acids in breast and colorectal cancer. *Eur J Cancer Prev* 8(3): 213–21, Jul 1999.

Franceschi, S. et al. The role of energy and fat in cancers of the breast and colon-rectum in a southern European population. *Ann Oncol* 10 Suppl 6: 61–3, 1999.

Hayashi, A. et al. Effects of daily oral administration of quercetin chalcone and modified citrus pectin. *Altern Med Rev* 5(6): 546–52, Dec 2000.

Kaeffer, B. et al. Biological properties of ulvan, a new source of green seaweed sulfated polysaccharides, on cultured normal and cancerous colonic epithelial cells. *Planta Med* 65(6): 527–31, Aug 1999.

Kampman, E. et al. Calcium, vitamin D, sunshine exposure, dairy products and colon cancer risk (United States). *Cancer Causes Control* 11(5): 459–66, May 2000.

Kidd, P.M. The use of mushroom glucans and proteoglycans in cancer treatment. *Altern Med Rev* 5(1): 4–27, Feb 2000.

Knekt, P. et al. Risk of colorectal and other gastrointestinal cancers after exposure to nitrate, nitrite and N-nitroso compounds: a follow-up study. *Int J Cancer* 80(6): 852–6, Mar 1999.

Levi, F. et al. Food groups and colorectal cancer risk. *Br J Cancer* 79(7–8): 1283–7, Mar 1999.

Martinez, M.E. et al. Leisure-time physical activity, body size, and colon cancer in women. Nurses' Health Study Research Group. *J Natl Cancer Inst* 89(13): 948–55, Jul 1997.

McIntosh, G.H. et al. A probiotic strain of *L. acidophilus* reduces DMH-induced large intestinal tumors in male Sprague-Dawley rats. *Nutr Cancer* 35(2): 153–9, 1999.

McIntosh, G.H. et al. The influence of dietary proteins on colon cancer risk. *Nutr Res* 21(7): 1053-1066, Jul 2001.

Narayanan, B.A. et al. IGF-II down regulation associated cell cycle arrest in colon cancer cells exposed to phenolic antioxidant ellagic acid. *Anticancer Res* 21(1A): 359–64, Jan/Feb 2001.

Ogimoto, I. et al. WCRF/AICR 1997 recommendations: applicability to digestive tract cancer in Japan. *Cance Causes Control* 11(1): 9–23, Jan 2000.

Saied, I.T. et al. Up-regulation of the tumor suppressor gene p53 and WAF1 gene expression by IP6 in HT-29 human colon carcinoma cell line. *Anticancer Res* 18(3A): 1479–84, May/Jun 1998.

Scheppach, W. et al. Effect of nutrition factors on the pathogenesis of colorectal carcinoma. *Zentralbl Chir* (German) 125 Suppl 1: 5–7, 2000.

Schneider, Y. et al. Anti-proliferative effect of resveratrol, a natural component of grapes and wine, on human colonic cancer cells. *Cancer Lett* 158(1): 85–91, Sep 2000.

Sesink, A.L. et al. Red meat and colon cancer: dietary haem, but not fat, has cytotoxic and hyperproliferative effects on rat colonic epithelium. *Carcinogenesis* 21(10): 1909–15, Oct 2000.

Sinha, R. et al. Role of well-done, grilled red meat, heterocyclic amines in the etiology of human cancer. *Cancer Lett* 143(2): 189–94, Sep 1999.

Tanaka, T. et al. Citrus limonoids obacunone and limonin inhibit azoxymethane-induced colon carcinogenesis in rats. *Biofactors* 13(1–4): 213–8, 2000.

Voorrips, L.E. et al. Vegetable and fruit consumption and risks of colon and rectal cancer in a prospective cohort study: The Netherlands Cohort Study on Diet and Cancer. *Am J Epidemiol* 152(11): 1081–92, Dec 2000.

Wenzel, U. et al. Dietary flavone is a potent apoptosis inducer in human colon carcinoma cells. *Cancer Res* 60(14): 3823–31, Jul 2000.

Weyer, P.J. et al. Municipal drinking water nitrate level and cancer risk in older women: the Iowa Women's Health Study. *Epidemiology* 12(3): 327–38, May 2001.

Upper Digestive Tract Cancer Nutrition Action Plan

Actis, A.B. et al. N-3, n-6 and n-9 dietary fatty acids modulate the growth parameters of murine salivary gland tumors induced by dimethylbenzanthracene. *Prostaglandins Leukot Essent Fatty Acids* 61(4): 259–65, Oct 1999.

Alhasan, S.A. et al. Genistein-induced cell cycle arrest and apoptosis in a head and neck squamous cell carcinoma cell line. *Nutr Cancer* 34(1): 12–9, 1999.

Bosetti, C. et al. Food groups and risk of squamous cell esophageal cancer in northern Italy. *Int J Cancer* 87(2): 289–94, Jul 2000.

Bosetti, C. et al. Risk factors for oral and pharyngeal cancer in women: a study from Italy and Switzerland. *Br J Cancer* 82(1): 204–7, Jan 2000.

Castellsague, X. et al. Influence of mate drinking, hot beverages and diet on esophageal cancer risk in South America. *Int J Cancer* 88(4): 658–64, Nov 2000.

Chyou, P.H. et al. Diet, alcohol, smoking and cancer of the upper aerodigestive tract: a prospective study among Hawaii Japanese men. *Int J Cancer* 60(5): 616–21, Mar 1995.

Cornee, J. et al. A case-control study of gastric cancer and nutritional factors in Marseille, France. *Eur J Epidemiol* 11(1): 55–65, Feb 1995.

De Stefani, E. et al. Diet and risk of cancer of the upper aerodigestive tract. *Oral Oncol* 35(1): 17–21, Jan 1999.

De Stefani, E. et al. Diet and risk of cancer of the upper aerodigestive tract — II. Nutrients. *Oral Oncol* 35(1): 22–6, Jan 1999.

De Stefani, E. et al. Plant foods and risk of laryngeal cancer: A case-control study in Uruguay. *Int J Cancer* 87(1): 129–32, Jul 2000.

ElAttar, T.M. et al. Effect of tea polyphenols on growth of oral squamous carcinoma cells in vitro. *Anticancer Res* 20(5B): 3459–65, Sep/Oct 2000.

ElAttar, T.M. et al. Modulating effect of resveratrol and quercetin on oral cancer cell growth and proliferation. *Anticancer Drugs* 10(2): 187–93, Feb 1999.

ElAttar, T.M. et al. The inhibitory effect of curcumin, genistein, quercetin and cisplatin on the growth of oral cancer cells in vitro. *Anticancer Res* 20(3A): 1733–8, May/Jun 2000.

Fernandes, A.O. et al. Inhibition of benzopyrene-induced forestomach tumors by field bean protease inhibitor. *Carcinogenesis* 16(8): 1843–6, Aug 1995.

Fioretti, F. et al. Risk factors for oral and pharyngeal cancer in never smokers. *Oral Oncol* 35(4): 375–8, Jul 1999.

Franceschi, S. et al. Diet and thyroid cancer: a pooled analysis of four European case-control studies. *Int J Cancer* 48(3): 395–8, May 1991.

Gao, C.M. et al. Protective effect of allium vegetables against both esophageal and stomach cancer: a simultaneous case-referent study of a high-epidemic area in Jiangsu Province, China. *Jpn J Cancer Res* 90(6): 614–21, Jun 1999.

Garcia-Closas, R. et al. Intake of specific carotenoids and flavonoids and the risk of gastric cancer in Spain. *Cancer Causes Control* 10(1): 71–5, Feb 1999.

Hoshiyama, Y. et al. A case-control study of single and multiple stomach cancers in Saitama Prefecture, Japan. *Jpn J Cancer Res* 83(9): 937–43, Sep 1992.

Ji, B.T. et al. Dietary habits and stomach cancer in Shanghai, China. *Int J Cancer* 76(5): 659–64, May 1998.

Kaaks, R. et al. Nutrient intake patterns and gastric cancer risk: a case-control study in Belgium. *Int J Cancer* 78(4): 415–20, Nov 1998.

Kawabata, K. et al. Suppression of N-nitrosomethylbenzlamine-induced rat esophageal tumorigenesis by dietary feeding of auraptene. *J Exp Clin Cancer Res* 19(1): 45–52, Mar 2000.

Kidd, P.M. The use of mushroom glucans and proteoglycans in cancer treatment. *Altern Med Rev* 5(1): 4–27, Feb 2000.

Kikuchi, S. Risk factors of stomach cancer. *Gan To Kagaku Ryoho* (Japan) 28(2): 142–5, Feb 2001

Levi, F. et al. Food groups and risk of oral and pharyngeal cancer. *Int J Cancer* 77(5): 705–9, Aug 1998.

Li, S.D. et al. Association between body mass index and adenocarcinoma of the esophagus and gastric cardia. *Nutr Rev* 58(2 Part 1): 54–6, Feb 2000.

Nagao, M. et al. Genetic changes induced by HCAs. *Mutat Res* 376(1–2): 161–7, May 1997.

Nomura, A.M. et al. Serum micronutrients and upper aerodigestive tract cancer. *Cancer Epidemiol*

Biomarkers Prev 6(6): 407–12, Jun 1997.

Ogimoto, I. et al. WCRF/AICR 1997 recommendations: applicability to digestive tract cancer in Japan. *Cancer Causes Control* 11(1): 9–23, Jan 2000.

Ripamonti, C. et al. A randomized, controlled clinical trial to evaluate the effects of zinc sulfate on cancer patients with taste alterations caused by head and neck irradiation. *Cancer* 82: 1938–45, 1998.

Rogers, M.A. et al. Consumption of nitrate, nitrite, and nitrosodimethylamine and the risk of upper aerodigestive tract cancer. *Cancer Epidemiol Biomarkers Prev* 4(1): 29–36, Jan/Feb 1995.

Singh, S.V. et al. Mechanism of inhibition of benzoapyrene-induced forestomach cancer in mice by dietary curcumin. *Carcinogenesis* 19(8): 1357–60, Aug 1998.

Stoner, G.D. et al. Isothiocyanates and freeze-dried strawberries as inhibitors of esophageal cancer. *Toxicol Sci* 52(2) Suppl: 95–100, Dec 1999.

Takezaki, T. et al. Comparative study of lifestyles of residents in high and low risk areas for gastric cancer in Jaigsu Province, China; with special reference to allium vegetables. *J Epidemiol* 9(5): 297–305, Nov 1999.

Tamura, H. et al. Inhibitory effects of green tea and grape juice on the phenol sulfotransferase activity of mouse intestines and human colon carcinoma cell line, Caco-2. *Bio Pharm Bull* 23(6): 695–9, Jun 2000.

Ushida, J. et al. Chemopreventive effect of curcumin on N-nitrosomethylbenzylamine-induced esophageal carcinogenesis in rats. *Jpn J Cancer Res* 91(9): 893–8, Sep 2000.

Ward, M.H. et al. Dietary factors and the risk of gastric cancer in Mexico City. *Am J Epidemiol* 149(10): 925–32, May 1999.

Wattenberg, L.W. et al. Inhibition of polycyclic aromatic hydrocarbon-induced neoplasia by naturally occurring indoles. *Cancer Res* 38(5): 1410–3, May 1978.

Weber, U.S. et al. Antitumor-activities of coumarin, 7-hydroxy-coumarin and its glucuronide in several human tumor cell lines. *Res Commun Mol Pathol Pharmacol* 99(2): 193–206, Feb 1998.

████ ██ ██ ██ al. ██ ████████████ ██ ████████ ████ ████ ██ ████████ ███████ ███ ███████ ██ ████████ ███ founders. *Can Epid Bio Prev* 9(10): 1051–8, Oct 2000.

Yoshida, M. et al. The effect of quercetin on cell cycle progression and growth of human gastric cancer cells. *FEBS Lett* 260(1): 10–3, Jan 1990.

Yuan, J.M. et al. Preserved foods in relation to risk of nasopharyngeal carcinoma in Shanghai, China. *Int J Cancer* 85(3): 358–63, Feb 2000.

Zheng, G.Q. et al. Chemoprevention of benzoapyrene-induced forestomach cancer in mice by natural phthalides from celery seed oil. *Nutr Cancer* 19(1): 77–86, 1993.

Gynecologic Cancer Nutrition Action Plan

Ballard-Barbash, R. et al. Body weight: estimation of risk for breast and endometrial cancers. *Am J Clin Nutr* 63(3) Suppl: 437S–41S, Mar 1996.

Bartsch, H. et al. Effect of melatonin and pineal extracts on human ovarian and mammary tumor cells in a chemosensitivity assay. *Life Sci* 67(24): 2953–60, Nov 2000.

Bell, M.C. et al. Placebo-controlled trial of indole-3-carbinol in the treatment of CIN. *Gynecol Oncol* 78(2): 123–9, Aug 2000.

Butterworth, C.E. et al. Folate deficiency and cervical dysplasia. *J Amer Med Assoc* 226: 1421–4, 1973.

Cramer, D.W. et al. A case-control study of galactose consumption and metabolism in relation to ovarian cancer. *Cancer Epidemiol Biomarkers Prev* 9(1): 95–101, Jan 2000.

De, S. et al. Chemopreventive activity of quercetin during carcinogenesis in cervix uteri in mice. *Phytother Res* 14(5): 347–51, Aug 2000.

Goodman, M.T. et al. Association of soy and fiber consumption with the risk of endometrial cancer. *Am J Epidemiol* 146(4): 294–306, Aug 1997.

Goodman, M.T. et al. Diet, body size, physical activity and the risk of endometrial cancer. *Cancer Res* 57(22): 5077–85, Nov 1997.

Heinonen, P.K. et al. Serum vitamins A and E and carotene in patients with gynecologic cancer. *Arch Gynecol Obstet* 241(3): 151–6, 1987.

Hubbard, N.E. et al. Reduction of murine mammary tumor metastasis by conjugated linoleic acid. *Cancer Lett* 150(1): 93–100, Mar 2000.

Kanishi, Y. et al. Differential growth inhibitory effect of melatonin on two endometrial cancer cell lines. *J Pineal Res* 28(4): 227–33, May 2000.

Kidd, P.M. The use of mushroom glucans and proteoglycans in cancer treatment. *Altern Med Rev* 5(1): 4–27, Feb 2000.

Levy, J. et al. Lycopene is a more potent inhibitor of human cancer cell proliferation than either alpha-carotene or beta-carotene. *Nutr Cancer* 24(3): 257–66, 1995.

McCann, S.E. et al. Diet in the epidemiology of endometrial cancer in western New York (United States). *Cancer Causes Control* 11(10): 965–74, Dec 2000.

Miranda, C.L. et al. Antiproliferative and cytotoxic effects of prenylated flavonoids from hops in human cancer cell lines. *Food Chem Toxicol* 37(4): 271–85, Apr 1999.

Palan, P.R. et al. Decreased beta-carotene tissue levels in uterine leiomyomas and cancers of reproductive and nonreproductive organs. *Am J Obstet Gynecol* 161(6 Pt 1): 1649–52, Dec 1989.

Pawlega, J. et al. Ovarian cancer and selected life style habits. *Ginekol Pol* (Polish) 66(1): 41–5, Jan 1995.

Sagar, P.S. et al. Cytotoxic action of cis-unsaturated fatty acids on human cervical carcinoma (HeLa) cells in vitro. *Prostaglandins Leukot Essent Fatty Acids* 53(4): 287–99, Oct 1995.

Scambia, G. et al. Inhibitory effect of quercetin on OVCA 433 cells and presence of type II estrogen binding sites in primary ovarian tumors and cultured cells. *Br J Cancer* 62(6): 942–6, Dec 1990.

Shu, X.O. et al. A population-based case-control study of dietary factors and endometrial cancer in Shanghai, People's Republic of China. *Am J Epidemiol* 137(2): 155–65, Jan 1993.

Studzinski, Z. et al Initial estimation effect of body mass on survival of patients with endometrial carcinoma. *Ginekol Pol* (Poland) 70(2): 81–7, Feb 1997.

Sturgeon, S.R. et al. Diet and the risk of vulvar cancer. *Ann Epidemiol* 1(5): 427–37, 1991.

Webb, P.M. et al. Milk consumption, galactose metabolism and ovarian cancer (Australia). *Cancer Causes Control* 9(6): 637–44, Dec 1998.

Weyer, P.J. et al. Municipal drinking water nitrate level and cancer risk in older women: the Iowa Women's Health Study. *Epidemiology* 12(3): 327–38, May 2001.

Yuan, F. et al. Anti-estrogenic activities of indole-3-carbinol in cervical cells: implication for prevention of cervical cancer. *Anticancer Res* 19(3A): 1673–80, May/Jun 1999.

Leukemia Nutrition Action Plan

Amir, H. et al. Lycopene and 1,25-dihyrdoxyvitamin D_3 cooperate in the inhibition of cell cycle progression and induction of differentiation in HL-60 leukemic cells. *Nutr Cancer* 33(1): 105–12, 1999.

Bernhard, D. et al. Resveratrol causes arrest in the S-phase prior to Fas-independent apoptosis in CEM-C7H2 acute leukemia cells. *Cell Death Differ* 7(9): 834–42, Sep 2000.

Buckley, J.D. et al. Pesticide exposures in children with non-Hodgkin's lymphoma. *Cancer* 89(11): 2315–21, Dec 2000.

Conney, A.H. et al. Some perspectives on dietary inhibition of carcinogenesis: studies with curcumin and tea. *Proc Soc Exp Biol Med* 216(2): 234–45, Nov 1997.

Harada, H. et al. Selective antitumor activity in vitro from marine algae from Japan coasts. *Biol Pharm Bull* 20(5): 541–6, May 1997.

Hirota, A. et al. 1,1-Diphenyl-2-picrylhydrazyl radical-scavenging compounds from soybean miso and antiproliferative activity of isoflavones from soybean miso toward the cancer cell lines. *Biosci Biotechnol Biochem* 64(5): 1038–40, May 2000.

Ito, Y. et al. The novel triterpenoid 2-cyano-3,12-dioxoolean-1,9-dien-28-oic acid induces apoptosis of human myeloid leukemia cells by a caspase-8-dependent mechanism. *Cell Growth Differ* 11(5): 261–7, May 2000.

Kawaii, S. et al. Effect of coumarins on HL-6- cell differentiation. *Anticancer Res* 20(4): 2505–12, Jul/Aug 2000.

Matsuda, M. et al. Clinical roles of vitamins in hematopoietic disorders *Nippon Rinsho* (Japan) 57(10): 2349–55, Oct 1999.

Nagabhushan, M. et al. Curcumin as an inhibitor of cancer. *J Am Coll Nutr* 11, 192–198, 1992.

Polkowski, K. et al. Anticancer activity of genistein-piperazine complex. In vitro study with HL-60 cells. *Acta Pol Pharm* 57(3): 223–32, May/Jun 2000.

Sastry, P.S. et al. Prevention of progression in chronic myeloid leukemia by altering DNA methylation with a pyridoxine analogue. *Med Hypotheses* 53(6): 488–9, Dec 1999.

Sergediene, E. et al. Prooxidant toxicity of polyphenolic antioxidants to HL-60 cells: description of quantitative structure-activity relationships. *FEBS Lett* 462(3): 392–6, Dec 1999.

Shoff, S.M. et al. Concentration-dependent increase of murine P388 and B16 population doubling time by the acyclic monoterpene geraniol. *Cancer Res* 51(1): 37–42, Jan 1991.

Uddin, S. et al. Quercetin, a bioflavonoid, inhibits the DNA synthesis of human leukemia cells. *Biochem Mol Biol Int* 36(3): 545–50, Jul 1995.

Lung Cancer Nutrition Action Plan

Batkin, S. et al. Antimetastatic effect of bromelain with or without its proteolytic and anticoagulant activity. *J Cancer Res Clin Oncol* 114(5): 507–8, 1988.

Carpenter, C.L. et al. Alcoholic beverage consumption and lung cancer risk among residents of Los Angeles County. *J Nutr* 128(4): 694–700, Apr 1998.

Chung, F.L. The prevention of lung cancer induced by a tobacco-specific carcinogen in rodents by green and black tea. *Proc Soc Exp Biol Med* 220(4): 244–8, Apr 1999.

Chung, F.L. et al. Inhibition of tobacco-specific nitrosamine-induced lung tumorigenesis by compounds derived from cruciferous vegetables and green tea. *Ann NY Acad Sci* 686, 186–201, May 1993.

D'Agostini, F. et al. Interactions between NAC and ascorbic acid in modulating mutagenesis and carcinogenesis. *Int J Cancer* 88(5): 702–7, Dec 2000.

Ghielmini, M. et al. Double-blind randomized study on the myeloprotective effect of melatonin in combination with carboplatin and etoposide in advanced lung cancer. *Br J Cancer* 80(7): 1058–61, Jun 1999.

Hecht, S.S. Inhibition of carcinogenesis by isothiocyanates. *Drug Metab Rev* 32(3–4): 395–411, Aug 2000.

Hecht, S.S. et al. Evaluation of butylated hydroxyanisole, myoinositol, curcumin, esculetin, resveratrol and lycopene as inhibitors of benzoapyrene plus 4-(methylnitrosamino)-1-(3-pyridyl)-1-butanone-induced lung tumorigenesis in A/J mice. *Cancer Lett* 137(2): 123–30, Apr 1999.

Kidd, P.M. The use of mushroom glucans and proteoglycans in cancer treatment. *Altern Med Rev* 5(1): 4–27, Feb 2000.

Lai, S.L. et al. Impact of nutritional status on the survival of lung cancer patients. *Chung Hua I Hsueh Tsa Chih* (Taipei) 61(3): 134–40, Mar 1998

LeMarchand, L. et al. Intake of flavonoids and lung cancer. *J Natl Cancer Inst* 92(2): 154–60, Jan 2000.

Li, Y. et al. Effects of curcumin derivatives on the GJIC of normal and tumor cells. *Zhongguo Yi Xue Ke Xue Yuan Xue Bao* (China) 18(2): 111–5, Apr 1996.

Lian, F. et al. p53-independent apoptosis induced by genistein in lung cancer cells. *Nutr Cancer* 33(2): 125–31, 1999.

Maehle, L. et al. Growth of human lung adenocarcinoma in nude mice is influenced by various types of fat and vitamin E. *Anticancer Res* 19(3A): 1649–55, May/Jun 1999.

Mohr, D.L. et al. Southern cooking and lung cancer. *Nutr Cancer* 35(1): 34–43, 1999.

Rauscher, G.H. et al. Relation between body mass index and lung cancer risk in men and women never and former smokers. *Amer J Epidemiol* 152, 506–13, Sep 2000.

Sinha, R. et al. Dietary heterocyclic amines and the risk of lung cancer among Missouri women. *Cancer Res* 60(14): 3753–6, Jul 2000.

Stoner, G.D. et al. Isothiocyanates and plant polyphenols as inhibitors of lung and esophageal cancer. *Cancer Lett* 114(1–2): 113–9, Mar 1997.

Veierod, M.B. et al. Dietary fat intake and risk of lung cancer: a prospective study of 51,452 Norwegian men and women. *Eur J Cancer Prev* 6(6): 540–9, Dec 1997.

Yang, C.S. et al. Mechanisms of inhibition of chemical toxicity and carcinogenesis by diallyl sulfide (DAS) and related compounds from garlic. *J Nutr* 131(3S): 1041S–5S, Mar 2001.

Zhang, J. et al. Fish consumption is inversely associated with male lung cancer mortality in countries with high levels of cigarette smoking or animal fat consumption. *Int J Epidemiol* 29(4): 615–21, Aug 2000.

Melanoma Nutrition Action Plan

Albino, A.P. et al. Cell cycle arrest and apoptosis of melanoma cells by DHA: association with decreased pRb phosphorylation. *Cancer Res* 60(15): 4139–45, Aug 2000.

Bogenrieder, T. et al. Analysis of pentacyclic triterpene-mediated antiproliferative effects on malignant melanoma cells (Meeting abstract). *Proc Annu Meet Am Assoc Cancer Res* 38: A1458, 1997.

Caltagirone, S. et al. Flavonoids apigenin and quercetin inhibit melanoma growth and metastatic potential. *Int J Cancer* 87(4): 595–600, Aug 2000.

Casagrande, F. et al. Effects of structurally related flavonoids on cell cycle progression of human melanoma cells: regulation of cyclin-dependent kinases CDK2 and CDK1. *Biochem Pharmacol* 61(10): 1205–15, May 2001.

Danielsson, C. et al. Differential apoptotic response of human melanoma cells to 1 alpha, 25-dihydroxyvitamin D_3 and its analogues. *Cell Death Differ* 5(11): 946–52, Nov 1998.

Danielsson, C. et al. Positive and negative interaction of 1,25 dihydroxyvitamin D_3 and the retinoid CD437 in the induction of human melanoma cell apoptosis. *Int J Cancer* 81(3): 467–70, May 1999.

DiSorbo, D.M. et al. In vivo and in vitro inhibition of B16 melanoma growth by vitamin B_6. *Nutr Cancer* 7(102): 43–52, 1985.

Drewa, G. et al. Influence of quercetin on B16 melanotic melanoma growth in C57BL/6 mice and on activity of some acid hydrolases in melanoma tissue. *Neoplasma* 48(1): 12–8, 2001.

Erickson, K.L. Dietary fat influence on murine melanoma growth and lymphocyte-mediated cytotoxicity. *J Natl Cancer Inst* 72(1): 115–20, Jan 1984.

Fu, Y.M. et al. Focal adhesion kinase-dependent apoptosis of melanoma induced by tyrosine and phenylalanine deficiency. *Cancer Res* 59(3): 758–65, Feb 1999.

Fu, Y.M. et al. Tyrosine and phenylalanine restriction induces G0/G1 cell cycle arrest in murine melanoma in vitro and in vivo. *Nutr Cancer* 29(2): 104–13, 1997.

He, L. et al. Isoprenoids suppress the growth of murine B16 melanomas in vitro and in vivo. *J Nutr* 127(5): 668–74, May 1997.

Iwashita, K. et al. Flavonoids inhibit cell growth and induce apoptosis in B16 melanoma 4A5 cells. *Biosci Biotechnol Biochem* 64(9): 1813–20, Sep 2000.

Jimenez-Orozco, F.A. et al. Cytostatic activity of coumarin metabolites and derivatives in the B16-F10 murine melanoma cell line. *Melanoma Res* 9(3): 243–7, Jun 1999.

Martin-Cordero, C. et al. Cytotoxic triterpenoids from Erica andevalensis. *Z. Naturfosch* 56(1–2): 45–8, Jan/Feb 2001.

Moon, J, et al. Induction of G(1) cell cycle arrest and p27(KIP1) increase by panaxydol isolated from *Panax ginseng. Biochem Pharmacol* 59(9): 1109–16, May 2000.

Palozza, P. et al. Canthaxanthin induces apoptosis in human cancer cell lines. *Carcinogenesis* 19(2): 373–6, Feb 1998.

Pelayo, B.A. et al. Decreased tissue plasminogen activator and increased plasminogen activator inhibitors and increased activator protein-1 and specific promoter 1 are associated with inhibition of invasion in human A375 melanoma deprived of tyrosine and phenylalanine. *Int J Oncol* 18(4): 877–83, Apr 2001.

Pelayo, B.A. et al. Inhibition of B16BL6 melanoma invasion by tyrosine and phenylalanine deprivation is associated with decreased secretion of plasminogen activators and increased plasminogen activator inhibitors. *Clin Exp Metastasis* 17(10): 841–8, 1999.

Ramsewak, R.S. et al. Cytotoxicity, antioxidant and anti-inflammatory activities of curcumins I-III from Curcuma longa. *Phytomedicine* 7(4): 303–8, Jul 2000.

Reich, R. et al. Eicosapentaenoic acid reduces the invasive and metastatic activities of malignant tumor cells. *Biochem Biophys Res Commun* 160(2): 559–64, Apr 1989.

Xiaoguang, C. et al. Cancer chemopreventive and therapeutic activities of red ginseng. *J Ethnopharmacol* 60(1): 71–8, Feb 1998.

Yan, L. et al. Effect of dietary supplementation of soybeans on experimental metastasis of melanoma cells in mice. *Nutr Cancer* 29(1): 1–6, 1997.

Yokota, T. et al. The inhibitory effect of glabridin from licorice extracts on melanogenesis and inflammation. *Pigment Cell Res* 11(6): 355–61, Dec 1998.

Non-Hodgkin's Lymphoma Nutrition Action Plan

Baris, D. et al. Epidemiology of lymphomas. *Curr Opin Oncol* 12(5): 383–94, Sep 2000.

Basu, M. et al. Beta-carotene prolongs survival, decreases lipid peroxidation and enhances glutathione status in transplantable murine lymphoma. *Phytomedicine* 7(2): 151–9, Apr 2000.

Gross, K.L. et al. Effect of fish oil, arginine, and doxorubicin chemotherapy on remission and survival time for dogs with lymphoma: a double blind, randomized placebo-controlled study. *Cancer* 88(8). 1916–28, Apr 2000.

Han, S.S. et al. Curcumin causes the growth arrest and apoptosis of B cell lymphoma by downregulation of egr-1, c-myc, bcl-XL, NF-kappa B, and p53. *Clin Immunol* 93(2): 152–61, Nov 1999.

Koide, T. et al. Antitumor effect of hydrolyzed anthocyanin from grape rinds and red rice. *Cancer Biother Radiopharm* 11(4): 273–7, Aug 1996.

Mukhopadhyay, P. et al. Influence of dietary restriction and soybean supplementation on the growth of a murine lymphoma and host immune function. *Cancer Lett* 78(1–3): 151–7, Apr 1994.

Park, J.W. et al. Chemopreventative agent resveratrol, a natural product derived from grapes, reversibly inhibits progression through S and G2 phases of the cell cycle in U937 cells. *Cancer Lett* 163(1): 43–9, Feb 2001.

Ramanathan, R. et al. Cytotoxic effect of plant polyphenols and fat-soluble vitamins on malignant human cultured cells. *Cancer Lett* 62(3): 217–24, Mar 1992.

Ranjan, D. et al. Enhanced apoptosis mediates inhibition of EBV-transformed lymphoblastoid cell line proliferation by curcumin. *J Surg Res* 87(1): 1–5, Nov 1999.

Saeki, K. et al. Apoptosis-inducing activity of polyphenol compounds derived from tea catechins in human histiolytic lymphoma U937 cells. *Biosci Biotechnol Biochem* 63(3): 585–7, Mar 1999.

Tavani, A. et al. Diet and risk of lymphoid neoplasms and soft tissue sarcomas. *Nutr Cancer* 27(3): 256–60, 1997.

Thorn, A. et al. Mortality and cancer incidence among Swedish lumberjacks exposed to phenoxy herbicides. *Occup Environ Med* 57(10): 718–20, Oct 2000.

Ward, M.H. et al. Dietary factors and non-Hodgkin's lymphoma in Nebraska (United States). *Cancer Causes Control* 5(5): 422–32, Sep 1994.

Ward, M.H. et al. Drinking water nitrate and the risk of non-Hodgkin's lymphoma. *Epidemiology* 7(5): 465–71, Sep 1996.

Zheng, W. et al. Diet and risk of non-Hodgkin's lymphoma in older women. *JAMA* 275(17): 1315–21, May 1996.

Zhang, S. et al. Dietary fat and protein in relation to risk of non-Hodgkin's lymphoma among women. *J Natl Cancer Inst* 91(2): 1751–8, Oct 1999.

Zhang, S.M. et al. Intakes of fruits, vegetables, and related nutrients and the risk of non-Hodgkin's lymphoma among women. *Cancer Epidemiol Biomarkers Prev* 9(5): 477–85, May 2000.

Pancreatic Cancer Nutrition Action Plan

Barber, M.D. et al. The effect of an oral nutritional supplement enriched with fish oil on weight loss in patients with pancreatic cancer. *Br J Cancer* 81(1): 80–6, Sep 1999.

Binstock, M. et al. Coffee and pancreatic cancer: an analysis of international mortality data. *Am J Epidemiol* 118(5): 630–40, Nov 1983.

Bueno de Mesquita, H.B. et al. Intake of foods and nutrients and cancer of the exocrine pancreas: a population-based case-control study in The Netherlands. *Int J Cancer* 48(4): 540–9, Jun 1991.

Burke, Y.D. et al. Inhibition of pancreatic cancer growth by the dietary isoprenoids farnesol and geraniol. *Lipids* 32(2): 151–6, Feb 1997.

Crowell, P.L. et al. Antitumorigenic effects of limonene and perillyl alcohol against pancreatic and breast cancer. *Adv Exp Med Biol* 401: 131–6, 1996.

Gonzales, N.J. et al. Evaluation of pancreatic proteolytic enzyme treatment of adenocarcinoma of the pancreas, with nutrition and detoxification support. *Nutr Cancer* 33(2): 117–24, 1999.

Hoppin, J.A. et al. Pancreatic cancer and serum organochlorine levels. *Cancer Epidemiol Biomarkers Prev* 9(2): 199–205, Feb 2000.

Howe, G.R. et al. A collaborative case-control study of nutrient intake with pancreatic cancer within the Search programme. *Int J Cancer* 51: 365–372, 1992.

Howe, G.R. et al. Nutrition and pancreatic cancer. *Cancer Causes Control* 7(1): 69–82, Jan 1996.

Lai, P.B. et al. Cell cycle arrest and induction of apoptosis in pancreatic cancer cells exposed to EPA in vitro. *Br J Cancer* 74(9): 1375–83, Nov 1996.

Lyon, J.L. et al. Dietary intake as a risk factor for cancer of the exocrine pancreas. *Cancer Epidemiol Biomarkers Prev* 2(6): 513–8, Nov/Dec 1993.

Majima, T. et al. Inhibitory effects of beta-carotene, palm carotene, and green tea polyphenols on pancreatic carcinogenesis initiated by N-nitorsobis(2-oxopropyl)amine in Syrian golden hamsters. *Pancreas* 16(1): 13–8, Jan 1998.

Olsen, G.W. et al. Nutrients and pancreatic cancer: a population-based case-control study. *Cancer Causes Control* 2(5): 291–7, Sep 1991.

Porta, M. et al. Serum concentrations of organochlorine compounds and K-ras mutations in exocrine pancreatic cancer. PANKRAS II Study Group. *Lancet* 354(9196): 2125–9, Dec 1999.

Roebuck, B.D. Dietary fat and the development of pancreatic cancer. *Lipids* 27(10): 804–6, Oct 1992.

Rosenthal, G.A. L-canaline: a potent antimetabolite and anti-cancer agent from leguminous plants. *Life Sci* 60(19): 1635–41, 1997.

Ura, H. et al. Growth inhibition of pancreatic cancer cells by flavonoids. *Gan To Kagaku Ryoho* 20(13): 2083–5, Oct 1993.

Woutersen, R.A. et al. Modulation of pancreatic carcinogenesis by antioxidants. *Food Chem Toxicol* 37(9–10): 981–4, Sep/Oct 1999.

Zatonski, W. et al. Nutritional factors and pancreatic cancer: a case-control study from southwest Poland. *Int J Cancer* 48(3): 390–4, May 1991.

Prostate Cancer Nutrition Action Plan

Agarwal, S. et al. Tomato lycopene and its role in human health and chronic diseases. *CMAJ* 163(6): 739–44, Sep 2000.

Awad, A.B. Peanuts as a source of beta-sitosterol, a sterol with anticancer properties. *Nutr Cancer* 36(2): 238–41, 2000.

Darzynkiewicz, Z. et al. Chinese herbal mixture PC SPES in treatment of prostate cancer (review). *Int J Oncol* 17(4): 729–36, Oct 2000.

De Stefani, E. et al. Alpha-linolenic acid and risk of prostate cancer: a case-control study in Uruguay. *Cancer Epidemiol Biomarkers Prev* 9(3): 335–8, Mar 2000.

Dorai, T. et al. Therapeutic potential of curcumin in human prostate cancer. *Mol Urol* 4(1): 1–6, Spring 2000.

Fullerton, S.A. et al. Induction of apoptosis in human prostate cancer cells with beta-glucan (Maitake mushroom polysaccharide). *Mol Urol* 4(1): 7–13, Spring 2000.

Giovannucci, E. Nutritional factors in human cancers. *Adv Exp Med Biol* 472, 29–42, 1999.

Hayashi, A. et al. Effects of daily oral administration of quercetin chalcone and modified citrus pectin. *Altern Med Rev* 5(6): 546–52, Dec 2000.

Jain, M.G. et al. Plant foods, antioxidants, and prostate cancer risk: findings from case-control studies in Canada. *Nutr Cancer* 34(2): 173–84, 1999.

Kampa, M. et al. Wine antioxidant polyphenols inhibit the proliferation of human prostate cancer cell lines. *Nutr Cancer* 37(2): 223–33, 2000.

Kolonel, L.N. et al. Vegetables, fruits, legumes and prostate cancer: a multiethnic case-control study. *Cancer Epidemiol Biomarkers Prev* 9(8): 795–804, Aug 2000.

Lamm, D.L. et al. Enhanced immunocompetence by garlic: role in bladder cancer and other malignancies. *J Nutr* 131(3S): 1067S–70S, Mar 2001.

Ramon, J.M. et al. Dietary fat intake and prostate cancer risk: a case control study in Spain. *Cancer Causes Control* 11(8): 679–85, Sep 2000.

Shamsuddin, A.M. et al. Inositol hexaphosphate inhibits growth and induces differentiation of PC-3 human prostate cancer cells. *Carcinogenesis* 16(8): 1975–9, Aug 1995.

Shen, J.C. et al. Low-dose genistein induces cyclin-dependent kinase inhibitors and G(1) cell-cycle arrest in human prostate cancer cells. *Mol Carcinog* 29(2): 92–102, Oct 2000.

Small, E.J. et al. Prospective trial of the herbal supplement PC-SPES in patients with progressive prostate cancer. *J Clin Oncol* 189210: 3595–603, Nov 2000.

Tzonou, A. et al. Diet and cancer of the prostate: A case-control study in Greece. *Int J Cancer* 80(5): 704–8, Mar 1999.

Xing, N. et al. Quercetin inhibits the expression and function of the androgen receptor in LNCaP prostate cancer cells. *Carcinogenesis* 22(3): 409–14, Mar 2001.

Other Cancers Nutrition Action Plan

Connolly, J.M. et al. Effects of dietary fatty acids on DU145 human prostate cancer cell growth in athymic nude mice. *Nutr Cancer* 29(2): 114–119, 1997.

Kari, F.W. et al. Roles for Insulin-like growth factor in mediating the anti-carcinogenic effects of caloric restriction. *J Nutr Hlth Age* (3)2, 92, 101, 1999.

McCarty, M.F. Vegan proteins may reduce risk of cancer, obesity, and cardiovascular disease by promoting increased glucagon activity. *Med Hypotheses* 53(6): 459–85, Dec 1999.

Owen, R.W. et al. Phenolic compounds and squalene in olive oils: the concentration and antioxidant potential of total phenols, simple phenols, secoiridoids, lignans and squalene. *Food Chem Toxicol* 38(8): 647–59, Aug 2000.

Owen, R.W. et al. The antioxidant/anticancer potential of phenolic compounds isolated from olive oil. *Eur J Cancer* 36(10): 1235–47, Jun 2000.

Rose, D.P. Dietary fat, fatty acids and breast cancer. *Breast Cancer* 4(1): 7–16, Mar 1997.

Shen, J.C. et al. Low dose genistein induces cyclin-dependent kinase inhibitors and G(1) cell-cycle arrest in human prostate cancer cells. *Mol Carcinog* 29(2): 92–102, Oct 2000.

Glossary

Absolute neutrophil count The number of circulating white blood cells that combat bacterial infections, inflammatory disorders, stress, and certain drugs.

Achalasia Inability of the smooth muscle of the esophagus to relax during swallowing.

Allopathic The treatment of disease by conventional medical practices, i.e., to treat the physical symptoms of a particular medical condition.

Angiogenesis The development of new blood vessels to a tissue.

Antiemetic An agent that prevents nausea or vomiting.

Antineoplastic An agent that prevents the development of cancer cells.

Antioxidant A compound that prevents or delays cellular deterioration caused by oxygen.

Apoptosis Cellular destruction.

Atrophy Wasting away of cells, tissues, organs, or parts of the body.

Cachetic A weak, emaciated condition related to malnutrition.

Cancer cachexia A weak, emaciated condition related to advanced cancer where weight and strength are lost despite adequate caloric intake.

Carcinogen Any substance that causes cancer.

Carcinogenesis The production of a cancerous new growth.

Cruciferous A family of vegetables that contain indoles and isothiocyanates. Members include bok choy, broccoli, Brussels sprouts, cabbage, cauliflower, collards, kale, kohlrabi, mustard greens, rutabaga, turnips, and turnip greens.

Cytotoxic Causing cellular destruction and death.

Dysbiosis A state of altered bacterial flora in the gut.

Endoscope An instrument used to examine the inside of the GI tract.

Free radical An extremely reactive molecule that can cause cellular damage.

Gastrectomy Surgical removal of part or all of the stomach.

Gastroesophageal reflux A return flow of stomach contents into the esophagus.

Hepatocytes Liver cells.

Hypermetabolism An increased metabolic rate.

Hypoglycemia A condition of low blood sugar.

Metabolic Refers to the nature of metabolism.

Metabolism The method providing energy for all physical and chemical processes in the body.

Metastasis Movement of cancer from one part of the body to another.

Mutations A change in the genetic material of a cell.

Neuropathy A decrease in the function of the nervous system.

Nitrosamines Carcinogenic forms of nitric acid derived from nitrates in food.

Olfactory Pertaining to the sense of smell.

Oncology The study of tumors.

Oxidation A chemical reaction that removes electrons from an atom.

Peristalsis The movement of the GI tract used to propel its contents.

pH A symbol used to express an acid or alkaline condition.

Pharmacological Having the property of a prescription drug.

Physiological Refers to the normal functioning of the body.

Phytochemicals Compounds found in plants that may protect humans.

Phytoestrogens Hormones produced naturally in plants.

Procarcinogens A substance that only becomes carcinogenic after it is altered by a metabolic reaction.

Proliferation The reproduction or multiplication of cells.

Prooxidant A compound that promotes oxidation.

Sphincter A ring-like band of muscle fibers that constricts a passage, as in the esophageal sphincter.

Synergism Combining nutrients to create a greater effect than if they were taken individually.

Resources

Internet Sites

Alliance for Lung Cancer Advocacy, Support and Education (www.alcase.org)

AMC Cancer Research Center, Cancer Information and Counseling Line (www.amc.org)

American Botanical Council (http://www.herbalgram.org/abcmission.html)

American Cancer Society (www.cancer.org)

American Institute for Cancer Research (www.aicr.org)

Cancer Care, Inc. (www.cancercare.org)

Cancer Hope Network (www.cancerhopenetwork.org)

Cancer Treatment Centers of America (www.cancercenter.com)

Cancer Treatment Research Foundation (www.ctrf.org)

Colon Cancer Alliance (www.ccalliance.org)

ConsumerLab (www.consumerlab.com) Conducts dietary supplement analysis

Conversations: The International Ovarian Cancer Connection (www.ovarian-news.org)

Cure for Lymphoma Foundation (www.cfl.org)

Environmental Working Group (www.ewg.org or www.foodnews.org)

Health World Online (www.healthy.net/index/html)

International Myeloma Foundation (www.myeloma.org)

Joy of Soy (www.joyofsoy.com)

Kidney Cancer Association (www.kidneycancerassociation.org)

The Leukemia and Lymphoma Society (www.leukemia-lymphoma.org)

Mothers and Others (www.consciouschoice.com)

Multiple Myeloma Research Foundation (www.multiplemyeloma.org)

National Cancer Institute (www.nci.nih.gov)

National Center for Complementary and Alternative Medicine (www.nccam.nih.gov)

National Cervical Cancer Coalition (www.ncc-online.org)

The Oley Foundation (www.wizvax.net/oleyfdn)

R.A. Bloch Cancer Foundation, Inc. (www.blochcancer.org)

Rodale Institute (www.rodaleinstitute.org)

Pancreatic Cancer Action Network (www.pancan.org)

The Skin Cancer Foundation (www.skincancer.org)

Stretch Island Fruit, Inc. (www.stretch-island.com)

Support for People with Oral and Head and Neck Cancer, Inc. (www.spohnc.org)

United Soybean Board (www.soybean.org)

United States Department of Agriculture Nutrient Data Laboratory (www.ag.uiuc.edu)

Vegetarian Resource Group (http://envirolink.org/arrs/VRG/heart.html)

WebMD (www.webMD.com)

Y-ME (www.y-me.org)

Healthcare Provider Organizations

American Association of Naturopathic Physicians   703 610-9037   (www.naturopathic.org)

American College of Allergy, Asthma and Immunology   800 842-7777 (www.allergy.mcg.edu)

American Dietetic Association   800 877-1600   800 366-1655 (automated referral system)   (www.eatright.org)

American Gastroenterological Association   301 654-2055   (www.gastro.org)

American Society of Clinical Oncology   703 299-0150   (www.asco.org)

Recommended References

Beating Cancer with Nutrition, by Patrick Quillin

The Detox Diet, by Elson Haas

Encyclopedia of Nutritional Supplements, by Michael Murray

Food Allergies, written for the American Dietetic Association by Celide Koerner
and Anne Furlong

Food Values of Portions Commonly Used, by Jean Pennington

Fresh Vegetables and Fruit Juices, by N.W. Walker

The Healing Power of Herbs, by Michael Murray

The Healthy Home, by Linda Mason Hunter

Herbs of Choice, by Varro Tyler

A Manual of Laboratory Diagnostic Tests, by Frances Fischbach

The Natural Pharmacy, by Lininger, Wright, Austin, Brown and Gaby

Nutritional Assessment and Support, by Grant and DeHoog

The Real Vitamin & Mineral Book, Using Supplements for Optimal Health, by
Shari Lieberman and Nancy Bruning

Tissue Cleansing through Bowel Management, by Bernard Jensen

Nutritional Supplements

Botanic Lab (PC SPES) 800 242-5555

Cambridge Nutraceuticals (glutamine) 800 443-7802

Enzymatic Therapy 800 225-9245

Frontier Herbs 800 786-1388

Gaia Herbs 800 994-9355

Nature's Herbs 800 437-2257

Twin Lab 800 645-5626

Magazines, Newsletters, and Public Information

American Institute for Cancer Research Newsletter 800 843-8114

Cancer Resource Center 800 940-2822

Cooking Light 800 336-0125

Coping with Cancer 615 790-2400

Environmental Nutrition Newsletter 800 829-5384

Nutrition Action Healthletter 202 332-9110

Prevention 800 813-8070

Produce for Better Health Foundation 302 235-2329

Tuft's University Diet & Nutrition Letter 800 274-7581

United Soybean Board Soy Hotline 800 TALK-SOY

Vegetarian Times 877 717-8923

Cookbooks

The American Cancer Society Cookbook: A Menu for Good Health, by Anne
Lindsay

In the Kitchen with Rosie, by Rosie Daley

Lean and Luscious and Meatless, by Bobbie Hinman and Millie Synder

The Low Fat Good Food Cookbook, by M. and T. Katahn

Mediterranean Light, Bantam Books

Moosewood Restaurant Low-Fat Favorites, Clarkson/Potter

*Quick and Healthy Recipes for People Who Say They Don't Have Time to Cook
Healthy Meals,* by Brenda Ponichtera

Simply Vegan, by Debra Wasserman

The Versatile Grain and Elegant Bean, by Sheryl and Mel London

Health Food Mail Order Businesses

Apple Valley Market 800 237-7436

Crusoe Island 800 724-2233

Dixie USA, Inc. 800 347-3494

Gold Mine Natural Food Co. 800 862-2347

Hodgson Mill 800 525-0177

The Mail Order Catalog 800 695-2241

Melissa's World Variety 800 588-0151

Natural Lifestyle Supplies 800 752-277

Index

5-FU, 60, 202, 247

A

abdominal cramping, 57-59, 68
Acesulfame-K, 102
adrenal glands, 81, 82
Adriamycin, 69, 202, 206, 207, 210, 221, 247, 206
advanced nutrition support, 41
aerobic conditioning, 9-10
alcohol, 205, 208, 240 254, 268, 278, 288, 290, 292, 335
allergies, food, 52, 64-65, 69, 76, 197
allicin, 150, 224, 267, 279, 358
aloe vera, 58, 67, 81, 83, 202,223
American Cancer Society, 331
American College of Sports and Medicine, 9
American Dietetic Association, 26, 170, 187, 277
American Institute for Cancer Research, 174, 263, 274, 276, 286, 298, 310, 332, 354, 387, 376
amino acids, 29, 90-91, 92, 218, 229, 345
            L-carnitine, 247
            L-cysteine, 246
            L-glutamine, 246, 247
            L-lysine, 70
anemia, 29, 30, 31, 206, 214
angiogenesis, 227
anthocyanidins, 150-51, 276, 288, 388
antiangiogenesis, 218
antibiotics, 215, 237, 256
            and GI tract, 49-50, 61
            in food supply, 237
antiemetic, 72-74
antiesophageal reflux, 47, 66, 67, 72, 230
antioxidants, 29, 87, 147, 149, 150, 151, 152, 153, 155, 156, 168, 200, 201, 202, 203, 205, 206, 212, 215, 218, 232, 226, 229, 239,
artificial sweeteners, 102-03, 252
ascorbic acid. See vitamin C.
Aspartame, 102, 142, 252
astragalus, 29, 49, 224-25
avocado, 31, 38, 93, 113, 118, 124, 175

B

bacterial infection, 51, 52, 53, 65, 131, 223, 245, 270
beans, 70, 117, 174-75, 240

    as fiber, 58, 173-75
    difficult to digest, 61, 65
    glandular support, 81
    protein source, 97
belching, 65-66
beneficial behaviors, 5-7
beta carotene, 151, 201, 202, 204-05, 211
betaine HCl, 52, 53, 65, 66, 67, 83
bile acids
            eliminating, 55
            from sugars, 170
Biotene, 63
bladder cancer, 150, 185, 186, 217
            dietary supplements for, 267
            nutrition action plan, 262-72
Bleomycin, 69, 247
body scans, 6-7
boron, 230
boswellia, 347
bowel obstructions, 56, 187
bowel spasms, 75-77, 83
brain metastasis, 226, 259, 275
BRAT diet, 60
breast cancer, 6, 8, 9, 26, 112, 121, 125, 130, 146, 151, 152, 153, 155, 156, 169, 170, 185, 186, 187, 202, 210, 211, 215, 219, 220, 221, 223, 226, 227, 230, 252, 255, 256, 312
            dietary supplements for, 278-79
            estrogen-receptor positive, 186, 277, 312
            nutrition action plan, 273-84
butter vs. margarine, 119

C

cachexia, 9, 20, 332, 365
calcium, 34, 56, 59, 66, 67, 69, 97, 138, 170, 176, 184, 209, 210, 211, 212-13, 214
calorie density, 38,94
calories, counting 93-94
cancer cells, 3-4
cancer prevention diet, 386-95
cancer treatments
            and stress, 7-8
            dietary supplementation, 200-03
cancers, hormonally based, 9

candida, 25, 49, 52, 53, 54-55, 83, 130, 131, 140, 150, 220,
canola oil, 38, 93, 113, 116, 121, 123, 124
caprylic acid, 54, 83, 220
capsaicin, 152
carbohydrates
    complex, 89, 98, 131, 143
    simple sugars, 88, 102, 103, 129, 131
cascara sagrada, 56, 57, 83
catechins, 152, 276, 288, 299
cells
    cancer, 4
    normal, 3
cervical cancer, 9, 151, 154, 208, 210, 309, 311. *See also gynecological cancers.*
chamomile, 58, 72, 76
characteristics, winning, 15-16
charcoal tablets, 66
chemistry panel, 28, 31
chemotherapy
    and digestion, 46-47
    dietary supplements to decrease, side effects of, 247
    dietary supplements to enhance, effectiveness, 202
chromium, 138, 140, 141, 213, 213, 369
Cisplatin, 71, 186, 201, 202, 207, 219, 224, 247
citrus bioflavonoids, 152-53
cobalamin, 55, 62, 122, 153, 155, 167, 168, 169, 202, 209, 212, 217, 219, 220, 286, 289. *See also vitamin B$_{12}$.*
colitis, 75
colon cancer, 55, 62, 122, 153, 155, 167, 168, 169, 202, 209, 212, 217, 219, 220, 286, 289. *See also colorectal cancer.*
colorectal cancer, 130, 153, 168, 185, 211, 223
    dairy product consumption, 289
    dietary supplements for, 290-91
    nutrition action plan, 285-96
    prevention, 168-69
    red meat consumption, 288-89
complete blood count, 28-30
complementary proteins, 92
complex carbohydrate, 165
constipation, 46, 49, 51, 55-56, 122, 130, 167, 181, 236
copper, 138, 170, 209, 213, 214, 230, 267, 303
copper cookware, 78
CoQ10, 207, 220-21, 230, 247
cottonseed oil, 113, 125, 252
coumarins, 153, 276, 299, 323, 334, 344
crackers, healthy, 178
cravings, sugar, 140-41
curcuma root, 291, 325, 336, 358, 380
curcumins, 153, 201
cutting fats, 115-17
Cytoxan, 71, 202, 247

D

Dacarbazine, 71
daidzein, 156, 185, 187, 324

dairy products, 38, 58, 61, 76, 116, 127, 212, 240, 250
    colon cancer, 289
    ovarian cancer, 313
    prostate cancer, 378
dandelion, 222-23, 246
deglycyrrhizinated licorice, 58, 67, 81, 347
dental health, 59
detoxification, 51, 52, 56, 156, 164, 200, 202, 203, 206, 219, 235-256
    benefits of, 237-38
    colonics, 237-38
    diet, 238-41
    dietary supplements for, 202, 206, 219 246
    environmental pollutants, 252-54
    exercise, 255
    fasting, 237-38
    food additives, 250-52
    juicing, 164, 245-46
    lifestyle, 255-56
    safety of, 227-28
    side effects, 247-48
detoxifiers, 222-23
development of cancer, 3
diarrhea, 32, 42, 46, 60-61, 62, 64, 68, 76, 77, 83, 104, 138, 210, 241, 251, 263, 310
diet, 12-15
    adding fruits and vegetables to, 158-62
    amount of carbohydrate, 88
    amount of fat, 93
    amount of fiber, 169-71
    amount of protein, 89
    BRAT, 60
    calories 93-94
    deprivation, 15
    detoxification, 238-41
    for stress, 81-82
    making changes, 15, 88, 237
    meal planning, 13-15
    serving size, 35, 96, 100, 118, 149
    weight control, 94-96
dietary fats, 63, 93, 115, 117, 119
    avocado, 31, 38, 93, 113, 118, 124, 125,
    balancing, 123
    borage, 113
    canola oil, 38, 93, 113, 116, 121, 123, 124
    connection to cancer, 111-12
    corn, 100, 113
    cottonseed oil, 223, 125, 252
    counting grams, 113
    cutting, 115-17
    evening primrose oil, 113
    flax oil, 58, 67, 83, 113, 121-23, 220, 221, 230, 271, 275
    hydrogenation, 101, 113, 116, 117, 124, 126, 127, 175, 191, 239, 240
    olive oil, 38, 74, 93, 113, 116, 121-4, 127, 158, 196

Index

peanut oil, 93, 113, 124-25, 252
safflower, 93, 113
sunflower, 113,
substitutes, 127-28, 251
unhealthy, 125-27
unsaturated, 113
dietary supplements, 14, 30, 67, 82, 199-232,
aloe vera, 223
astragalus, 29, 49, 224-25
beta carotene, 151, 201, 202, 204-05, 211
calcium, 184, 209, 210, 211, 212-13,
214
caprylic acid, 54, 83, 220
chromium, 213
cobalamin, 209
copper, 138, 140, 141, 213-14, 369
CoQ10, 207, 220-21, 230, 247
dandelion, 222-23, 246
detoxification, 202, 206, 219,246
detoxifiers, 222-23
digestive enzymes, 37, 46, 53, 56, 57, 58,
61, 65, 66, 67, 64, 76, 83, 89,
173, 175, 208, 217-18
echinacea, 29, 49, 225
EPA, 119, 121, 219-20, 230,
Essiac, 58, 67, 226
fiber, 165, 171, 180, 181, 182
flaxseed oil, 58, 67, 83, 113, 121, 219,
220, 221, 230
flor-essence, 226
folic acid (folate), 12, 30, 124, 168, 174,
202, 208, 209, 289, 291, 315
garlic, 53, 54, 58, 60, 72, 79, 83, 99, 107,
149, 150, 158, 196, 223-24, 243,
247
gastrointestinal supporters, 223-24
ginger, 60, 72, 73, 74, 75, 80, 83, 224,
244
glandulars, 24, 49, 54, 82, 216-17
glutathione, 55, 201, 202, 206, 215,
218, 219, 235, 247
grape seed extract, 150, 222, 279
green tea, 152, 202, 222
guidelines for choosing, 227-31,
gynecological cancers, 314-15
herbs, 221-25, 226-27, 232
immune enhancers, 224-25
inositol hexaphosphate, 185, 226
iron, 29, 30-32, 66, 67, 78, 97, 170,
174, 177, 209, 214, 230
magnesium, 34, 53, 56, 67, 81, 83, 121,
138, 170, 174, 177, 213, 214,
215, 217, 246
melatonin, 201, 221, 247
milk thistle, 55, 223, 246, 247
modified citrus pectin, 220, 291, 380
mushroom extracts, 225
niacin, 121, 202, 206, 207
panothenic acid, 81, 207

probiotics, 49, 53, 54, 56, 61, 66, 69,
76, 83, 217-18
prostate cancer, 380
pyridoxine, 207-08. See also vitamin B_6.
quercetin, 70, 83, 152, 153, 202, 247
reliable brands, 231
riboflavin, 121, 206
saw palmetto, 227
selenium, 49, 54, 79, 82, 200, 205, 211,
215-16, 217, 246, 247,
shark cartilage, 227
soy, 187-88, 190, 193
thiamin, 205
upper digestive tract cancer, 303
vitamin A, 79, 148, 151, 176, 201, 203-4
vitamin C, 29, 30, 32, 34, 56, 59, 83,
121, 173, 182, 200, 202, 209,
210, 211, 213, 214, 217, 218
vitamin D, 211, 213, 230
vitamin E, 64, 70, 79, 82, 83, 120, 124,
152, 153, 174, 184, 200, 202,
204, 211-12, 217, 230, 247
digestion, 45-82
effect of chemotherapy, 46-47
effect of radiation, 46-47
digestive enzymes, 37, 46, 53, 54, 56, 57, 58, 61, 65,
66, 67, 69, 76, 83, 89, 173, 175, 209, 217, 218
digestive process, 45-46
dining out, 104-09, 159
doctors, relationship with, 8
dry mouth, 62-63

E

echinacea, 29, 49, 225
ELISA food allergy test, 53, 55, 58, 64, 65
ellagic acid, 153-54, 201, 243
endometrial cancer, 26, 112, 146, 169, 185, 187, 310,
311, 312. See also gynecological cancers.
enteral feeding, 41-43
environmental pollutants, 252-54
HCAs (heterocyclic amines), 239, 252
PAHs (polycyclic aromatic hydrocarbons)
252-3
PCBs (polychlorinated biphenyls) 253,
368
EPA (eicopentaenoic acid), 119, 121, 230
Epirubicin, 69
Epogen, 30
esophageal cancer, 7, 66, 79, 150, 153, 154, 155,
169, 206, 216, 222, 225, 255, 297, 299, 300,
301, 302. See also upper digestive tract cancer.
Essiac, 58, 67, 226
estrogen, 6, 9, 154, 156, 168, 170, 184, 186, 227, 230
estrogen-sensitive cancer, 187, 312
exercise, 9, 10, 16, 52, 53, 55, 56, 58, 65, 67, 71, 72,
77, 81, 255
and lymphedema, 11

F

fake fats, 127, 128, 251
fasting, 237-38

fat grams, 113
fat. *See dietary fats.*
fatty acids, 93, 113, 211, 219-20, 241
    monounsaturated, 113, 116, 119, 122,
        127
    omega-3, 42, 119, 120, 121, 123, 168,
        184, 202, 219-20, 239, 247
    polyunsaturated, 113, 275
    saturated, 113, 123
    superunsaturated, 113
    trans, 115, 117, 119, 126, 127
    unsaturated, 113
feverfew, 70
fiber, 49, 51, 55-56, 58, 60, 76, 103-04, 165-81
    amount required, 169-71
    beans, 174-75
    cancer fighting properties, 167-68, 169
    colorectal cancer prevention, 168-69
    increasing your intake, 172-73
    insoluble, 166
    soluble, 121, 166, 167, 176
    whole grain, 167-68, 176-77
fiber supplements, 180-81
flaxseed oil, 58, 67, 83, 113, 121-23, 220, 221, 230,
    271, 275, 253, 272, 277
Flor-essence, 226
fluid intake, 51, 53, 55, 56, 60, 62, 78, 240, 242,
    266, 268, 278, 290, 292, 302, 304, 306, 314,
    316, 324, 326, 335, 337, 346, 348, 357, 359,
    368, 370, 378, 381, 390, 391
folic acid (folate), 12, 30, 124, 168, 174, 202, 208,
    209, 289, 291, 315
food additives, 250-52
food allergies, 52, 64-65, 69, 76
    and stress, 65
food intolerances, 57, 59
food labeling, 100-04
food records, 34-36
food safety, 248-50
food sensitivities, 55, 64-65, 83
foods, serving size, 35, 96, 100, 118, 149
foods, toxins, 4
Fruit n' Nut Sundaes, 50
fruits and vegetables
    adding to diet, 158-62

G

G.I. tract. *See gastrointestinal tract.*
gamma-oryzanol, 58, 67
garlic, 53, 54, 58, 60, 72, 79, 83, 99, 107, 149, 150,
    158, 196, 223-24, 243, 247
gas, 32, 49, 54, 65-6, 68, 76, 83, 130, 131, 170, 173,
    175, 214
gastrointestinal cancer, 152, 205, 217
gastrointestinal supporters, 223-24
gastrointestinal tract healing, 67, 79, 81, 83
gastrointestinal tract, 41, 42, 44, 46, 53, 67, 166, 246,
    263-64, 275, 286, 287, 299, 310-11,
    322, 333, 343, 354-55, 365, 376, 387
    abdominal cramping, 57-58

antibiotics, 49-50
bad breath, 51-52
bloating, 52-53
bowel obstructions, 56
bowel spasms, 75-77
candidiasis, 54-55
constipation, 55-56
diarrhea, 60-61
difficulty swallowing, 62-63
dry mouth, 62-63
food allergies, 64-65
food sensitivities, 64-65
gas or belching, 65-66
greasy or fatty stools, 63-64
heartburn, 66-67
lactose intolerance, 68-69
mouth sores, 69-71
nausea and vomiting, 71-75
poor dental health, 59
stress, 81
taste changes, 77-79
toxic burden, 130
ulcers, 79, 81
genes, 3
genetic mutations, 3, 153
genistein, 156, 185, 186, 187, 202, 219
ginger, 60, 72, 73, 74, 75, 80, 83, 224, 244
gingko biloba, 247
glandulars, 216-17
glucose, 9, 88, 102, 132, 139, 140, 142, 173, 206,
    213, 239
glutathione, 55, 201, 202, 206, 215, 218, 219, 235,
    247
goldenseal, 61, 70
grape seed extract, 150, 222, 279
grapefruit seed extract, 61
green tea, 152, 202, 222, 266, 268, 270, 278, 282,
    290, 292, 294, 302, 306, 314,, 316, 318, 326,
    328, 331, 335, 337, 339, 346, 348, 350, 353,
    357, 359, 361, 368, 370, 372, 379, 381, 383,
    390, 391, 393
gut dysbiosis, 52
gynecological cancers,
    dairy product consumption, 313
    dietary fat, 311
    dietary supplements, 314-15
    nutrition action plan, 309-20
    soy consumption, 212-13

H

halitosis, 51-52
head and neck cancer, 42, 62, 78, 79, 297, 301. *See
    also upper digestive tract cancer.*
heartburn, 66-67, 72, 214
helicobacter pylori, 66, 81, 214
hematocrit, 28-30
hemoglobin, 28-30
herbs, 221-25
    aloe vera, 58, 67, 81, 202, 223
    astragalus, 29, 49, 224, 225

boswellia, 347
cascara sagrada, 56, 57, 83
chamomile, 58, 72, 76
dandelion, 222-23, 246
deglycyrrhizinated licorice, 58, 67, 88
echinacea, 29, 49, 225
feverfew, 70
gamma-oryzanol, 58, 67
garlic, 53, 54, 58, 60, 72, 79, 83, 99,
    107, 149, 150, 158, 196, 223-24,
    243, 247, 267, 271, 272, 276, 279,
    283, 284, 288, 295, 296, 299, 307,
    308, 312, 319, 320, 334, 340, 334,
    340, 344, 351, 352, 358, 362, 363,
    377, 384, 385, 388, 394, 395, 405
ginger, 60, 72, 73, 74, 75, 90, 224, 244,
    330
gingko biloba, 247, 267, 303, 315, 337
goldenseal, 61,70
grape seed extract, 150, 222, 279
grapefruit seed extract, 61
green tea, 152, 202, 222
melissa extract, 70
milk thistle, 76, 223, 246, 247
peppermint oil, 76
rosemary, 58, 77, 128, 150, 150
saw palmetto, 227
senna, 56, 57
slippery elm, 70, 226
tea tree oil, 59, 70
valerian root, 58, 77
heterocyclic amines, 239, 252-54
hidden fats, 101
honey, 102, 144, 250
hormonally based cancers, 9, 168
Hot n' Spicy Soy Nuts, 190
Hurricaine, 71
hydrogenation, 101, 113, 124, 126, 127
hypochlorhydria, 52, 66, 67, 212

I

immune enhancers, 224-25
immune response, effect of sugar, 131
immune system, 4, 15, 25, 54,, 59, 60, 81, 88, 43,
    94, 131, 139, 147
    diet, 4, 12, 123, 136, 236, 241, 245
    free radicals, 4
    stress, 4
    supplements to support, 29, 49, 201,
        208, 215, 217, 224, 247
immunocompetence, 12
indoles, 154, 239
inflammaory bowel diseases, 57, 58, 60
information resources, 6
inositol hexaphosphate (IP-6), 226, 279, 291, 380,
    462, 185, 206
isolated soy protein, 60, 187, 190, 193-4, 267, 291,
    303, 325, 336, 345, 347, 358, 380, 390
insoluble fiber, 166
insulin, 9, 130-31, 136, 168

insurance benefits, 5
intravenous feeding, 44
iron, 30, 66, 67, 170, 174, 236
    deficiency, 31, 32, 214
    supplementation, 30, 214
irritable bowel syndrome, 58, 60, 75, 76, 77
isoflavones, 156, 183-89
isothiocyanates, 154-55

J

juices, 60, 72, 79, 162, 173, 240
juicing, 137, 241, 245-46

K

Kaopectate, 61
kidney cancer, 26, 112
Kytril, 73

L

L-carnitine, 247
L-cysteine, 246
L-glutamine, 246-47
L-lysine, 70
label reading, 100-04
    fats, 101-02
    sugars, 103
laboratory tests, 27-33
    anemia, 29-31
    CBC, 28-30
    chemistry panel, 31-33
    protein panel, 32-33
    RBC, 29-30
    WBC, 29
LactAid, 53, 69
lactobacillus, 50
lactose intolerance, 53, 56, 60, 68-69, 71
laxatives, 56
legumes, 92, 166
leeks, 150
leukemia, 150, 153, 155, 156, 185, 209, 224 226
    dietary supplements, 325
    nutrition action plan, 321-330
liver cancer, 155, 202, 214, 215, 219, 226, 253
Lomotil, 61
lung cancer, 151, 152, 154, 155, 203, 204, 210, 226
    and obesity, 9, 332
    dietary supplements for, 336-37
    nutrition action plan 331-41
    saccharin and, 141, 252
lymphedema, 11
lymphocytes, 9

M

macrophages, 9
magnesium, 34, 58, 66, 67, 81, 83, 121, 138, 170,
    215, 174, 177, 213, 214, 217, 246
malnutrition, 19-44, 46-47, 59, 76, 200
    avoiding, 24-28
    myths of, 20-22
    risks of, 21-22
margarine vs. butter, 119
Marinol, 39

massage therapy, 8
MCT oil, 63-64
meal planning, 13-15
meals, fast and easy, 73-75, 77
medical records, 5
Megace, 39
melanoma
    dietary supplements, 346-47
    nutrition action plan, 342-52
    vegetarian diet, 345
melatonin, 201, 221, 279, 315, 336, 380
melissa extract, 70
metabolic profile, 31
metastasis, 11, 121, 169, 275, 345
Methotrexate, 208
milk thistle, 55, 223, 246, 247
miso, 192, 194
modified citrus pectin, 220
monoterpenes, 155
mouth cancer, 255. *See also upper digestive tract cancer.*
mouth sores, 69-71
mushroom extracts, 225

N

NAC, 218-19
National Cancer Institute, 166, 147, 149, 169
nausea and vomiting, 71-75
    stress, 71
    Kytril, 73
    Zofran, 73
Navelbine, 55, 60
niacin, 121, 202, 206-07
nitrates, 59, 239, 251
non-Hodgkin's lymphoma, 150, 212
    dietary supplements, 358
    nutrition action plan, 353-63
non-toxic lifestyle, 255-56
normal cells, 3
nutrients, 87-109
    amino acids, 90-91
    calories 93-94
    carbohydrates, 88-89, 102-03
    dietary fats, 93, 101-02, 111-28
    fiber, 103-04, 165-82
    labeling, 100-04
    phytochemicals, 146-47, 150-56
    portion size, 96
    protein, 89-92
nutrition action plan
    bladder cancer, 262-72
    breast cancer, 273-84
    cancer prevention, 386-95
    colorectal cancer, 285-96
    gynecological cancer, 309-20
    leukemia, 321-30
    lung, 331-41
    melanoma, 342-52
    non-Hodgkin's lymphoma, 353-63
    other cancers, 386-95
    pancreatic cancer, 364-74

prostate cancer, 375-85
    upper digestive tract cancer, 297-308
nutrition action plans, 256-395
nutrition, 12-15
    dietary supplements, 199-233
    food record keeping, 34-36
    meal planning, 13-15
nutritional requirements, 26-27
nutritional supplements. *See dietary supplements. See also herbs.*
nutritional support, 41-44
    enteral feeding, 41-43
    intravenous feeding, 44

O

obesity, 26, 130, 67, 274, 332
Olestra, 127, 128, 251
oils, storing, 120
olive oil, 38, 74, 93, 113, 116, 121-24, 127, 158, 196
omega-3 fatty acids, 42 119-21, 123, 168 104, 202, 219-20, 239, 247
oncogenes, 3
oral cavity cancer. *See upper digestive tract cancer.*
ovarian cancer, 169, 170, 187, 221. *See also gynecological cancers.*

P

Pancrease, 64, 365
pancreatic cancer, 130, 155, 219
    dietary supplements, 369
    nutrition action plan, 364-74
Pancreatin, 64, 365
pantothenic acid, 87, 207
parasitic infection, 52, 53
parenteral feeding, 44
patients, positive behaviors, 5-7
PC-SPES, 227, 380
peanuts, 124-25
pediatric brain cancer, 186
peppermint oil, 76
Pepto Bismol, 81
periodontal disease, 51
pesticides, 236, 237, 241, 254, 255, 256
pharynx cancer, 146, 169, 206. *See also upper digestive tract cancer.*
phenolic acids, 122, 155, 265, 288, 299, 366, 377
physical activity. *See exercise.*
phytates, 184-85
phytochemicals, 150-156
    allicin, 150, 224
    allylic sulfide, 150
    anthocyanidins, 150-51
    beta carotene and carotenoids, 151, 201, 202, 204-05, 211
    capsaicin, 152
    catechins, 152
    citrus bioflavonoids, 152-53
    coumarins, 153
    curcumins, 153, 201
    ellagic acid, 153-54, 201, 243
    indoles, 154, 239

isothiocyanates, 154-55
monoterpenes, 155
phenolic acids, 122, 155
phthalides, 156
phytoestrogens, 156
quinones, 156
triterpenoids, 156
phytoestrogens, 156
phytosterols, 184, 195
postmenopausal breast cancer, 26
potassium bromate, 251
Prednisone, 39
Prevacid, 81
Prilosec, 81
probiotics, 49, 51, 53, 54, 56, 59, 61, 66, 69, 217-18
produce
cancer-fighting, 146, 147-48
phytochemicals, 146-47, 150-56
safety, 162-63
spray wash, 163
prostate cancer, 9, 112, 125, 151, 152, 153, 155, 169, 170, 185, 205, 211, 215, 220, 221, 222, 223, 224, 226, 227, 230, 256
dairy product consumption, 378
dietary supplements for, 380
nutrition action plan, 375-85
protein status, 32-33
protein, 12, 89-92
pyridoxine, 207-08

Q

quinones, 156

R

radiation
and digestion, 46-47
dietary supplementation during, 200-03
side effects of, 20
recipes
Fast & Easy meals, 73-75, 77
Fruit n' Nut Sundaes, 50
Glorious Morning Muffins, 179
Hot n' Spicy Soy Nuts, 190
Seasoned bagel chips, 99
Spicy Rice & Beans, 180
Splendid Soy Shake, 197
Super Smoothie, 33
Tofu Egg Salad, 196
recombinant BGH, 256
rectal cancer, 185. See also colorectal cancer.
red blood count, 29-30
red meat consumption, 78, 91, 95, 113, 239, 252, 288-89
reflux. See antiesophageal reflux.
regaining weight, 21, 24-25
Reglan, 53
relaxation techniques, 8
religion, 8, 11-12
rest, 8
restaurant food, 104-09
retreats, 8

riboflavin, 121, 206
rosemary, 58, 77, 128, 150, 156
roughage. See fiber.

S

saccharaomyces bouldardii, 61
saccharin, 103, 141, 252
saw palmetto, 227
Seasoned Bagel Chips, 99
selenium, 205, 215-16
senna, 56, 57
serum albumin, 32-33
serving size, 149
shark cartilage, 227
side effects of detoxification, 247-48
Simplesse, 127, 251
skin cancer, 155, 226
slippery elm, 70, 226
snacks, 98, 160
soluble fiber, 121, 166, 167, 176
soy, 58, 60, 65,69, 91, 97, 123, 183-96
anti-cancer potential, 184-87
cooking, with, 195
daidzein, 185
dietary supplements, 187-88
genistein, 156, 185-86, 187, 202, 219
phytates, 184-85
phytosterols, 184-85
soy flour, 192-93
soy foods, 191-94
soy milk, 191
soy protein isolates, 193-94
soybean oil, 193
spastic colon, 75, 217
Spicy Rice & Beans, 180
spirituality, 11-12
Splendid Soy Shake, 197
squamous cancers, 79, 153, 185
stevia, 104, 143-44
stir-fry, 66, 127
stomach cancer, 130, 300. See also upper digestive tract cancer.
strength training, 10
stress, 58
and bowel spasms, 77
and cancer treatments, 7-8
and exercise, 9-11
and food allergies, 65
and nausea, 71
coping with, 81-82
gastrointestinal ulcers, 81
heartburn 67
mouth sores, 70-71
reducing 7-9
Sucralose, 142
sugar. See also carbohydrates. See also artificial sweeteners.
alternative sweeteners, 143-44
and candida, 140
and immune response, 131
craving, 134, 140-41

metabolizing, 138
sugar alcohols, 61, 102, 103, 104
sugar substitutes, 141-43. *See also artificial sweeteners.*
sugars
    concentrated, 136-37
    hidden, 137-38
sulfites, 239, 257
Super Smoothie, 33
support groups, 7-8
surgery
    bowel rest after, 58, 78
    side effects of, 20
survivors, winning characteristics, 15-16
swallowing difficulties, 62-63
sweeteners, alternative, 143-44. *See also artificial sweeteners.*

T

Tagamet, 67
Tamoxifen, 277, 312
taste changes, 77-79
Taxol, 60
Taxotere, 60, 69
tea tree oil, 59, 70
Temodal, 55
tempeh, 192
texturized vegetable protein, 192
thiamin, 205
thyroid cancer, 300
tofu, 191
Tofu Egg Salad, 196
toxins, 4, 235-256
TPN. *See intravenous feeding.*
trans-fatty acids, 115, 117, 119, 126, 127, 356
treatment options, 5
triterpenoids, 156
tube feeding. *See enteral feeding.*
tumor suppressor genes, 3
turmeric, 153
Tums, 67

U

undernutrition. *See malnutrition.*
unsaturated fats, 113
upper digestive tract cancer
    dietary supplements for, 303
    nutrition action plan, 297-308
    salt intake, 301
    treatment side effects, 299-300
uterine cancer, 9, 185, 187. *See also gynecological cancer.*

V

valerian root, 58, 77
vegetarian diet, 345
Veggie Wash, 163
Vincristine, 57, 186
vitamin A, 79, 148, 151, 176, 201, 203-04
vitamin C, 29, 30, 32, 34, 56, 59, 83, 121, 173, 182, 200, 202, 209, 210, 211, 213, 214, 217, 218
vitamin D, 211, 213, 230

vitamin E, 64, 70, 79, 82, 83, 120, 124, 152, 153, 174, 184, 200, 202, 204, 211-12, 217, 230, 247

W

weight control, 94-96
weight loss, 25-26
weight, regaining, 21
white blood count, 29
whole grains, 168, 176-77
whole soybeans, 191

X

Xylocaine, 71

Y

yeast infections. *See candidiasis.*

Z

zinc, 29, 58, 61, 64, 66, 70, 79, 121, 138, 170, 214, 216, 230, 246
zinc deficiencies, 79
Zofran, 73